Routledge International Handbook of Participatory Design

Participatory Design is about the direct involvement of people in the co-design of the technologies they use. Its central concern is how collaborative design processes can be driven by the participation of the people affected by the technology designed. Embracing a diverse collection of principles and practices aimed at making technologies, tools, environments, businesses and social institutions more responsive to human needs, the *Routledge International Handbook of Participatory Design* is a state-of-the-art reference handbook for the subject.

The Handbook brings together a multidisciplinary and international group of highly recognised experts to present an authoritative overview of the field and its history and discuss contributions and challenges of the pivotal issues in Participatory Design, including heritage, ethics, ethnography, methods, tools and techniques and community involvement. The book also highlights three large-scale case studies which show how Participatory Design has been used to bring about outstanding changes in different organisations.

The book shows why Participatory Design is an important, highly relevant and rewarding area for research and practice. It will be an invaluable resource for students, researchers, scholars and professionals in Participatory Design.

Jesper Simonsen is Professor of Design Studies in the Department of Communication, Business and Information Technologies at Roskilde University, Denmark. Since 1991 he has conducted research in collaboration with industry on Participatory Design, developing theories and methods for IT design in an organisational context. His publications include *Participatory IT Design: Designing for Business and Workplace Realities* (MIT Press, 2004), and *Design Research: Synergies from Interdisciplinary Perspectives* (Routledge, 2010).

Toni Robertson is Professor of Interaction Design in the Faculty of Engineering and Information Technology at the University of Technology, Sydney (UTS). Her research focuses on understanding and designing the interaction between people, their activities and technology, and the issues surrounding the use of technology in actual work and social settings. Her work has been published widely in the Interaction Design, Participatory Design, Human–Computer Interaction and Computer Supported Cooperative Work literature.

Routledge International Handbook of Participatory Design

Edited by
Jesper Simonsen and Toni Robertson

NEW YORK AND LONDON

First published 2013
by Routledge
711 Third Avenue, New York, NY 10017

Simultaneously published in the USA and Canada
by Routledge
2 Park Square, Milton Park, Abingdon, Oxon, OX14 4RN

Routledge is an imprint of the Taylor & Francis Group, an informa business

First issued in paperback 2013

British Library Cataloguing in Publication Data
A catalogue record for this book is available from the British Library

Library of Congress Cataloging-in-Publication Data
Routledge international handbook of participatory design / edited by Jesper Simonsen and
Toni Robertson.
    p. cm.
    Summary: "Participatory Design is about the direct involvement of people in the co-design
of the technologies they use. Its central concern is how collaborative design processes can be
driven by the participation of the people affected by the technology designed. Embracing a
diverse collection of principles and practices aimed at making technologies, tools,
environments, businesses, and social institutions more responsive to human needs, the
International Handbook of Participatory Design is a state-of-the-art reference handbook for
the subject. The Handbook brings together a multidisciplinary and international group of
highly recognized and experienced experts to present an authoritative overview of the field
and its history and discuss contributions and challenges of the pivotal issues in Participatory
Design, including heritage, ethics, ethnography, methods, tools and techniques and
community involvement. The book also highlights three large-scale case studies which show
how Participatory Design has been used to bring about outstanding changes in different
organisations. The book shows why Participatory Design is an important, highly relevant and
rewarding area for research and practice. It will be an invaluable resource for students,
researchers, scholars and professionals in Participatory Design" -- Provided by publisher.
Includes bibliographical references and index.
    1. System design. 2. Human-computer interaction. I. Simonsen, Jesper. II. Robertson,
Toni. III. Title: International handbook of participatory design. IV. Title: Participatory design.
    QA76.9.S88R675 2012
    003--dc23
                                    2012002306

ISBN: 978-0-415-69440-7 (hbk)
ISBN: 978-0-203-10854-3 (ebk)
ISBN: 978-1-136-26619-5 (online/web)
ISBN: 978-0-415-72021-2 (pbk)

Typeset in Bembo
by Taylor & Francis Books

Contents

List of illustrations   vii
List of contributors   ix
Preface   xix

1   Participatory Design: an introduction   1
    Toni Robertson and Jesper Simonsen

SECTION I
Participatory Design – contributions and challenges   **19**

2   Heritage: having a say   21
    Finn Kensing and Joan Greenbaum

3   Design: design matters in Participatory Design   37
    Liam J. Bannon and Pelle Ehn

4   Ethics: engagement, representation and politics-in-action   64
    Toni Robertson and Ina Wagner

5   Ethnography: positioning ethnography within Participatory
    Design   86
    Jeanette Blomberg and Helena Karasti

6   Methods: organising principles and general guidelines for Participatory
    Design projects   117
    *Tone Bratteteig, Keld Bødker, Yvonne Dittrich, Preben Holst Mogensen
    and Jesper Simonsen*

7   Tools and techniques: ways to engage telling, making and enacting   145
    Eva Brandt, Thomas Binder and Elizabeth B.-N. Sanders

Contents

8 Communities: Participatory Design for, with and by communities   182
   Carl DiSalvo, Andrew Clement and Volkmar Pipek

SECTION II
Outstanding applications of Participatory Design   **211**

 9 Integrating Participatory Design into everyday work at the Global Fund
    for Women   213
    Randy Trigg and Karen Ishimaru

10 Health Information Systems Programme: Participatory Design within the
    HISP network   235
    Jørn Braa and Sundeep Sahay

11 ACTION for Health: influencing technology design, practice and policy
    through Participatory Design   257
    Ellen Balka

    Index   281

Illustrations

Figures

6.1	Dimensions of information technology design (based on Andersen et al. 1990)	120
6.2	The STEPS model (Floyd, Reisin and Schmidt 1989). With kind permission from Christiane Floyd and Springer Science+Business Media	122
6.3	The MUST method's four types of resources for a Participatory Design project	124
6.4	CESD conceptual model	127
6.5	The use-oriented design cycle	128
7.1	The tell–make–enact diagram	150
7.2	Games	151
7.3	Atlantis experiences	154
7.4	Further Atlantis experiences	154
7.5	Use of mock-ups	156
7.6	Paper doll toolkits	157
7.7	A three-dimensional 'dollhouse' toolkit	157
7.8	Cultural probe kits	158
7.9	Static! Energy Curtain	159
7.10	Examples of generative toolkits	160
7.11	Dream devices	162
7.12	The aging worker acts out an envisioned future situation using the dream devices he has made	162
7.13	The digital noticeboard	163
7.14	Using the digital noticeboard and the 'popularity log'	163
7.15	The SeniorInteraction Project	165
7.16	Scenario from the COMIT project	167
7.17	The 'magic thing'	169
7.18	The stakeholders	170
7.19	The shop owner, Allan, and the resident, Lillian, enact scenarios in situ	171
7.20	The COMIT project workshops	174
8.1	St Chris House: participants in the ASE needs assessment exercise	187
8.2	St Chris House: flipchart from the ASE needs assessment exercise	188
8.3	The Neighbourhood Networks project: measuring air quality in a neighbourhood park	194
8.4	The Neighbourhood Networks project: collaborative mapping of air quality in the neighbourhood	195

9.1   The Global Fund for Women's classification categories as of October 2011   216
10.1 Design for integration in South Africa, 1995   239
10.2 Semi-online DHIS 2 design and implementation in Kenya   250
11.1 Technology Trouble logo   266

Tables

5.1   Principles of ethnography and participatory design   88
5.2   Ethnographers' institutional and disciplinary affiliation for the three formative
      research programmes   94
6.1   Knowledge domains for mutual learning (adapted from Kensing and
      Munk-Madsen 1993)   133
8.1   Adapted from 'How to infrastructure' (Star and Bowker 2002) and
      'Infrastructuring' (Pipek and Wulf 2009)   202
9.1   The 'flat' list of the Global Fund for Women classifications as of March 2001 217

Contributors

Ellen Balka, Professor, PhD, School of Communication, Simon Fraser University, Canada. Beginning with her graduate studies in the 1980s, Ellen has conducted Participatory Design projects with varied partners, including women's organisations and other non-profits and health care agencies. Her work and research group have focused on supporting participation prior to and during implementation, and using insights gained to inform technology design. Balka's publications have included a book aimed at community non-profit organisations seeking to computerise, and three co-edited collections about varied aspects of the computerisation of work, including *Gender, Health and Information Technology in Context* (Palgrave, 2009). Recent articles have appeared in *Scandinavian Journal of Information Systems*, *Journal of Computer Supported Cooperative Work*, *Social Studies of Science*, *Information Systems Frontiers*, *Journal of Computer-Mediated Communication* and *Canadian Journal of Communication*.

> *Why am I engaged in Participatory Design?* 'In the early 1980s I was exposed to the idea that technology was not neutral and value free, but rather was socially biased and "bears the social imprint of its authors." In practical terms this meant that influencing how people experienced technological change would require altering the values embedded in technology during design. Participatory Design offered an avenue for influencing technology design processes, and hence how people experienced technological change.'

Liam J. Bannon is Honorary Professor in Human–Computer Interaction at Aarhus University, Denmark, Visiting Professor in the School of Medicine, University College, Cork, Ireland, and Adjunct Professor in the Department of Computer Science and Information Systems at the University of Limerick, Ireland. He was the Founder, and acted as Director, of the Interaction Design Centre at the University of Limerick from 1996 until 2009. His research interests range over the gamut of human–technology relations, including cognitive ergonomics, Human–Computer Interaction, Computer Supported Cooperative Work, computer-supported collaborative learning, new media, interaction design, and social dimensions of new technologies. He was a founding editor of *CSCW: The Journal of Collaborative Computing* and is serving, or has served, on the editorial boards of *Journal of Cognition, Technology, and Work*, *Requirements Engineering Journal*, *Universal Access in the Information Society Journal*, *International Journal of Cognitive Technology*, *International Journal of Web-Based Communities*, *CoDesign Journal*, *Behaviour and Information Technology Journal* and *Journal of Computer Assisted Learning*.

Why am I engaged in Participatory Design? 'I am engaged in Participatory Design because I fully support the notion that people are entitled to be actively involved in the design and evaluation of their evolving working and living environments.'

Thomas Binder is Associate Professor at the Royal Danish Academy of Fine Arts, School of Design, and PhD in Science and Technology Studies. He is part of the co-design research cluster engaging open design collaborations and Participatory Design in the context of workplace change, interaction design and social innovation. His research includes contributions to methods and tools for experimental design research and open innovation processes with a particular emphasis on participation and learning. He has contributed to several books, including *Social Thinking – Software Practice* (MIT Press, 2002), *(Re-)Searching the Digital Bauhaus* (Springer, 2008), *Rehearsing the Future* (Danish Design School Press, 2010), *Design Research through Practice* (Morgan Kaufman, 2011) and *Design Things* (MIT Press, 2011) and chaired the Participatory Design Conference in 2002 and the Nordic Design Research Conference in 2005.

Why am I engaged in Participatory Design? 'To me the Participatory Design community offers an important and vibrant environment for debates on how design and design research engage in social change.'

Jeanette Blomberg is a Research Scientist and Programme Manager for practice-based service innovation at IBM Research. Her research explores issues in social aspects of technology production and use, ethnographically informed organisational interventions, participatory design and practice-based service innovation. Prior to assuming her current position, Jeanette was a member of the Work Practice and Technology group at the Xerox Palo Alto Research Center (PARC), Director of Experience Modeling Research at Sapient Corporation, and Industry-affiliated Professor at the Blekinge Institute of Technology in Sweden. Jeanette received her PhD in anthropology from University of California, Davis, and before embarking on her career in high tech she was a visiting professor and lecturer in cultural anthropology and sociolinguistics at University of California, Davis.

Why am I engaged in Participatory Design? 'I have been involved in Participatory Design since the first Participatory Design conference was held in Seattle in 1990 and have served as programme co-chair for two Participatory Design conferences. My commitment to Participatory Design and the community that supports it is motivated by a belief that workers, citizens and just plain folks should have the ability to shape their futures, particularly as they evolve in relation to information and communication technologies.'

Keld Bødker, Associate Professor, PhD, Department of Communication, Business and Information Technologies, Roskilde University, Denmark. Since the late 1980s he has conducted Participatory Design research in collaboration with labour union groups and industry – focusing on how information technology designers can cooperate with users and their management especially when relating to the clarification of goals, formulation of needs, and design and evaluation of coherent visions for change. Book contributions include: *Participatory IT Design: Designing for Business and Workplace Realities* (with Finn Kensing and Jesper Simonsen, MIT

Press, 2004). He has published in internationals conferences and journals within Participatory Design, information systems and health care and IT.

Why am I engaged in Participatory Design? 'To become really useful, even the most simple information technology artefact has to be appropriated and put into use in a complex pattern of use practices and a host of other artefacts. The only way to do this in a smart way is of course to involve the user. This goes for gadgets acquired in the market place for personal use, for example as part of leisure, and it goes for more complex systems developed for a work context: only the conditions and processes for involving the user are different.'

Jørn Braa, Professor, Department of Informatics, University of Oslo, Norway. Has since 1992 conducted Participatory Design research in Africa and Asia in collaboration with local health authorities and researchers. He initiated the Health Information Systems Programme – HISP – in South Africa in 1994, and has been engaged in the development of HISP as a global network since then. Jørn has since 2004 been engaged in globally distributed and participative open source software development of the DHIS2 platform, which is being implemented in many countries in Africa and Asia. He has published research on Participatory Design and action research in various outlets such as the *Scandinavian Journal of Information Systems*, *MIS Quarterly* and *Information Technology for Development*.

Why am I engaged in Participatory Design? 'Research in HISP has shown that user participation in system development is of particular importance in developing countries and resource-constrained contexts more generally. Reasons for this range from the pragmatic rationale for Participatory Design and the need for users and developers to mutually learn about what is possible and useful technical solutions in contexts with limited prior experience, to the political rationale for Participatory Design, and the need to empower marginalised communities and regions that are excluded from technological and socio-economic development.'

Eva Brandt, PhD, is Associate Professor at the Royal Danish Academy of Fine Arts, School of Design. Here she is part of the co-design research cluster engaging in open design collaborations and Participatory Design in the context of workplace change, interaction design and social innovation. Eva has been involved in research within Participatory Design since 1995. Her major fields of interest are to develop design approaches, methods and techniques for participation, experimentation and learning based on collaborative enquiry and Participatory Design. Recent book contributions include: *Design Spaces* (Edita Publishing Ltd IT Press, 2005), *Rehearsing the Future* (Danish Design School Press, 2010), *Facilitating Change – Using Interactive Methods in ?Organisations, Communities and Networks* (Polyteknisk Forlag, 2011). Eva has a PhD in user-centred design and an MA in engineering design from the Technical University of Denmark.

Why am I engaged in Participatory Design? 'For me Participatory Design approaches are powerful and sensitive. They include political and ethical concerns. They are the answer to many of the environmental, social and cultural challenges that we face today. It is through joint Participatory Design practices which involve and empower the people affected by new design solutions and other stakeholders that we are better able to design for future changes.'

Tone Bratteteig (DrPhilos) is Associate Professor at the Department of Informatics, University of Oslo, Norway. She has been involved in Participatory Design research for almost three decades, starting with the Florence project. Her research projects include collaboration with both public sector and industry. The research projects have focused on the process of Participatory Design: how designers and users collaborate on developing and implementing design ideas, and on the design result: how technical artefacts can contribute to users' autonomy. Her theoretical work concerns the integration of design theories with Participatory Design, emphasising Participatory Design as a social and technical work process. Book contributions include: *Exploring Digital Design* (with Ina Wagner and Dagny Stuedahl, Springer Verlag, 2010). She has published in international conferences and journals within Participatory Design, HCI, information systems, design research, and health care.

> *Why am I engaged in Participatory Design?* 'The research area of Participatory Design concerns information technology as an integral part of our social practices and gives me the possibility to include ethical, political and social questions in information technology design, not just technical matters: the fact that a design is possible may not mean that it is also desirable. The Participatory Design area is multidisciplinary – like its subject – and is the perfect place for researchers who like both people and machines.'

Andrew Clement is a Professor in the Faculty of Information at the University of Toronto, where he coordinates the Information Policy Research Program and is a co-founder of the Identity, Privacy and Security Institute. With a PhD in Computer Science, he has had long-standing research and teaching interests in the social implications of information/communication technologies and human-centred/participatory information systems development. His research has focused on community networking, public information policy, Internet use in everyday life, digital identity constructions, and public participation in information/communication infrastructure development. His recent research relates most directly to citizen-centred perspectives on identity, privacy and surveillance.

> *Why am I engaged in Participatory Design?* 'I first became interested in Participatory Design in the 1980s when, inspired by the Scandinavian experiments, I saw its potential for democratising systems development in North American settings. My initial focus on participatory approaches in workplaces shifted in the 1990s to "community" settings, especially in non-profit organisations and for policy advocacy. Now more than ever, with growing crises in our collective well-being, I'm keen to help citizens find an effective voice in re-shaping our shared socio-technological infrastructures.'

Carl DiSalvo, Assistant Professor, PhD, School of Literature, Communication, and Culture, Georgia Institute of Technology, Atlanta, GA, USA. Since 2001 DiSalvo has worked actively at the intersection of design, art, communities and politics. His research in Participatory Design focuses on developing and theorising new modes of community engagement with emerging technologies that emphasise the creative and critical aspects of design and the role of design in the construction of publics. He has recently published in the proceedings of the ACM Conferences on Human Factors in Computing Systems (CHI) and Participatory Design, the journal *Design Issues*, and contributed a chapter to the book *From Social Butterfly to Engaged Citizen* (MIT Press, 2010). His first book *Adversarial Design* was published by MIT Press in spring 2012.

Why am I engaged in Participatory Design? 'I am engaged in Participatory Design because I believe that fostering participation in the making of products and services is essential to a democratic culture. By doing and studying Participatory Design we can contribute to a greater agency of individuals and communities. In addition, the Participatory Design community is one of the places within the broader design community where there is open discussion and debate on the politics of design.'

Yvonne Dittrich, Dr, works as an Associate Professor the IT-University of Copenhagen. Her research interests are use-oriented design and development of software, and especially the flexibilisation of software and software processes in order to accommodate the co-development of work practices and technology. She developed an empirical research approach, Cooperative Method Development, together with industrial partners, which can be described as applying Participatory Design to software development methodology. In a recent project, she applied this approach to investigate the development, customisation and appropriation of software products.

Why am I engaged in Participatory Design? 'Participatory Design has for me two important dimensions: It promotes the design and development of useful and usable software. And it democratises the design of technology: Users become designers of information technology, rather than consumers.'?

Pelle Ehn is Professor at the School of Arts and Communication, Malmö University, Sweden. He has for four decades (!) been involved in the research field of Participatory Design and in bridging design and information technology. Participatory Design research projects include DEMOS from the 1970s on information technology and workplace democracy, UTOPIA from the 1980s on user participation and skill based design, ATELIER from the last decade on architecture and technology for creative environments, and during recent years Malmö Living Labs, on open design environments for social innovation. His publications include *Computers and Democracy* (Avebury, 1987), *Work-oriented Design of Computer Artifacts* (Lawrence Erlbaum Associates, 1988), *Manifesto for a Digital Bauhaus* (Taylor & Francis, 1998), and as one of the voices of A.Telier *Design Things* (MIT Press, 2011). In 2008 he received the biannual ACM Rigo Award for a lifetime contribution to the field of communication design.

Why am I engaged in Participatory Design? 'It was a question of politics (which voices could be heard in design), it became a rewarding design game (engaging collaboration with all kinds of interesting people and artefacts), now it is becoming an anxious act of political love.'

Joan Greenbaum. Professor Emerita, PhD Environmental Psychology and Interactive Technology and Pedagogy, City University of New York, Graduate Center, USA. She has written and lectured extensively on issues of design and interactive use of technology. Her books include: *In the Name of Efficiency* (Temple University Press, 1979); *Design at Work*, with Morten Kyng (Erlbaum Press, 1991) and *Windows on the Workplace* (Monthly Review Press, 1995 and 2004 edition). She is currently doing research on digital cafe squatting and visual analysis of the places where people work.

Why am I engaged in Participatory Design? 'Back in the 1980s when "users" were invented to fit into Human–Computer Interaction models, I was deeply disappointed in the passive tone of research – the assumption that "users" were some kind of test-car dummies sitting in chairs hitting keys. Some of us rebelled against this notion actively and thus began a movement toward understanding cooperative design and the participatory and social nature of how we engage with the digital world. There is still so much to learn and do, down this path of engagement, and I am delighted to be a part of it.'

Karen Ishimaru, Information Management Officer, Global Fund for Women, San Francisco, California. For the past four and a half years, she has utilised Participatory Design strategies in supporting the development and maintenance of the organisation's database systems. She has a master's degree in public policy from UCLA and has worked in the non-profit sector for over ten years. Prior to joining Global Fund, she worked with a consulting firm providing evaluation and information-based services to philanthropic and non-profit organisations.

Why am I engaged in Participatory Design? 'Since being introduced to Participatory Design by my colleague at the Global Fund for Women, I have found the approach to be essential in our work and personally fulfilling. Participatory Design fosters deeper understandings between people and is the foundation for real and substantive partnerships at the organisation. Within the Participatory Design framework, I believe people find that their opinions and experience matter and that their input can have direct implications for the women we support.'

Helena Karasti, PhD (University of Oulu), docent (University of Turku), Academy of Finland Research Fellow, Information Processing Science, University of Oulu, Finland, and Professor, Digital Curation, Data and System Science, Luleå Technical University, Sweden. Helena started exploring integrations of ethnographic work practice studies and Participatory Design in clinical radiology contexts in the mid-1990s. She continued the theme in Long-Term Ecological Research (LTER) networks, beginning with her postdoctoral year at the University of California, San Diego, in 2002. Both longitudinal empirical domains, e-health and large-scale scientific collaborations (e-research) have been transitioning from material to digital mediation. She recently added Science and Technology Studies (STS) to her interdisciplinary interests and was a visiting scholar at IAS-STS, Graz, Austria. Helena's work appears in international conferences, journals and edited books in Participatory Design, Computer Supported Cooperative Work, Information Systems, Gender and Information Technology, Medical Informatics, Digital Curation, and EcoInformatics disciplines. She recently co-edited a special issue of *CSCW Journal* titled 'Sociotechnical Studies of Cyberinfrastructure and e-Research: Supporting Collaborative Research'.

Why am I engaged in Participatory Design? 'I value that Participatory Design takes user participants seriously and encourages multivoicedness, and that in addition to socio-technical issues involved in design and change, Participatory Design also responsibly embraces ethical and political concerns.'

Finn Kensing, Professor, Dr Scient., Centre for IT Innovation, University of Copenhagen, Denmark. He has conducted research on Participatory Design since the late 1970s, first in one of the pioneering Scandinavian trade union projects, later also with management, IT professionals and users. Currently he focuses on Participatory Design research in order to improve communication and collaboration in the network of patients and health care professionals. He has published in, among others, *Communications of the ACM*, *Human–Computer Interactions*, *CSCW Journal* and *Scandinavian Journal of Information Systems*. He contributed to *Professional Systems Development* (Prentice Hall, 1990) and to *Participatory IT Design: Designing for Business and Workplace Realities* (MIT Press, 2004).

Why am I engaged in Participatory Design? 'I am engaged in Participatory Design for three reasons: I consider involving those for whom a given design is intended to increase the likelihood that it will be meaningful, useful and usable. Further, when what gets designed is intended for workplace settings I think that people should have the right to have a say. Finally, when it comes to research I appreciate the opportunity to learn from people "inhabiting" the area of concern.'

Preben Holst Mogensen, Associate Professor, PhD, Department of Computer Science, Aarhus University, Denmark. Since 1989 he has conducted Participatory Design research in collaboration with public authorities and industry – focusing on collaborative design and implementation of solutions between users, management, other stakeholders, developers, designers and work analysts. He has participated in, managed and coordinated numerous national and international research projects on this topic, and has published in international conferences and journals within Participatory Design, CSCW, object-oriented development and emergency response.

Why am I engaged in Participatory Design? 'I am engaged in Participatory Design because I see it as one of the most powerful and, at the same time, sensitive approaches to design and implementation of information technology applications to support and enhance practices. Participatory Design is not only the appropriate approach when designing for actual use; it is also a very creative endeavour that very often provides new and thought provoking insights.'

Volkmar Pipek, Assistant Professor, received a PhD in Information Processing Science from the University of Oulu, Finland. Currently he works in the field of Computer Supported Cooperative Work with the University of Siegen, Germany. He did design-oriented research with a strong ethnographic/participatory component in the fields of knowledge management, ERP systems and e-democracy. Currently he works on end-user development and crisis management infrastructures for the public. He has published more than 50 papers at peer-reviewed conferences in the fields of HCI, PD, CSCW and Information Systems, and served on the programme committees of the most important conferences in these fields (CHI, CSCW, ECSCW, PDC, ICIS, etc.). He has also edited books about knowledge management and end-user development.

Why am I engaged in Participatory Design? 'Technology development methods tend to underestimate the innovation strength of users. But with computers conquering more and more segments of our everyday lives, appropriate modes of technology production need to transcend disciplinary boundaries that manifested in the user–designer dichotomy and come to a design thinking that supports the creativity of all actors involved in the successful establishment of technology usages. The Participatory Design community reflects the desired values as well as the necessary interdisciplinarity to work towards this goal.'

Toni Robertson is Professor of Interaction Design in the Faculty of Engineering and Information Technology at the University of Technology, Sydney (UTS). Her research has focused on understanding and designing the interaction between people, their activities and technology, and the issues surrounding the use of technology in actual work and social settings. She is a specialist in the application of qualitative and participatory research and design methods and the use of phenomenological perspectives to understand actual human experience of technology use. She established and leads the Interaction Design and Human Practice Lab and initiated and co-directs the UTS Human Centred Technology Design Research Strength.

> *Why am I engaged in Participatory Design?* 'In the 1970s and 80s I was a graphic designer and poster printer, deeply involved in early Community Arts in Australia and aware of early local initiatives to increase participation in architecture and community planning. So when I started working in information technology design I sought out those working in that field who shared the participatory ideals that were already familiar to me. Participatory Design enables me to express basic political and ethical commitments to human rights, civil society and democratic process.'

Sundeep Sahay completed his PhD in 1992 from Florida International University, USA. Since 2000, he has been a Professor at the Department of Informatics, University of Oslo, Norway. He has been an active participant in the Health Information Systems Programme, having worked in various countries with a significant focus on India. He has published extensively in various journals from the domains of IS, Organisation Studies and also Public Health. He is a reviewer in various journals.

> *Why am I engaged in Participatory Design?* 'I have for more than a decade engaged with research and practice around the implementation of HIS globally with a specific focus on India. The Health Information Systems Programme is unique in its focus on Participatory Design, inspired by a larger Scandinavian tradition, and has reformulated its focus given the constantly changing environment of countries, technologies, political environment and users. By being in the unique position of supervising students from different countries studying aspects of Participatory Design in their respective countries, I have had the possibility of understanding how Participatory Design is a context-specific phenomenon. Currently, I am trying to understand the implications of new technologies, such as mobiles, web and cloud, on Participatory Design, as they offer rich potential and possibilities, but also introduce challenges of excluding users, and domain-specific knowledge so critical for establishing effective systems.'

Elizabeth B.-N. Sanders joined the Design Department at The Ohio State University as an Associate Professor in 2011 after having worked as a design research consultant in industry for over 30 years. She has practised Participatory Design research within and between all the design disciplines. Her research today focuses on Participatory Design research, collective creativity and transdisciplinarity. Her goal is to bring participatory, human-centred design thinking and co-creation practices to the challenges we face for the future. Liz has a PhD in Experimental and Quantitative Psychology and a BA in both Psychology and Anthropology.

> *Why am I engaged in Participatory Design?* 'We face significant environmental, social and cultural challenges today. Design innovation can help, but only if we open up the design

process to everyone. Co-creation puts tools for creativity and communication in the hands of the people who will be served through design. It is only through collective thinking and acting that we will be able to use design to help address the challenges we face today. All people are creative and can participate in co-designing if they are provided with relevant tools and the settings for their use.'

Jesper Simonsen, PhD, Professor of Design Studies, Department of Communication, Business and Information Technologies, Roskilde University, Denmark. Since 1991 he has conducted Participatory Design research in collaboration with industry – focused on how information technology designers can cooperate with users and their management, especially when relating to the clarification of goals, formulation of needs, and design and evaluation of coherent visions for change. He published his first PDC paper in 1994, and was Programme Chair of PDC'2008 and General Chair of PDC'2012. Recent book contributions include: *Participatory IT Design: Designing for Business and Workplace Realities* (MIT Press, 2004) and *Design Research: Synergies from Inter-disciplinary Perspectives* (Routledge, 2010). Recent articles have appeared in *Design Issues, Communications of the ACM, Communications of the Association for Information Systems, Scandinavian Journal of Information Systems*, and *International Journal of Medical Informatics*.

Why am I engaged in Participatory Design? 'The Participatory Design community constitutes a research community with a unique and special quality: it acknowledges that what you succeed in doing as a researcher has valuable meaning for yourself and for society as a whole, and further that you inevitably have to take responsibility for your professional work as a researcher and take a stand for your views within the community and society within which you work.'

Randy Trigg, Senior Information Management Officer, Global Fund for Women. Received his PhD in Computer Science from the University of Maryland. His research at Xerox PARC and for three years as a professor at the University of Aarhus, Denmark, focused on Participatory Design, hypermedia, tailorable systems and Computer Supported Cooperative Work. As part of the Work Practice and Technology Group at Xerox PARC, he brought ethnographic methods and Participatory Design to bear on the work of technology design and development. His publications include a special issue of *Human–Computer Interaction* on Participatory Design. He is also the co-author, with Kaj Grønbæk, of *From Web to Workplace: Designing Open Hyper-media Systems* (MIT Press, 1999). Since 2000, he has been a practitioner of Participatory Design in the implementation and maintenance of non-profit databases.

Why am I engaged in Participatory Design? 'In the 1980s, I saw the inspiring documentary *Computers in Context* (California Newsreel, 1986), featuring many of the founders of Participatory Design. I later worked with some of these same Scandinavian researchers, and helped bring their system design approaches to the US. To me, the respectful and empowering premises of Participatory Design are just as essential and relevant today as they were 25 years ago.'

Ina Wagner is Emeritus Professor for Multidisciplinary Systems Design and Computer-Sup-ported Co-operative Work (CSCW) at the Faculty of Informatics, Vienna University of Technology, where she has built up an interdisciplinary research unit, bringing together expertise in sociology, ethnography and computer science for the study of work practices and organisations, as well as the design of supporting technologies. Her major intellectual project is to achieve a deeper understanding of (collaborative) work practices and technology use in fields as varied as health care, architecture and urban planning, and other professional contexts. Ina has an Adjunct Professor position at the University of Oslo; since 2001 she has been a member of the Austrian Bioethics Committee, where she focuses on ethical aspects of technology development. She has published widely.

Why am I engaged in Participatory Design? 'I enjoy the practice-oriented view of the Participatory Design community and its political commitment to designing better "futures".'

Preface

This is the new reference handbook for Participatory Design. Participatory Design is about the direct involvement of people in the co-design of the information technologies they use. Its central concern is how collaborative design processes can be driven by the participation of the people who will be affected by the technology that is being designed.

Participatory Design embraces a diverse collection of principles and practices aimed at making technologies, tools, environments, businesses and social institutions more responsive to human needs. It brings together a multidisciplinary and international group of software developers, researchers, social scientists, managers, designers, practitioners, users, cultural workers, activists and citizens who both advocate and adopt distinctively participatory approaches in the development of information and communication artefacts, systems, services and technology.

It is our hope that this book will become the basis for Participatory Design courses at colleges and universities worldwide and that it will endure and remain a relevant reference for the next decade and beyond. The book's target audience is researchers and practitioners who are already working within Participatory Design, are interested in doing so, or who wish to obtain an authoritative overview of the field and its history. We hope especially to inspire new researchers to join our research community. The book provides an introduction and a reference to core areas of Participatory Design including thorough literature reviews, discussions of central contributions and challenges for current and future research areas, as well as chapters demonstrating the practical large-scale application of Participatory Design.

The book has been written by a group of highly recognised, very experienced and profoundly engaged[1] Participatory Design researchers and practitioners with first-hand knowledge of the discourse that has shaped the field over the last decades. We have endeavoured to illustrate why Participatory Design is such a valuable approach to thinking about design. We demonstrate why Participatory Design is an important, relevant and most rewarding area for research and practice.

Participatory Design has so much to offer to those living and working in environments where technologies are designed and used. Some of the most obvious examples include: clarifying design goals, formulating needs, designing coherent visions for change, combining business-oriented and socially sensitive approaches, initiating participation and partnerships with different stakeholders, using ethnographic analysis as part of the design process, establishing mutual learning processes among heterogeneous participants, conducting iterative experiments aiming at organisational change, managing stepwise implementation based on comprehensive evaluations, and providing a large toolbox of different practical techniques to encourage and enable participation. Most importantly, its defining commitment to ensuring active and genuine participation offers a principled design approach and practice to those seeking to harness the benefits of new technology for greater human good.

The Participatory Design community meets every second year at the biennial Participatory Design conferences. The idea for this book was fostered at the 10th Anniversary Conference on Participatory Design held in Bloomington, Indiana, USA, in 2008. The theme of this conference, *Experiences and Challenges*, was chosen to celebrate the fact that the Participatory Design community had been meeting for 20 years since the first conference held in 1990. At the conference, a need for a new handbook was voiced and discussed. Other very popular books have been published on Participatory Design, but the need for an updated book was obvious. The two books published by Lawrence Erlbaum (*Design at Work: Cooperative Design of Computer Systems* from 1991, edited by Greenbaum and Kyng; *Participatory Design: Principles and Practices*, from 1993, edited by Schuler and Namioka) have, to date, been the key handbooks available on Participatory Design and they are still widely cited.

We were the programme chairs for the 2008 conference and encouraged to initiate this book. We developed a proposal and invited 22 Participatory Design experts to join the project. All contributors met at a full day workshop held at the 11th Participatory Design Conference in Sydney, Australia, in 2010. At this workshop, we reviewed and discussed a 140-page draft for the book. During 2011 there was one major review round for all chapters and an additional review round for selected chapters. All have received from six to ten extensive reviews by the authors and editors as well as one or two editorial meta-reviews analysing and commenting on the collection of reviews. Drafts for each chapter and summaries of the chapters have been circulated between the contributors to ensure quality, consistency and proper cross-references. We will celebrate the final publication of the book at the 12th Participatory Design Conference in Roskilde, Denmark, in August 2012. A workshop will be held at the 13th Participatory Design Conference in 2014 where we will discuss our experiences in using the book in university courses at advanced bachelor, graduate or PhD levels.

As editors we have enjoyed immensely our numerous conversations, discussions, reflections and exchanges of draft materials with the authors in this book. We hope that you will enjoy reading the book, share the insights it provides, and participate in the discussions that it raises.

December 2011
Jesper Simonsen and Toni Robertson

Note

1 See all contributors' biographies and answers to the question 'Why am I engaged in Participatory Design?' in the section *List of contributors*.

Participatory Design

An introduction

Toni Robertson and Jesper Simonsen

The aim of this book is to provide a current account of the commitments and contributions of research and practice in the Participatory Design of information technologies. An overview of the central concepts that have defined and shaped the field is provided as an introduction to the more detailed focus of later chapters. The target audience is identified and the structure of the book explained. A short description of each chapter highlights its particular contributions as well as the associated challenges facing designers and researchers engaged in participatory approaches. The chapter concludes with some guidance and recommendations for further reading.

An introduction to Participatory Design is followed by explanations of how practitioners and researchers in the field understand participation and practice and how design is approached as a process driven by social interaction and engagement. The structure of the book is described, individual chapters introduced and further relevant publications listed.

Essentially this chapter introduces, motivates and grounds the book and the chapters that follow. It provides basic definitions of the core concepts of Participatory Design and explains both their origins and ongoing relations to the motivations and commitments of researchers and practitioners who use participatory approaches in their work. The chapter provides the foundation to account for the structure of the book: one section focusing on some of the different perspectives in the field and their particular contributions and challenges and another section that presents case studies of three outstanding applications of Participatory Design.

If we are to design the futures we wish to live, then we need those whose futures they will be to actively participate in their design. This is why it is so important that Participatory Design keeps developing the design processes, tools, techniques and methods needed to enable full and active participation in all kinds of design activities.

Introduction

The beginnings of Participatory Design lie among the various social, political and civil rights movements of the 1960s and 70s, when people in many Western societies demanded an increased say in decision-making about different aspects of their lives and were prepared to participate in collective action around shared interests and values. Some designers and design researchers responded to these events by investigating how they might relate to their own practices. For example, the theme for the 1971 conference of the Design Research Society, held in Manchester, was *Design Participation* (Cross 1972) and, around the same time, some architects and town planners began to seek ways to involve people in the design of various aspects of their everyday built environments (e.g. Sanoff 1978). The Participatory Design of information technology was pioneered in Europe and especially in Scandinavia as part of what became known as the workplace democracy movement during the 1970s (e.g. Nygaard and Bergo 1975; Sandberg 1979; Bjerknes et al. 1983). In particular it was a response to the transformation of workplaces driven by the introduction of computers. The aim was to provide people with better tools for doing their jobs, eventually enabling them to extend their skills while automating the tedious and repetitive parts of work. It is the motivation behind this aim and the context from which it emerged that has been so important to the development of Participatory Design.

The focus of this book is the tradition of Participatory Design that originated in Scandinavia and has concentrated on the design of information and communications technologies and technology-enabled systems (we will refer to these in the remainder of this book more simply as *information technologies*). At the heart of this tradition is an unshakable commitment to ensuring that those who will use information technologies play a critical role in their design. As such, the Participatory Design tradition is defined by a perspective that always looks forward to the shaping of future situations. A diverse collection of Participatory Design principles and practices has been developed, driven by ongoing efforts to deepen our understanding of how collaborative design processes can enable the participation of those who will, in the future, be affected by their results. Increasingly, designers committed to participatory approaches have extended their concerns to involving people in the design of the tools, environments, businesses and social institutions in which these technologies are embedded.

While Participatory Design has matured as a research discipline and field of design practice, it has been some years since a comprehensive volume of writings on the field has been published. In that time many of its insights, tools and techniques have become part of other design fields. Other designers and researchers have begun to use participatory approaches in their own work and new generations of both have sought to contribute to and extend the project that unites the different expressions of Participatory Design: directly involving people in the co-design of the artefacts, processes and environments that shape their lives.

The aim of this book is to provide a current account of the commitments and contributions of Participatory Design. In essence, Participatory Design can be defined as

> a process of investigating, understanding, reflecting upon, establishing, developing, and supporting mutual learning between multiple participants in collective 'reflection-in-action'. The participants typically undertake the two principal roles of users and designers where the designers strive to learn the realities of the users' situation while the users strive to articulate their desired aims and learn appropriate technological means to obtain them.

These two principal roles reflect two fundamental aspects of Participatory Design. The first is that it seeks to enable those who will use the technology to have a voice in its design, without needing to speak the language of professional technology design. This is achieved through interactions with prototypes, mock-ups and other tools that can represent developing systems and future practices. The second is that people who are not professional technology designers may not be able to define what they want from a design process, without knowing what is possible. A process of mutual learning for both designers and users can inform all participants' capacities to envisage future technologies and the practices in which they can be embedded.

By 'designers' we mean, at least initially, those participants who are professionally 'responsible for the information technology design project, underscoring the importance of the element of design in such projects and, in turn, the analogy to the function of the architect in construction' (Bødker et al. 2011, p. 117). By 'users' we refer to those participants who will interact with the information technologies being designed. But while this identification of the two principal roles of designers and users is useful in any simple definition of Participatory Design, in practice the roles have at times been contested and generally used with some unease. Throughout this book these roles will be challenged and elaborated to include much more than just one group's *design* of technology and another group's *use* of it. This is not just because changing technologies have continued to blur both the separation of designers and users as well as much of the gap between design and use. It is also because in Participatory Design the relations between humans and information technologies have always differentiated (among others) the users, who apply the technology for certain purposes; the customers, who order and pay for it; employees and management, who, because Participatory Design is also a political process, are involved in different ways in the conflicts and dilemmas that accompany it; and other participants, who might have first-, second- and third-hand knowledge of use-processes that, in turn, entail consequences for the tools and techniques which are helpful and relevant to apply in bringing that knowledge to bear (ibid.).

Many of the authors of the different chapters in this book have explicitly stressed that Participatory Design is not defined by formulas, rules and strict definitions but by a commitment to core principles of participation in design. These, in turn, are informed by a rich heritage of projects, methods, tools and techniques that we can bring to bear on each specific design context in which we participate. Both the shared principles of Participatory Design and many of the ways these have been expressed and experienced have informed the structure of this book and are examined from different perspectives in its pages.

We continue in this introductory chapter by providing an overview of the central concepts of Participatory Design. We discuss the motivation behind its basic commitment to participation, what we understand by participation and practice, and how design is understood as a process driven by social interaction and engagement. From there the chapter identifies its target audiences and explains the structure of the book, paying particular attention to how its chapters articulate the contributions of Participatory Design as well as the challenges that lie ahead. For those who want to read more, the chapter closes with some suggestions for further reading and provides a comprehensive list of Participatory Design publications.

Taking a stand

Writing of the early Scandinavian Participatory Design projects of the 1970s and 1980s, Morten Kyng observed: 'As part of the transformation of the workplace working conditions for many end users have changed dramatically, and not always for the better' (1988, p. 178). Discussions about these changes, between designers, users, trade unions and other stakeholders, highlighted that when those who would use these new computer-based systems were not actively involved and influential in their development and use, they were unable to create visions of future working conditions and practices that would improve or even match their current ones. Participatory Design researchers and trade unions initiated a range of activities to question existing approaches to the computerisation of the workplace and to influence legislation on the changing work environment. Active involvement from those who would use these systems was the key characteristic of these newly initiated activities; they were intended to achieve their aims through creating visions of different kinds of future workplaces and practices and to design the new computer-based systems that would shape them (ibid.). This meant that new ways of designing systems needed to be developed that, in turn, relied on finding new ways of cooperating between users and designers.

Then, as now, participatory designers viewed those who would use the new technologies as experts in their work domains while the designers acted as experts in theirs, contributing as experts and facilitators of the design process, technical consultants and often through involvement in the actual development of new systems. So Participatory Design was, in the first instance, about designing information technologies that would allow people to change and further develop their work practices to incorporate both the use of computer systems and improved working conditions. Its roots in the workplace democracy movement meant that those whose new work practices were being designed were centrally engaged in the process. This engagement was itself defined and enabled by the development of new design methods, tools and techniques that were intended to enable all those involved in the design process to imagine and move towards new visions of the future.

The commitments of Participatory Design to new ways of designing and to people's agency in shaping their work marked a clear move away from the formalised models of work that were, at the time, dominant in information systems design, business planning and related areas. Joan Greenbaum and Morten Kyng devoted a major part of their introduction to *Design at Work* (Greenbaum and Kyng 1991a, pp. 1–24) to critiquing the cultural, political and economic values inherent in formalised models of human activities and explicitly connected these models to the deeply rooted practices of the rationalist tradition of Western philosophy. They cited the summary provided by Winograd and Flores (1986, p. 15) of how these practices characterise situations in terms of identifiable objects with well-defined properties; find general rules that apply to situations in terms of those objects and properties; and then apply the rules logically to the situation of concern in order to draw conclusions about what should be done (Greenbaum and Kyng 1991a, p. 7). The effects include a top-down view of the organisation that formalises work into disembodied, algorithmic procedures and makes invisible the social, embodied and contingent nature of everyday work practices. Indeed, critiques of formalised representations of work are common in the early Participatory Design and related literature (e.g. Suchman 1983, 1987, 1995; Ehn and Kyng 1984; Kyng 1988, 1995; Greenbaum and Kyng 1991a; Star 1991). These critiques extended to the way such models informed developing approaches to system development contributing both to the failure of new systems and to the reduced workplace conditions that had motivated the early Participatory Design initiatives.

> Traditional methods and practices are firmly rooted in engineering and natural sciences origins of computer science. They are designed for implementing clear-cut specifications (as if such things exist), but they are far removed from actual practice. In fact, traditional methods, with their emphasis on step-by-step procedures, effectively prevent creative and cooperative sparks between system designers and users.
>
> *(Greenbaum and Kyng 1991b, p. viii)*

Participatory Design has always sought its theoretical and conceptual inspiration in those fields and approaches that shared both its critical stance towards rationalist accounts of human practice and its focus on the primacy of human experience, social agency and institution-shaping behaviour (e.g. Winograd and Flores 1986; Suchman 1987; Ehn 1988; Greenbaum and Kyng 1991a). Most importantly, Participatory Design has always given primacy to human action and people's rights to participate in the shaping of the worlds in which they act. In their critique of rationalist approaches to technology design, widely read and cited within the early years of Participatory Design, Winograd and Flores wrote: 'We encounter the deep questions of design when we recognize that in designing tools we are designing ways of being' (1986, p. xi). Here, then, is the crux of where and why we *take a stand*. Design is, fundamentally, about designing futures for actual people. Designing technologies that people rely on in their work shapes, in essential ways, how it is possible for people to do their work and how they experience their working lives. There is an ethical stand underlying Participatory Design that recognises an accountability of design to the worlds it creates and the lives of those who inhabit them. Designing in genuine partnership with those who will use the technologies we build is our way of taking a stand about who we can be as designers and design researchers.

Much has happened and many, many things have changed since these early Participatory Design projects in Scandinavian workplaces. Many of those reading this book will never experience a workplace or even a living space that has not been deeply shaped by information technologies. These technologies have moved off the desktops and out of workplaces into our homes, our public spaces, our pockets, handbags and backpacks, our leisure time and our social relationships. Such developments have constantly posed wonderfully interesting but also major challenges to those working within Participatory Design; we need to ensure that our under-standings of design and our design processes, methods, techniques and tools could enable the design of new and emerging technologies for changing and expanding contexts. This book is intended to give an account of some of the ways that those working within Participatory Design have met the challenges of change and how Participatory Design has developed in the process as well as outlining the challenges ahead that current and future Participatory Design researchers need to address.

Participation

Participation is the core of Participatory Design. The fundamental developments in the field have come from efforts to investigate, understand, support and practise what can be labelled as 'genuine' participation in design (Bødker et al. 2004). By 'genuine' participation, we refer to the fundamental transcendence of the users' role *from* being merely informants *to* being legitimate and acknowledged participants in the design process. This role is established – for example – when users are not just answering questions in an interview about their point of view or knowledge of a particular issue, but are asked to step up, take the pen in hand, stand in front of the large whiteboard together with fellow colleagues and designers, and participate in drawing and sketching how the work process unfolds as seen from their perspectives. Inviting users to such collective discussions and reflections requires a trustful and confiding relationship between all participants. Any user needs to participate willingly as a way of working both *as themselves* (respecting their individual and group's/community's genuine interests) and *with themselves* (being concentrated present in order to sense how they feel about an issue, being open towards reflections on their own opinions) as well as *for the task and the project* (contributing to the achievement of the shared and agreed-upon goals of the design task and design project at hand) (Storm Jensen 2002). Such participation demands acknowledgement of the users' interests as fully legitimate elements of the design process. It includes addressing questions such as: what does participation mean in terms of actual power to make decisions; who needs to participate and how can this be managed and supported; how can the design process itself be designed so people can participate in it; and what kinds of design tools and methods do we need?

Participatory Design has had a profound influence on the current recognition and acceptance of the value of user participation in design. Improving both the quality of the product (e.g.

Grudin 1991; Grønbæk et al. 1993) and the quality of the process (e.g. Bødker et al. 2004) have always been central commitments. Involving people with everyday knowledge of a particular domain of human activity in the design of technologies for that domain offers a way to increase product and service quality because the resulting technologies work better. Using design-by-doing methods, such as mock-ups and prototypes, is another central commitment of Participatory Design because these have enabled 'ordinary workers' to use their practical skills when participating in the design process (e.g. Ehn 1993). Using these methods enhances participant engagement in the process and encourages more robust communication and shared understandings between designers, users and other stakeholders in design. These days, participation within information technology design is routinely advocated in many textbooks (for example, within Human–Computer Interaction) through iterative design techniques such as mock-ups and prototyping.

There are both pragmatic and political rationales for genuine participation in design. The pragmatic rationale stresses the need for users and developers to learn together about possible and useful technical solutions. So *mutual learning* and the setting up of *mutual learning processes* are defining commitments of Participatory Design. The mutual learning process typically includes ideas and visions for change as they evolve through a design project 'that reveals goals, defines problems, and indicates solutions, with the aim of designing sustainable uses of IT based on a specific problem within the company' (Bødker et al. 2004, p. 13).

Mutual learning is an ongoing activity throughout the Participatory Design process. Users need knowledge of potential technological options as well as of how these options can be provided. Designers are the source of this knowledge, as well as of relevant design expertise. The designers need knowledge about the users, their practices and the use situation (often the work domain) in question. The users are the source of this knowledge and relevant domain expertise. They provide experiential knowledge of their expertise, the work domain and practices. During a Participatory Design process all participants increase their knowledge and understandings: about technology for the users, about users and their practice for designers, and all participants learn more about technology design. Kensing and Blomberg summed up the pragmatic argument for full and genuine participation in design: 'The epistemological stand of participatory design is that these types of knowledge are developed most effectively through active cooperation between workers [end-users] (and increasingly other organizational members) and designers within specific design projects' (1998, p. 172). Mutual learning supports the design of technology based on the logic of the practice it is intended to support. This makes the solution more robust and sustainable (e.g. Bjerknes and Bratteteig 1988).

The political rationale for genuine participation in design reflects a commitment to ensuring that the voices of marginalised groups and communities are heard in decision-making processes that will affect them. The motivation was and remains democratic and emancipatory: participation in Participatory Design happens, and needs to happen, because those who are to be affected by the changes resulting from implementing information and communications technologies should, as a basic human right, have the opportunity to influence the design of those technologies and the practices that involve their use. This emancipatory commitment will be explained and explored further all through this book, particularly in Chapter 2 on the heritage of Participatory Design and Chapter 4 on ethics and design. Expressed simply, if we are to be able to design the futures we wish to live, then we need those whose futures they will be to actively participate in their design. This is why it is so important that Participatory Design keeps developing the design processes, tools and methods needed to enable full and active participation in design activities. As we work together to design solutions to all kinds of complex issues that confront us, not only those involving new information technologies, we need to ensure not just that we have the best processes, tools and methods available to work with but that these can enable the successful development of inclusive and democratic design solutions.

Practice

> Through practice we produce the world, both the world of objects and our knowledge about this world. Practice is both action and reflection. But practice is also a social activity; it is produced in cooperation with others. However, this production of the world and our understanding of it takes place in an already existing world. The world is also a product of former practice. Hence, as part of practice, knowledge has to be understood socially – as producing or reproducing social processes and structures as well as being the product of them.
>
> *(Ehn 1993, p. 63)*

Participatory Design is driven by a consistent socio-technical approach that appreciates the context in which the technology will be used and the processes and practices within that context. The term *practice* is used to refer to what people really do. Its use emphasises that what people really do is often very different from the way their activities might be described by others or depicted in, for example, work flow diagrams and similar kinds of representations of work, or presented as what people should do, ought to do or might ideally do 'in theory' (Schmidt et al. 2007). Understanding practice is fundamental to Participatory Design for many reasons, most importantly because so much of what we do is guided by the recognition that designing the technologies people use in their everyday activities shapes, in crucial ways, how those activities might be done. Suchman and Trigg summarised: 'Effective design involves a co-evolution of artefacts with practice' (1991, p. 72). They explained:

> Because of the intimate relation between work and technology, the development of the artefacts with which people work and the development of their work practices go hand in hand. Available technologies afford certain resources and constraints on how the work gets done and people's ways of working give the technologies their shape and significance.
>
> *(Suchman and Trigg 1991, p. 65)*

Rich accounts of practice and the understandings they enabled were considered early in the development of Participatory Design as alternatives to the formal diagrams and abstracted work procedures that had guided so much early technology design. At the time this commitment to the empirical study of practice, in order to understand work and inform the design of technologies that could be used in that work, separated Participatory Design approaches from other technology and work design traditions. The focus on practice recognises the role of everyday practical action in shaping the worlds we live in. That is, practice plays a central epistemological role in Participatory Design that complements its rejection of formalised models of both work and design along with their focus on individual work tasks. Most importantly, practice is, by definition, a social activity; 'it is the community, rather than the individual, that defines what a given domain of work is and what it means to accomplish it successfully' (ibid., p. 73). Participatory Design has developed a range of design techniques, such as various kinds of design and future workshops, to support participants working together to develop detailed accounts and other representations of both current and desired future practices. These are explored further in Chapter 7 of this book.

The work by Lucy Suchman and her Work Practice and Technology Group at Xerox Palo Alto Research Center (PARC) was a major inspiration for the importance of understanding practice in both Participatory Design and Computer Supported Cooperative Work (CSCW).

There has always been a close relationship and much crossover between researchers and practitioners in Participatory Design and CSCW. Appreciating the realities of a work-oriented organisational context implies viewing work as a socially organised and situated activity, where the actual behaviour, because of its situatedness, cannot be fully described by plans (and other formal descriptions) that guide and/or help coordinate a practice (Suchman 1987, 2007). Both Participatory Design and CSCW recognise that human activities are carried out in cooperation with others and so new technologies need to be designed to support cooperation. They also share a major reliance on applying ethnographic methods to support the development of a thorough understanding of current practices, within the particular design domain, as a basis for the specification of new technologies (e.g. Blomberg et al. 1993). As described in Chapter 5, such methods are an important means within Participatory Design to develop experiential understandings of actual practice and have been used extensively from its earliest days (e.g. Bjerknes and Bratteteig 1995).

Practice evolves over time as practitioners actively engage in reviewing and modifying their practice in response to all kinds of changes and developments, not just those resulting from the introduction of new technologies. But the introduction of new technologies will always change the practice they are part of, in ways that were predicted and in ways that were not, no matter how well the original domain was understood. Planned or anticipated changes may or may not happen while other changes can emerge spontaneously or as a result of the new possibilities experienced from using the technology (e.g. Orlikowski and Hofman 1997). There are variations in the same basic practice across different local settings and there are deviations from them. Specific practices and how they are defined can be questioned, evaluated, debated, undermined, and challenged, but also defended, promoted, adopted, applied, enforced, and upheld by instruction, training, and sanction (Schmidt et al. 2007).

Understandings of practice developed and used in Participatory Design include what is routinely done in some kind of human activity and how the activity is actually accomplished by the actions of those participating in it. It is the latter that provides the major link into the design of future practices and the technologies that will be part of them. The aim is to design technology not just to support cooperation between those using it but also to enable people to take advantage of the new technologies, to (re-)configure and appropriate them and to redesign their practice in positive ways over time. As we will see in the following section and in greater detail in Chapters 6 and 7, Participatory Design has also developed a range of methods, tools and techniques to assist future users, designers and other stakeholders envisage, experience and reflect on the future practices that new technologies might enable.

Design

Participatory Design is driven by social interaction as users and designers learn together to create, develop, express and evaluate their ideas and visions. Shared experimentation and reflection are essential parts of the design process. Pelle Ehn (1993) wrote: 'the origin of design is in involved practical use and understanding, not detached reflection, and design is seen as an interaction between understanding and creativity' (p. 62). So Participatory Design has much in common with Schön's (1983) articulation of design as 'reflection-in-action', a process engaged in by an experienced and reflective design-practitioner. But while Schön takes the perspective of the individual designer, the direct involvement of future users in a Participatory Design process involves collective 'reflection-in-action' between multiple participants. Within Participatory Design, what is being designed is both the technological *product* or artefact and the *process* that enables different participants to engage in designing this product. Indeed, Participatory Design has a strong focus on the 'how' of designing, i.e. a focus on the process of designing and the particular participatory practices that different processes can enable (see Chapter 9 for an elaborated practical example).

The development and use of a variety of design methods, tools and techniques to support collective 'reflection-in-action' have historically formed a substantial part of the Participatory Design agenda since the pioneering projects in the 1970s, and these are among the major contributions Participatory Design has made. Workshops with designers and users using techniques such as mock-ups, scenarios, prototypes and various types of design games have been central to Participatory Design since it began. These enable ongoing design experiments to visualise, simulate and experiment with selected elements of envisioned technologies, in use, prior to their development and implementation. They enable the participants in the design process to propose, represent, interrogate and reflect on different aspects of the developing design continually throughout that process. These shared cycles of design experiment and evaluation are the essence of the Participatory *Design* process. The ideas and visions for new technologies are based on understandings of the actual use context, but the implementation and use of new technologies changes the way activities are done. This fosters new possibilities in two ways: by providing a (new) starting point for the current design situation and new experiences and understandings of how different technological options might support new practices in the future.

Initially, Participatory Design mostly addressed small-scale and custom-made systems (Clement and van den Besselaar 1993; Oostveen and van den Besselaar 2004) or the initial parts of larger-scale information technology development followed by a conventional contractual bid (Kensing 2000; Bødker et al. 2004). But organisations now are increasingly buying generic software (Bansler and Havn 1994) as off-the-shelf systems or development frameworks offering standardised, domain-specific 'building blocks' that can be rapidly configured to support individual requirements. At the same time the growing use of technologies outside the work context and the availability and wide uptake of various social technologies have massively extended the domains where Participatory Design is being used.

New technologies and domains of use have enabled the expansion of Participatory Design to embrace implementation and real use of the technologies as well as ongoing redesign and reconfiguration (Büscher et al. 2004; Hansen et al. 2006; Simonsen and Hertzum 2010, 2012). Using actual technologies during the Participatory Design process offers valuable opportunities. Simulated use of technologies through mock-ups, prototypes and design games can investigate and evaluate anticipated change, but using the actual technologies means that unanticipated changes can also emerge, including inappropriate, undesirable or disastrous side effects as well as unforeseen opportunities and unintended advantageous and desirable possibilities.

The recognition that design is completed in use was shared by many of those involved in Participatory Design and has become more central in recent years (e.g. Balka and Kahnamoui 2004). During the 1990s it manifested as a marked interest in the tailorability of systems (e.g. Trigg and Bødker 1994; Robertson 1998) so users could adapt them to suit their needs after implementation. Tailorability extended to configurability with the increasing availability of off-the-shelf products and the rise of domestic, mobile and embedded technologies. Configurability has more to do with assembling and recombining components into useful devices and services (Balka et al. 2005). But the Participatory Design literature increasingly includes studies of technology use and reconfigurations of technologies in support of new and unanticipated use. This can be generalised as a move to 'designing for design after design', which deliberately defers some aspects of design until after a design project is completed as a way to explicitly support the potential for redesign for unanticipated use or other unanticipated change (A.Telier 2011).

Chapter 3 of this book is devoted to a detailed account of how those using participatory approaches have conceptualised and practised design in their work.

Target audience, aims and structure

This international handbook is written by well-known and experienced researchers and practitioners of Participatory Design who are all deeply embedded in the field and familiar with its development, especially as it has unfolded within the Participatory Design conferences.

Our aims for this book are that it will become the major text for Participatory Design courses at colleges and universities worldwide and that it will endure and remain a relevant reference for the next decade and beyond. Our goal has been to produce a state-of-the-art reference handbook that provides an introduction to, and detailed exploration of, core areas of Participatory Design including thorough literature reviews of both central research contributions and current and future research areas and application domains.

The book's target audience is researchers and practitioners who are already working within Participatory Design, those who are interested in doing so, or those who wish to obtain an authoritative overview of the field and its history. In particular it is intended for:

- *Young researchers* looking for a scholarly handbook on Participatory Design. The book provides emerging researchers, for example graduate students and PhD candidates, with a thorough overview of Participatory Design and a familiarity with the aims and interests of the Participatory Design community. It is also intended to provide insights into potential challenging research areas that these readers might wish to address in their future careers. The contributors to the book have each provided personal statements about why they are so engaged in Participatory Design. These statements reflect the very special qualities of this research area.
- *Senior researchers* who may enjoy the book as the new major reference handbook for Participatory Design. It provides updated overviews of the major areas of the field that may be secondary yet important supplements to existing research interests and expertise. The book is designed to make available the basic literature for teaching advanced bachelor, graduate or doctoral courses. It includes an introduction to Participatory Design, accounts of what the field can offer theoretically, methodological approaches, techniques and tools supporting specific activities, and detailed examples of practical application.
- *Practitioners* who use, or wish to use, participatory approaches in their design practice. As we have discussed in this chapter, a defining characteristic of Participatory Design research is the consistent and systematic engagement with practice. Indeed, very early on Participatory Design was described as research in 'Systems design for, with, and by the users' (Briefs et al. 1983) with action research in collaboration with industry as the preferred research approach. Practitioners might especially value the impressive collection of practical applications of Participatory Design given in Section II. These could also be used as preliminary readings to entice practitioners into the theoretical and methodological material and issues presented in Section I.

Other very popular books have been published on Participatory Design. The two books published by Lawrence Erlbaum (Greenbaum and Kyng 1991a; Schuler and Namioka 1993) have been to date the key handbooks available on Participatory Design and they are widely cited. However, they are out of date in some important areas and do not address the major developments in the field over the past 20 years. This has meant that readings in Participatory Design have needed to be heavily supplemented with various newer articles and papers. This book is intended to encourage reflection on, and learning from, the considerable achievements of Participatory Design research and practice over the past three decades. Most importantly, it is also intended to encourage those contributing to Participatory Design to consider how we might take up the challenges of changing societies, technologies and contexts for technology use today and in the future. It demonstrates why Participatory Design is such a valuable approach to design in general, describes the Participatory Design community and explains why its members have embraced Participatory Design as an important, highly relevant and most rewarding area for research and practice.

The book is structured into two sections.

- *Section I* includes seven chapters each representing a distinct and influential area of Participatory Design. Each chapter presents major research contributions and future research agendas and application domains based on thorough reviews of the literature from the last 30 years (see note at the end of this chapter for a list of sources). Together these seven chapters provide a thorough review of the important areas of Participatory Design research to date, while also looking forward to possible future trends, phenomena, developments, views, etc. that will challenge both the traditions and the current wisdom in the field.
- *Section II* includes three chapters demonstrating the practical, large-scale application of Participatory Design. Each chapter describes and reflects on a project that received the Participatory Design Conference's Artful Integration Award (in 2004, 2006 and 2008 respectively). This award is given to projects nominated and recognised by the Participatory Design community as outstanding achievements by a group of people who, in exceptionally creative ways, have together designed new and useful configurations of technologies and practices. While traditionally design awards have gone to individual designers or single objects or products, the Artful Integration Award emphasises the importance of collaborative participation in design, viewing good design as the effective alignment of diverse collections of people, activities and artefacts.

Section I: Participatory Design – contributions and challenges

Chapter 2 opens this section with a review of the history and heritage of Participatory Design. This history begins with the world famous projects conducted in collaboration with trade unions in Scandinavia during the 1970s and the early struggles to give a voice to those who traditionally lack power in the development process. It continues with the Participatory Design movements in the USA and Canada in the 1980s, where the society of Computer Professionals for Social Responsibility (CPSR) was formed, along with growing recognition that design and development must be situated in the real, everyday actions of people using technology. From there the chapter proceeds through the 1990s, when the Participatory Design Conferences began, to the present, when Participatory Design has become influential even in commercial large-scale information technology projects and has gained widespread academic recognition in a broad range of conferences and journals. The discussion of the heritage of Participatory Design demonstrates how difficult it is to go beyond just 'involving' users in design, to bringing about more equal power relations and genuinely fostering emancipatory participation in actual design projects.

Chapter 3 investigates and elaborates on the design concept. It provides a detailed account of how those using participatory approaches have conceptualised and practised design in their work. Relations and influences between various design traditions and Participatory Design are discussed from the birth of the design movement in 1919, the Bauhaus, to the current design research movement. The historical account of design traditions is complemented by a discussion of the challenges that confront Participatory Design today and how these challenges might be addressed in a 'designerly' way. Recent research initiatives are outlined, pointing to how Participatory Design reinvents itself to face the changing political, economic, social and technological environments. The chapter finally argues that Participatory Design should shift the frame of reference from design projects to design *things* – referring to an 'assembly' around 'matters of concern', which takes place at a certain time and in a certain place. A Participatory Design thing strategy is especially relevant when aspects of democratisation are at stake.

Chapter 4 is dedicated to the ethics of Participatory Design. Participatory Design is exceptional as an international community of researchers and practitioners who expect, and are expected to, engage in the ethics of their practice and who take that engagement very seriously. The chapter explores the defining role of ethics in the development of Participatory Design. An overview of different approaches to ethics is followed by an exploration of the ethical issues of working with users. Its discussion of core ethical issues of Participatory Design is grounded in particular examples drawn from the literature where the expression of these principles has been negotiated by designers and other participants. The chapter calls for new and extended participatory methods, tools and processes that can enable and improve genuine participation, not just in the design of new technologies but in the shaping of future societies. In particular it identifies the need for new and extended Participatory Design methods and tools that can help us envision and resolve ethical issues that might arise in the use of future technologies.

Chapter 5 re-examines the relationship between ethnography and Participatory Design. It provides a much-requested invaluable update on the earlier, influential and much-cited chapter on ethnographic methods and their relation to design (Blomberg et al. 1993) which was included in *Participatory Design: Principles and Practices* (Schuler and Namioka 1993). The chapter examines the commitments and guiding principles of ethnography and Participatory Design, revisits foundational research on the application of ethnography to Participatory Design and explores how ethnography can support the important role of reflexivity in Participatory Design. Given the challenges of designing for large-scale systems, global connections and the need for the participation of people from diverse cultures and socio-economic circumstances, the chapter explains how the sensibilities of ethnography can continue to make an important contribution to the future of Participatory Design.

Chapters 6 and 7 review and discuss ways to do Participatory Design and engage with users in Participatory Design projects. Chapter 6 is devoted to methods and Chapter 7 to tools and techniques. Methods are considered as 'recipes' for how to do Participatory Design, and include tools and techniques as well as general guidelines and organising principles. A rich repertoire of Participatory Design tools and techniques has been developed that can be combined, adapted and extended to be used in new and existing methods and other participatory practices.

Chapter 6 explores how various fundamental commitments of Participatory Design can be translated to ways of organising Participatory Design projects and general guidelines for the design process itself. A selection of Participatory Design methods are described and examined, and inherent perspectives relevant for all Participatory Design methods are discussed in terms of having a say, mutual learning and co-realisation. This chapter addresses some of the fundamental challenges of actually doing Participatory Design projects while maintaining its defining aims and commitments. These include: the challenges of ensuring users continue to have a say in design within the current specialisation of information technology design; how new technologies imply that design increasingly continues after they are implemented; and the challenges to managing the scope and effect of user participation as the organisation of work continues to change.

Chapter 7 presents a rich variety of tools and techniques that can be used in Participatory Design projects to enable various practices of participation. Using a range of examples the chapter explains how these tools and techniques are not intended to be rigidly applied, but instead used in ways that can support participants in making a variety of things, telling stories and enacting aspects of future design and, in the process, forming new, temporary communities that can enable the collective envisioning of future practices. Participatory tools and techniques avoid the formal models and abstract representations of traditional design approaches, and allow designers and users to experiment and evaluate various innovative design possibilities. In turn, this means they can be used and extended to meet the challenges of designing new technologies and practices, with different and diverse groups of users in new and changing design contexts.

Chapter 8 recognises community-based Participatory Design as a distinctive field of Participatory Design research. It draws together and examines a collection of previously published Participatory Design projects that cover different notions of 'community' based in, for example, actual community-based organisations, loosely coupled communities such as local neighbourhood networks, and online communities facilitated by Web 2.0 technologies such as Twitter, Facebook, etc. The complexities, potentials and pitfalls of community-based Participatory Design are considered and the chapter argues for the use and further development of pluralistic approaches to employing and analysing Participatory Design practices across the diverse contexts of different communities and the issues that affect them. The authors suggest that this will require inventiveness with new modes of infrastructuring, attentiveness to new forms of politics and the exploration of new opportunities for community-based Participatory Design.

Section II: Outstanding applications of Participatory Design

Chapter 9 provides one of this section's three cases of practical large-scale applications of Participatory Design. Randy Trigg (former Participatory Design researcher from Xerox PARC) and the Global Fund for Women organisation received the first Artful Integration Award, which was given in 2004. This chapter describes a Participatory Design project that has been ongoing for more than ten years. The project has resulted in the design of a database system for a non-profit organisation that brings together fundraising and grantmaking in ways that accommodate the continually evolving work practices of the organisation. The Global Fund's developing infrastructure weaves together Randy and his colleague Karen Ishimaru's long-standing commitment to cooperative design practices with the Global Fund's commitment to democratic forms of resource mobilisation. The Fund makes grants to seed, support and strengthen local women's rights groups based outside the United States working to address human rights issues. The Global Fund has developed a unique grantmaking process based in a global network of sister organisations, and is recognised and admired for its respectful and responsive relations to its grantees. Since 1987, the Global Fund has granted $90 million to more than 4,000 women's organisations in 172 countries.

Chapter 10 describes the second Artful Integration Award initiative: the Health Information Systems Programme (HISP), an extensive, ongoing international collaboration in health information systems for public health and higher education. HISP comprises a network of related systems development projects, as well as a dual international master's programme in Information Systems and Public Health of the informatics and medical faculties of the University of Oslo, Norway, and the University of Eduardo Mondlane, Mozambique, with additional collaborations including the University of the Western Cape, South Africa, and the University of Dar es Salaam, Tanzania. More than two dozen international and Norwegian doctoral and master's students participate in this programme as teachers, trainers, mentors and advisors for and with health care personnel, as well as pursuing their own research. The open source HISP software development and implementation collaboration now extends to a growing network of countries including India, China, Malawi and Vietnam. Emerging cloud-based infrastructure means that local capacity in the new technologies needs to be developed, offering further opportunities for the use and development of participatory approaches.

Chapter 11 presents the ACTION for Health project that was initiated in 2003 and ended in 2008. The project focused on the social implications of information technology and its introduction into the health system, and aimed to fill gaps about existing knowledge of Canada's health information infrastructure. Health technology in Canada, as in many other countries, is reviewed in terms of its clinical and cost effectiveness. ACTION for Health goes beyond the limits of such traditional assessment by considering the social, ethical and legal aspects of introducing new technologies into the health sector. Through innovative Participatory Design approaches, the project enhanced health technology assessments, leading to improved policies and practices. The chapter draws attention to and explores power relations in Participatory Design projects, providing examples of how these were negotiated during the project and suggestions for those who might find themselves in similar situations.

Further reading

Today, Participatory Design is a well-established area of research and an emerging practice within many areas of information technology design. The Participatory Design research community have since 1990 met at the biennial international Participatory Design Conferences (PDCs).[1] Participatory Design is also represented in many other local and international conferences, as well as in a number of books and special journal issues.[2]

For those who wish to know more about Participatory Design we have in the endnotes provided a list of further readings. This includes a full list of the Participatory Design Conferences (and their themes) from 1990 until 2012. All conference proceedings from 1990 until today are available from http://pdcproceedings.org (1990–2002 as free downloads and from 2004 via the ACM Digital Library). The list also includes the major books on Participatory Design, other related books and the special issues of international journals that have published Participatory Design research.

Notes

1 Below is a list of the Participatory Design Conferences (and their themes) held from the start in 1990 and until 2012:
1990, Seattle, WA, USA (Namioka and Schuler 1990)
1992, MIT, Cambridge, MA, USA (Muller et al. 1992)
1994, Chapel Hill, NC, USA (Trigg et al. 1994)
1996, Cambridge, MA, USA (Blomberg et al. 1996)
1998, Seattle, WA, USA: Broadening Participation (Chatfield et al. 1998)
2000, New York, NY, USA: Designing Digital Environments (Cherkasky et al. 2000)
2002, Malmö, Sweden: Inquiring into the Politics, Contexts and Practices of Collaborative Design Work (Binder et al. 2002)
2004, Toronto, Canada: Interweaving Media, Materials and Practices (Clement et al. 2004a, 2004b)
2006, Trento, Italy: Expanding Boundaries in Design (Jacucci et al. 2006a, 2006b)
2008, Bloomington, Indiana: Experiences and Challenges (Simonsen et al. 2008)
2010, Sydney, Australia: Participation :: The Challenge (Bødker et al. 2010)
2012, Roskilde, Denmark: Embracing New Territories of Participation (Halskov et al. 2012)

2 Books on Participatory Design:

Bjerknes, G., P. Ehn and M. Kyng (eds) (1983) *Computers and Democracy – A Scandinavian Challenge*, Aldershot: Avebury, Gower.

Briefs, U., C. Ciborra and I. Schneider (eds) (1983) *Systems Design for, with, and by the Users*, Amsterdam: North-Holland.

Greenbaum, Joan and Morten Kyng (eds) (1991) *Design at Work: Cooperative Design of Computer Systems*, Chichester: Lawrence Erlbaum Associates.

Schuler, Douglas and Aki Namioka (eds) (1993) *Participatory Design: Principles and Practices*, London: Lawrence Erlbaum Associates.

Other related books:

Ackerman, M. S., C. A. Halvorson, T. Erickson and W. A. Kellog (eds) (2008) *Resources, Co-Evolution and Artifacts*, London: Springer.

Bødker, K., Finn Kensing and Jesper Simonsen (2004) *Participatory IT Design: Designing for Business and Workplace Realities*, Cambridge, MA: MIT Press.

Dittrich, Y., C. Floyd and R. Klischewski (eds) (2002) *Social Thinking –Software Practice*, Cambridge, MA: MIT Press.

Grønbæk, Kaj and Randall Trigg (1999) *From Web to Workplace: Designing Open Hypermedia Systems*, Cambridge, MA: MIT Press.

Simonsen, J., J. O. Bærenholdt, M. Büscher and J. D. Scheuer (eds) (2010) *Design Research: Synergies from Interdisciplinary Perspectives*, London: Routledge.

Special journal issues on Participatory Design:

CACM: *Communications of the ACM*, 36(4), 1993 (eight articles).

CoDesign: *International Journal of CoCreation in Design and the Arts*, 8(2–3), 2012 (six articles).

CSCW: *Computer Supported Cooperative Work: The Journal of Collaborative Computing*, 7(3–4), 1998 (nine articles).

DI: *Design Issues*, 28(3), 2012 (eight articles).

HCI: *Human–Computer Interaction*, 11(3), 1996 (five articles).

SJIS: *Scandinavian Journal of Information Systems*, 21(1), 2009 (three articles).

SJIS: *Scandinavian Journal of Information Systems*, 22(1), 2010 (one article and debate section).

References

A.Telier (Thomas Binder, Pelle Ehn, Giulio Jacucci, Giorgio De Michelis, Per Linde, Ina Wagner) (2011) *Design Things*, Cambridge, MA: MIT Press.

Balka, E. and F. Kahnamoui (2004) 'Technology trouble? Talk to us, findings from an ethnographic field study', *Proceedings of the PDC 2004*, Toronto: CPSR, 224–34.

Balka, E., I. Wagner and C. B. Jensen (2005) 'Reconfiguring critical computing in an era of configurability', *Proceedings of the 4th Decennial Conference on Critical Computing*, Portland, OR: ACM, 79–88.

Bansler, J. and E. Havn (1994) 'Information systems development with generic systems', *Proceedings of the Second European Conference on Information Systems*, Nijenrode: Nijenrode University Press, 707–15.

Binder, T., J. Gregory and I. Wagner (eds) (2002) *Proceedings of the 7th Biennial Participatory Design Conference, PDC 2002, Malmö, Sweden, 23–25 June 2002: Inquiring into the Politics, Contexts and Practices of Collaborative Design Work*, Palo Alto, CA: CPSR.

Bjerknes, G. and T. Bratteteig (1988) 'The memoirs of two survivors – or evaluation of a computer system for cooperative work', *Proceeding of CSCW '88*, Portland, OR: ACM, 167–77.

Bjerknes, G. and T. Bratteteig (1995) 'User participation and democracy: a discussion of Scandinavian research on systems development', *Scandinavian Journal of Information Systems*, 7(1): 73–98.

Bjerknes, G., P. Ehn and M. Kyng (eds) (1983) *Computers and Democracy – A Scandinavian Challenge*, Aldershot: Avebury, Gower.

Blomberg, J., J. Giacomi, A. Mosher and P. Swenton-Hall (1993) 'Ethnographic field methods and their relation to design', in D. Schuler, and A. Namioka (eds) *Participatory Design: Principles and Practices*, London: Lawrence Erlbaum Associates, 123–55.

Blomberg, J., F. Kensing and E. Dykstra-Erickson (eds) (1996) *Proceedings of the 4th Biennial Participatory Design Conference, PDC 1996, Cambridge, MA, USA, 13–15 November 1996*, Palo Alto, CA: CPSR.

Bødker, K., F. Kensing and J. Simonsen (2004) *Participatory IT Design: Designing for Business and Workplace Realities*, Cambridge, MA: MIT Press.

Bødker, K., T. Bratteteig, D. Loi and T. Robertson (eds) (2010) *Proceedings of the 11th Biennial Participatory Design Conference, PDC 2010, Sydney, Australia, November 29 – December 3, 2010: Participation: The Challenge*, New York: ACM.

Bødker, K., F. Kensing and J. Simonsen (2011) 'Participatory Design in information systems development', in H. Isomäki and S. Pekkola (eds) *Reframing Humans and Information Systems*, Berlin: Springer, 115–34.

Briefs, U., C. Ciborra and I. Schneider (eds) (1983) *Systems Design for, with, and by the Users*, Amsterdam: North-Holland.

Büscher, M., M. A. Eriksen, J. F. Kristensen and P. H. Mogensen (2004) 'Ways of grounding imagination', *Proceedings of the Eighth Participatory Design Conference*, Portland, OR: ACM, 193–203.

Chatfield, R. H., S. Kuhn and M. Muller (eds) (1998) *Proceedings of the 5th Biennial Participatory Design Conference, PDC 1998, Seattle, WA, USA, 12–14 November 1998: Broadening Participation*, Palo Alto, CA: CPSR.

Cherkasky, T., J. Greenbaum, P. Mambrey and J. K. Pors (eds) (2000) *Proceedings of the 6th Biennial Participatory Design Conference, PDC 2000, New York, NY, USA, 28 November – 1 December 2000: Designing Digital Environments*, Palo Alto, CA: CPSR.

Clement, A. and P. van den Besselaar (1993) 'A retrospective look at participatory design projects', *Communications of the ACM*, 36(6): 29–37.

Clement, A., F. D. Cindio, A.-M. Oostveen, D. Schuler and P. van den Besselaar (eds) (2004a) *Proceedings of the 8th Biennial Participatory Design Conference, PDC 2004, Toronto, Canada, July 27–31, 2004: Interweaving Media, Materials and Practices, Volume 1*, New York: ACM.

Clement, A., F. D. Cindio, A.-M. Oostveen, D. Schuler and P. van den Besselaar (eds) (2004b) *Proceedings of the 8th Biennial Participatory Design Conference, PDC 2004, Toronto, Canada, July 27–31, 2004: Interweaving Media, Materials and Practices, Volume 2*, Palo Alto, CA: CPSR.

Cross, N. (ed.) (1972) *Design Participation*, London: Academy Editions.

Ehn, P. (1988) *Work-Oriented Design of Computer Artifacts*, second edition, Hillsdale, NJ: Lawrence Erlbaum Associates.

Ehn, P. (1993) 'Scandinavian design: on participation and skill', in D. Schuler and A. Namioka (eds) *Participatory Design: Principles and Practices*, Hillsdale, NJ: Lawrence Erlbaum Associates, 41–78.

Ehn, P. and Kyng, M. (1984) 'A tool perspective on design of interactive computer support for skilled workers', in M. Saaksjarvi (ed.) *Report of the Seventh Scandinavian Research Seminar on Systemeering*, Helsinki: ECIS, 211–42.

Greenbaum, J. and M. Kyng (eds) (1991a) *Design at Work: Cooperative Design of Computer Systems*, Chichester, UK: Lawrence Erlbaum Associates.

Greenbaum, J. and M. Kyng (1991b) 'Preface: memoires of the past', in J. Greenbaum and M. Kyng (eds) *Design at Work: Cooperative Design of Computer Systems*, Chichester, UK: Lawrence Erlbaum Associates, vii–x.

Grønbæk, K., J. Grudin, S. Bødker and L. Bannon (1993) 'Achieving cooperative system design: shifting from a product to a process focus', in D. Schuler and A. Namioka (eds) *Participatory Design: Principles and Practices*, London: Lawrence Erlbaum Associates, 79–97.

Grudin, J. (1991) 'Interactive systems: bridging the gaps between developers and users', *IEEE Computer*, 24 (4): 59–69.

Halskov, K., J. Simonsen and K. Bødker (eds) (2012) *Proceedings of the 12th Biennial Participatory Design Conference, PDC 2012, Roskilde, Denmark, August 12–16, 2012: Embracing New Territories of Participation*, New York: ACM.

Hansen, T. R., J. E. Bardram and M. Soegaard (2006) 'Moving out of the laboratory: deploying pervasive technologies in a hospital', *IEEE Pervasive Computing*, 5(3): 24–31.

Jacucci, G., F. Kensing, I. Wagner and J. Blomberg (eds) (2006a) *Proceedings of the 9th Biennial Participatory Design Conference, PDC 2006, Trento, Italy, August 1–5, 2006: Expanding Boundaries in Design, Volume 1*, New York, NY: ACM.

Jacucci, G., F. Kensing, I. Wagner and J. Blomberg (eds) (2006b) *Proceedings of the 9th Biennial Participatory Design Conference, PDC 2006, Trento, Italy, August 1–5, 2006: Expanding Boundaries in Design, Volume 2*, Palo Alto, CA: CPSR.

Kensing, F. (2000) 'Participatory Design in a commercial context – a conceptual framework', *PDC 2000 Proceedings of the Participatory Design Conference*, Palo Alto, CA: CPSR, 116–26.

Kensing, F. and J. Blomberg (1998) 'Participatory Design: issues and concerns', *Computer Supported Cooperative Work*, 7(3–4): 167–85.

Kyng, M. (1988) 'Designing for a dollar a day', *CSCW '88 Proceedings of the Conference on Computer Supported Cooperative Work*, Palo Alto, CA: ACM, 178–88.

Kyng, M. (1995) 'Making representations work', *Communications of the ACM*, 38(9): 46–55.

Muller, M. J., S. Kuhn and J. A. Meskill (eds) (1992) *Proceedings of the Second Biennial Participatory Design Conference, PDC 1992, MIT, Cambridge, MA, 6–7 November 1992*, Palo Alto, CA: CPSR.

Namioka, A. and D. Schuler (eds) (1990) *Proceedings of the First Biennial Participatory Design Conference, PDC 1990, Seattle, WA, March 31 – April 1, 1990*, Palo Alto, CA: CPSR.

Nygaard, K. and Bergo, O. T. (1975) 'The trade unions – new users of research', *Personnel Review*, 4(2): 5–10.

Oostveen, A.-M. and P. van den Besselaar (2004) 'From small scale to large scale user participation: a case study of participatory design in e-government systems', *Proceedings of the Eighth Participatory Design Conference 2004, Artful Integration: Interweaving Media, Materials and Practices (PDC 2004)*, Palo Alto, CA: ACM, 173–82.

Orlikowski, W. and D. Hofman (1997) 'An improvisational model for change management: the case of groupware technologies', *Sloan Management Review*, 38(2): 11–22.

Robertson, T. (1998) 'Shoppers and tailors: participative practices in small Australian design companies', *Computer Supported Cooperative Work: The Journal of Collaborative Computing*, 7(2–3): 205–21.

Sandberg, Å. (1979) *Computers Dividing Man and Work: Recent Scandinavian Research on Planning and Computers from a Trade Union Perspective*, Stockholm: Arbetslivscentrum.

Sanoff, H. (1978) *Designing with Community Participation*, New York: McGraw-Hill.

Schmidt, K., I. Wagner and M. Tolar (2007) 'Permutations of cooperative work practices: a study of two oncology clinics', *GROUP '07. Proceedings of the Conference on Supporting Group Work*, Florida: ACM, 1–10.

Schön, D. A. (1983) *The Reflective Practitioner: How Professionals Think in Action*, New York: Basic Books.

Schuler, D. and A. Namioka (eds) (1993) *Participatory Design: Principles and Practices*, London: Lawrence Erlbaum Associates.

Simonsen, J. and M. Hertzum (2010) 'Iterative participatory design', in J. Simonsen, J. O. Bærenholdt, M. Büscher and J. D. Scheuer (eds) *Design Research: Synergies from Interdisciplinary Perspectives*, London: Routledge, 16–32.

Simonsen, J. and M. Hertzum (2012) 'Sustained Participatory Design: extending the iterative approach', *Design Issues*, 28(3).

Simonsen, J., T. Robertson and D. Hakken (eds) (2008) *Proceedings of the 10th Biennial Anniversary Conference on Participatory Design, PDC 2008, Bloomington, Indiana, October 1–5, 2008: Experiences and Challenges*, New York: ACM.

Star, S. L. (1991) 'The sociology of the invisible: the primacy of work in the writings of Anselm Strauss', in D. R. Maines (ed.) *Social Organization and Social Process: Essays in Honor of Anselm Strauss*, New Brunswick, NJ: AldineTransaction, 265–83.

Storm Jensen, O. (2002) 'Krop, selv og virkelighed – Skal vi snakke om selvet eller være os selv?' [Body, self and reality – should we talk about the self or be ourselves?], in P. Bertelsen, M. Hermansen and J. Tønnesvang (eds) *Vinkler på selvet – En antologi om selvbegrebets anvendelse i psykologien, [Perspectives on the Self – An Anthology on the Concept of Self and its Use in Psychology]*, Århus: Klim, 119–46.

Suchman, L. (1983) 'Office procedure as practical action: models of work and system design', *ACM Transactions on Office Information Systems*, 1(4): 320–8.

Suchman, L. (1987) *Plans and Situated Actions: The Problem of Human–Machine Communication*, Cambridge: Cambridge University Press.

Suchman, L. (1995) 'Making work visible', *Communications of the ACM*, 38(9): 46–55.

Suchman, L. (2007) *Human–Machine Reconfigurations: Plans and Situated Action*, second edition, Cambridge: Cambridge University Press.

Suchman, L. and R. Trigg (1991) 'Understanding practice: video as a medium for reflection and design', in J. Greenbaum and M. Kyng (eds) *Design at Work: Cooperative Design of Computer Systems*, Hillsdale, NJ: Lawrence Erlbaum Associates, 65–89.

Trigg, R. and S. Bødker (1994) 'From implementation to design: tailoring and the emergence of systemisation in CSCW', *CSCW '94, Proceedings of the Conference on Computer-Supported Cooperative Work, Chapel Hill, North Carolina, October 22–26, 1994*, New York: ACM, 45–54.

Trigg, R., S. I. Anderson and E. Dykstra-Erickson (eds) (1994) *Proceedings of the 3rd Biennial Participatory Design Conference, PDC 1994, Chapel Hill, NC, October 27–28 1994*, Palo Alto, CA: CPSR.

Winograd, T. and F. Flores (1986) *Understanding Computers and Cognition*, New York: Addison-Wesley.

Section I
Participatory Design –
contributions and challenges

2

Heritage

Having a say

Finn Kensing and Joan Greenbaum

This chapter focuses on the early history of Participatory Design projects up to the first Participatory Design Conference in 1990. It explains how the political and social movements of the 1970s and 80s formed a stage for translating participatory research into development of computer applications. Some of the early action projects are described in order to give readers an understanding of the problems and challenges. A central focus is on the roots of Participatory Design in enabling workers to gain a voice in the technologies that affect their working lives. It concludes with reviewing theoretical underpinnings as well as summarising some guiding principles.

The Introduction focuses on the motivations and struggles in early work-oriented design. The general political context is described in order to situate the early projects in the complexity of enabling workers to gain a voice in decision-making about technology. Both action-based projects and theoretical sources are used to explain the development of Participatory Design's guiding principles.

Readers will learn about the early struggles to give voice to those who traditionally lack power in the development process. Equalising power relations and mutual learning are both a motivation and an outcome of the Participatory Design heritage. Of equal importance is the understanding that design and development must be situated in the real, everyday actions of people using technology. The early history is *not* intended as a 'birth story' but rather as a series of struggles that grew out of some mistakes and into new ways of looking at computer system development, traces of which can be seen today in many design situations.

The early heritage demonstrates how difficult it is to do more than 'involve' users in design. Bringing about more equal power relations and actually fostering emancipatory participation remains a critical challenge. The projects discussed here each begin with motivating factors and conclude with lessons learned and the need for further research. Participatory Design history tells us that mistakes and unanswered questions still abound.

Introduction

The roots of Participatory Design are deep and broad. We begin here in the 1970s when progressive ideas spread from the society at large into emerging computer system development in the workplace. This early heritage is intriguing in many ways because the seeds of later participatory approaches have inherited some of the victories of earlier projects as well as some of the continuing challenges.

This chapter lays out some of the struggles in the history of the now maturing – after more than four decades of growth – field of Participatory Design. We discuss some of the lessons learned in the 1970s and 1980s as we address the following questions: What motivated initial projects for choosing a Participatory Design approach? What was in fact designed? How may the heritage be conceptualised? What does the heritage have to offer to those who strive to apply Participatory Design inspired approaches today? Our focus is on Participatory Design action projects where the needs of groups of workers drove researchers to take note of how previously unheard voices could be important in design of technologies. These early projects are discussed within the political context of the 1960s, 70s and 80s, a cold war environment that gave rise to the importance of strong voices speaking out on social issues that affected groups with access to fewer resources. The chapter takes us up to the first Participatory Design Conference in 1990, where the ideas and practices in the early period began to be pulled together into a coherent set of principles. The following chapters will cover later developments within Participatory Design.

We start in Scandinavia in the 1970s with some exemplary cases of projects with what was then known as data processing. In some ways it is no surprise that the heritage discussed here starts in places where trade unions and collective bargaining were strong and able to influence power relations in the workplace. These cases involved trade union activists who sought ways to influence the fast-paced automation that was emerging on their shop floor. The early trade union work set out to ask systems researchers as 'experts' to help them better cope with workplace problems – and indeed Participatory Design helped the workers do this, but it also flipped the project on its ear by introducing the system designers to a whole new set of problems.

We then proceed with a short introduction to another strong inspiration for Participatory Design – ethnographic studies about the introduction of technology into workplaces. These types of studies gave voice to office workers and technicians as they experienced the consequences of workplace change. Chapter 5 gives more detail about the ethnographic approach.

Finally, the chapter provides an overview of some of the main theoretical roots of participation; a topic that will be further explored in Chapter 3. The more specific principles, practices and techniques that Participatory Design has provided may be – and have indeed been – used for other purposes and with other intentions. Understanding and appreciating the theoretical roots of participation are seen as necessary for obtaining what this chapter will begin to describe as genuine participation. And we conclude with some principles we feel are instrumental for carrying out contemporary, genuine and action-based Participatory Design.

While this book describes concepts and practices affecting tools that are applied now to a wide range of digital artefacts – going well beyond the workplace – this chapter focuses on the work-oriented heritage of this field. But the lessons learned bear repeating, as without history we are often left to repeat some of the same mistakes – and as we know too well, the challenges of multi-party participation combined with constantly changing technologies are fertile ground for making mistakes! The participatory perspective we introduce here brings those issues back up to the surface.

The need for participation, in essence, recognises that tensions exist between those with some form of knowledge and power and those without. Kensing (1983) argues that basic requirements for genuine participation include access to information, resources (time, money and expert assistance) and the power to influence decisions. In an extensive review of

Participatory Design projects, Clement and van den Besselaar (1993) suggest further that appropriate participatory development methods and organisational and technical flexibility are also needed.

Political context

What came to be known as Participatory Design started as a reaction to changes in society at large, rooted in local communities as well as in workplaces. In Germany and Austria, for example, where some community groups were experimenting with ways to actively involve citizens in local issues, a new type of process, called a 'Future Workshop', engaged citizens in important issues (see Jungk and Müllert 1987). In the US, where burning social issues such as civil rights and urban problems needed to be addressed through grass-roots action, Participatory Action Research (PAR) began to gain serious hold in the research and public sector communities (see Whyte 1991). Also in the US, the war in Vietnam propelled activists to examine technology through groups such as Computer People for Peace and, later, Computer Professionals for Social Responsibility (CPSR), which became involved in key influencing political policies around technology issues, and which sponsored the Participatory Design conferences from the very start. In England the path-breaking socio-technical approach, among other activities, evolved to directly confront the fact that technology had social and political roots (Mumford 1972). The socio-technical approach spread well beyond England and was, in fact, used widely in Scandinavia among employers' associations.

Within the field of computer science the times and tensions were also reflected through the lens of professional organisations. Until the later 1980s, most computer programs were custom designed for huge mainframe computers; there were no generic applications to re-apply to different companies or situations. Systems analysis and design – the process of developing mainframe computer systems – was strongly influenced by management principles that controlled the flow of how programs were designed. Classic textbooks on design (e.g. Yourdon 1982; Demarco 1979) advocated a 'waterfall model' where problems were defined by management with no input from those who would be using the system. In the early 1980s as micro-computers (precursors to mini and desktop computing) began to emerge, the concept of 'users' began to emerge. Human–Computer Interaction, and its professional association Computer Human Interaction (CHI), focused on how then-emerging interfaces could be designed for presumed 'users'. Computer Human Interaction, however, borrowed the cognitive assumption from earlier computer system design, establishing a set of procedures that stemmed from how designers thought users might think. From a participatory perspective, this cognitive approach is considered a central fallacy in that it assumes that individual users' thoughts could be transcribed into programmed interfaces and applications. Even when users were invited to laboratories to test out interface designs, the focus was on 'capturing' user eye movement or keystrokes, rather than actually involving the users in the context of their own work. Computer Supported Cooperative Work (CSCW), a professional conference group, distanced itself from the single-user cognitive approach, focusing instead on the social and cooperative nature of work. CSCW's origins coincided with the beginning of network and distributed systems in the late 1980s as it introduced ethnographic and social science analysis into computer system design. But CSCW also had a central fallacy to many who moved into what later became Participatory Design: namely, the focus levelled work and workers with management and failed to examine the political nature of work and its power relations. The CSCW conference of 1988 gave birth to a sub-group that was concerned with the conflicting and politically sensitive issues of workers and their muted voices. This sub-group created the first Participatory Design Conference in 1990, joining forces with CSCW colleagues, yet giving voice to the politics behind all design.

Early action projects

The action-based stories in this chapter begin in Norway, where workers in the Iron and Metal union teamed up with Kristen Nygaard, a computer scientist, and Olav Terje Bergo, an economist, from the Norwegian Computing Centre (Norsk Regnesentral) in order to have a say at the bargaining table about how computers should be introduced at the workplace.

Kristen Nygaard, who pioneered this stream of work in Norway in the early 1970s, referred to it as a 'knowledge strategy' for trade unions (Nygaard and Bergo 1975a). Nygaard, an early developer of what is considered the first object-oriented computer language,[1] stressed that in order to have a say in relation to the ways in which technology is introduced at the workplace, workers and their organisations have to build up a 'knowledge base' to draw on when they met with management. While unions had the right to bargain about wages and working conditions, the idea of having the right to bargain about the type of technology-mediated change brought into the workplace was very radical for its time. Yet, as we shall see, the knowledge-base strategies worked up to a point. Nygaard and the unions soon found that other forces came into play.

Out of these early experiences grew three types of projects that tried to take workplace actions and workers seriously; each addressed concerns that didn't have clear problem definitions or methods for solving them, and each brought forth new lessons for new problems that still need to be attacked. The first we call Knowledge Strategy projects, which began to unravel the very unequal balance between workers, who knew little about technology, with system developers who, like designers today, spoke in a language that was hard for the workers to understand and relate to. The second set of early projects are called Design and Intervention projects where, building on and expanding the knowledge base of workers, the concern was to show, by concrete examples, that there are technological alternatives, and that those alternatives reflect different starting values. Indeed, this is very much the case with social networking and communication design situations now: the clear need to demonstrate alternative visions. The third type of projects involved ethnographic analyses of relations between work, workers and technology. As a reaction to the decontextualised studies of such relations that were most common at the time, American anthropologists, who were affiliated with the Xerox Palo Alto Research Center (located in Silicon Valley, California), applied their skills in the interest of understanding a new domain. Today various versions of ethnographically informed analysis have found their way – with or without anthropologists – to the design of many different kinds of technologies.

Knowledge strategy projects

The idea of involving workers in decisions about technology didn't suddenly spring out of the air; two significant management and political situations acted as triggers. One factor, not unique to Scandinavia, was the widespread use of management strategies to divide and conquer workers' power by automating tasks and de-skilling workers. For an elaborate discussion of such issues see Greenbaum (1975) and Sandberg (1979). These management actions, while having precursors at the turn of the twentieth century in Scientific Management, sought to standardise and simplify work tasks in order to create interchangeable workers as well as interchangeable manufactured parts. Standardisation and simplification were intended to lower wages and better control the workforce (see Greenbaum 1979). Charlie Chaplin's film *Modern Times* (from 1936) illustrates the outrageous effects on workers whose skill is removed and inserted into automated equipment. The process of de-skilling workers can still be seen in jobs such as those in call centres, where work practices are standardised to reduce labour costs and fit into computerised routines. The Norwegian Iron and Metal workers were experiencing this as Nygaard and Bergo began working with them in the early 1970s.

The second factor was indeed unique to Scandinavia, where legislation and workplace agreements had been written in the late 1960s and through the 70s allowing workers the right to information and some degree of co-determination over the conditions of their work. The limitations in these arrangements, however, were contested in the knowledge strategy projects described here, where workers often had to fight for information about management's technology plans.

The Norwegian NJMF[2] project from 1970 to 1973 (Nygaard and Bergo 1975a, 1975b), the Swedish DEMOS[3] project from 1975 to 1980 (Ehn and Sandberg 1983; Ehn 1988) and the Danish DUE[4] project from 1977 to 1980 (Kensing 1981; Jacobsen et al. 1981; Kyng and Mathiassen 1982) were based on similar concerns. While we discuss lessons learned from all these projects, we have chosen to give a detailed account of the rationale and activities of only one of these, the NJMF project, as it became an inspiration for later work.

In these early projects workers and researchers analysed the specific problems with new technology at the workplace and developed strategies to boost workers' power in relation to management's technology initiatives. The projects were carried out as action research and were organised as a reaction to workers' experiences from a vast number of co-determination experiments carried out cooperatively between the employers' federation and the labour movements in each of the Scandinavian countries. In the Danish case, for instance, workers reported that these experiments stopped before any substantial changes towards real influence had been achieved, and workers were reluctant to press for more influence for fear of reprisals (Tjørnehøj 1976; Ehn and Kyng 1987). These experiments were inspired by socio-technical research at the Tavistock Institute in England (see e.g. Trist et al. 1963; Trist 1981; Mumford 1983).

The English projects were rooted in the path-breaking notion that technology was a result of a social and political process, and therefore attention to technical design was embedded in all levels of discourse from the shop floor through political action. Since the early 1970s, Mumford and associates had worked on a socio-technical approach (see Mumford 1972, 1993a, 1993b; Mumford et al. 1978) advocating development of the social and technical systems more or less parallel to each other. This approach strove for efficient use of technology and increased job satisfaction for the intended users. The approach was heavily critiqued by Scandinavian researchers involved in trade union projects in the mid to late 1970s. The critique was twofold (Ehn and Sandberg 1979; Kyng and Mathiassen 1982). From an ideological point of view, the approach to workers' participation was evaluated as too narrow, because workers were mainly participating as informants in a process dominated by managers and their specialists. Further, the proposed techniques for decision-making in projects were evaluated as naïve, because they suggested that decisions should be taken by voting, thus not reflecting the distribution of power at the workplace. However, the socio-technical approach should be acknowledged for insisting on a focus on organisational as well as technical issues, and also for introducing prototyping as early as 1978 (Mumford et al. 1978, p. 250).

The Iron and Metal project

The Iron and Metal project started as workers realised that their deteriorating working process involved dislocation, de-skilling and less influence on their own working conditions. Additionally they saw the need to push co-determination rights to include the right to information about technology (see Nygaard and Bergo 1975a).

Nygaard and Bergo (1975b) report on an important lesson they learned at the very beginning of the project, and one that pops up again and again: namely, that the best-laid plans are not the way the project will end up! So though plans are helpful resources for action (Suchman 1987) in complex situations, participatory designers need to be prepared to alter plans as they learn more about the situation and the context. When the Iron and Metal project began, there had been very few projects that had taken the interests of trade unions as their starting point, so there was little experience to build on. Initially, Nygaard and Bergo describe that they had planned the project in a rather traditional way, *without* the active participation of the workers, relying instead on the researchers to conduct the analysis. This comprised:

- mapping the goals and interests of the workers and their union;
- analysing three other management systems used in Norway, showing how the purpose and mechanisms inscribed in these systems affected the interests of the workers and their union;
- formulating workers' requirements for these systems;
- analysing the trade union's earlier experience with building competences;
- analysing which competencies were needed in relation to information technology and management.

In the initial plan these activities were to be carried out by the researchers, while workers and the union were to be involved mainly through interviews.

The reaction from trade unionists was that it would be interesting to see the results, but that they couldn't see any practical relevance. How were the workers supposed to make use of the knowledge produced? The two researchers then realised that they were in the process of producing reports that would end up unread on the bookshelves in the trade union hall. The results they were about to produce did not fit into the reality of the workers' lives; they could not use the knowledge developed as a resource for action.

In order to fill this gap, Nygaard and Bergo got together with the workers and their union and began to apply action research practices in order to build technical and organisational knowledge for the workers to use in negotiations with employers and their management experts. Action research, an important component of Participatory Design, seeks to engage both the affected workers and the outside researchers in studying and remedying existing problems (Greenwood and Levin 1998).

Nygaard and Bergo describe the rationale for the new research design, involving action research, in the following way:

- The purpose is to develop new knowledge geared towards the workers' ability to take action to increase their say over the ways in which the computer systems are introduced at the workplace.
- Actions for change require that the goals are discussed (and shared) among the workers, and that the actions are part of a plan.
- Results of the research are not reports and papers, but all *actions* taken by workers, at the local or the central level, that are based on the research project, and that intend to increase the influence of workers on information technology and management in the companies.
- Therefore reports and papers are useful only if they lead to such actions among workers.

Thus, the project had a triple focus on what Wagner and Gärtner (1996) later called Arenas A, B and C: namely the individual project arena (A), the company arena (B) and the national arena (C).

Based on such a rationale, the new research design had the following elements:

- A strategy report focusing on *actions* that would call for new knowledge
- Iterative development of *teaching materials*
- A *working process*: at the four participating companies 20–30 workers in smaller groups met every other week for a few hours to discuss problems with computer systems and management – and how to deal with such problems. The researchers functioned as lecturers and consultants and sometimes as students, as they realised they had much to learn about how mainframe management systems worked in practice. The groups then produced reports that were primarily written by the workers.

While the first research design was oriented towards analysis and proposals made by the researchers, the second research design focused on establishing a *learning cycle within the union*, where actions for change generated needs for new knowledge, which furthered new actions. And the workers involved found their own voice and technical vocabulary to use in negotiations with management.

And here, through the first mistakes, we find a key argument for what is now called Participatory Design. Literature in the field commonly bases the need for participation on several arguments. One, a political argument, emphasises that people *should have the right* to influence their working conditions. Another central argument is pragmatic. Its focus is that in the process of involving people who will be affected as active participants, learning will take place between the 'experts' and the participants which can result in better designs. And as we will see, this process of learning between and among the different power groups came to be known as 'mutual learning', a cornerstone of Participatory Design.

For Nygaard and Bergo it was both arguments and at the same time – not one without the other. It is through participation that new ideas and knowledge would be produced or sought for, and this was part of the process for standing up for one's rights. The project showed that rights were not something given by those in power – rather, rights were something workers had to fight for through knowledge-based negotiations.

Voicing participation

In this way, what we call genuine participation as practised by proponents of Participatory Design is significantly different from participation as seen by other traditions such as user-centred design, contextual design and user-driven innovation (Norman and Draper 1986; Beyer and Holtzblatt 1998), and other approaches that offer some form of 'user empowerment', which have become more 'mainstream' today. While Participatory Design differentiates itself from these other approaches we place the practice within a spectrum of ways that prospective users of a technology can get involved. However, Participatory Design as an emancipatory approach has little regard for approaches that solely involve users as informants through interviews, focus groups or other one-way techniques in a process otherwise controlled by information technology designers and their clients/managers. Such one-way data-gathering approaches we do not consider to be genuine participation.

In addition to the local achievements obtained by active participation of union members, the early Scandinavian projects also contributed with other types of results that should be briefly mentioned. For instance, the Scandinavian researchers reacted against the idea that technology at the workplace should take place solely under the co-determination agreements that were in place in their countries. Instead, in the Swedish DEMOS project, Ehn and Sandberg (1979) proposed that introduction of technology at the workplace should be based on negotiation within collective bargaining rights, just as wages and working conditions are negotiated. Second, and perhaps more significantly in terms of lasting effect, the Iron and Metal project was the basis for the formulation of the Norwegian technology agreement signed by the trade unions and the employers' federation in 1975 (see Ciborra and Schneider 1983; Mathiassen et al. 1983). Third, many tools and techniques that have been developed within Participatory Design (see, for example, Kensing and Blomberg 1998, and also Chapter 7 of this volume) have been adopted by other approaches, although more often than not without the emancipatory rationale upon which Participatory Design approaches are founded. Fourth, another long-lasting result came from the Danish DUE project. For more than a decade, up to ten one-week technology courses for trade unionists were organised by the researchers, who had also developed the teaching materials (Kyng and Mathiassen 1982). Finally, the researchers also developed new university courses on technology analysis and design based on their experiences with the trade unions. Such courses, in updated versions, are still offered at bachelor's and master's levels. Further, master's and PhD theses were produced and contributed to building an additional branch of computer science and information systems called Human–Computer Interaction and Computer Supported Cooperative Work.

Not all issues were dealt with in these early projects. Indeed, the Iron and Metal workers did not end up implementing any new technology; rather, the outcome was a new process. The most apparent missing link was probably the idea that in order for workers to gain real influence on technology at their workplace, new technologies have to be designed based on workers' interests and values. This became a key issue in the subsequent projects.

Design and intervention projects

The knowledge strategy projects began to nibble away at the problem of how workers could learn more about computers and how the systems designers/researchers could learn more about what workers really needed in the workplace. But then came the problem that if workers really got involved – not just as users but as participants – would the design of alternative systems be different? The answer, as we will see, is still part of an ongoing conundrum, lurking today at the heart of designing truly new tools and applications.

While participants in the earlier projects did not engage themselves directly in the design and implementation of new information technology applications, this became the focal point of later strategies like UTOPIA (1981–4) and Florence (1984–7) and many subsequent projects. The rationale for this was that while experience from the early projects had shown that strong unions may increase the workers' influence on technology, this was a necessary but not a sufficient condition for real changes to take place. It appeared to be necessary to create alternative technologies as well as to fight vendors' monopoly over technological choices.

The UTOPIA project was carried out by computer and social science researchers at the Swedish Centre for Working Life, the Royal Institute of Technology, also in Sweden, and Aarhus University in Denmark. The project cooperated with a supplier Liber/TIPS and a Swedish and a Danish newspaper. It focused on typographical issues such as page make-up and image processing in the newspaper industry. The goals of the UTOPIA project were to develop technology for graphical workers that contributed to high-quality newsprint products, skilled work and a democratic organisation of work, goals that sharply contrasted with the management-driven objective of de-skilling workers (Ehn and Kyng 1984; Bødker et al. 1987; Ehn 1988). The project aimed at creating technological alternatives with an involved trade union based on their interests and concerns. The researchers set up a technology laboratory, in which trade union representatives participated as skilled workers in prototyping technology for page make-up and image processing. For the workers, control over their work process and the quality of work and results were paramount issues.

The motivation for engaging in alternative technology production was that the knowledge strategy projects of the 1970s in Norway (Iron and Metal), Sweden (DEMOS) and Denmark (DUE) had realised that existing production technology more and more often constitutes an insurmountable barrier preventing the realisation of trade union demands for the quality of work and a meaningful job (Bødker et al. 1987). Further, the rationale was that it could be more realistic to try to develop technology applicable for a whole industry rather than local unions formulating alternatives for each of their employers to implement. The project therefore set out to produce a 'demonstration example', showing that trade union development of technology would be a feasible strategy (ibid.).

The idea of cooperating with the technology companies and the newspapers aimed to bring the research prototypes closer to commercially viable products that could be tested in real-life situations. However, it turned out, not too surprisingly, that management and even the funding research agency were not interested in the changes in work organisation and training that the research project had crafted. Further, the journalists' union also lost interest in the idea as they began to pursue other interests – an issue that occurs all too frequently in participatory projects, as workers and community groups also have other things to do (Ehn 1988). As a result, the prototypes were never turned into commercial products. Interestingly, the problems of vendor monopoly and worker or user lack of interest still loom large in the challenges facing participatory practitioners.

However, through the technology laboratory, the UTOPIA project went one step further than the earlier work: it brought workers out of their workplace into a joint space where they could freely experiment and imagine the types of digital tools they might need. This was long before prototyping and off-the-shelf applications were common, and so it was difficult to help spark people's imagination of future alternatives. Even now, with all the building blocks of interface designs, applications and social networking software, the problem of *imagining* alternative solutions still rears its head. The UTOPIA project's concept of setting up laboratory-like settings where designers/researchers and prospective users could work together to mock-up or prototype new technologies and new ways of working, is one of the lessons that still stay with us. Further, the UTOPIA project developed and designed new ways of looking at future possibilities that inspired and influenced Participatory Design methods (see Chapter 6) and Participatory Design tools and techniques (see Chapter 7).

The Florence project was another example of a research project with design and intervention strategies. Unlike the UTOPIA research, though, it brought the focus directly back into the workplace (Bjerknes and Bratteteig 1987, 1988). A motivation for the project was to build computer systems for nurses' daily work, focusing on communication and the professional language and skills of nurses in order for them to gain control over the computer systems and their own working conditions. And a central idea was that technological solutions should be tested in real work situations. Florence was also carried out by researchers and workers, this time nurses at two hospitals in Oslo, Norway, and two computer scientists and an anthropologist from the university, although in this case the union was not a partner.

As with earlier projects, Florence focused on workers whose voices were rarely heard, and feminist concepts from the period were an important influence, particularly in relation to fostering an environment where nurses felt comfortable to speak out about what was important in their work. While the project did not involve unions it did actively engage nurses who saw their work through the eyes of their patients, rather than through the lens of doctors' orders or computerised procedures.

The project made a prototype based on the existing paper-based 'kardex' – the nurses' equivalent to the physicians' medical record. Reflecting on the final evaluation meeting, the researchers note (Bjerknes and Bratteteig 1988) that while the nurses used the system, it was not easy to grasp how the system actually fitted their work. Developing an understanding of the way work gets done and listening to the voices of the actual people in the field remain key lessons that still live on with Participatory Design today – lessons that continue to present an enormous challenge in the national and international development of medical records systems.

The Florence project was among the pioneers – for the purpose of designing new computer applications – in applying observations of real work situations in combination with more detached techniques such as interviews and workshops. Inspiration for this came from, and overlapped with the work of, American anthropologists, as we shall see in the next section.

While the motivation for Florence was to help the nurses give voice to their concerns at work, a strict workplace orientation on the nursing profession was difficult to maintain; other occupational groups, like physicians and nursing assistants, wanted to be considered as well. This is a problem that remains today as different groups or stakeholders within an organisation may have conflicting power relations and thus differing views about what activities an application should support. There are no easy fixes for this problem, but as we will see in the concluding part of this chapter and in subsequent chapters, there are principles and tools and techniques that help groups speak for themselves.

Ethnographic analysis of relations between work and technology

Another important part of the Participatory Design heritage is the influence of the work practice and technology research area at the Xerox Palo Alto Research Center (PARC) on early explorations of the role of ethnography in Participatory Design. Anthropologists at PARC were involved in studies of the relations between people, technology and work in the service sector in the US. They performed detailed analyses of the ways work gets done, the in situ rationales that workers apply, and the technologies and other resources they bring to bear. They were able to show how new technologies, when introduced into the workplace, shape the working practices of office workers and service technicians and the people with whom they interact. Their work demonstrated the consequences of relying solely on the managers' or information technology designers' understanding of work, and began to argue for the importance of involving workers in the design of new technologies.

These workplace studies dealt with: office workers (Wynn 1979; Suchman 1983; Suchman and Wynn 1984; Blomberg 1987); service technicians (Orr 1990); and ground operations at an airport (Brun-Cottan et al. 1991). In her much acclaimed book *Plans and Situated Actions,* Suchman gives a profound critique of the then dominant cognitive science approach to technology design as it relied on an understanding of human activity where plans direct action. She advocated an alternative view, where plans are seen as potential resources for action but need to be understood as they unfold in situ (Suchman 1987, 2007).

Later, the anthropologists at PARC joined forces with computer scientists to find ways that such detailed studies of work practices could inform a participatory approach to the design of technology. Here we will just mention some of the earlier works, as Chapter 5 goes into more detail. Suchman and Trigg (1991) and Jordan and Henderson (1995) describe how video recordings may be used for analysis and design. Blomberg et al. (1990; further developed in Blomberg et al. 1993) were among the first to provide a methodological introduction to the guiding principles of ethnographically informed analysis when it is conducted as part of technology design. Ethnographic approaches strive to gain an appreciation for what workers are doing and how they see things. Blomberg et al. (1993) describe 'four main principles that guide much ethnographic work':

- [Ethnographers make] a commitment to study the activities of people in their everyday settings … as opposed to a laboratory or experimental setting.
- [Ethnographers hold] a belief that particular behaviours can only be understood in the everyday context in which they occur.
- Ethnographers describe how people actually behave, not how they ought to behave.
- [E]thnographers are concerned with describing behavior in terms relevant and meaningful to study participants. This contrasts with the requirements of survey research where relevant categories must be known before the study begins.

(Blomberg et al. 1993, pp. 125–6)

In the rest of the book you will find many examples of how ethnographically informed analysis has found its way – with or without the involvement of anthropologists – into the design of work-related technologies, as well as other forms of Participatory Design.

Voice and democracy: theoretical roots for participation

In the deep-rooted system of Participatory Design heritage, there are many theoretical currents that have served to nurture active involvement in technological design. It was apparent in the cases described in this chapter that supporting new voices meant breaking with the Cartesian dualism inherent in traditional computer development work. As Ehn, one of the UTOPIA project researchers, explained it in *Work-Oriented Design of Computer Artifact*s,

> The prototypical Cartesian scientist or system designer is an observer. He does not partici-pate in the world he is studying, but goes home to find the truth about it by deduction from the objective facts that he has gathered.

(Ehn 1988, p. 52)

And, growing out of the Xerox PARC studies mentioned earlier, Lucy Suchman's book *Plans and Situated Actions* (1987) set the stage for understanding that human actions – in and outside the workplace – are not simple steps followed according to plans, but rather actions situated in the concrete situations before us.

From inside the world of computer science, influential works such as Winograd and Flores's *Understanding Computers and Cognition: A New Foundation for Design* (1986) critiqued the Cartesian and rationalistic traditions of system design, and set in motion a new framework for under-standing that 'in designing tools we are designing ways of being' (p. xi). And setting these ideas in motion, Schön's book, *The Reflective Practitioner* (1979), helped early experimenters under-stand how both workers and designers could actively reflect on their work in the midst of concrete situations.

Here we focus on three crucial roots in the early history that both inspired projects and helped set up working principles and practices: (1) *Political economy*, workers' movements and rights in the struggles between workers and management/capital; (2) *Democracy*, the belief in the right of people to express themselves in governments and communities, and its extension in the workplace and in the design of technology; and (3) *Feminism*, the grass-roots movement of women asking questions and initiating change through direct actions.

There are, in addition, multiple strands of influential thinkers and writers whose work has influenced the need for participatory actions about technologies. Clearly, a movement as broad as this has numerous starting points and what are often called 'birth stories'. Our intention is not to seek out these 'birth' myths, but rather to weave heritage stories together in a pattern that newcomers can understand. It should be noted that computer system design, as technological practice, was embedded in top-down thinking, and that books like *Understanding Computers and Cognition* (Winograd and Flores 1986), as well as Herbert and Stuart Dreyfus's *Mind over Machine* (Dreyfus and Dreyfus 1986), were instrumental in breaking down the barriers that formal rule-oriented computer science placed in the way of user participation.

The early Iron and Metal workers project in Norway was based in a Marxist critique of capital and the mechanism through which the power of capitalist control pushed workers into corners where their skills and knowledge were taken away in the interest of faster, cheaper production. Later projects, such as UTOPIA with the graphic workers, sought to directly confront management rule with creative worker involvement. These works were inspired by Braverman's *Labor and Monopoly Capital* (1974), which showed that management, acting in the 'best interests' of corporate boards and shareholders, got more labour out of workers by a process called 'de-skilling' – removing the knowledge of workers from their daily tasks and embedding it into the control of technical systems – both administrative and machine- (computer) driven. In *In the Name of Efficiency* (Greenbaum 1979) Greenbaum showed that the de-skilling process, while being transported to the very computer programmers and operators who were thought of as 'highly' skilled, was not a natural or inevitable occurrence, and therefore could be fought.

For many, the pragmatic philosophy of John Dewey has been inspirational as it addresses active engagement in creating and maintaining democratic practices. While much of Dewey's writing has been directly applied to education, it has resounding notes for Participatory Design of technologies. At root is the concept of bottom–up active engagement through personal experience. This means, of course, that ideas and actions that grow out of one's experience in a work situation, as in an educational experience, form a cornerstone in shaping the tools that are applied to that experience. In essence, Dewey's beliefs go far beyond the idea of user involvement, or simple user-centred design. Like the early heritage cases described in this chapter, his work seeks not only to help people gain (and retain) knowledge but to use that knowledge towards broader, more fundamental goals such as freedom and democratic rights.

On the issue of freedom, for example, Dewey argues that:

> There can be no greater mistake, however, than to treat freedom as an end in itself … For freedom from restrictions, the negative side is to be prized only as a means to freedom which is power; power to frame purposes; to judge wisely, to evaluate desires by the consequences, which will result from acting upon them; power to select and order means to select chosen ends into operation.
>
> *(Dewey 1938, p. 64)*

Feminism is a third strand underpinning participatory actions. An integral part of feminism gives voice to personal experience. In the 1960s, women around the developed world acted upon their experience and developed grass-roots practices to gain and regain voice and control over their own lives. By the 1970s and 80s these actions were supported by a wealth of literature giving voice to previously invisible thoughts and actions. In the sciences, for example, Evelyn Fox Keller (1985) asked why 'objectivity' and 'impersonal judgment' were the basis of what was considered good science. And, by extension, research like the Florence project with nurses asked why computer systems designed for nurses should be designed by systems professionals without the experience and personal knowledge of nurses' daily work (Greenbaum 1990). In fact, today, feminist movements, including those now strongly based in developing countries, are giving voice to previously invisible questions and actions, examples of which will be given in Chapter 10.

Reflecting on heritage: guiding principles

The heritage of Participatory Design is not set in stone. Movement from simple involvement to active participation has many beginnings in different situations. However, for those entering the field we offer our interpretation of a set of basic principles. Further, we acknowledge that such principles have been practised in different ways because of power relations in local conditions, as well as the ethical and political concerns of individual Participatory Design projects.

Understanding the conditions for and the consequences of 'in some way' actively including people in technology design and implementation has been the glue that keeps this maturing field of academics and professionals together. The principles and practices of these groups have further been stimulated by ongoing discussions of the theoretical and political underpinning of participation, as well as experimenting with new ways of developing methods that facilitate participation.

While the early cases described in this chapter grew out of strong union movements, the basic set of beliefs and practices lives on in areas where trade unions are not a central focus of power relations or may not exist. These principles are based firmly on:

- *Equalising power relations* – finding ways to give voice to those who may be invisible or weaker in organisational power structures. Clearly, in the workplace settings described in this chapter both management and technical experts had more power than the workers on the shop floor, thus giving voice to workers was a critical starting point. In community and local government settings it is important to help people with less money, power or influence to find ways of asserting their needs to those in power. This is an integral part of:
- *Democratic practices* – putting into play the practices and role models for equality among those some call 'stakeholders'. Democracy is often thrown around as a concept that is assumed to happen by itself but, as Dewey and others point out, it requires educated and engaged people acting on their own interests and in the interests of the common good. The projects described here made strides in attempting to bring participants up to speed in this process by educating them in technical jargon, where necessary, and engaging them in the process of project-building. But democracy does not happen in the abstract, and is rooted in:
- *Situation-based actions* – working directly with people in their workplace or homes to understand actions and technologies in actual settings, rather than through formal abstractions. As we saw from the studies in this chapter, the early projects broke the mould by moving away from formal, abstract technical description towards activities by and with people in their working environment. These actions gave rise to:
- *Mutual learning* – encouraging and enhancing the understanding of different actors by finding common ground and ways of working. As people with technical expertise work with workers on the shop floor – when they actually engage and listen and take note of conditions and questions – then both the technical experts and the workers have a chance to learn from each other. The process of mutual learning can give rise to:
- *Tools and techniques* – that actually, in practical situations, help different actors express their needs and visions. These early projects developed a range of techniques for active engagement through training programmes, paper-based mock-ups, prototypes and workshops. Later chapters will describe additional tools and techniques that have been added to a participatory repertoire. These tools are important for helping people develop:

- *Alternative visions about technology* – whether it be in the workplace, home, public place or elsewhere – ideas that can generate expressions of equality and democratic practices. And as mentioned earlier, alternative visions about technical choice are difficult to imagine, even with new software tools and applications. But the book returns to this issue later on.

The pre-1990 heritage cases described in this chapter each experimented with confronting several of these guiding principles in order to give people a voice in technology that affected their daily lives. The following chapters proceed from these roots, expanding on lessons learned and problems left unsolved.

Notes

1 Simula, considered the first object-oriented programming language, was designed to simulate traffic flow patterns for streets. Instead of the focus on procedures, which marked all earlier programming languages, Simula introduced the concept of objects – or data elements which could be integrated into any part of the program.
2 NJMF is a Norwegian acronym for Norwegian Iron and Metal Workers Union.
3 DEMOS is a Swedish acronym for Democratic Control and Planning in Working Life.
4 DUE is a Danish acronym for Democracy, Development and EDP (Electronic Data Processing).

References

Beyer, H. and K. Holtzblatt (1998) *Contextual Design: Defining Customer Centered Systems*, Waltham, MA: Morgan Kaufmann.

Bjerknes, G. and T. Bratteteig (1987) 'Florence in Wonderland: System development with nurses', in G. Bjerknes, P. Ehn and M. Kyng (eds) *Computers and Democracy: A Scandinavian Challenge*, Aldershot: Avebury, 279–95.

Bjerknes, G. and T. Bratteteig (1988) 'The memoirs of two survivors', *Proceedings of the ACM Conference on Computer Supported Cooperative Work*, New York: ACM.

Blomberg, J. (1987) 'Social interaction and office communication: effects on users' evaluation of new technologies', in R. Kraut (ed.) *Technology and the Transformation of White Collar Work*, Hillsdale, NJ: Lawrence Erlbaum Associates, 195–210.

Blomberg, J., J. Giacomi, A. Mosher and P. Swento-Wall (1990) 'Ethnographic field methods and their relation to design', in A. Namioka and D. Schuler (eds) *Proceedings of the First Biennial Participatory Design Conference, PDC 1990, Seattle, WA, March 31 – April 1, 1990*, Palo Alto, CA: CPSR.

Blomberg, J., J. Giacomi, A. Mosher and P. Swento-Wall (1993) 'Ethnographic field methods and their relation to design', in D. Schuler and A. Namioka (eds) *Participatory Design: Principles and Practices*, Hillsdale, NJ: Lawrence Erlbaum Associates, 123–55.

Bødker, S., P. Ehn, J. Kammersgaard, M. Kyng and Y. Sundblad (1987) 'A Utopian experience', in G. Bjerknes, P. Ehn and M. Kyng (eds) *Computers and Democracy: A Scandinavian Challenge*, Aldershot: Avebury, 251–78.

Braverman, H. (1974) *Labor and Monopoly Capital: The Degradation of Work in the Twentieth Century*, New York: Monthly Review Press.

Brun-Cottan, F., K. Forbes, C. Goodwin, M. H. Goodwin, B. Jordan, L. Suchman and R. Trigg (1991) *Workplace Project: Designing for Diversity and Change Video*, Palo Alto, Xerox PARC Video Production, Xerox Palo Alto Research Center. Videotape.

Ciborra, C. and L. Schneider (1983) 'Technology bargaining in Norway', in U. Briefs, C. Ciborra and L. Schneider (eds) *Systems Design for, with, and by the Users: Proceedings of the IFIP WG 9.1 Working Conference on Systems Design for, with, and by the Users, Riva De Sole, Italy, 1982*, Amsterdam: North-Holland, 20–24.

Clement, A. and P. van den Besselaar (1993) 'A retrospective look at PD projects', *Communications of the ACM*, 36(6): 29–37.

Demarco, T. (1979) *Structured Analysis and System Specification*, New York: Prentice Hall.

Dewey, J. (1938) *Experience and Education*, New York: Macmillan.

Dreyfus, H. and Dreyfus, S. (1986) *Mind over Machine: The Power of Human Intuition and Expertise in the Era of the Computer*, New York: Free Press.

Ehn, P. (1988) *Work-Oriented Design of Computer Artifacts*, Stockholm: Arbetslivscentrum.

Ehn, P. and M. Kyng (1984) 'A tool perspective on design of interactive computer support for skilled workers', in M. Saaksjarvi (ed.) *Report of the Seventh Scandinavian Research Seminar on Systemeering*, Helsinki: ECIS, 211–42.

Ehn, P. and M. Kyng (1987) *Computers and Democracy: A Scandinavian Challenge*, Avebury: Aldershot.

Ehn, P. and Å. Sandberg (1979) *Företagsstyrning och Löntagarmakt*, Falköping: Prisma (in Swedish).

Ehn, P. and Å. Sandberg (1983) 'Local union influence on technology and work organization: some results from the DEMOS Project', in U. Briefs, C. Ciborra and L. Schneider (eds) *Systems Design for, with, and by the Users: Proceedings of the IFIP WG 9.1 Working Conference on Systems Design for, with, and by the Users, Riva De Sole, Italy, 1982*, Amsterdam: North-Holland, 427–37.

Greenbaum, J. (1975) 'Automation and unemployment: a look at the basic assumptions in the computer field', *Computers and Society*, 6(3): 4–5.

Greenbaum, J. (1979) *In the Name of Efficiency: Management Theory and Shopfloor Practice in Data Processing Work*, Philadelphia, PA: Temple University Press.

Greenbaum, J. (1990) 'The head and the heart: using gender analysis to study the social creation of computer systems', *Computers and Society*, 20(2): 9–17.

Greenbaum, J. and M. Kyng (1991) *Design at Work: Cooperative Design of Computer Systems*, Hillsdale, NJ: Lawrence Erlbaum Associates.

Greenwood, D. and M. Levin (1998) *Introduction to Action Research: Social Research for Social Change*, Thousand Oaks, CA: Sage.

Jacobsen, H., F. Kensing, M. Kyng and L. Mathiassen (1981) *Klubarbejde og EDB*, Copenhagen: Fremad (in Danish).

Jordan, B. and Henderson, A. (1995) 'Interaction analysis: foundation and practice', *Journal of Learning Sciences*, 4(1): 39–103.

Jungk, R. and Müllert, N. (1987) *Future Workshops: How to Create Desirable Futures*, London: Institute for Social Inventions.

Keller, E. (1985) *Reflections on Gender and Science*, Cambridge, MA: Yale University Press.

Kensing, F. (1981) 'Handlingsorienteret partsforskning med fagbevægelsen', in Å. Sandberg (ed.) *Forskning for forandring*, Stockholm: Arbeidslivscentrum (in Danish).

Kensing, F. (1983) 'The trade unions' influence on technological change', in U. Briefs, C. Ciborra and L. Schneider (eds) *Systems Design for, with, and by the Users: Proceedings of the IFIP WG 9.1 Working Conference on Systems Design for, with, and by the Users, Riva De Sole, Italy, 1982*, Amsterdam: North-Holland.

Kensing, F. and J. Blomberg (1998) 'PD meets CSCW – issues and concerns', *Computer Supported Cooperative Work – The Journal of Collaborative Computing*, 7: 3–4.

Kyng, M. and L. Mathiassen (1982) 'Systems development and trade union activities', in N. Bjørn-Andersen (ed.) *Information Society, For Richer, For Poorer*, Amsterdam: North-Holland, 247–60.

Mathiassen, L., B. Rolskov and E. Vedel (1983) 'Regulating the use of EDP by law and agreement', in U. Briefs, C. Ciborra and L. Schneider (eds) *Systems Design for, with, and by the Users: Proceedings of the IFIP WG 9.1 Working Conference on Systems Design for, with, and by the Users, Riva De Sole, Italy, 1982*, Amsterdam: North-Holland, 251–64.

Mumford, E. (1972) 'Job satisfaction: a method of analysis', *Personnel Review*, 1(3): 48–57.

Mumford, E. (1983) *Designing Human Systems for New Technology: The ETHICS Method*, Manchester: Manchester Business School.

Mumford, E. (1993a) 'The ETHICS approach', *Communications of the ACM*, 36(6): 82.

Mumford, E. (1993b) 'The participation of users in system design: an account of the origin, evolution, and use of the ETHICS method', in D. Schuler and A. Namioka (eds) *Participatory Design: Principles and Practices*, Hillsdale, NJ: Lawrence Erlbaum Associates, 257–70.

Mumford, E., F. Land and J. Hawgood (1978) 'A participative approach to the design of computer systems', *Impact of Science on Sociology*, 28(3): 235–53.

Norman, D. and S. Draper (1986), *User-Centered System Design: New Perspectives on HCI*, New York: CRC Press.

Nygaard, K. and O. T. Bergo (1975a) 'The trade unions – new users of research', *Personnel Review*, 4(2): 5–10.

Nygaard, K. and O. T. Bergo (1975b) *En vurdering av styrings-og informasjonssystemet KVPOL*, Tiden Norsk Forlag (in Norwegian).

Orr, J. E. (1990) 'Sharing knowledge, celebrating identity: war stories and community memory in a service culture', in D. Middleton and D. Edwards (eds) *Collective Remembering: Memory in Society*, Newbury Park, CA: Sage, 169–89.

Sandberg, Å. (1979) *Computers Dividing Man and Work: Recent Scandinavian Research on Planning and Computers from a Trade Union Perspective*, Stockholm: Arbetslivscentrum.

Schön, D. (1979) *The Reflective Practitioner: How Professionals Think in Action*, London: Temple Smith.

Suchman, L. (1983) 'Office procedures as practical action: models of work and system design', *ACM Transactions on Office Information Systems*, 1(4): 320–8.

Suchman, L. (1987) *Plans and Situated Actions: The Problem of Human–Machine Communication*, New York: Cambridge University Press.

Suchman, L. and R. Trigg (1991) 'Understanding practice: video as a medium for reflection and design', in J. Greenbaum and M. Kyng (eds) *Design at Work: Cooperative Design of Computer Systems*, Hillsdale, NJ: Erlbaum Associates, 65–90.

Suchman, L. and E. Wynn (1984) 'Procedures and problems in the office', *Office: Technology and People*, 2(2): 133–54.

Tjørnehøj, H. (1976) *Arbejdsmiljøet i jernindustrien*, Aarhus, Denmark: Modtryk (in Danish).

Trist, E. (1981) *The Evolution of Socio-technical Systems*, Toronto: Quality of Working Life Center.

Trist, E., G. W. Higgin, H. Murray and A. B. Pollock (1963) *Organizational Choice*, London: Tavistock.

Wagner, I. and J. Gärtner (1996) 'Mapping actors and agendas: political frameworks of systems design and participation', *Human–Computer Interaction*, 11(3): 187–214.

Whyte, W. (1991) *Participatory Action Research*, Newbury Park, CA: Sage.

Winograd, T. and F. Flores (1986) *Understanding Computers and Cognition: A New Foundation for Design*, Norwood, NJ: Ablex.

Wynn, E. (1979) 'Office conversation as an information medium', unpublished PhD thesis, University of California, Berkeley.

Yourdon, E. (1982) *Managing the System Life Cycle: A Software Development Methodology Overview*, New York: Yourdon Press.

3

Design

Design Matters in Participatory Design

Liam J. Bannon and Pelle Ehn

This chapter focuses on design in Participatory Design, enquiring into why and how design matters to the field. It traces the relations between various design traditions, from the Bauhaus and the modern design movement, through socio-technical and systems design, to the design research movement. It engages with the design frameworks of Herbert Simon and Donald Schön, and discusses challenges to Participatory Design from contemporary 'critical design' practices. It continues by addressing the design challenges facing Participatory Design as it confronts changing social, economic, technical and political landscapes. It examines the emergence of social media and the generation of new social spaces – arenas for public participation and the generation of new forms of peer production. Finally it suggests that a major design challenge for future Participatory Design is to 'draw together' controversial 'things'.

The chapter begins with a prologue that introduces the birth of the design movement, the Bauhaus, with its goal of uniting art and technology. It then proceeds to discuss a series of developments in the design field and outlines their influence on Participatory Design. The next section of the chapter outlines a variety of challenges – social, economic, political and technological – that confront Participatory Design today, and indicates how Participatory Design might address these challenges in a 'designerly' way. Finally, in the epilogue it advocates that Participatory Design should attempt to engage in creating things as matters of concern, and shows what this might mean for a future Participatory Design practice.

The chapter provides a brief historical account of certain Participatory Design-related design traditions, also noting design topics and themes that are emerging as of importance within the Participatory Design field. It provides some pointers to recent research that engages with issues of social innovation, through the use of new social media, and design platforms and infrastructures. While acknowledging earlier work in Participatory Design, the chapter raises questions as to the future of Participatory Design in a changing world, and suggests avenues for further exploration.

Much of the chapter is concerned with outlining a set of challenges which confront the field of Participatory Design, as it reinvents itself to face the changing political, economic, social and technological environment which it now encounters. New technical infrastructures, new socio-economic arrangements, new conditions of work, all impinge on Participatory Design practices, and several such topics are discussed here. How does design matter in all of this, and how can Participatory Design confront these new challenges?

Prologue: Bauhaus – the birth of modern design and the design object

Design as a profession, concept and movement emerged during hard times – in the socially, economically, and politically unstable aftermath of World War I. A distinctive moment was the inauguration of the *Bauhaus* in 1919, as a new kind of art school different from the fine arts, engaging in a practical way with social change (Droste 1998).

The Bauhaus laid the foundation for what we today think of as *modern design* – 'useful', functionalist, transparent *objects of design*: buildings, furniture and utensils, combining traditional materials like glass and leather with 'modern' materials like steel and reinforced concrete and, later, plastic composite materials and information technology. 'Art and Technology – a new Unity' became after a few years the constructivist motto for turning social utopias into industrially oriented product design and architecture. Buildings and other artefacts should be designed in order to engender social change. By the design of progressive social and cultural values into artefacts, these were then viewed as vehicles for change – through creating the necessary conditions.

Early modern design was also, if not explicitly participatory, at least programmatically collaborative. The Bauhaus was inspired by the notion of the *Bauhütten* – the medieval organisation of craftspeople involved in building cathedrals. Except that the Bauhaus was more about the cathedral of the future – that is, mundane objects that would support people in their everyday, secularised life. It was collaborative and interdisciplinary, as we would say today, joining the different design competences of art, craft, architecture and technology – in order to build a *Gesamtkunstwerk*, a genuinely collaborative design work. The foundation for this work was the collaborative building activities that took place in the Bauhaus *workshops*.

The project was controversial and political, advocating a modernist lifestyle, embodying socially progressive and democratic values, at a time when the influence of Nazism was steadily growing, thus linking its ultimate fate to the 'wrong' side of the political divide in Germany and resulting in its demise in 1933. Now it was the Third Reich that should be realised, and in this design there was no place for the socially radical Bauhaus school, with its rational functionalism as a meeting place for art, culture and technology.

On the international scene the reception of the Bauhaus figures and ideas was quite different. In exile, key figures from the Bauhaus, such as Gropius, Moholy-Nagy and van der Rohe, enjoyed great success in the US. They became the design *avant-garde* for the modern international style (Wolfe 1982). While the Bauhaus was justly celebrated for developing modern design and the international style, it was also criticised by some for its overly harsh forms in steel, glass and reinforced concrete, which were replicated uniformly around the world. The slogan 'architecture or revolution' seemed to imply that a revolution could only be avoided if the modern architects and designers were given the freedom and power to change the world (Berman 1982). The original social engagement in this form of modern design at times became transformed into an undemocratic professional elitism.

Modern design also flourished in Europe after World War II. The Scandinavian countries became internationally known for Nordic design. However, the real breakthrough for functionalism and the impact of the Bauhaus came earlier, with the 1930 Stockholm exhibition and the *acceptera* (accept) manifesto produced by leading functionalist architects and designers (Asplund et al. 1931). Here the espoused vision of the interplay between art, technology and politics was made very clear. The belief in the link between industrial development and social progress was strong. Social problems could be solved with scientific rationality. Salubrious and functional apartments, clothes and everyday objects for the masses were to be produced industrially. Craftwork was to be subsumed under this industrial production. 'Funkis', as functionalism was nicknamed, became synonymous with the growing working class, or at least with the social democratic parties and their welfare ideology of *folkhemmet*. The legacy was obvious in what became known as Nordic Design, but the forms were somewhat more inviting and warmer – soft curves rather than German exactness, wood rather than metal, and more nuances than the basic colours proclaimed by the Bauhaus. In Denmark it was clearly the cultivated bourgeois middle class who made the style their own. What in Sweden, first and foremost, was perceived as a political conviction, was in Denmark more of a style, literally known as the 'white style'. And in Sweden, despite the initial utopian visions, the reality of Nordic design was perhaps more of an elitist doctrine from above than an approach based on democracy and participation of all concerned.

Where does this leave Participatory Design as a design field? Even if the Bauhaus and modern design concepts in general, with their specific social and aesthetic considerations, were not part of the early Participatory Design movement, we would argue that they were implicit in the background thinking of the Participatory Design pioneers. For instance, the first Participatory Design attempts in Scandinavia in the early 1970s, pioneered in collaboration with the Norwegian Metal Workers Union in the field of computers in the workplace, shared some of the social and democratic values of modern design, especially Nordic Design (for more information, see Chapter 2). Initially the Participatory Design focus was on the shared concerns with the labour movement and its values, rather than on its conception of modern design per se. However, we believe that by the 1980s these modern design ideals had become more explicit in Participatory Design thinking and design practice. A good practical example of this influence is the oft-cited Nordic Participatory Design project UTOPIA, in which computer scientists, social scientists, industrial designers and graphic designers worked together with graphic workers and their unions to design 'tools for skilled work' (Bødker et al. 1987). The extensive use of material mock-ups and prototypes introduced by the industrial designers led to new ways of performing design in Participatory Design such as 'design-by-doing' and 'design-by-playing', actually extending the Bauhaus workshop to also include as designing participants those people who would ultimately be the users of the artefacts designed.

Later, in attempts to 'bring design to software', references to the Bauhaus design concepts once again became more explicit (e.g. Ehn 1988; Winograd 1996) and even institutionalised, as attempts were made to re-establish a latter-day Bauhaus as a 'Digital Bauhaus' (Ehn 1998; Binder et al. 2009). Today the link between these early modern design ideals and Participatory Design is more evident, as design thinking has been introduced into the computer systems and Human–Computer Interaction (HCI) fields, in the shape of the emerging new field of 'inter-action design'. This new field provides a more explicit link between the design movement and systems design thinking, by shifting some of the focus on human–machine interaction away from an engineering or human science perspective and towards more engagement with the design community, linking it to other design disciplines such as product design, communication design and architecture.

But now that Participatory Design has become more of an established design field, can we avoid the fate of the Bauhaus and its successor, modern design – i.e. becoming an overly rationalistic and somewhat elitist programme, filling the market with well-crafted functionalist modern design objects for mass consumption? Or is it an even bigger risk that Participatory Design, now incorporating design thinking and offering creative and collaborative environments for user-driven design and innovation, also ends up as the latest fashion in a further modern, market-driven, commodification process (Thrift 2006)? We believe these are major design challenges for the contemporary Participatory Design community, despite all the promising participatory and democratic intentions and statements in our field.

Introduction

This chapter examines the ways in which the field of Participatory Design engages with the field of design – as both a topic, a research field and a practice. We highlight what we consider are core themes in design, especially as they relate to Participatory Design concerns. The chapter is not intended as a review of the whole design field, nor is it a comprehensive overview of work being done by the Participatory Design community. Rather, our purpose is to mine both traditions for insights into the relation between design topics more generally and ongoing practices in the Participatory Design field.

Our aim, from the title of the chapter, is to address the question of whether, and in what way, design *actually matters* for the Participatory Design community. The intent is to show how Participatory Design work is inextricably bound up in more general design debates, even if the topic of design per se is not always a front-line issue. The structure of the chapter is as follows: we started the chapter with a prologue, focusing on the birth of the design movement, showing how its influence is still with us to this day. Next we provide a short account of certain key intellectual design traditions that have inspired researchers in Participatory Design. We then turn to a series of challenges confronting the Participatory Design field. Finally, in the epilogue we look to the future, exploring the implications for design of Bruno Latour's call for the design field to 'draw things together', and how that might be interpreted within Participatory Design. However, before we proceed with Part 1, we have a few general remarks on the design field and on the nature of Participatory Design.

Encountering design

One of the difficulties in any enquiry concerning the concept of design is that the term (in English) has so many different meanings that it can be difficult to determine exactly what kind of process, practice or product is being examined. The term 'design' comes originally from the Latin *signum* – meaning 'sign', to designate or appoint – via Italian and French, its meaning shifting to mean marking, and then drawing or sketching (marks). Indeed, the word 'design' is both a noun and a verb, and can refer to a process or a product. Design can be viewed as a specialised craft or field of study, or it can be viewed as a general ability inherent in almost all human endeavours. Design can be studied as moments of idiosyncratic individual illumination, where a novel solution to a problem occurs, or it can refer to a scheduled organisational development process. It grew out of the arts and crafts movements at the beginning of the last century offering collaborative *gesamtkunstwerk*, a joining of art and technology. It was also linked to the notion of 'the modern', a focus on rational ways of dealing with creativity and production. This tension between the more humanistic, historical, 'soft' arts and crafts tradition on the one hand, and the rationalistic, scientific, modernist, 'hard' approach on the other, permeates design to this day. Today, design is a major economic force, especially in Western capitalist societies, focusing on both production and consumption. Design thinking is fundamental to business strategies, partly replacing traditional market analysis, and designing and managing have become interwoven in interesting ways (e.g. Boland and Collopy 2004). Design has been credited with creating whole new markets, as witnessed by Apple's redefinition of several commercial arenas – mobile phones, music purchasing and listening, tablet computing, etc. Design companies, especially from Italy and Scandinavia, play a key role in the strategic positioning of products and services. Celebrity designers and design groups have become cultural icons. The role of Participatory Design in these developments is ambiguous. On the one hand, the involvement of 'users' in the design process, as pioneered by Participatory Design research, has become more accepted in mainstream design, e.g. in activities such as user-centred design practices and 'user-driven' innovation and user-experience design. At the same time, in our designer-led culture, the focus often seems to be on the cult of the designer or design team and their unique insights, which leaves little space for the inclusion of other groups into their design visions, and is inimical to Participatory Design concerns.

We will briefly examine design ideas emerging from these distinct sources – from the humanist, reflective craft tradition, and from the rationalist, modernist design tradition, where ideas of systems thinking have been influential across a variety of design domains, from computing through to product design.

Participatory Design

In exploring the field of Participatory Design, one can briefly start by analysing its constituent terms. The first element, 'participatory', seems to be self-explanatory. It has to do with participation, with how stakeholders – especially users, developers and planners – cooperatively make or adjust systems, technologies and artefacts in ways which fit more appropriately to the needs of those who are going to use them. Participation can be approached as an ideology, and also clearly refers to questions of ethics, politics, democracy and empowerment. This is discussed in several other chapters in this book (see especially Chapters 1, 2 and 4). The meaning of the term 'design' in Participatory Design is less clear, as noted earlier. What is meant by it, and how has it been applied in the field? Is it design as in the crafts tradition, or design as practised in product design, fashion design and architecture? How does design in Participatory Design relate to contemporary design thinking and to design theory? Is design in Participatory Design akin to the 'designerly' design (Cross 1984) we meet in the emerging discipline of interaction design – merging HCI and Computer Supported Cooperative Work (CSCW) with design fields?[1]

We believe that it is important to stress an overarching concern within the 'Participatory Design tradition', if we can call it that, on the 'how' of designing, i.e. a focus on the *practice of design* – the nature of design activities, the need for providing means for people to be able to be involved, the need for respect for different voices, the engagement of modes other than the technical or verbal, the concern with improvisation and ongoing evaluation throughout the design process, etc. It is this concern that may serve as the *leitmotiv* for this chapter. This orientation is distinct from that of others in the design community, where the focus is more on the content, the 'what' of design, rather than the 'how'. In related fields where Participatory Design has had some influence and where design themes can be taken up on occasion, for example in HCI, the emphasis on design practice per se is much less than in Participatory Design proper, and more focused on the resultant product, or service. Even where practice is itself sometimes studied, for instance in ethnographic studies of design, here the focus is usually on the content of the practices and implications for design, which, while of interest, is a perspective distinct from the pragmatic concerns of Participatory Design on the actual 'doing', i.e. design practice.

Part 1: Understanding design – core themes

While Participatory Design has been practised in a variety of areas, such as urban planning and community development, one of the major areas where its design aspect has been developed has been in the field of technology development and use in organisations. The work of Enid Mumford in the UK was explicitly concerned with issues of how to create more participatory methods for the design of information systems for the workplace (Mumford 1987). So also was the competing 'Scandinavian' systems development tradition of Kristen Nygaard and his colleagues in Scandinavia, although from a much more explicit and distinctive political stance. Both took inspiration from the action research projects on socio-technical systems conducted by the UK Tavistock group (see below). Participatory Design has been influenced by this action research tradition, in terms of attempting to change situations, not simply study them. In this section, we discuss socio-technical systems, action research, different views on design research, including the science of design and the reflective designer traditions, and briefly note other approaches to studying design that have had varying degrees of influence on the Participatory Design community.

Socio-technical systems

The socio-technical systems approach arose out of studies in UK workplaces after World War II. It became clear that the introduction of systems engineering solutions into organisations did not have the desired effect on productivity. This led to the development of an approach to work reorganisation that focused not only on the social subsystem, or the technical subsystem, but rather on how to jointly optimise the joint system. Failure to pay attention to the design of this social subsystem while simultaneously developing the technical subsystem led to project failures and poor performance. The articulation of this concept of 'socio-technical systems' was developed by researchers at the Tavistock Institute in London while working on studies of coal mining in the UK (Trist and Bamforth 1951).

This approach contradicted the technological imperative in work design, where work organisation was planned by engineers whose priority was fitting people to the requirements of the technology, and not vice versa. It was presumed that offering improved socio-economic conditions via 'human relations' activities could offset any difficulties with this approach. The latter approach, developed in the inter-war years, focusing on improved personnel relations and management–union negotiation, had done little to change the basic structure of jobs and the experience of work. Alienation remained in organisations where the social and the technical aspects of work had been treated as completely separate domains. From this came the conceptual reframing proposed by Trist and colleagues, viewing work organisations as socio-technical systems, and not simply distinct social and technical systems, which should be studied via action research. The term 'system' being used by the Tavistock researchers was developed in the context of the emerging work on 'open systems theory', as promulgated by the biologist/cyberneticist Ludwig von Bertalanffy (1950), whose paper 'The theory of open systems in physics and biology' had just been published. This highlighted the self-regulating and environmental factors involved. The Australian researcher Fred Emery while at the Tavistock substantially developed this 'systems' aspect of the socio-technical approach. The idea was that a work system consisted of both a social system and a technical system interacting with an external environment (both the organisation in which people are working, and the environment within which the firm operates) and that these subsystems needed to be 'in balance' in order for an optimal output from the overall system.

A key feature of this work was the realisation that the notion of system was something that was a perspective framed by the researcher, and not something already defined in the natural world. Also, the later Tavistock work argued for the need for greater industrial democracy (e.g. in the work in Norway of Emery and Thorsrud 1969, 1976) and for forms of worker participation in work changes. While the role of technology in work was studied by the Tavistock, they did not focus on technology design itself, but rather on how technology was introduced and used.

The 'Scandinavian' approach to systems design

The 'Scandinavian' approach to systems design, though sharing many of the insights of the socio-technical tradition, emerged as a political critique of the socio-technical perspective. This was seen as being overly concerned with a consensual model of participation, while the Scandinavian researchers focused more on the importance of local trade union involvement (Bjerknes et al. 1987). We have already alluded in the prologue to the Norwegian Metal Workers Union project headed by computer scientist Kristen Nygaard (Nygaard and Bergo 1975), one of the inventors of object-oriented programming, analysis and design. Besides being a pioneer in the Participatory Design movement. Nygaard's conception of design was a modelling and systems concept for describing, abstracting and simulating complex, real-life phenomena. Nygaard even developed the DELTA language (in Norwegian 'PARTICIPATE'), a specific high-level object-oriented design language aimed at supporting participatory descriptions of the world. It was assumed that this way of describing and simulating the world would be congenial with the emancipatory interests of the workers and their trade unions. Nygaard's view on design, objects and systems has had considerable influence on many researchers in the Participatory Design field, and continues to this day. The Norwegian experiment led to similar projects with unions being launched in Sweden and Denmark (Ehn and Kyng 1987; Bjerknes and Bratteteig 1987). Supporting workers in understanding the way computers and applications worked was a starting point, but the objective was to attempt to change how these systems worked, to allow for greater human flexibility in the use of systems. The realisation that what was needed was a clear move into the design of technology itself led to the launch of the UTOPIA project, the first Participatory Design project with a clear focus on design issues (Bødker et al. 1987; Ehn 1988).

Other early systems influences

Other systems design approaches that influenced early Participatory Design were 'soft systems methodology' by Peter Checkland (1981) in the UK, and the book *The Design of Inquiring Systems* by C. West Churchman (1971), the US systems theorist. The 'soft systems' analysis and design approach was developed by Checkland and colleagues at Lancaster University in the UK (Checkland 1981). It was one of the first more collaborative Participatory Design methodologies applied in several Participatory Design projects, encouraging professional designers to examine how they could engage 'users' in the design process (Andersen et al. 1990). The approach acknowledged the existence of a variety of stakeholders involved in any project, and their distinct interests, and how this might impact on the design of any system. Thus, the approach provided ways to support dialogue between competing interests and their (partial) resolution, in order to proceed with design. This approach, as used in Participatory Design, may also be seen as an early attempt to work with more narrative design tools – such as scenarios and storyboards, which later became more widely used within the Participatory Design and systems design community more generally (Chapter 7 gives a rich repertoire of such design tools.).

If 'soft systems' were influential for Participatory Design on the level of participatory tools and methods, the philosophical backbone of the 'systems approach' for many in Participatory Design was shaped by philosopher and pioneering systems thinker C. West Churchman, in his influential book entitled *The Design of Inquiring Systems* (Churchman 1971). While much of the systems engineering approach could be seen as an extension of an overly rationalist and technical approach to real-world problems, Churchman's view openly articulated multiple frames for viewing 'systems', showing how these different perspectives could influence the design of concrete system implementations. Design was seen as the design of knowledge systems.

Churchman shows how our philosophical perspective influences what kind of systems we create, contrasting, for instance, a design focusing on a system and its parts in harmony – which he frames in the context of the philosophy of Leibniz – with a design focusing on a synthesis of conflicting ideas, linking to the dialectical philosophy of Hegel. This way of thinking about design inspired some early Participatory Design thinking concerning the development of a more explicit Marxist design approach, an approach which took its point of departure, not in the synthesis of conflicting ideas, but in dealing with social and material controversies, developing local trade union negotiation design models (Ehn 1988). While the work of Churchman is not as visible in Participatory Design today, he has had a significant impact on the thinking of influential contemporary design researchers (e.g. Nelson and Stolterman 2003).

'Design' interventions: inspiration from action research

Though different in political orientation we note that both the socio-technical tradition and the Scandinavian systems design tradition shared an action-research inspiration for the kind of research and design interventions they developed. Kurt Lewin in the US pioneered the notion of action research during the war years. He wrote that the approach was: 'a comparative research on the conditions and effects of various forms of social action and research leading to social action' (Lewin 1946, p. 35). The key steps in the approach involved 'a spiral of steps, each of which is composed of a circle of planning, action, and fact-finding about the result of the action' (Lewin 1946, p. 38). This approach opened up new possibilities for researchers to engage with interested parties in changing their working/living conditions, and so is sometimes referred to as *participatory action research*. The researcher becomes engaged as one element in a change process, facilitating change, working with the parties concerned, planning change and reflecting on the process of change. This approach was subsequently developed in the UK by researchers at the Tavistock (Trist and Lewin collaborated, and their two research groups were responsible for the launch of the journal *Human Relations* after the war). For many researchers wishing to effect change in society, this research approach opened up new ways of thinking and, importantly, 'doing'. These ideas influenced, directly or indirectly, many subsequent change efforts by groups such as the Tavistock, researchers on socio-technical systems, and Scandinavian interventionist approaches to changing workplaces.

As action research became part of the early Scandinavian Participatory Design projects in the 1970s it also introduced accountability issues that are still central to Participatory Design (Suchman 2002). The early projects had a strong focus on *local accountability*, i.e. the Participatory Design researchers had to recognise that their work must be geared to local needs, and not simply to the production of knowledge for their research peers. For example, the Norwegian metal workers project defined knowledge contributions as knowledge that could support local actions (Nygaard and Bergo 1975; Sandberg 1981). In general there were genuine efforts made to reflect upon, and develop, the role of action-oriented research, knowledge production and democratic ideals (Sandberg 1981). It is also possible to think about this early action research orientation serving as a stimulus to later, more 'designerly' and 'reflective' design research interventions.

Design Research and Participatory Design

We have discussed the origins of the design movement after World War I, in the context of the work of the Bauhaus and others, in the prologue. Another area that influenced early Participatory Design work, and which took inspiration from the Modernist movement, was that of the Design

Research movement. This originated in a series of conferences in the UK in the 1960s that brought together a variety of designers and researchers in an attempt to systematise the understanding of design issues and the nature of design problems. Researchers pursued several lines of investigation, including models of the design process, the exploration of problem spaces, and more psychologically oriented experimental studies of designers as they worked on design problems. Out of this developed a number of books and articles, some attempts at formalising design issues, and also studies on how designers think (Gregory 1966a; Cross 1981, 1982, 1984, 1989; Alexander 1964; Jones 1970; Lawson 1980).

The futurist and inventor Buckminster Fuller, in the context of his thinking about a 'comprehensive anticipatory design science', originally developed the notion of a 'design science'. It was subsequently taken up and reinterpreted by Gregory, in his paper attempting to develop 'the scientific method for design' (Gregory 1966b). He stated:

> Design science is concerned with the study, investigation and accumulation of knowledge about the design process and its constituent operations. It aims to collect, organize and improve those aspects of thought and information which are available concerning design, and to specify and carry out research in those areas of design which are likely to be of value to practical designers and design organizations.
>
> *(Gregory 1996b, p. 323)*

The later work of Herbert Simon (see below) on a 'science of design' seems related to this approach. Later theorists have explored the multiple possible meanings of a design science or, alternatively, a science of design (cf. Cross 2002).[2]

Within a few years the early enthusiasm for formalising the design process and treating design as a field amenable to standard scientific methods faded, as researchers acknowledged that the problems designers were dealing with were so-called 'ill-structured' problems (Rittel and Webber 1973) which were not amenable to precise definition, nor were they suitable for the application of determinable methods to achieve the required result. Thus, while certain of the design methods developed and explored had a certain value, they did not provide an algorithmic solution. The upshot of this realisation was that the notion of a 'design science' that would lead to viewing design activity as involving a well-formulated plan of action and a rule set to be followed was not the way forward. That did not mean that one could not have a scientific approach to the study of design, in terms of using scientific methods to study elements of design, but that is not the same thing as having a design science, as pointed out by Cross (2001). (But see note 2, where we briefly discuss another version of 'design science' that has re-emerged in the information systems field.)

As a result, researchers began to call for a new field of research, and new methods to study the field of design, as distinct from the fields of the sciences and humanities. Archer (1979) has been one of the principal proponents of this third area of human knowledge. As Simon (1969, p. 11) notes, 'The natural sciences are concerned with how things are … design on the other hand is concerned with how things ought to be.' Archer (1981) articulated a notion of the 'designerly mode of enquiry' which he views as distinct from scientific and scholarly approaches. This notion was amplified in the later work of Nigel Cross, where he develops the notion of what he terms 'design intelligence' and 'design ability' (Cross 1982, 1995, 2001). It would be fair to say that this 'modern' design research movement has had a much greater influence on the understanding of design in Participatory Design research than the heritage from the Bauhaus modernist design programme. This is especially the case if we consider the tension between understanding design as rational problem-solving versus reflective practice, our next topic.

Design as rational problem-solving versus reflective practice

The two main approaches discussed in the design field are the *rational problem-solving* model and the *reflective practice* paradigm. The former can be represented by the work of the Nobel Prize winner in economics Herbert Simon, whose book *The Sciences of the Artificial* (1969) had a major impact on the design research community. In this approach, design is conceived as a rational search process, where the designer searches a problem space using formal methods in order to achieve a solution to the problem. With this view design comes very close to, for example, computer science, but it is far removed from the practice-based design approach articulated by the Bauhaus and the modern design movement. Simon's approach has merit and introduces important notions such as that of 'satisficing' rather than simply 'optimising', i.e. achieving a 'good enough' fit between desiderata and product. He also pays attention to the complexity of the task environment and its influence on the design problem, but many designers feel he underestimates the creative aspects of design and the mechanisms by which designers play with possibilities through, for example, sketching, and focusing on possible solutions from the outset. An alternative approach to design thinking, such as that reflected in the work of researcher Donald Schön, seemed more appealing for many Participatory Design researchers (Schön 1983).

Schön's view of the designer as a *reflective practitioner* has become the mainstay of many design frameworks, and has been an important reference point for many in Participatory Design. This view stands in contrast to the rational, problem-solving approach to design. Both Schön and Simon acknowledge the complexity and messiness of design problems or, rather, complex design situations. While Simon suggests ways to transform and reduce this messiness into a stable design space where systems thinking, standard logic and mathematics can be applied, Schön suggests that we pay attention to the ways professionals in their practice master this messiness and complexity 'in the swamp', acknowledging that a stable state is an illusion. The concepts of *reflection-in-action* and *conversations-with-the-material-of-the-situation* – as ways of understanding the professional designers' practice – have become standard references in the Participatory Design community.

This perspective on design as a designerly practice is heavily influenced by the pragmatist philosophy of John Dewey, who posited a general epistemology of creative and investigative processes, where 'experience', seen as growing out of encounters with real-life situations, is taken to be fundamental to understanding (Dewey 1934, 1938). According to Dewey, all creative activities across research and art (not least designerly skills) show a pattern of controlled enquiry: framing situations, searching, experimenting and experiencing, where both the development of hypotheses and the judgement of experienced aesthetic qualities are important aspects within this process. Experiments and learning-by-doing practices are fundamental to Dewey.

Early attempts to apply the pragmatic-reflective and practice approach to a Participatory Design setting was done by Giovanni Francesco Lanzara and Claudio Ciborra, with a focus on design thinking and collaboration (see, e.g., Lanzara 1983) and later by several Participatory Design researchers, with a focus on professional systems designers (Andersen et al. 1990). It has also been used by design theorist Erik Stolterman focusing on the hidden rationality of design work (Stolterman 1991; Nelson and Stolterman 2003; Löwgren and Stolterman 2004). Last, but not least, this pragmatic learning-by-doing perspective has been important for understanding the main Participatory Design design enquiry strategies of prototyping – design-by-doing and design-by-playing (Greenbaum and Kyng 1991).

Ethnography and the emergence of design anthropology

Early Participatory Design work involved learning about working conditions and practices in particular sectors as a prelude to intervention. There was a gradual 'opening up' within the Participatory Design community to the insights from ethnographic studies of work, i.e. field studies of work coming from a sociological or anthropological tradition. These provided fine-grained analyses of work practices and, more importantly, interpreted them within a framework that articulated members' practices. Their focus was on how workers made sense of each other's actions and they showed the artful ways people accomplished their work. The important cross-linkages between ethnography and design are extensively discussed in Chapter 5, so there is no need to elaborate here. However, we do wish to note the emergence of a body of work labelled as design anthropology.

In recent years, the confluence of ethnographers – many from an anthropological background – and designers, has led to the emergence of a new field, labelled design anthropology. While the field is still taking shape, a key characteristic of people working in this area is their attempt to meld the insights gained from an understanding of material culture and members' practices more directly into a more practical, action-oriented Participatory Design agenda. The approach attempts to go beyond performing ethnographic studies that may inform design, or celebrating the unique creative capacities of individual designers and design teams. Rather, they attempt to 'do design' directly, in and through the social settings of everyday life (Halse 2008). To paraphrase Shakespeare, this approach sees the entire world as a stage. As articulated in a recent manifesto set out in a project entitled the Design Anthropological Innovation Model (DAIM) (Halse et al. 2010): '"The Social" is increasingly acknowledged as an important part of the design materials available to the designer for experimentation' (p. 13). It will be interesting to track the evolution of this field and its interconnections with Participatory Design.

User-centred design approaches in HCI

The field of HCI, which emerged in the 1980s, initially focused on developing an applied psychology of the user, viewed as a human information-processing system (Card et al. 1983). Also, the field described the problems people had in using systems, deciphering instructions and recovering from 'errors'. This increased interest in the user and use situations led to a linkage between certain Participatory Design research on use activities and the user-centred design (UCD) field in HCI (Norman and Draper 1986). The UCD tradition helped in focusing attention on the overall system design and on how many supposedly human 'errors' could be traced to systems design flaws, rather than human operator errors per se. The growing understanding of the 'user' not simply as a component but as an active agent in a successful human–machine system provided further impetus to design frameworks that emphasised competent human actors within complex systems (Bannon 1986, 1991). However, despite the word 'design' in 'user-centred design' this HCI community focused overwhelmingly on use rather than design issues, and did not contribute significantly on the 'design' front. However, over the years a certain commingling of work in HCI and in Participatory Design had occurred, both conceptually and empirically (e.g. Bannon and Bødker 1991; Buur and Bødker 2000; Gulliksen et al. 2003).

The role of art and critical design studies

As noted earlier, the influence from the Bauhaus and modern design schools on Participatory Design has been somewhat indirect and rather marginal, compared to systems and socio-technical design thinking, design as reflective practice, and action research, but there has also been more direct inspiration from art and design schools suggesting that Participatory Design could also be performed as a form of 'critical design'.

While design schools are often seen as existing within the consumer society and its capitalist ethos, there has also been an emergence of a 'critical' design arena exemplified, for instance, by the work done by faculty and students at the Royal College of Art in London under the rubric of 'critical design studies'. Here, 'designs' are intended to provoke reflection and debate among users and viewers. The designers produce alternative provocative events, happenings, mock-ups and shows that hold up a mirror to society and challenge it. While in some cases artists prefer that their work stands for itself in terms of its interpretation, other artists and designers have developed an articulate critique of current fashion, style and discourse within their society, and view their role as not simply 'buying into' the prevailing culture, but wishing to hold up a mirror to it, or in some cases, shattering the images we have of ourselves. The work of designers such as Anthony Dunne and Fiona Raby is a good exemplar of this approach (e.g. Dunne 2005; Dunne and Raby 2001). The relevance of this work to people in Participatory Design is that it provides ideas and inspiration for challenging some of the taken-for-granted positions we adopt in relation to our society.

Other design-related work which questions our assumptions about the world can be found in the work of Bill Gaver and colleagues at Goldsmith's College, London (Gaver 2002). They have moved the debate about HCI and interaction design beyond functionality and efficacy, and have engaged in more searching questions as to the role of design in society and how to design evocative and transformative artefacts. The group engage with ideas of play and ambiguity in terms of the relations between people, activities and artefacts through their articulation of the 'ludic'. While still privileging the design discourse at times to professional designers, some of this work challenges our traditional views and notions of participation, design and use. In a related but more 'academic' mould, recent writings of Sengers and others argue for a new paradigm for design, which they label 'Reflective Design' (Sengers et al. 2005). Interestingly, they explicitly acknowledge the importance of the Participatory Design tradition in the development of their framework.

These approaches may be seen in a broader perspective of art, participation and design. From the time of the Dadaists onwards, artists have questioned our society and its values and have presented alternatives. This artistic background has been present in such movements as the Situationist International in the 1960s, and continues in a modified form in groups such as Reclaim the Streets and Adbusters today. One can, for example, see this in the work of Participatory Design-related artists such as Natalie Jeremijenko, in her work on what she terms 'experimental design', which is grounded in a severe critique of the status quo, with clear design elements. Her work bridges the worlds of art, design, the environment, society and technology itself in interesting and provocative ways. (Her work has been a stimulus for certain Participatory Design projects, and she has presented her work to the Participatory Design community, for example, as a keynote speaker at the biennial Participatory Design Conference in Bloomington in 2008.)

Our focus in Part 1 of this chapter has been to link the field of Participatory Design to a number of people, ideas and communities, in order to show the diversity of influences that have been interwoven in the debates about the role of 'design' in Participatory Design. There is no single path through this space; rather, there are a series of interleavings, each with its own unique features. Just as we have outlined a variety of approaches in the design research tradition, we also need to bear in mind that, while for convenience, we at times refer to 'the Participatory Design community' as a singular entity, we also have a variety of viewpoints and approaches within this community. In the next section, we investigate a set of design challenges for Participatory Design in the new millennium.

Part 2: Design challenges for Participatory Design

In the first part of this chapter, we have provided a brief outline of a series of research topics and traditions that we believe have informed the Participatory Design community. This community has in turn made substantive contributions to the design field, especially in terms of design practice. Such books as those by Greenbaum and Kyng (1991), Schuler and Namioka (1993) and Bødker, Kensing and Simonsen (2004) have provided a wealth of material about Participatory Design practices, in terms of how to perform Participatory Design, exemplary projects, etc. The biennial Participatory Design Conferences are also a key resource for those who are seeking the latest work in the field. In recent years, our approach to Participatory Design has had to change in various ways, as a result of a wave of social, economic, political and technological developments. While this is a very large canvas, in the next section we attempt to identify some of the key design challenges emerging from these developments.

Changing technology substrates: from systems to infrastructures

> Infrastructures subtend complex ecologies: their design process should always be tentative, flexible, and open.
>
> *(Star and Bowker 2002, p. 160)*

Organisational information systems

Much of the early exemplary work in Participatory Design stems from an era where the design of bespoke information systems for organisational units was the norm. However, this situation has changed drastically. Organisations have tended to develop a two-pronged strategy in dealing with the information technology function in their organisations. On the one hand, for larger strategic and operational planning purposes many have bought into large-scale enterprise systems (ERPs). On the other hand, many more local information technology-supported activities are accomplished through the use of simpler applications, and the coupling of a series of off-the-shelf systems, where local adjustments may be made, but the scope for reframing work activities through socio-technical redesign are more limited. The upshot of this change in purchasing is that the traditional kind of bespoke application development, familiar from the 1980s and 90s, is no longer as significant an area of activity. Thus the question becomes: what is the future of Participatory Design in organisational environments where these new forms of information systems are being introduced into the workplace? These kinds of infrastructures (e.g. in electronic patient records, or in customer relationship management) support multiple distinct applications, and allow for a certain amount of end-user modifiability. Indeed, whole new positions are created in developer organisations and in the host organisations to help facilitate the shaping of these generic systems to particular needs. That said, given the previous investment in generic infrastructure, there can be a host of issues as to the extent to which they can be modified to fit particular cases, and the relative (economic) cost of so doing. This challenge for Participatory Design is being addressed in certain research projects, for instance the work of the Danish MUST team (Bødker et al. 2004). Their Participatory Design method supports the work involved in preparing visions for competitive bids and a later implementation project. It addresses outsourcing situations, and the use of configurable standard solutions in various customer–supplier relations. Design in these contexts takes on a very different meaning than in the more traditional design paradigm and this is an area of growing interest and importance for Participatory Design. No longer are we discussing the development of bespoke information systems together with our local clients, but we have a situation where large-scale commercial infrastructures are being put in place, albeit with some space for building local applications on this infrastructure. We are slowly developing an understanding of the issues involved here, based on accounts of ongoing empirical research in the field, as for example that of Pollock and Williams (2008). Issues of globalisation, generification and personalisation are all involved in complex ways, and the issue is to develop further the methods and techniques of Participatory Design for these kinds of situations. Perhaps there will emerge new niche areas for software application facilitators or 'configuration engineers' who will work with end-user communities in order to tailor these infrastructures for local use. There is evidence that this is already happening (Simonsen and Hertzum 2008). We also see a growing Participatory Design interest in various forms of end-user development approaches that we note below, and we expect to see these issues being addressed more fully in future Participatory Design conferences. Note that these changes affect not only the Participatory Design field, but also other areas of computing and information systems. For example, the Requirements Engineering field has also had to confront this shift from traditional 'requirements' gathering to supporting the development and tailoring of more off-the-shelf systems.

From tinkering and tailoring to appropriation

There has always been a space, however small, where end-users of technology could make minor changes to their computer-based work environments. However, these local tailorings were often quite limited in scope. Over time, the level of tinkering with systems has been facilitated, to the extent that there is now a whole research domain that focuses on end-user programming and development, with their own conferences, workshops, books and papers (e.g. Eriksson and Dittrich 2009; Costabile et al. 2011). The field of Participatory Design has been active, both conceptually and pragmatically, in developing this whole arena. Also there has been a link between early HCI work on tailoring, and Participatory Design practices, in papers such as Henderson and Kyng (1991). Thus Participatory Design has been concerned about developing opportunities for end-users to shape their environments through modification of systems. Indeed, a more radical understanding of design realises that all systems only become operational through use, so the traditional distinction between design and use becomes somewhat problematic. The work of ethnographers such as Nardi (1993), and other Participatory Design-inspired researchers (e.g. Pipek and Wulf 2009; Spinuzzi 2003) has shown just how inventive users can be in reshaping computing systems to fit their needs.

New open-source software packages provide a plethora of opportunities for people to take, remake, shape and tailor software, and increasingly even hardware, to fit their particular purposes. In so doing, they are also contributing to the growth of the open source movement, and adding to the community know-how and expertise embedded within the corpus of open software libraries and packages available to all. Within such an active, open community space, the need for us to develop more 'designerly' concepts and methods to understand and support these practices is clear. There is a renewed interest in understanding bottom-up innovative practices in general, where people are taking a closer look at such vernacular expressions of 'making do' with resources at hand in areas with resource scarcity. The renewed interest in the topic of appropriation is also of interest. Part of the Participatory Design agenda has been to assist in giving people a voice, in challenging received opinion. In cases of appropriation, we can find instances where groups take over control and shape technologies to their own ends, and here appropriation can lead directly to empowerment (cf. Eglash et al. 2004; Stevens et al. 2010; Storni 2010).

Infrastructural variations: Ambient Intelligence or the Internet of Things?

We can observe some differences in the scenarios of future working and living environments currently being portrayed. All scenarios envision a ubiquitous technical infrastructure, a combination of new forms of pervasive computing, such as location-aware systems, networked sensor arrays, intelligent buildings and services, etc. In one scenario, we have a world where not only are our movements tracked, but our intentions are modelled, and even our emotions are supposedly discerned and acted on by 'intelligent' environments. The role of the human actor in the scenarios depicted in these 'ambient intelligence' (AmI) visions seems a rather passive one, as it is apparently the machines who perform most of the sensing, interpretation and even action in the scenarios, not the human. There are many conceptual and pragmatic difficulties with the ambient intelligence vision (e.g. Greenfield 2006; van Kranenburg 2008). It appears that this vision has begun to pall, even for its promoters, and in a recent paper Emile Aarts, one of the originators of the original AmI concept, now argues for a revised approach, AmI 2.0, entitled 'synergetic prosperity' (Aarts and Grotenhuis 2011).

A more open, and still developing, technological vision of the future can be discerned in the evolving debates on 'the Internet of Things' (IoT). The basis for this vision is one where objects in the world become networked together, so that the Internet address space is populated not simply with people and machines but with all kinds of objects that exist in the world. They are not only 'aware' of their state and location, but can also blog about it on the Net. The futurist and media commentator Julian Bleecker (2006) labels such objects 'blogjects' – objects that blog, close relatives of the even more futurist concept of 'Spime', objects that can talk about their interactions, trajectories, etc., as articulated by science fiction writer Bruce Sterling (2005) in his book *Shaping Things*. Exactly what it might mean to have such interconnections, and to what level these objects are not just 'on' the Net, but active agents, are items for debate. What is clear is that the IoT scenario allows for more heterogeneity than that of AmI, and is less closed in its operation. We need to address, as a matter of urgency, how people in the Participatory Design community might engage in the debate about various versions of AmI and IoT in a 'designerly' way. The distinction between things and objects, for example, is just one of the issues that has been addressed in more recent Participatory Design approaches (A.Telier 2011).

Social media

As information and communication technologies have moved from the desktop to the mobile phone and into people's homes, new electronic spaces have become pervasive, and have become interwoven into our lives. The way we organise our activities has changed; being always online is no longer a feature, but a taken-for-granted aspect of daily living. The changes in technology itself have provided some surprising openings for more participatory practices, albeit with a shifting notion of design. The rise of social media – Web 2.0 applications – has been striking, and has provided a wide range of services that allow people to engage in activities and share their interests and concerns. So, the framing of Participatory Design needs to reflect these changes. What we can clearly see today is a reorientation of software applications – beyond the workplace, and towards everyday life and the public sphere. The provision of such simple mechanisms as Wikis and blogs has allowed for new forms of participation and debate, operating from a local scale to the global (Jenkins 2006; Gauntlett 2011); Facebook and Twitter allow for new modes of expression, dissemination and comment. While we do not believe the overly naive arguments that these applications themselves have 'caused' revolutions, there is no doubt that they provide an opportunity for people to participate in emergent forums and spread news and opinions rapidly, and in viral-like ways, completely bypassing traditional media channels and thus allowing more open and immediate reporting, though at a cost of lack of editorial curatorship. There is an explosion in user-generated content; traditional separations between media and computing have disappeared. Cross-media platforms are being developed commercially for production and distribution, while audiences are no longer passive but can become active through a variety of alternative platforms, forming alternative communities. In his book on convergence culture Jenkins (2006) argues that the power of these changes lies not in the individual but in the formation of local communities of interest that can exert considerable power, often against traditional media oligarchies. While this has attracted much attention in media studies and among media activists, we can also see new design challenges for Participatory Design. These (media) communities are often as much about *making* as about *communicating*, as demonstrated by Gauntlett (2011). People are increasingly 'making media', producing their own Web 2.0 applications and platforms and mediating other forms of making, as in making food or knitting. Participatory Design practitioners are beginning to explore these developments, searching for new ways in which they can facilitate participation, change and development through these social technologies (Hagen and Robertson 2010). Examples from the recent Participatory Design conferences include: applying a Participatory Design approach to Web 2.0 (Clement et al. 2008), community design (Karasti and Baker 2008), urban planning (Botero and Saad-Sulone 2008; Nuojua et al. 2008) and shaping public spaces (Lindström and Ståhl 2010; Vina 2010).

Forms of participatory production

Just as new infrastructures have altered conditions and challenges for Participatory Design when it comes to information technology, there has been a similar development in the production sphere – from closed socio-technical production systems to more open innovation and partici-patory production. This is a development not without controversies and Participatory Design design challenges. In this section we will make some remarks on Participatory Design and design challenges from these emerging participatory production approaches and practices. By partici-patory production we think of such phenomena as open innovation and Living Labs, but also more open peer-production arenas from maker spaces like Fab Labs (Gershenfeld 2005) to social innovation in the public sphere. In many ways we believe that Participatory Design today is in a similar situation to when the field emerged in the early 1970s: participation by users and con-sumers is seen as fundamental to contemporary production, and now, as then, it is a question of which interests to support – narrow corporate managerial interests or broader more democratic participatory ones?

Open and user-driven innovation

Innovation activities may be distributed in complex ways through new media, often blurring the borders between citizens, private companies, the public domain and academia. This reorientation is also due to the fact that user-driven design and innovation has become widespread. This development demands that Participatory Design research consider how it relates to ideas and initiatives that concern open and user-driven design and innovation in other research traditions.

Traditional business models of innovation have undergone significant reworking over the past decade. Closed company innovation has given way to 'open' innovation models, where creativity, knowledge and expertise are co-opted wherever they are found (Chesbrough 2003). This more open innovation model raises some major challenges, one such being that a company product-centric view is being replaced by the 'co-creation' of value. While the view of the individual innovator is still common, it is becoming increasingly challenged by the collaborative business environment, seen as a basis for innovation (Prahalad and Krishnan 2008). 'Crowd-sourcing' is one of the new ways for companies to innovate by harnessing 'the wisdom of crowds' through new media (Surowiecki 2004) and 'lead users' (von Hippel 2005), putting them at the centre of attention for user-driven innovation. Much of this discussion is oriented to a narrow market-oriented business model removed from Participatory Design concerns. So, how can Participatory Design research and practice respond to this managerial version of user-driven design and innovation? What is the Participatory Design approach to design, democracy and participation in open innovation? Is there a research perspective on open innovation more in line with the values that once guided Participatory Design?

Defining what innovation is about, who innovates, where and under what conditions innovation occurs, is an important 'contested space' within society today. The recent work of Participatory Design researchers from such groups as SPIRE in Denmark (Buur and Matthews 2008; Buur and Larsen 2010), the Danish Design School (Halse et al. 2010) and Malmö Living Labs (Björgvinsson et al. 2010; Hillgren et al. 2011) are pushing these frontiers with their locally anchored Participatory Design-based innovation strategies, which we believe has great potential for revitalising the discussion about core Participatory Design values in a contemporary setting.

Living Labs and end-user participation

While we are outlining a series of critical issues for traditional Participatory Design practices in a changing world, we also, paradoxically, note how the Participatory Design field can take credit for the fact that many of the background assumptions of the Participatory Design approach and the methods developed through Participatory Design – e.g. a belief in the right of people to co-determination of their living and working conditions, an awareness of how participation can lead to more appropriable and usable systems, the need for the use of different modalities in workshops, the value of working with mock-ups and prototypes in the design process, etc. – have now become part and parcel of the general field of HCI, interaction design and information systems development. To that extent, some of the battles that have been fought, for example over opening up the design process and making it more participatory, have been 'won', at least in certain Western countries. However, nothing remains constant, and as we have been outlining, the debates and the conditions under which these debates happen have shifted significantly.

A closer look at some of the current topics of concern in information society technologies, at the EU and North American information systems landscape especially, shows an increased awareness of the need to engage in a more participatory way with all stakeholders in the design and development of new technological applications. For example, the Living Labs concept, which has become a major European science and technology policy platform, lays stress on the importance of end-user involvement at all stages of development, of stakeholder engagement, and of the need for early development of prototypes to be trialled extensively in actual working situations. Living Labs emerged as a response to innovation environments that were too closed, which often resulted in failure to innovate, partly because of limited and late interaction with potential markets (Stålbröst 2008). Foregrounding the importance of the users' role and real-life contexts in innovation has thus been central to the Living Labs approach. Common to many of these approaches is, however, a *product-centric* view. While the rhetoric surrounding the Living Labs concept seems to fit well with a Participatory Design orientation, again some caution is required, as the actual activities of many of the Living Labs do not seem to differ substantively from more traditional innovation models. Indeed, given the visibility of the concept, it is surprising how difficult it is to find more detailed evaluation studies that examine how the Living Labs concept has actually played out in practice, specifically concerning issues of participation, innovation and design.

There are, however, also approaches somewhat akin to that of Living Labs within Participatory Design research, for example 'design labs' (Binder 2007) that foreground active user participation. Such Participatory Design projects can be seen as collaborative learning environments where chains of translations occur across organisational and community boundaries. Another Participatory Design example is the 'Neighbourhood Networks Project', prompting critical engagements between people, technology and their urban environment, using technology in a rhetorical sense to create arguments for better living (DiSalvo et al. 2008). Still another example of critically linking Living Labs and Participatory Design traditions are the Malmö Living Labs, which have been in operation since 2007. With an interventionist action research-oriented approach, the labs constitute a milieu where an open-ended infrastructure for innovation allows a continuous match-making process and prompts quick contextual experiments, exploring whether innovation in practice can be about opening up spaces for questions and possibilities – rather than seeing innovation purely as producing novel products to be marketed. The labs explore in practice whether innovation must be delimited to specific privileged societal groups – experts and lead-users – or whether a more democratic approach is possible (Björgvinsson et al. 2010; Hillgren et al. 2011).

Fabrication Labs and open production

The Fabrication Labs concept (Fab Labs) can be seen as a combination of a Living Labs experimental environment with participatory ideas of open source and open innovation, though the idea is as old as the Participatory Design tradition. One of the first examples of fabrication spaces can be found in the shared machine workshops from the early 1970s which had enough basic tools, both hand and power driven, to make the building of demonstration models or test facilities a practical and everyday activity (Hess 1979). The concept today has re-emerged, with one focus around work at the MIT Media Lab (Gershenfeld 2005) concerned with packaging a suite of useful machines, tools and applications into a generic low-cost workshop accessible to everyone at very low, or nil, cost. These facilities allow people to fabricate for themselves novel prototypes and actual working models of new products and services. Besides the hands-on imperative, other distinctive features are a culture of sharing and peer-to-peer interactions.

Fab Labs have sprung up around the world, and some of the results of these experiments have indeed been fascinating (Gershenfeld 2005). Again, optimism needs to be tempered with caution, as the practical working through of the Fab Lab concept is not without difficulties, in terms of ownership of tools and of ideas and resulting products and services. In terms of product innovation the impact is still relatively small, the labs' innovation ecosystem is often limited, and they have not yet found a sustainable business model similar to that of open source software (Troxler 2010). There are, however, also promising experiences; the shift from a 'do-it-yourself' to a 'do-it-together' perspective leads to networks from which innovation can arise. 'Community' is one of the main achievements of Fab Labs (Troxler 2010; Seravalli 2011) and it seems that collaborative experiences are most promising when it comes to open source fabrication. For example, Openwear (openwear.org) is an online platform for open source fashion, boosting the development of micro-fashion initiatives, and Open Source Ecology (opensourceecology. org) is a project based in the US where a group of farmers are building their own machines for farming and construction. They are sharing their drawings and instructions under a project called the Global Village Set, which aims to collect information about how to build a set of machines that should lower the barriers to entry into farming, building and manufacturing. Fabriken is both a site and a community in Sweden which has developed as a merging of Participatory Design, open hardware and Fab Lab culture. This maker space joins Fab Lab machinery and hacker culture (mostly men) with, for example, traditional textile production tools (mostly women) and a bike repair shop (more mixed). Though developed from the perspective of developing new, more user-driven Participatory Design design practices, it also exhibits many controversies and challenges concerning openness, collaboration and democracy in shaping such forms of peer-to-peer production and innovation (Seravalli 2011).

Public participation and social innovation

Another contemporary design approach that can challenge and inspire Participatory Design is design for *social innovation*. Just as with open and user-driven innovation, this is a broad field with many different agendas ranging from politically conservative attempts to replace the welfare state with market-oriented social entrepreneurs, to grass-roots initiatives responding to local challenges. The key aspect of social innovation is its capacity to simultaneously meet social needs and create new social relations. The Young Foundation in the UK has been a major player in developing the social innovation perspective in theory and practice (Murray et al. 2010) and the British Design Council has, through different transformation design initiatives, pushed a design perspective (Design Council 2004, 2010; see also SILK 2010). Italian designer and researcher Ezio Manzini and the international group around him in Milan and elsewhere have also been spreading design practices where new ideas emerge from a variety of actors directly involved in the problem to be addressed: end-users, grass-roots designers, technicians and entrepreneurs, local institutions and civil society organisations. In this perspective, design is no longer just a tool for the development of functional innovative consumer products, but is increasingly seen as a process for radical change – developing services, systems and environments supporting more sustainable lifestyles and consumption habits. A key concept for Manzini and his colleagues is 'collaborative services'. The role of the designer is initially to support the development of new concepts and later to make them attainable so they can result in 'social' enterprises (Jégou and Manzini 2008). The design critic John Thackara has also been highlighting the design possibilities of such approaches (Thackara 2005; see also Dott Cornwall 2010). There is a strong potential for Participatory Design to contribute to social innovation initiatives, but this also involves a number of challenges: appropriating design practices to fit into working in settings where no object is being designed, where local actors with different agendas and resources interact, and where the Participatory Design researcher is but one of the professional actors claiming the responsibility for promoting social change (Hillgren et al. 2011).

Epilogue: 'Drawing together' through design things

Design, under the label of design thinking, has become a central issue in modern design discourse and rhetoric, not least in the business sector (Brown 2009; Verganti 2009). Tim Brown, head of the world-renowned design firm IDEO, pushes the design community to think beyond both the omnipotent designer and the obsession with products, objects or things. What he suggests is that designers should be more involved in the big picture of socially innovative design, beyond the economic bottom line. He argues that design should be viewed as a collaborative effort where the design process is spread among diverse participating stakeholders and competences; ideas have to be envisioned, 'prototyped' and explored hands-on, tried out early on in the design process, in a process characterised by human-centredness, empathy and optimism. What is striking about this business rhetoric is how so many of its elements have been foreshadowed in earlier Participatory Design projects. Some recent business design manifestos similarly articulate a view of design more open to participation and appropriation than is normally the case when designers or design companies take the stage (e.g. Nokia Design Manifesto 2008). We might note how much of the current debate about design in the public arena has come from those closely connected with the industrial practice of design – Philips, Nokia, IDEO, etc. While their various manifestos and arguments are interesting and show an increased openness to social and global economic and environmental concerns such as climate change, social equity, etc., this debate is mainly taking place within the framework of a Western neo-liberal consumer perspective which is certainly open to question. Is this how Participatory Design has become modern? Is the most efficient way to Participatory Design yet another heap of products and services, or is there still a search for participatory, designerly alternatives that go beyond the market agenda?

We have argued that Participatory Design needs to reform in the light of new challenges – technical, socio-economic and political. How to deal with these design challenges must, however, remain open to debate and practical interventions. So, rather than ending this chapter with conclusions, we provide in this epilogue a way to 'open up' thinking about Participatory Design, a way that goes beyond the traditional design project, that acknowledges heterogeneity and conflicts of interest, as well as new forms of participation and engagement. At the same time it addresses questions of democracy and participation that have been at the core of Participatory Design from the very beginning.

The challenge is to 'draw things together', or at least that is how it was formulated by the influential French science and technology scholar Bruno Latour at the Design History Society gathering in Cornwall in a speech in 2008 (Latour 2008). In that talk he observed that designers ever since the time of the Bauhaus and modern design, and even long before that, have demonstrated great skill in designing objects, in 'drawing' architectural sketches, mechanical blueprints, scale models, prototypes, etc. But in this design work he did not find the controversies and the many contradicting stakeholders that these objects bring with them, and he suggested that the designerly 'drawing' skills of designers could be put into play – not just to design single objects, but rather to draw things together, by 'opening-up' controversial things.

The background for this challenge is his position that 'we have never been modern' (Latour 1993). He suggests that the modern separation of nature/object from social/individual is a fake division and that processes of socio-material hybridisation are performed all the time. This would then be the case both before Bauhaus and modern design and after. The implied critique of modern design is towards its obsession with the isolated object, but is this also the case with Participatory Design? The latter has, on the one hand, devised modern and much-appreciated participatory tools and methods for user-driven design and innovation of new products and services. On the other hand, it has also remained traditional, focusing on the role of artefact–human hybrids, be they as collectives of prototypes, designers and users in design projects, or as hybrids of skilled workers and their machines-in-use, where we intervene. Our Participatory Design practices have much of the time been performed in the sphere of hybrids as constructed nature and naturalised social facts. 'Thank God, we never really managed to become modern!' we could exclaim, but beyond that how should we respond to the challenge of drawing things together? Where should Participatory Design then go as a design field, if not as the most participatory and democratic of modern designs? What is needed are designerly ways of doing Participatory Design that capture, in Latour's words, what has always been the hidden practice of modernist innovation: 'matters of fact have always been matters of concern, objects have always been projects' – and, we might add, projects are preferably approached as 'design things'.

The main approach in Participatory Design has been to organise projects with identifiable stakeholders within an organisation, paying attention to power relations and providing resources with a view to the empowerment of weak and marginalised groups. This has been the main rationale for Participatory Design in contributing to 'democracy at work'. However, design today is rather heterogeneous, partly open and public, engaging users and other stakeholders across organisational and community borders. To capture this change we think it may be useful to shift the frame of reference – from design *projects* to design *things* (A.Telier 2011). The etymology of the English word 'thing' is revealing. Its early usage referred to an 'assembly' around 'matters of concern', taking place at a certain time and in a certain place. Only later did its meaning as 'an entity of matter' or a material 'object' come into use. *Things* in ancient Nordic and Germanic societies were originally assemblies, rituals and places where disputes were dealt with and political decisions made. Latour has called for a contemporary 'thing philosophy' and to make things 'public' (Latour and Weibel 2005). Things are not cut off from human relations, but rather are socio-material 'collectives of humans and non-humans' through which 'matters of concern' or controversies are handled. (At the same time, a designed object/thing – 'an entity of matter' – is potentially a *thing* made public, since once it is delivered to its participants it becomes a matter of concern for them with new possibilities of interaction.)

Hence, it may be constructive to think of Participatory Design assemblies as things, especially if aspects of democratisation are at stake. This helps to explore these design environments as socio-material frames for 'matters of concern' and the alignment of controversies, ready for unexpected use, opening up new ways of thinking and behaving. This perspective may also inform designers as to how they may act in a public space where a heterogeneity of perspectives are in evidence among the actors, in finding alignments of their conflicting matters of concern.

Given this, we might also see a desirable shift in the main Participatory Design design *thing* strategy: from 'use-before-use' (Redström 2008), engaging users and 'prototypes' in a project and collaboratively exploring potential future use, to 'design-after-design', designing for a continuous appropriation and redesign where *infrastructuring* work becomes the main activity. Infrastructure is a central issue, since contemporary design demands extensive collaboration over time and among many stakeholders. But this demands, as Star argues, that we see infrastructure not as a substrate that other actions can run on top of, but rather as an ongoing alignment between contexts (Star and Ruhleder 1996). This is difficult design work, where various contexts or practices and technologies concurrently undergo change, and therefore demand continuous infrastructuring and aligning of partly conflicting interests.

Hence, infrastructuring can be seen as an ongoing process, and should not be seen as being limited solely to the design project phase in the development of a free-standing system. Infrastructuring entangles and intertwines potentially controversial, a priori infrastructure design activities such as development and deployment, along with everyday design activities in actual use – such as mediation, interpretation and articulation, as well as actual design-in-use such as adaptation, appropriation, tailoring, redesign and maintenance (Karasti and Baker 2008; Twidale and Floyd 2008; Pipek and Wulf 2009). As a consequence, what needs to be established are *things* as long-term relationships through artful integration, in which continuous co-creation can be realised, in which those involved pay attention to, and work with, the way technology connects to wider systems of socio-material relation in the form of the collective interweaving of people, objects and processes (Suchman 2002; Björgvinsson et al. 2010).

When reflecting upon the design thinking of Donald Schön and his key impact on Participatory Design, we referred back to the influence of pragmatist philosopher John Dewey. Just as his views on art, science, learning and doing have been very influential in Participatory Design, so his lesser-known views on topics such as controversies and the public may be of interest in the context of our argument here, not least since on these matters Schön seems to deviate from his philosophical heritage. Schön never formally endorsed the concept of Participatory Design per se. He favoured 'conversational design', by which he meant dialogue with stakeholders in a situation, but he was hesitant in his support for the political or democratic side of Participatory Design, in the sense of building a 'constitution' (a republic) to handle controversies (Binder 1996). To Dewey, however (Dewey 1927; Marres 2005) the public is characterised by heterogeneity and conflict. It may be challenging enough to design for, by and with stakeholders, where common social objectives are already established, institutionalised, or at least within reasonable reach. These are social communities supported by relatively stable infrastructures. But the really demanding challenge is to design where no such consensus seems to be within immediate reach, where no social community exists. In short, to design where a political community, a public characterised by heterogeneity and difference with no shared object of design, is in need of a platform or infrastructure, an 'agonistic' public space (Mouffe 2000), not necessarily to solve conflict, but to constructively deal with disagreements – public controversial matters where heterogeneous design *things* can unfold, and actors engage in alignments of their conflicting objects of design. Participatory Design projects that wish to take on the design challenge of 'drawing together' can improve further by adopting designerly skills from the Bauhaus, but they cannot ignore passionate engagement in controversial design *things*.

Acknowledgements

The authors would like to thank the large number of reviewers who offered critiques and advice concerning several versions of this paper. They include book co-authors: Thomas Binder, Jeanette Blomberg, Carl DiSalvo, Helena Karasti, Toni Robertson, Jesper Simonsen and Ina Wagner. We would like to thank Erling Björgvinsson, Anders Emilsson, Parag Deshpande, Per-Anders Hillgren, Anna Seravalli and Cristiano Storni for many debates and discussions, as well as textual comments. We have attempted to take on board many of their criticisms and suggestions, but are keenly aware that we have not been able to respond to all of their concerns.

Notes

1 One of the most influential of all design researchers, Nigel Cross, argues that there is a distinct set of 'designerly' capabilities that designers learn and use, different from other scientific and scholarly activities. These capabilities characterise their approach to problems – i.e. being solution-focused rather than problem-focused – and relate to their knowledge of materials, etc. (Cross 1982, 2001).

2 The notion of a 'design science' has resurfaced in the field of information systems as a result of work by Hevner and others (Hevner et al. 2004). An emerging IS community has developed around this concept, resulting in a new conference series, labelled DESRIST. We do not have space to critically discuss this work in the context of the chapter but our initial opinion on this approach is that their 'design science' concept is used in ways which appear rather removed from the design concerns of Cross and others. Thus it appears of limited relevance to the Participatory Design community, at least at this stage, given the limited role provided for human actors in the design process. (See Hovorka and Germonprez 2011 for a short critique.)

References

A.Telier (T. Binder, G. de Michelis, P. Ehn, G. Jacucci, P. Linde, I. Wagner) (2011) *Design Things*, Cambridge, MA: MIT Press.

Aarts, E. and F. Grotenhuis (2011) 'Ambient intelligence 2.0: towards synergetic prosperity', *Journal of Ambient Intelligence and Smart Environments*, 3: 3–11.

Alexander, Christopher (1964) *Notes on the Synthesis of Form*, New York: McGraw-Hill.

Andersen, N. E., F. Kensing, J. Lundin, L. Mathiassen, A. Munk-Madsen, M. Rasbech and P. Sørgaard (1990) *Professional Systems Development: Experience, Ideas and Action*, Englewood Cliffs, NJ: Prentice-Hall.

Archer, B. (1979) 'The three Rs', *Design Studies*, 1(1): 18–20.

Archer, B. (1981) 'A view of the nature of design research', in R. Jacques and J. A. Powell (eds) *Design: Science: Method. The Design Research Society Conference, Portsmouth, 1980*, Guildford: Westbury House, 30–47.

Asplund, G., W. Gahn, G. Paulsson, E. Sundahl and U. Åhren (1931) *Acceptera*, Stockholm: Tiden.

Bannon, L. J. (1986) 'Issues in design – some notes', in D. Norman and S. W. Draper (eds) *User Centered Design*, London: Lawrence Erlbaum Associates.

Bannon, L. J. (1991) 'From human factors to human actors: the role of psychology and human–computer interaction studies in systems design', in J. Greenbaum and M. Kyng (eds) *Design at Work: Cooperative Design of Computer Systems*, Hillsdale, NJ: Lawrence Erlbaum Associates, 25–44.

Bannon, L. J. and S. Bødker (1991) 'Beyond the interface: encountering artifacts in use', in J. M. Carroll (ed.) *Designing Interaction: Psychology at the Human–Computer Interface*, New York: Cambridge University Press, 227–53.

Berman, M. (1982) *All that is Solid Melts into Air: The Experience of Modernity*, New York: Simon and Schuster.

Binder, T. (1996) 'Learning and knowing with artifacts: an interview with Donald A. Schön', *AI and Society*, 10: 51–7.

Binder, T. (2007) 'Why design: labs?', in *Design Inquiries*, Stockholm: Nordes Conference.

Binder, T., J. Löwgren and L. Malmborg (eds) (2009) *(Re)searching the Digital Bauhaus*, London: Springer Verlag.

Bjerknes, G. and T. Bratteteig (1987) 'Florence in Wonderland – systems development with nurses', in G. Bjerknes, P. Ehn and M. Kyng (eds) *Computers and Democracy: A Scandinavian Challenge*, Brookville, VT: Avebury.

Bjerknes, G., P. Ehn and M. Kyng (eds) (1987) *Computers and Democracy: A Scandinavian Challenge*, Brookville, VT: Avebury.

Björgvinsson, E., P. Ehn and P.-A. Hillgren (2010) 'Participatory Design and democratizing innovation', in K. Bødker, T. Bratteteig, D. Loi and T. Robertson (eds) *Proceedings of the 11th Biennial Participatory Design Conference (PDC '10), November 29 – December 3, 2010, Sydney, Australia*, New York: ACM, 41–50.

Bleecker, Julian (2006) 'A manifesto for networked objects – cohabitating with pigeons, arphids and aibos', in *The Internet of Things*, February. Published on his research blog at http://research.techkwondo.com/blog/julian/185.

Blomberg, J., J. Giacomi, A. Mosher and P. Swenton-Wall (1993) 'Ethnographic field methods and their relation to design', in D. Schuler and A. Namioka (eds) *Participatory Design: Perspectives on Systems Design*, Hillsdale, NJ: Lawrence Erlbaum Associates, 123–55.

Blomberg, J., L. Suchman and R. Trigg (1997) 'Back to work: renewing old agendas for cooperative design', in M. Kyng and L. Mathiassen (eds) *Computers and Design in Context*, Cambridge, MA: MIT Press, 267–87.

Bødker, K., F. Kensing and J. Simonsen (2004) *Participatory IT Design: Designing for Business and Workplace Realities*, Cambridge, MA: MIT Press.

Bødker, S., P. Ehn, J. Kammersgaard, M. Kyng and Y. Sundblad (1987) 'A Utopian experience', in G. Bjerknes, P. Ehn and M. Kyng (eds) *Computers and Democracy: A Scandinavian Challenge*, Aldershot: Avebury, 251–78.

Boland, R. J. and F. Collopy (2004) *Managing as Designing*, Palo Alto, CA: Stanford University Press.

Botero, A. and J. Saad-Sulone (2008) 'Co-designing for new city–citizen interaction possibilities', in J. Simonsen, T. Robertson and D. Hakken (eds) *Proceedings of the 10th Biennial Anniversary Conference on Participatory Design, PDC 2008, Bloomington, Indiana, October 1–5, 2008: Experiences and Challenges*, New York: ACM.

Brown, T. (2009) *Change by Design: How Design Thinking Transforms Organizations and Inspires Innovation*, New York: HarperCollins.

Buur, J. and S. Bødker (2000) 'From usability lab to "design collaboratorium": reframing usability practice', in D. Boyarski and W. A. Kellogg (eds) *Proceedings of the 3rd Conference on Designing Interactive Systems: Processes, Practices, Methods, and Techniques*, New York: ACM, 297–307.

Buur, J. and Larsen, H. (2010) 'Crossing intentions in participatory innovation', in K. Bødker, T. Bratteteig, D. Loi and T. Robertson (eds) *Proceedings of the 11th Biennial Participatory Design Conference, PDC*

2010, Sydney, Australia, November 29 – December 3, 2010: Participation: The Challenge, New York: ACM, 251–5.

Buur, J. and B. Matthews (2008) 'Participatory innovation', *International Journal of Innovation Management*, 12 (3): 255–73.

Card, S., T. Moran and A. Newell (1983) *The Psychology of Human–Computer Interaction*, Hillsdale, NJ: Lawrence Erlbaum Associates.

Checkland, P. (1981) *Systems Thinking, Systems Practice*, Chichester: John Wiley.

Chesbrough, H. (2003) *Open Innovation: The New Imperative for Creating and Profiting from Technology*, Harvard, MA: Harvard Business School Press.

Churchman, C. W. (1971) *The Design of Inquiring Systems: Basic Concepts of Systems and Organization*, New York: Basic Books.

Clement, A., T. Costantino, D. Kurtz and M. Tissenbaum (2008) 'Participatory Design and Web 2.0: the case of PIPWatch, the collaborative privacy toolbar', in J. Simonsen, T. Robertson and D. Hakken (eds) *Proceedings of the 10th Biennial Anniversary Conference on Participatory Design, PDC 2008, Bloomington, Indiana, USA, October 1–5, 2008: Experiences and Challenges*, New York: ACM.

Costabile, M. F., Y. Dittrich, G. Fischer and A. Piccinno (eds) (2011) *End-user Development 2011, Proceedings of the 3rd International Symposium, IS-EUD, Torre Canne, Italy, June 7–10*, New York: Springer; LNCS 6654.

Cross, N. (1982) 'Designerly ways of knowing', *Design Studies*, 3(4): 221–7.

Cross, N. (ed.) (1984) *Developments in Design Methodology*, Chichester: John Wiley.

Cross, N. (1989, 1994) *Engineering Design Methods*, Chichester: John Wiley.

Cross, N. (1990) 'The nature and nurture of the design ability', *Design Studies*, 11(3): 127–40.

Cross, N. (1995) 'Discovering design ability', in R. Buchanan and V. Margolin (eds) *Discovering Design: Explorations in Design Studies*, Chicago, IL: Chicago University Press.

Cross, N. (2001) 'Designerly ways of knowing: design discipline versus design science', *Design Issues*, 17(3): 49–55.

Cross, N. (2002) 'Design as a discipline', presentation at the Inter-disciplinary Design Quandary Conference, 13 February, De Montfort University, UK. Text available at: http://nelly.dmu.ac.uk/4dd/DDR3-Cross.html.

Cross, N., J. Naughton and D. Walker (1981) 'Design method and scientific method', *Design Studies*, 2(4): 195–201.

Design Council (2004) *RED* (online). 'RED is a "do tank" that develops new thinking and practice on social and economic problems through design-led innovation'. Available at: www.designcouncil.info/mt/RED/about/ (accessed 24 November 2011).

Design Council (2010) *Public Services by Design* (online). Available at: www.designcouncil.org.uk/our-work/Support/Public-Services-by-Design/ (accessed 24 November 2011).

Dewey, J. (1927) *The Public and Its Problems*, New York: Henry Holt.

Dewey, J. ([1934] 1980) *Art as Experience*, New York: Berkeley Publishing Group.

Dewey, J. ([1938] 1969) *Logic: The Theory of Inquiry*, New York: Henry Holt

DiSalvo, C., I. Nourbakhsh, D. Holstius, A. Akin and M. Louw (2008) 'The Neighborhood Networks Project: a case study of critical engagement and creative expression through Participatory Design', in J. Simonsen, T. Robertson and D. Hakken (eds) *Proceedings of the 10th Biennial Anniversary Conference on Participatory Design, PDC 2008, Bloomington, Indiana, USA, October 1–5, 2008: Experiences and Challenges*, New York: ACM.

Dott Cornwall (2010) *What's Dott?* (online). Available at: www.dottcornwall.com/about-dott/whats-dott (accessed 24 November 2011).

Droste, M. (1998) *Bauhaus 1919–1933*, Köln: Benedikt Taschen Verlag.

Dunne, A. (2005) *Hertzian Tales: Electronic Products, Aesthetic Experience, and Critical Design*, Cambridge, MA: MIT Press.

Dunne, A. and F. Raby (2001) *Design Noir – The Secret Life of Electronic Objects*, London: August/Birkhäuser.

Eglash, R., J. L. Croissant, G. Di Chiro, and R. Fouché (eds) (2004) *Appropriating Technology: Vernacular Science and Social Power*, Minneapolis: University of Minnesota Press.

Ehn, P. (1988) *Work-Oriented Design of Computer Artifacts*, Hillsdale, NJ: Lawrence Erlbaum Associates.

Ehn, P. (1998) 'Manifesto for a digital Bauhaus', *Digital Creativity* 9(4): 2007–216.

Ehn, P. and M. Kyng (1987) 'The collective resource approach to systems design', in G. Bjerknes, P. Ehn and M. Kyng (eds) *Computers and Democracy: A Scandinavian Challenge*, Brookville, VT: Avebury.

Emery, F. E. and E. Thorsrud (1969) *Form and Content in Industrial Democracy*, London: Tavistock.

Emery, F. E. and E. Thorsrud. (1976) *Democracy at Work*, Leiden: Martinus Nijhoff.

Eriksson, J. and Y. Dittrich (2009) 'Achieving sustainable tailorable software systems by collaboration between end-users and developers', in S. Clarke (ed.) *Evolutionary Concepts in End User Productivity and Performance: Application for Organizational Progress*, Hershey, PA: IGI Global.

Gauntlett, D. (2011) *Making is Connecting: The Social Meaning of Creativity, from DIY and Knitting to YouTube and Web 2.0*, Cambridge: Polity Press.

Gaver, B. (2002) 'Designing for Homo ludens', *EU 13 Magazine*, 12 (June).

Gershenfeld, N. A. (2005) *Fab: The Coming Revolution on your Desktop – From Personal Computers to Personal Fabrication*, New York: Basic Books.

Greenbaum, J. and M. Kyng (eds) (1991) *Design at Work: Cooperative Design of Computer Work*, Hillsdale, NJ: Lawrence Erlbaum Associates.

Greenfield, A. (2006) *Everyware: The Dawning Age of Ubiquitous Computing*, Berkeley, CA: New Riders.

Gregory, S. A. (1966a) *The Design Method*, London: Butterworth.

Gregory, S. A. (1966b) 'Design science', in S. A. Gregory (ed.) *The Design Method*, London: Butterworth, 323–30.

Gulliksen, J., B. Goransson, I. Boivie, S. Blomkvist, J. Persson and Å. Cajander (2003) 'Key principles for user-centred systems design', *Behaviour and Information Technology*, 22(6): 397–409.

Hagen, P. and T. Robertson (2010) 'Social technologies: challenges and opportunities for participation', in K. Bødker, T. Bratteteig, D. Loi and T. Robertson (eds) *Proceedings of the 11th Biennial Participatory Design Conference, PDC 2010, Sydney, Australia, November 29 – December 3, 2010: Participation: The Challenge*, New York: ACM.

Halse, J. (2008) 'Design anthropology: borderland experiments with participation, performance and situated intervention', PhD thesis, Copenhagen, IT University.

Halse, J., E. Brandt, B. Clark and T. Binder (2010) *Rehearsing the Future*, Copenhagen: Danish Design School Press.

Henderson, A. and M. Kyng (1991) 'There's no place like home: continuing design in use', in J. Greenbaum and M. Kyng (eds) *Design at Work: Cooperative Design of Computer Systems*, Hillsdale, NJ: Lawrence Erlbaum Associates, 219–40.

Hess, K. (1979) *Community Technology*, New York: Harper and Row.

Hevner, A. R., S. T. March, J. Park and S. Ram (2004) 'Design science in information systems research', *MIS Quarterly*, 28(1): 75–105.

Hillgren, P.-A., A. Seravalli and A. Emilsson (2011) 'Prototyping and infrastructuring in design for social innovation', *Co-Design* 7(3–4): 169–83.

Hovorka, D. and M. Germonprez (2011) 'Reflecting, tinkering, and tailoring: implications for theories of information system design', in S. Pekkola and H. Isomaki (eds) *Reframing Humans in Information Systems Development,* London: Springer, 135–49.

Jégou, F. and E. Manzini (2008) *Collaborative Services: Social Innovation and Design for Sustainability*, Milan: Poli Design.

Jenkins, Henry (2006) *Convergence Culture: Where Old and New Media Collide*, New York: New York University Press.

Jones, J. Christopher (1970) *Design Methods: Seeds of Human Futures*, London: John Wiley.

Karasti, H. and K. Baker (2008) 'Community design: growing one's own information infrastructure', in J. Simonsen, T. Robertson and D. Hakken (eds) *Proceedings of the 10th Biennial Anniversary Conference on Participatory Design, PDC 2008, Bloomington, Indiana, October 1–5, 2008: Experiences and Challenges,* New York: ACM.

Lanzara, G. F. (1983) 'The design process: frames, metaphors and games', in U. Briefs, C. Ciborra and L. Sneider (eds) *Systems Design for, with and by the Users*, Amsterdam: North-Holland.

Latour, B. (1993) *We Have Never Been Modern*, Cambridge, MA: Harvard University Press.

Latour, B. (2008) *'A Cautious Promethea? A few steps toward a philosophy of design (with special attention to Peter Sloterdijk)',* keynote lecture for the Networks of Design meeting of the Design History Society, Falmouth, Cornwall, 3 September.

Latour, B. and P. Weibel (eds) (2005) *Making Things Public: Atmospheres of Democracy*, Cambridge, MA: MIT Press.

Lawson, Bryan (1980, fourth edition 2006) *How Designers Think: The Design Process Demystified*, Amsterdam: Elsevier.

Lewin, K. (1946) 'Action research and minority problems', *Journal of Social Issues*, 2(4): 34–46.

Lindström, K. and Å. Ståhl (2010) 'Threads – a mobile sewing circle: making private matter public in temporary assemblies', in K. Bødker, T. Bratteteig, D. Loi and T. Robertson (eds) *Proceedings of the 11th*

Biennial Participatory Design Conference, PDC 2010, Sydney, Australia, November 29 – December 3, 2010: Participation: The Challenge, New York: ACM.

Löwgren, J. and E. Stolterman (2004) *Thoughtful Interaction: A Design Perspective on Information Technology*, Cambridge, MA: MIT Press.

Marres, N. (2005) 'Issues spark a public into being', in B. Latour and P. Weibel (eds) *Making Things Public: Atmospheres of Democracy*, Cambridge, MA: MIT Press.

Mouffe, C. (2000) *The Democratic Paradox*, London: Verso.

Mumford, E. (1987) 'Sociotechnical systems design – evolving theory and practice', in G. Bjerknes, P. Ehn and M. Kyng (eds) *Computers and Democracy: A Scandinavian Challenge*. Brookville, VT: Avebury.

Murray, R., J. Caulier-Grice and G. Mulgan (2010) *The Open Book of Social Innovation*, London: Young Foundation, NESTA.

Nardi, B. A. (1993) *A Small Matter of Programming: Perspectives on End User Computing*, Cambridge, MA: MIT Press.

Nelson, H. and E. Stolterman (2003) *The Design Way*, Englewood Cliffs, NJ: Educational Technology Publications.

Nokia Design Manifesto (2008). Available to download at hiltonbarbour.com/assets/Manifesto-A5-Final.pdf.

Norman, D. A. and S. W. Draper (eds) (1986) *User Centred Systems Design*, Hillsdale, NJ: Lawrence Erlbaum Associates.

Nuojua, J., A. Juustila, T. Räisänen, K. Kuutti and L. Soudunsaari (2008) 'Exploring Web-based participation methods for urban planning', in J. Simonsen, T. Robertson and D. Hakken (eds) *Proceedings of the 10th Biennial Anniversary Conference on Participatory Design, PDC 2008, Bloomington, Indiana, October 1–5, 2008: Experiences and Challenges,* New York: ACM.

Nygaard, K. and O. T. Bergo (1975) 'The trade unions – new users of research', *Personal Review*, 4(2): 5–10.

Pekkola, S. and H. Isomaki (eds) (2011) *Reframing Humans in Information Systems Development*, London: Springer.

Pipek, V. and V. Wulf (2009) 'Infrastructuring: toward an integrated perspective on the design and use of Information Technology', *Journal of the Association of Information Systems*, Special Issue, 10(5): 447–73.

Pollock, N. and R. Williams (2008) *Software and Organisations: The Biography of the Enterprise-Wide System or How SAP Conquered the World*, Abingdon: Routledge.

Prahalad, C. K. and M. S. Krishnan (2008) *The New Age of Innovation: Driving Co-created Value through Global Networks*, New York: McGraw Hill.

Redström, J. (2008) 'Re:definitions of use', *Design Studies*, 29(4): 410–23.

Rittel, H. and M. Webber (1973) 'Dilemmas in a general theory of planning', *Policy Sciences*, 4: 155–69.

Sandberg, Å. (ed.) (1981) *Forskning för förändring* (Research for Change), Stockholm: Arbetlivscentrum.

Schön, Donald A. (1983) *The Reflective Practitioner: How Professionals Think in Action*, London: Temple Smith.

Schuler, D. and A. Namioka (1993) *Participatory Design: Principles and Practices*, Mawah, NJ: Lawrence Erlbaum Associates.

Sengers, P., K. Boehner, J. David and J. J. Kaye (2005) 'Reflective design', *Procedures of the 4th Decennial Conference on Critical Computing*, New York: ACM, 49–58.

Seravalli, A. (2011) 'Democratizing production: challenges in co-designing enabling platforms for social innovation', paper presented at 'The Tao of Sustainability', an international conference on sustainable design strategies in a globalisation contest, Beijing, 27–29 October.

SILK (2010) *Social Innovation Lab for Kent* (online). Available at: http://socialinnovation.typepad.com/silk/ (accessed 24 November 2011).

Simon, Herbert (1969, 1996) *The Sciences of the Artificial*, third edition. Cambridge, MA: MIT Press.

Simonsen, J. and M. Hertzum (2008) 'Participatory Design and the challenges of large-scale systems: extending the iterative PD approach', in J. Simonsen, T. Robinson and D. Hakken (eds) *Proceedings of the 10th Anniversary Conference on Participatory Design: Experiences and Challenges, September 30 – October 4, 2008, Bloomington, Indiana*, New York: ACM, 1–10.

Spinuzzi, C. (2003) *Tracing Genres through Organizations: A Sociocultural Approach to Information Design*, Cambridge, MA: MIT Press.

Stålbröst, A. (2008) 'Forming future IT: the living lab way of user involvement', doctoral thesis, Luleå University of Technology.

Star, S. L. and G. Bowker (2002) 'How to infrastructure,' in L. A. Lievrouw and S. Livingstone (eds) *Handbook of New Media – Social Shaping and Consequences of ICTs*, London: Sage, 151–62.

Star, S. L. and K. Ruhleder (1996) 'Steps toward an ecology of infrastructure: design and access for large information spaces', *Information Systems Research*, 7(1): 111–34.

Sterling, Bruce (2005) *Shaping Things*, Cambridge, MA: MIT Press.

Stevens, G., Pipek, V. and Wulf, V. (2010) 'Appropriation infrastructure: mediating appropriation and production work', *Journal of Organizational and End User Computing*, 22(2): 58–81.

Stolterman, E. (1991) 'Designarbetets dolda rationalitet' [The hidden rationality of design work], PhD thesis, Umeå University.

Storni, Cristiano (2010) 'Multiple forms of appropriation in self-monitoring technology: reflections on the role of evaluation in future self-care', *International Journal of Human–Computer Interaction*, 26(5): 537–61.

Suchman, L. (2002) 'Located accountabilities in technology production', *Scandinavian Journal of Information Systems*, 14(2): 91–105.

Surowiecki, J. (2004) *The Wisdom of Crowds*, New York: Anchor Books.

Thackara, John (2005) *In the Bubble: Designing in a Complex World*, Cambridge, MA: MIT Press,

Thrift, N. (2006) 'Re-inventing invention: new tendencies in capitalist commodification', *Economy and Society*, 35(2): 279–306.

Trist, Eric L. (1981) 'The sociotechnical perspective: the evolution of sociotechnical systems as a conceptual framework and as an action research program', in Andrew H. van de Ven and William F. Joyce (eds) *Perspectives on Organization Design and Behavior*, New York: John Wiley. (Also published in substantially the same form and cited as Trist, Eric L. (1981) 'The evolution of socio-technical systems: a conceptual framework and an action research program', *Issues in the Quality of Working Life: Occasional Papers*, no. 2, June, Toronto: Ontario Ministry of Labour.)

Trist, Eric and K. Bamforth (1951). 'Some social and psychological consequences of the longwall method of coal getting', *Human Relations*, 4: 3–38.

Troxler, Peter (2010) 'Commons-based peer-production of physical goods: is there room for a hybrid innovation ecology?' paper presented at the 3rd Free Culture Research Conference, Berlin, 8–9 October 2010. Available at: http://ssrn.com/abstract=1692617.

Twidale, M. and I. Floyd (2008) 'Infrastructures from the bottom-up and the top-down: can they meet in the middle?' in J. Simonsen, T. Robertson and D. Hakken (eds) *Proceedings of the 10th Biennial Anniversary Conference on Participatory Design, PDC 2008, Bloomington, Indiana, October 1–5, 2008: Experiences and Challenges,* New York: ACM.

van Kranenburg, R. (2008) 'The Internet of Things: a critique of ambient technology and the all-seeing network of RFID', *Network Notebooks 02*, Amsterdam: Institute of Network Cultures.

Verganti, R. (2009) *Design-Driven Innovation*, Boston, MA: Harvard Business Press.

Vina, Sandra (2010) 'Engaging people in the public space – ANIMATO, a design intervention', in K. Bødker, T. Bratteteig, D. Loi and T. Robertson (eds) *Proceedings of the 11th Biennial Participatory Design Conference, PDC 2010, Sydney, Australia, November 29 – December 3, 2010: Participation: The Challenge,* New York: ACM.

von Bertalanffy, L. (1950) 'The theory of open systems in physics and biology', *Science*, 3: 22–9.

von Hippel, E.(2005) *Democratizing Innovation*, Cambridge, MA: MIT Press.

Winograd, T. (1996) *Bringing Design to Software*, Reading, MA: Addison-Wesley.

Wolfe, T. (1982) *From Bauhaus to Our House*, London: Jonathan Cape.

4

Ethics

Engagement, representation and politics-in-action

Toni Robertson and Ina Wagner

This chapter explores a range of different approaches to ethics and their relevance to Participatory Design as background to the ethical issues of designing with users. The discussion highlights the strong connections between ethical practices in design, the inclusiveness of the design processes, the choice of design methods and the responsibilities and accountabilities of those participating. The chapter calls for increased attention to the ways that design is completed in use and for new and extended Participatory Design methods and tools to better foresee and imagine ethical issues that might arise in the use of future technologies.

An overview of different approaches to ethics is followed by an exploration of the ethical issues of working with users. Ethical issues of designing for and within use are the focus of the following section. Finally, we return to a reflection on the essential relations of ethics to Participatory Design.

Using examples drawn from the literature, the chapter explores the defining role of ethics in the development of Participatory Design. The discussion of core ethical issues of Participatory Design is grounded in particular examples where the expression of these principles has been negotiated by designers and other participants. This enables the chapter to, first, emphasise the ongoing negotiations and reflection that have faced designers when their ethical ambitions collide with the pragmatic decisions that define any design practice, and second, to identify specific design questions addressed by designers in their efforts to bring the principles of Participatory Design to their projects.

Changing times and technologies demand new and extended Participatory Design methods, tools and processes that can enable and improve genuine participation in the shaping of future societies. In particular we need to develop tools that can help us envision and resolve ethical issues that might arise in current and future use.

We are accountable for the present in that we are responsible for those present possibilities that become actual through our actions.

(Gatens 1996, p. 105)

Ethics and Participatory Design

Practitioners of Participatory Design share a commitment to those worldviews that recognise people as active participants in the shaping of the world around them. Participatory Design, then, has at its core an ethical motivation to support and enhance how people can engage with others in shaping their world, including their workplaces, over time. This ethical motivation is not some optional extra to accessorise any understandings and specific practices of Participatory Design. It is its essence and structures its definition and ongoing development. In the same way that a human body needs to breathe to live, Participatory Design cannot continue to exist without this commitment to working together to shape a better future.

There are a number of principles underlying Participatory Design (e.g. Greenbaum 1993; Kensing and Blomberg 1998; Beck 2002). One is that the people who do a particular activity (including work) know most about how it gets done. So involving them in the design of the technologies they will use means that the outcomes are more likely to be successful. But this principle also expresses the ethical stance that respects people's expertise and their rights to represent their own activities to others, rather than having others do this for or to them. The important point for our discussion here is that the ethical stance about the making of the technology is not incidental to the quality and value of the outcomes. This is why, for example, it is so important in Participatory Design that representations of people and activities, such as personas and scenarios, are developed by and with those whose activities they are.

A second principle calls for the development and use of processes and tools that enable designers, technology users and other stakeholders to learn from each other through understanding each other's perspectives and priorities. This leads to more robust communication among those involved in the design, which leads, in turn, to outcomes that are more likely to be successful. But, again, it also expresses the ethical stance that different voices need to be heard, understood and heeded if a design process is to be genuinely participatory. The success of the outcome is fundamentally linked to the different voices who have been able to contribute to its design. This is why, for example, ethnographic studies of practice are so common in Participatory Design projects; they enable designers to develop understandings of the lived experience of those who will use the new technology and the context in which they will use it. It is also why prototyping has always been so important to Participatory Design; prototypes function as models of some aspect of the developing design that can be seen, interrogated and reflected upon by a potentially diverse group of people participating in the design process. Developing design methods that enable people to work together to imagine and then design new kinds of technologies, spaces and products has always been a strength and focus of Participatory Design research and practice, and among its major contributions.

Perhaps the core principle of Participatory Design is that people have a basic right to make decisions about how they do their work and indeed any other activities where they might use technology. This is also the most contested aspect of Participatory Design, its most directly stated ethical commitment and its main point of difference to more mainstream user- or human-centred design approaches. It is why, for example, Participatory Design has important political agendas expressed by its close collaboration with identifiable political movements that are informed and underpinned by ethical discourses around human rights and a robust civil society. This emancipatory agenda is shared by participatory approaches within other areas of design such as architecture and town planning. The Participatory Design of information technology originated in the workplace democracy movement in Scandinavia in the 1970s and much of its early work was done with the trade union movement. Since then, projects within developing countries and with marginalised and vulnerable groups in society have also been major expressions of the human rights agenda that defines Participatory Design.

These constitutive relations between ethics and Participatory Design are explored further in the remainder of this chapter. Ethics is a very broad area and there are a number of different approaches ranging from the more abstract perspectives of moral philosophy to those motivated by a need to directly support decision-making in everyday practice. We begin with a consideration of a range of approaches to ethics identifying how these have been expressed in different aspects of Participatory Design. The chapter continues with an exploration of the ethical issues of working with users, highlighting the strong connection between ethical practice in design, the inclusiveness of the design processes, the choice of design methods, the responsibilities and accountabilities of those participating, including designers, and the importance of mutual learning and the development of trust between the designers and other participants. Participatory Design is about envisioning future use and those working within it have argued that design is only ever completed in use. Ethical issues of designing for and within use are the focus of the final major section of the chapter. We suggest that these have not so far been as well explored and understood as they need to be within Participatory Design. We identify some of the difficulties that have challenged those who have sought to work in these areas as well as some of the major areas of concern that still need to be addressed. The chapter closes with some suggestions for tools that designers may find useful as they seek to address the ethical issues that will always arise in any design project. We recommend that increased attention be paid to the ways that design is completed in use as a way to contribute to resolving ethical issues/conflicts that arise in use. Finally, we encourage the development of new and extended Participatory Design methods and tools that build on ethical case deliberation as a way to foresee and imagine ethical issues that might arise in future use.

About ethics

The subject matter of ethics, or moral philosophy, has to do with questions relating to how we should live to live a good life (what is a good life?), what kind of society we should have (how to distribute goods and burdens?) and how we should treat others. Typical ethical terminology includes the notions of right and wrong, good, bad and evil, rights and duties, and responsibility and obligation. In 'A lecture on ethics' Wittgenstein (1965, p. 6) writes:

> Ethics is the enquiry into what is valuable, or, into what is really important, or I could have said Ethics is the enquiry into the meaning of life, or into what makes life worth living, or into the right way of living. I believe if you look at all these phrases you will get a rough idea as to what it is that Ethics is concerned with.

While definitions of ethics are expressed in terms of the quest for how to live a good life and generally illustrated by a number of accompanying questions, the answers to these questions depend on the perspectives of those providing the answers. Various dominant ethical discourses have been criticised as legitimating existing power structures by those who do not benefit from those structures. For example, feminists have argued that the history of ethics has been developed from a male perspective and relies on a range of assumptions that are not gender neutral (e.g. Gilligan 1982; Held 1993). Other dominant perspectives that have influenced particular ethical priorities at different times in history have included – and may still include – the current ruling classes, the hierarchies in various mainstream religions or those who benefit from defining rights and behaviours on the basis of someone's race. These perspectives too have been extensively critiqued by those arguing for an ethics informed by commitments to human rights and civil society. When ethics extends from the realm of moral philosophy into the realm of everyday life – that is, when it moves from exploring abstract questions about how to live a good life to influencing how people actually do things – then people need to take a stand on various issues that affect them and shape the society in which they live (Singer 1993); for example the treatment of refugees, the use of animals for food or research, obligations to the environment, of the wealthy to the poor and, in our case, of designers to the future worlds that they can shape through their work. It is here that the overlap between ethics and politics is made visible. When different ethical perspectives compete, then supporting one over another is a political act motivated by an ethical commitment. Ethics-in-practice and politics-in-practice become blurred. In the remainder of this section a number of ethical traditions and perspectives are introduced and discussed to emphasise how aspects of each resonate with the ethical commitments of Participatory Design.

Ethical theories

Normative ethical theories seek answers regarding the standards of moral right and wrong and the grounds for making decisions about what would be the right thing to do; in other words, how we should meet our obligations in a given situation. Valid moral reasoning and sources of our duties have been seen as resting either on single principles such as the *greatest happiness principle* proposed by the utilitarian philosopher J. S. Mill, or the *categorical imperative* (in its different versions) formulated by the German thinker Immanuel Kant, or on pluralistic theories (see, for example, McNaughton 1988). Mill and Kant's views on the rightness or wrongness of an act depend either on the consequences of the act (Mill) or on its correspondence with a duty (Kant). The so-called common morality pluralist view on ethics has been a particularly popular approach in the field of health care ethics. Possibly the single best-known piece of literature in biomedical ethics, written by Beauchamp and Childress, *Principles of Biomedical Ethics* (for example fourth edition, 1994) introduces such a pluralistic common morality approach for analysing ethical problems in the health care setting. The authors defend a four-principles approach to biomedical ethics: autonomy, justice, beneficence and non-maleficence. This approach has dominated much of the bioethical discussion during the 1980s and 1990s. Practitioners in medicine and nursing found it understandable and applicable to their fields.

Virtue theory as an approach to ethics places value on the cultivation of the character of individuals. Plato and Aristotle, for example, conceived of ethics in terms of virtues instead of terms such as right, wrong or obligation (see, for example, Frankena 1973). Related to virtue ethics, the ethics of care originally emerged as a feminist critique to traditional theorising (see the pioneering work of Gilligan 1982). It focuses especially on personal relationships and character traits that are valued in them. It has been reformulated as an ethics of responsibility, which, with respect to science and modern technology, stresses issues of accountability and liability.

In their discussion of the 'collective designer' Ehn and Badham (2002) refer to the Aristotelian vision of ethical life and in particular to the virtue of *phronesis*:

> In phronesis, wisdom and artistry, as well as art and politics are one. Phronesis concerns the competence how to exercise judgment in particular cases. It is oriented towards the analysis of values and interests in practice, based on a practical value rationality, which is pragmatic and context-dependent. Phronesis is experience-based ethics, oriented towards action.
>
> *(Ehn and Badham 2002, p. 6)*

Ehn and Badham see cultivating the virtue of *phronesis* as supporting the 'collective designer' in handling the many ethical and political dilemmas that arise when engaging in the 'politics of practice' of Participatory Design.

A broad distinction can be made between theories representing an absolutist or relativist view of morality: the absolutist view holds that the grounds for judging human conduct are always the same, independent of people involved and time and place, while the proponents of the relativist view claim that the grounds vary with social and individual needs, customs and historical evolution (see, for example, Abelson and Friquegnon 1995). Haraway goes beyond thinking in terms of 'either/or' (in this case absolutist/relativist), arguing: 'Relativism is the perfect mirror twin of totalisation in the ideologies of objectivity; both deny the stakes in location, embodiment, and partial perspective; both make it impossible to see well' (Haraway 1988, p. 584). We *always* speak from somewhere and the ethical stance we take, what we judge as right or wrong, good or bad, always reflects our particular situation and with that the particular context in which ethical issues may arise.

Normative ethical theories and the principles on which they build may help address some of the general ethical issues at stake in the making of technologies. They can guide thinking about questions related to autonomy, responsibility, the right to privacy, and so forth. Taking an ethical stance in Participatory Design is about an ethical practice that allows the identification of these issues as they arise in design and use.

Moreover, Participatory Design explicitly connects to the notion of 'civil society', a normative concept with different meanings and discourses in different cultures and languages. It shares its process dimension with Participatory Design, building on discourse, conflict and negotiation; and, most importantly, it shares its commitment to designing futures that challenge power relationships and transform patterns of exclusion and social injustice. Advocates of civil society argue from a strong moral basis, referring to values such as autonomy, democratic self-realisation, self-organisation and solidarity. This strong link with civil society points to the need for Participatory Design to broaden its focus to embrace more general questions of human-centred social change. As we will demonstrate, a stronger focus on ethics can help to put these more general questions in focus.

Practical, situated ethics

A practical, situated approach to ethics is often connected to the work of Levinas (1985), who suggests that one's ethical self is defined by the ability to recognise the humanity of the other. Regard for the other is the central principle for dialogic ethics, requiring that one see one's self in the place of the other. Levinas has been appreciated by feminists and by marginalised groups in society more generally because his work demands that the other is defined on its own terms and not in relation to dominant values; that is, as different to but equal. This dialogical relation with others is at the heart of Participatory Design. Bakhtin (Holquist et al. 1990) argues such a relation requires a 'loving and value-positing consciousness'. He considered Kant's system as too abstract and too prescriptive. 'Dialogue as it occurs within the everyday lifeworld' in Bakhtin's understanding 'establishes a relation of mutuality, shared responsibility (or answerability), and unsolicited concern between human beings that supersedes the dictates of a systematic or formalised morality' (Gardiner 1996, p. 32).

Hall (2002) proposed an approach, based on the work of Johnson (1993), who sees the basis for moral sensitivity in the 'moral imagination'. Her notion of narrative ethics puts imagination and interpretation at the centre of ethical decision-making. Narrative ethics proceeds through constructing and telling one's own story and comprehending the story of others. This may include decisions such as: What is my story? What is important to relate? What is the best way to express what I consider to be the ethically most relevant material? Narratively crafting our understanding allows us entry into a decision-making process, which includes contextual elements. The imaginative capacity is revealed in the images, metaphors and symbolism the narrator uses, and in the small details s/he fills in. Hall stresses that narrative ethics and arguing on the basis of rules and principles are not mutually exclusive but can complement each other.

The notion of 'narrative ethics' resonates well with methods of ethical case deliberation that recognise the moral intuitions embedded in narratives. Participants are encouraged to bring forward/argue through stories, and organisers of a deliberation process are required to provide suitable case descriptions. It also resonates well with Participatory Design, which also seeks to build rich representations of practice that are used to collaboratively examine a current situation and envision future, technology-supported practices. In this way Participatory Design already provides the empirical material for ethical case deliberation.

Ethical case deliberation has a tradition in the clinical field where it is mainly used for evaluating clinical cases. It has also been used in studies assessing an individual's moral reasoning (e.g. by Kohlberg 1981 and Gilligan 1982). Steinkamp and Gordijn (2003) suggest a protocol for reasoning about ethical issues that is based on an analogy between clinical judgement and the structure of ethical reflection. It assumes that there is no agreed-upon order of moral values and norms that can be simply applied and that 'it is accepted to be impossible to anticipate a sound solution in a moral conflict without elaborate actual deliberation' (ibid., p. 236). Ethical principles are understood in analogy to scientific hypotheses, as providing a tentative orientation rather than a solution. The ethics consultation is to be guided by an expert ethicist. The process should start with carefully analysing the clinical details of a case, taking into account its ambiguity and complexity. According to Dewey (1991), the quality of such an analysis rests on open, democratic deliberation and suspended judgement. All the relevant stakeholders are invited to share their particular perspectives on an issue. It requires 'contextual factors' to be taken into account in 'concentric circles. Implying first and foremost the perspectives of the other professional groups as well as their contributions to care giving' (Steinkamp and Gordijn 2003, p. 237). Narrative elements, representing moral intuitions and stories are to be included. Institutional policies have to be examined. Finally, classical casuistry is to be practised, making comparisons to other, similar cases. This practice is common in law and philosophy and is about analysing cases for debating and resolving particular ethical issues. We should add that clinical pragmatism accounts for the fact that moral problems do not typically take on the shape of moral conflicts.

Again we can say that Participatory Design fits well into this tradition as it builds its own cases for bringing out issues of use and examining openings into the future. At the same time there is a point in the practice of casuistry, which could be strengthened in the Participatory Design community: systematically examining different cases (not just one's own) for bringing out moral issues of future use. For example, in the ACTION for Health project (see Chapter 11 in this book) ethnographic fieldwork material was used for constructing vignettes: short, narrative accounts of a 'case' from the field that illustrate one or more ethical issues (Balka et al. 2007). Ideally, vignettes should be written so that readers understand the context (of people, tasks, information technology support, organisation, cultured practices, history, etc.) in which ethical issues arise. Some of these vignettes were used in focus group discussions with stakeholders in hospital-based information technology projects.

Ethics and technology

In 1979, the phenomenologist philosopher Hans Jonas, published *The Imperative of Responsibility: In Search of an Ethics for the Technological Age*, which examines the ethical issues surrounding modern technology (English edition 1984). His starting point was that ethics needed to respond to the massively increased capacities of human actions and the wider effects and longer durations of these actions that the development of modern technologies enabled. Jonas argued that the rapid development of modern technology had changed the making of technology from a response to human necessity to the essential purpose of human effort (Jonas 1984, p. 32). He was concerned that there had been little place or time in this process of constant redevelopment and rapid technological change for reflection on that growth, where it might be directed or even if it ought to continue at all. The result is a process of change that appears to drive itself with no time for its own self-correction or regulation. As a consequence, recovering from bad decisions and fixing or removing damaging technologies becomes more and more difficult and the freedom to make changes becomes more and more restricted (ibid.). Jonas argued for the ethical importance of finding ways to better predict the effects of new technologies as a way to strengthen and improve our decision-making about their design and use:

> the indefinite future, rather than the contemporary context of the action, constitutes the relevant horizon of responsibility. This requires imperatives of a new sort. If the realm of making has invaded the space of essential action, then morality must invade the realm of making, from which it had formerly stayed aloof.
>
> *(Jonas 1984, p. 9)*

Designing is a central activity within the realm of making. As stated in the introduction to this book, there is an ethical stance underlying Participatory Design that recognises the accountability of design to the worlds it creates and the lives of those who inhabit them. Participatory designers have consistently sought ways to fully engage people in the design of their own futures. The motivation behind many of the basic tools and methods developed over the years has been to set up rich design contexts that can support imagining better futures, using existing expertise and mutual learning and understanding between different stakeholders. The development of tools and methods, to enable genuine and meaningful participation in the design of new and emerging technologies in a range of different contexts, remains a central concern of Participatory Design.

People are formed both by their own physical and other genetic dispositions and by the contexts within which they live. Who particular people can be in the future depends very much on their present contexts and the options for action within them. The crucial point for technology design is that as present possibilities become what actually 'is', they become increasingly embedded not just in the technology itself and the social and organisational protocols surrounding its use, but in the specific embodied histories, capacities and social identities of particular people (Robertson, 2006). Dewey (1991) argued that morality is bound up in all our actions. It is not some optional extra that can be added or removed so that we can choose to be accountable for some of our actions but not for others. Instead our identities are generated by our actions and interaction with others. Similarly, Foucault's consideration of ethics as 'the relationship you have to yourself when you act' (Foucault 1994, p. 131) recognises the defining role of morality in our actions and the resulting relations to the people we can be.

These approaches share an important focus on the ethical importance of how we act in everyday practice in the myriad of small decisions we make as designers and researchers. We can recognise that some solutions to design problems are better than others because they enable human action differently. Some solutions enhance the possibilities for human agency, others diminish it. Some can support important human capabilities, such as flexibility, creativity, sociability and learning, while others can, in everyday practice, preclude them. This means that there can be a moral basis for choosing between alternative design decisions that might otherwise be considered equivalent in terms of the functionality and usability of the technology

(Robertson 2006). As designers we contribute both our design expertise and our understandings of technology to the Participatory Design process. An informed awareness of the potential implications of different aspects of the design of future technologies on human action is a crucial part of our contribution.

Ethical issues of working with users

Participatory Design has a long tradition of engaging with users in a process that seeks both to arrive at a profound understanding of their work and to create 'trial use situations as part of the design process, so as to stage users' hands-on experience with the future' (Bødker 2000, p. 62). In this section we explore ethical issues involved in this process of engaging, learning and envisioning. As Halloran et al. (2009) have argued:

> users express values whether or not one looks for them. From worries about depersonali-sation, through issues with responsibility, to the idea that technology has to be fun, we found that users frame technology – what it is for, what it does, how it should be designed and evaluated – in terms of spontaneously expressed values. Listening to and acting on these serve important purposes in co-design.
>
> *(ibid., p. 246)*

This leads us to address problems that are commonly encountered within a Participatory Design project by adding a specific ethical perspective to these problems. We look at the ethical aspects of four questions:

- Who do we engage with in a Participatory Design project?
- How do we engage with participants?
- How do we represent participants and their work?
- What can we offer participants?

Who do we engage with in a Participatory Design project?

As stated by Greenbaum (1993), people have the right to influence their own workplace, including the use of computer technology. While identifying the 'legitimate' participants in a small project may be straightforward, it can become a problem in complex settings with many participants and multiple dependencies. Also, those who actually do the work may not necessarily want to be included for their own good reasons; their contribution may be limited by time constraints; some may even have to use their free unpaid time for engaging with the project. Who has the time to participate and whether this participation is acknowledged as part of their regular work are critical questions for Participatory Design and highlight the notion of 'voluntary and unconstrained participation' (Byrne and Alexander 2006) as an issue to be considered.

Extending our reach to internal and external stakeholders, beyond those who actually perform the work, further complicates the issue. For example, Wagner et al. (2009) have engaged with participants – urban planners and specialists, members of the municipality and representatives of the local community – in an urban project in France, offering and evaluating with them participatory tools for envisioning the future of an urban site. Negotiating in particular the participation of 'normal citizens' turned out to be a highly sensitive political issue, since municipalities feared having to include critical views. The question that arises then is how to identify those who have been excluded and their views on the project. This may be a particularly salient issue in community projects, where 'those who are younger or very old, female, of low status groups and/or poor, deprived, disabled and weak will tend to be left out unless care is taken to find them and bring them in' (Chambers 1999, p. 183, quoted in Byrne and Alexander 2006).

In many organisations there are hierarchical and professional boundaries to be taken into account. For example, in a project introducing a new 'oncology system' into Austrian hospitals, nurses were invited to the first user meeting by project management. However, they decided that the system was of no interest for them, the main reason being that they were already engaged in another project introducing a nursing documentation system (Reidl et al. 2008). Their decision reflects the clear occupational boundaries as well as the separation of medical and nursing documentation that are common to many health care systems; but it also precludes the opportunity to question this separation in a Participatory Design project.

The ethical problems these examples point to are twofold. First, they illustrate that defining those who may have the 'right to participate' is made difficult by constraining forces – political power, organisational and professional boundaries; and that some of those who may contribute to and benefit from participating may even not be 'found'. Second, they point to problems of responsibility and accountability. Pedersen (2007) has made an interesting distinction between 'representatives' and 'constituencies', arguing that participants in a Participatory Design project not only represent particular knowledges and interests which they bring to bear on how present and future work is understood and embedded in technologies. They are also accountable to the communities to which they belong: the design community, the research community, different communities of practice within an organisation. In making this distinction Pedersen refers to his own Participatory Design project in the area of maintenance work, critically examining his (and his co-researcher's) efforts at making this work 'public' and 'demonstrating promising results' to the participating stakeholders. He states that the pressure in a project to be 'constructive' may obliterate the desire and obligation of a researcher to be critical. Moreover, he describes how the fieldwork itself had to be formatted for different uses and the constraints of having to avoid conflict with the people under study. Pedersen concludes with these observations: 'People are *partially* connected and ethnographies have *dual* loyalties and are *double agents* … [they] may find themselves in a precarious situation in balancing between the demands of their constituency and those of their collaborators' (ibid., pp. 123, 126). It may be difficult in some situations to sort out these dual loyalties, and to make them transparent so that the ethical conflicts they may imply can be openly discussed.

This resonates with the argument made earlier in this book (see Chapters 1 and 2) that 'taking a stand' is a political *and* ethical issue and an example of how ethics-in-practice and politics-in-practice can become blurred in Participatory Design projects. It involves negotiating issues of non-discrimination and equality of access, as well as of responsibility and account-ability. The examples we discuss show how complicated the politics of ethical negotiations can become in a Participatory Design project.

How do we engage with participants?

A core principle of Participatory Design has always been to acknowledge participants as experts in their own work situation. This presumes respect for their expertise as well as mutual trust. Büscher et al. (2002) think of the sharing of responsibilities and trust building as a matter of 'practical politics' in a Participatory Design project. They identify 'membership', a 'space for imagining', as well as the willingness to make a project work as prerequisites of mutual trust and describe 'how trust is practically worked up in the face of specific risks and gains that surround processes of co-realisation' (ibid., p. 184).

In the tradition of ethical reviewing, 'informed consent' is a key instrument that addresses some of these concerns in a formal way. It is a requirement for ethical clearance of a project. In a design project 'informed consent', which must be signed by all participants, has to take account of conditions that do not necessarily apply to a research project. First, in a design project outcomes are usually open and a project may even fail. This entails risks and responsibilities for all participants that need to be addressed. Second, sensitive issues may arise in a project and their disclosure may cause harm to participants or people connected to them. From the point of view of ethics, trust also implies non-disclosure of possibly incriminating details of the present situation or of possibly critical views. Third (and in part related to the last point), given the multiplicity and heterogeneity of stakeholders included in a project, the handling of conflicts between perspectives and loyalties may have to be addressed. A related concern is vulnerable and frail participants, such as children, people with disabilities including dementia, refugees, immigrants and in general people in marginalised situations. We use 'vulnerability' here as a term indicating that some groups of users may require special sensibility and care.

Our first example comes from a Participatory Design project developing a tool for severely ill children in a Norwegian hospital on a mobile device. As the children were too ill to participate, other healthy children took their place in the project. The tool was also to be used by doctors and nurses, and this made it more difficult for the children to have their voices heard in the design discussion. Moreover, the children were given a limited role in the design and their input was used as an inspirational resource rather than a 'serious' design option. A critical examination of the process comes to the conclusion:

> The children's ideas were fitted into a logic based in the profession of the information receivers. The children's choices were limited with respect to both the overall solution and the details of it – and even the setting of the problem to be solved. The doctors' and nurses' needs for information defined the scope of the project and therefore limited the possibilities for maintaining an openness in the design that enabled the (sick) children to discuss how they could communicate with doctors and nurses – or even others – by means of ICTs.
>
> (Bratteteig et al. 2010, p. 23)

While in this project the most vulnerable stakeholders – the severely ill children – were 'protected', this also excluded their views and experiences from the design solution.

What makes this case interesting from an ethical point of view is that it shows some of the limitations Participatory Design may have to face. The healthy children were involved in what might be defined as a combination of user research and user-centred design: developers learned how children express certain symptoms, they built on the colourful screen layouts the children had produced and had them test the prototype. The children contributed but they were not 'full participants' and theirs was only one and not the most important voice. The ethical issue that arises here is not only how to make limitations to participation transparent but how to make the decision on where the limitation comes in and why: is the limitation due to legal constraints or costs; is it due to medical concerns; or is it just simpler working with healthy children?

Our second example is taken from a project which aimed at making toilet facilities better suited for older people and people with disabilities. For the users, active participation meant contributing personal information to questionnaires regarding difficulties experienced in toileting and in toilet facilities, and trying out the components of the system by showing their toileting routines in user trials. The test users were only asked to simulate the use of the toilet and they were not asked to remove their clothes.

One test user broke into tears during the coffee break, possibly as a reaction to having failed in a task he had been asked to perform. The task required a capacity in the participant, namely raising his voice, which had been affected as a result of his recent stroke. A successful rehabilitation made the man physically appear a healthy volunteer to the research team. What the team could not foresee was how the man's failure to activate an alarm with his voice would mean a sad reminder of the loss of health and control in his life. The participant's unexpected emotional response made the team members reflect on what they could have done differently to prevent the feeling of failure. There was – in hindsight – some indication of the user's hesitance with regard to the task as he attempted to tell the test leader that the feature might not suit stroke patients. But it was not obvious for the research team that the user wanted to discontinue.

(Rauhala 2011, p. 56)

This case is typical of many others that deal with frail users. It involves addressing at least the following questions with ethical dimensions: how to deal with sensitive topics in a test situation (in this case the taboo topic of toileting); how can users be made to feel confident and secure in the test situation and how can the risks of embarrassment or unpleasant surprises be avoided; what steps are necessary to protect the participants' privacy; and considering the users' frailty, how can their safety in test situations be ensured?

Our last example is taken from a project to develop an indigenous knowledge management system in a community in Namibia (Winschiers-Theophilus et al. 2010). As in many other traditional rural African communities, 'participation' was a well-established value in this community and directly incorporated in collaborative day-to-day activities such as storytelling, inclusive decision-making and participatory community meetings. This meant that the focus of the designers' facilitation was less on joining individuals in activities such as design workshops and more on directing the interactions of the community towards design within their local participation practices. The different focus reflected the fact that different understandings of participation are held by different societies and are based on local value systems. Major gaps existed between the international team of design researchers and the local participants based on 'contrasting sense of self, individuality and community, orality versus print-based literacy, and technological skills versus local situational knowledge' (ibid., p. 2). Recognising these differences enabled the designers to carefully select and review the methods they used so that participation appropriate to the underlying value system of the design context could be used. This could mean an appropriation by the community of the design process. Designers needed to also recognise that these differences were not deficiencies to be remedied, that the values inherent in Western readings of participation can displace other knowledge traditions and that as they conformed to community ethics they needed to rethink their role as part of the particular community of participants. Acting well in these situations relies on traditional Participatory Design core commitments such as mutual learning, but also insists that we rethink what this means in contexts very different from those of traditional workplaces, organisations or Western democracies (see also the HICS project in Chapter 10 of this book).

The 'practical politics' of how to engage with participants involves a diversity of complex issues, most importantly the question of how trust can be established and the sharing of responsibilities ensured in very specific situations. These include: those in which there are limitations to participation (in our example, due to the vulnerability of severely ill children); those in which highly personal and sensitive issues are at stake (in our example, toileting practices of people with disabilities); or those in which the value systems and understandings of researchers and users differ (as in the case of community projects in rural Africa). We cannot escape the fact that these issues need to be negotiated and managed. Such an awareness is itself valuable because it can mean that space is made available within project planning for such negotiations. It also opens another rich area for future work.

How do we represent participants and their work?

Another principle of Participatory Design is not to tell users what their work is or what it means to them. Producing representations of work can be seen in analogy to the creation of 'ethnographic accounts' (and in fact ethnography has an important role in Participatory Design projects). Clifford argues that all ethnographic accounts are partial truths, written from specific perspectives, adding:

> Once 'informants' begin to be considered as co-authors, and the ethnographer as scribe and archivist as well as interpreting observer, we can ask new, critical questions of all ethno-graphies; however monological, dialogical, or polyphonic their form, they are hierarchical in their arrangement.
>
> *(Clifford 1986, p. 17)*

When, during a design process, we tell a story or represent a social practice or site in some other way, we are constructing a representation that we intend to contribute to shaping the future social practices or site. Design representations have a performative function that we are accountable to in that they are constitutive of the worlds in which ourselves and others will live (Gibson–Graham 1996). Representations are not only partial truths, they are not 'innocent' in that they carry 'persuasion', invite others into a dialogue or preclude such a dialogue from taking place (Latour 1986). The production of representations is critical to Participatory Design (e.g. Bødker 1998) and the literature discusses different methods for arriving at 'good' representations. Here we want to point out the ethical issues involved in their creation.

A first example is taken from an early design project for the editorial board (the body responsible for making grants) of a film board in Denmark (Simonsen and Kensing 1997). The designers developed a first design based on interviews with the secretaries and editors involved in accepting and responding to grant applications. However, they realised that the editors had struggled to formulate their needs for the new system because they could not see the relation-ship between the problems they encountered in their work and computer systems. So a second stage of research was done, involving ethnographic fieldwork focusing on observation of key activities that the editors nominated as defining their work. Accompanying the editors as they performed these activities set up the context for mutual learning about the work of the editors and the scope of the new system. The result was a second design that decisively changed the first.

This example highlights how representations of work, even well-meaning ones developed within Participatory Design projects, can 'silence' or just completely miss the perspective of one whole group of participants who will be affected by the new system. One design was devel-oped with the perspective of the editors missing from it. Importantly, in this case, the ongoing reflection and iteration, so defining of Participatory Design, enabled the designers to recognise the issue. They could then engage in further fieldwork to ensure that the voices of all those affected were represented. The important point for our discussion here is that only by working with the editors in ways that enabled both the designers and editors to learn together about the work that the new system would support were the designers able to develop representations of the editors' work that could adequately reflect their concerns in the design of the new system.

75

In their account of 'litigation support' in a law firm, Blomberg et al. (1996) quote a senior attorney who described the process of document coding as made up of two types: what he termed *subjective*, or issues coding done by attorneys, and *objective* coding which he described as follows:

> You have, you know, 300 cartons of documents and you tear through them and say, I'm going to put Post-Its on the ones we have to turn over to the other side. And then, ideally, you hire chimpanzees to type in From, To, Date. And then, ideally, you then have lawyers go through it again and read each document, with their brain turned on.
>
> *(ibid., p. 252)*

Blomberg et al. (1996) relate how they came to realise that the work of coding documents was invisible to lawyers in the firm, and when they started observing both types of work they saw that

> the work of the attorneys revealed no small measure of mundane or tedious activities, which when brought into the attorneys' awareness were accepted by them, albeit ruefully, as inevitable accompaniments of their practice. At the same time, the more we looked into the work of document coding and data entry, the more we saw the judgmental and interpretive work that the document coders were required to bring to it.
>
> *(ibid., p. 253)*

This is another compelling example of how work may get 'misrepresented' when it is not observed directly and the representation is not co-produced with those who perform it. It also raises the issue of 'invisible work' that has been described so convincingly in Star and Strauss (1999). They describe different mechanisms through which work or part of this work is made invisible: creating a non-person, disembedding background work, and abstracting and manipulation of indicators. In their book *Sorting Things Out*, Bowker and Star (1999) cite the wonderful example of a nursing classification system that has been developed bottom up, by the nurses themselves, and in which, among others, the category 'humour' has been specified in great detail:

> contained within the nursing classification is an anatomy of what it is to be humorous, and a theory of what humour does ... One should determine the types of humour appreciated by the patient; determine the patient's typical response to humour (e.g. laughter or smiles); select humorous materials that create moderate arousal for the individual (for example picture a forbidding authority figure dressed only in underwear); encourage silliness and playfulness and so on to make a total of fifteen sub-activities: any one of which might be scientifically relevant. A feature traditionally attached to the personality of the nurse (being a cheerful and supportive person) is now attached through the classification to the job description as an intervention, which can be accounted for.
>
> *(Berg and Bowker 1997, p. 528)*

As a representation of work that has been co-authored by practising nurses, this example is especially interesting. Aspects of work have been made visible that are partly highly personal and contingent, begging questions of cultural sensitivity and appropriateness for different groups of patients. For example, why is 'picture a forbidden authority figure dressed only in underwear' presented as an example of humour? Is it related to the position that nurses occupy in hospital hierarchies and is it appropriate for a general or unknowable audience? Examples such as this raise the ethical questions of 'where to stop', 'what to make visible' and 'in which ways'. One of

Bowker and Star's arguments is that what is not made visible in representations of work often does not 'count', is neither valued nor remunerated. But should 'humour' be remunerated? As stated earlier: representations are not innocent and digging deeper may bring forth numerous political and ethical questions connected to the description of practices.

Bowker and Star (1999) also point to another aspect of this problem: the desire to 'normalise' practices and their descriptions and, connected to this, the importance of attending to 'residual categories':

> Simply put, a residual category is that which is left over after a classification is built – 'none of the above' and 'not otherwise specified' are typical locutions. A system without the possibility to understand the history and sociology of its residual categories desiccates stories it already labels 'unknowable'.
>
> *(Star and Bowker 2007, p. 274)*

Star and Bowker point at the processes of what they call 'double silencing': 'double' because these residuals and the practices or people they represent have been put into a 'garbage can' and because we may not understand why, historically and sociologically, they have been labelled as 'none of the above'. Star and Bowker argue for resistance as well as engagement for 'a politics of the other'.

A conclusion from the point of view of ethics is, first, not only to engage with users as co-producers of representations but also to focus attention on parts of work that may be invisible (occasionally also to users themselves); and second, to question established practices of sorting and explore residual categories, 'listening to those who inhabit them' (ibid., p. 280). While ethnography in combination with participative methods offers good instruments for making things visible and creating good representations, what may be considered 'residual', albeit important, to people's lives is much more difficult to capture. But as we can see from the example of 'humour', reflecting on such residual categories can add to researchers' and practitioners' understanding of a practice and the difficulties in representing and supporting it adequately.

What can we offer participants?

In the best of all cases a Participatory Design project results in a well-functioning system or application, amenable to users' reconfiguring and redesigning to fit evolving uses. But what happens when this is not possible? We are often 'creating future forms of technology that will not become completely viable within the scope of the project. The gap between existing conditions and our vision can only be closed through imagination and improvisation' (Büscher et al. 2002, p. 191). This means that the emerging design will not be available to users who have participated in its creation. Moreover, project time often ends before we can support users in integrating what has been designed with their everyday practice. This also means not being able to observe, understand and heed the evolving new practices around a system or application.

In Participatory Design projects we often experience that we receive more than we can give, which is not only to do with the incompleteness of the designs we are able to deliver within project time but also with the very different situations of users and designers. For example, designers working in a research environment often have the benefit of a full-time involvement in a project and their own reward structures, which allow them to harvest findings even from a 'failed' project, whereas users may be left with the feeling that their time and effort did not lead to the changes they may have desired and in fact needed.

Taking responsibility in design requires reflecting on what designers can offer participants. Participatory Design methods offer a variety of ways of making engagement in a project a worthwhile endeavour for users. From the point of view of research ethics, commitment to involving participants in the co-creation of 'partially truthful' accounts of their situation is a part of responsible Participatory Design practice from which participants benefit. Participatory Design is a reflective practice (see e.g. Ehn 2002) and it builds on mutual learning (see e.g. Bratteteig 2004). A Participatory Design project can offer participants the experience of participation as a creative, joyful and reflective activity. Many of the tools and techniques used have been inspired by other creative areas such as art making and theatre, and some Participatory Design projects have a particular focus on how to encourage and support reflection. Gaver et al. (2003) argued for and experimented with 'ambiguity' as stimulating reflection on ethical and political issues. Mörtberg and Elovaara (2010) used 'cartographic exercises' to create space and time for sharing and reflection of their stories by the participating women in an e-Government project and Johansson and Linde (2005) explored how playfulness and games can be used as a way of doing design based on field studies, and how 'the ambiguous nature nourishes a *dialogue* between different actors in the design process' (ibid., p. 8).

A major strength of Participatory Design is that there is a robust connection between ethical practice and the choice of methods, tools and techniques. We interpret this not only as the responsibility of designers and researchers to foster mutual learning. It also calls on them to reflect deeply and systematically on the politics of the organisations or communities they engage with and the resulting limitations for participation and learning. This is of course not a new concern. Blomberg et al. (1996) formulated a series of requests to designers:

> Understand the politics of change and where you stand within them … Understand how extended contexts (e.g. institutional, global) constrain the scope of what can be accomplished in a given setting, and attempt to question or take advantage of those contexts as appropriate.
>
> *(ibid., pp. 260f)*

This is already very difficult in work-related projects but may be even more difficult in community-related projects. For example Brereton and Buur (2008, p. 107), reflecting on their experience with a community design project state: 'If the project is to grow, the next step potentially involves working out issues such as business models, public/private ownership, open sourcing and location of other noticeboards.' They address the need to get involved in the different political aspects of a community if a project is to be successful. They see this as part of their responsibility as designers and researchers.

Ethical issues of technology design in and for use

Participatory Design is about envisioning future use. This implies among other things anticipating ethical issues that may arise in use, to think of strategies for resolving them or embedding some protection in the design. In this section we seek to point out some of the major issues that may arise in use, also taking account of future and emerging technologies. In this endeavour, which is about envisioning, ethical principles provide useful anchors for thinking about future use.

The challenges

Eevi Beck (2002) argued that Participatory Design should be narrowed to exclude work that uses participation just as a design tool without contributing to understanding or challenging patterns of dominance: 'Participatory Design must develop a stronger demand for analyses of societal/ political/ethical consequences of ICT development, management, adoption, or use' (ibid., p. 77). Taking up this argument we may say that Participatory Design has perhaps not devoted sufficient effort to systematically addressing ethical issues of use. There are a variety of practical reasons for this, some of which we mentioned before. They include the fact that a Participatory Design project often ends before we can support users to analyse and resolve issues that might only become visible once the system is in use. A second reason may be that some ethical issues, such as those connected to monitoring and surveillance, frequently are less a technical than an organisational issue and participants may have to face situations of limited control over the 'privacy' aspects of a design. Finally, assessing some of the questions that directly concern power and dominance cannot be always resolved by anticipating use but would require an extensive study of use on the one hand and the negotiation of power within the organisation on the other. Shapiro (2005) in discussing the potential involvement of Participatory Design in large-scale systems development projects concludes: 'we would have, at the limit, to be prepared to walk away from a project where such matters are not negotiable' (ibid., p. 35).

These reflections remind us that the recognition that design is completed in use is constitutive of Participatory Design. Early Scandinavian Participatory Design in the 1970s may, through its alliance with unions, have found more opportunities to see this completion in use and do a thorough analysis of political/ethical issues connected with a design. This has become even more difficult today, due to changes in the political and policy-making context, as well as the changing nature of technologies and of the work required to flexibly configure and deploy them in contexts that reach into leisure, museums, community services, and the collaborative design of services and products (see also Chapter 3 in this book). We also see changes in the participants in Participatory Design projects, with more and more researchers collaborating with particularly vulnerable participant groups (e.g. with old people developing home care technologies), as well as engaging in projects in 'distant' social and cultural contexts, including developing countries. Looking at the new areas that are affected by emergent technologies, we should not forget that workplaces continue to be subject to technological and organisational change. When we look beyond the Western world, let's say to China where working conditions in many areas are still poor, we witness a generation of young educated migrant workers organising strikes. As the *New York Times* reported:

> They fired off cellphone text messages urging colleagues to resist pressure from factory bosses. They logged onto a state-controlled Web site – workercn.cn – that is emerging as a digital hub of the Chinese labour movement. And armed with desktop computers, they uploaded video of Honda Lock's security guards roughing up employees … they have also tapped into a broader communications web enabling the working class throughout China to share grievances and strategies. Some strike leaders now say they spend much of their time perusing the Web for material on China's labor laws.
>
> *(New York Times, 16 June 2010)*

As Schmidt (2011) shows in his analysis, events such as these make the actual degradation of work in many parts of the world visible. These workers are making use of modern technologies to exercise their voice and 'By turning the Taylorist system around, that is, by using the carefully designed just-in-time workflow so as to identify strategic weak spots, and then paralyzing these by walking out – and thereby showing the essential value of their work' (ibid.). Political action is taking place making use of mobile and ubiquitous technologies, and it is for Participatory Design to reflect on and learn from these examples.

How can an analysis of ethical problems of technology use contribute to Participatory Design?

There are ethical issues that potentially concern all technologies, current and future ones, and as Jonas argued we need to examine them in order to improve our decision-making about design and use. Participatory Design, with the richness of techniques of envisioning future use and its commitment to actively engaging future users in genuine participation in design, is a most suitable approach to address the ethical issues of technology use.

Some of the key ethical issues to take account of are connected to monitoring and surveillance. Much has been written about how modern – in particular novel 'pervasive' – technologies threaten the right to privacy and confidentiality. Altman (1977) has argued that the boundaries between public and private are dynamic and open to continuous negotiation. Hence, technologies have to be examined as to whether they support users in regulating these boundaries according to their needs. As restricting technology-supported monitoring and surveillance is more often an organisational than a technical issue, Participatory Design may have to face situations of limited control over aspects of a design with strong ethical implications. On the other hand, designing for the configurability of public–private boundaries is a considerable challenge for any design project.

Both mobile and social technologies enable new forms of participation and opportunities for design to be completed in use. They have already been useful tools for Participatory Design but introduce their own ethical issues for both participants and designers (e.g. Hagen and Robertson 2010). For example, if participants are asked to gather data about their own lives then they may also, intentionally or otherwise, document the lives of others. This allows for richer understandings about potential situations of use but it raises questions about anonymity, ownership of data, safety (for example if there are children involved), privacy and consent, especially in public spaces. There may even be issues about participant safety and legality if they are documenting in places where this might be forbidden, or require sensitive negotiation or some kind of official consent. Hagen and Robertson point to the tight coupling of design and use inherent in social technologies, suggesting that this also opens new ways of identifying and addressing ethical issues, for example using mobile diaries as well as hybrid exploratory prototypes that help propose and experiment with different design options in ad hoc, and therefore easily changeable, ways.

Our next example refers to the fact that many systems have not only and primarily been designed to support practitioners but require the additional work of accounting for managerial and other purposes. These have been called 'systems of accountability' (Suchman 1993). Berg (1999) critically discusses expectations connected with electronic patient records. A substantial part of health data included in the record does not refer directly to the clinical situation, but is collected to satisfy other needs such as those of cost control and containment, planning, epidemiological studies and other research. Often, current electronic record designs make nurses and doctors responsible for the production of standardised 'transportable' data for these multiple secondary purposes. They have to fill in coded forms, write explanations, take account of the information needs of management, etc. This example points at the politics and control that are built into such systems and how these can actually get in the way of people doing good work. It raises issues that form part of an ethics of work: what kind of work other than the work directly related to the clinical care situation can be legitimately expected from health professionals; and how does this affect their workload and their attention to their primary function as caretakers?

Our last example is taken from the area of home care to illustrate some of the challenges for Participatory Design when it engages in designing home care devices and services. This is a relatively new and fast developing area that offers an enormous new market to providers. Much of the ethical discussion connected to home care technologies focuses on safety and privacy issues. However, there are many unresolved issues connected to responsibility and autonomy. Programmes in the area of home care technologies build on the generalised and largely unquestioned ethical premise that allowing people with chronic diseases to live in their homes will offer them a better quality of life. Willems (2004) points out that when transferring a technology away from hospital and into the home we need to ask what impact this will have on the quality of the patient's living conditions and what demands it places on patients and their care-giving family members. For example, patients can receive respiratory care at home using invasive or non-invasive methods. While some patients only need to be ventilated at night, others require it around the clock. Studies generally show that the possibility of carrying out artificial respiration at home enhances both the patient's quality of life and his or her life expectancy. However, it places a great deal of strain on the care-giving relatives, especially in situations where an interruption of ventilation would immediately lead to death (Austrian Federal Chancellery 2009). Ambrosino and Vianello (2002) ask whether this type of long-term treatment is even compatible with life within a family.

In a Participatory Design project involving the design of home care technologies we have to examine questions such as:

> Which aspects of a task can be entrusted to technologies or to informal caregivers? How does life change, not just for the patients, but also for their informal caregivers? Under which circumstances may they initiate measures, which are legally reserved to physicians? To what extent can informal caregivers be held to account for the consequences of errors when interpreting and operating complex technologies?
>
> *(Austrian Federal Chancellery 2009, p. 16)*

Defining responsibility and the sharing of it in a complex network of affected people, their families, nurses, medical doctors, service providers, etc., is not a straightforward issue. Moreover, what may increase the autonomy of chronically ill people may have a downside; as Loewy (1996) argues: 'Unthinkingly and unfeelingly abandoning persons to their supposed autonomy is the flip side of paternalism' (ibid., p. 77). Responsibility has individual, organisational and legal aspects, each of which have to be taken into consideration when designing for future use.

The strength of Participatory Design is that nurturing participation as well as using ethnographic methods can certainly be expected, as Shapiro (2005) puts it, 'to reclaim and to emphasise the complex, multi-faceted and resourceful ways in which all forms of work are carried out, regardless of how they may be officially or conventionally characterised, and so to retrieve respect for its accomplishment' (ibid., p. 35). But is this sufficient? It is not only the case that users of home care technologies are vulnerable and designers and researchers may have limited access to them. There are many 'external' but also many 'personal' factors that influence how these technologies are embedded into users' home environments and how all the resulting highly sensitive dependencies are 'managed'. In turn this can affect how and whether resulting ethical problems get resolved.

We want to express with these examples a crucial direction for Participatory Design to engage with more intensely in the future. This is to find different ways of observing and monitoring a design in use and through this not only analyse 'societal/political/ethical consequences of ICT development, management, adoption, or use' (Beck 2002, p. 77) but use participation as a means for resolving conflicts that emerge in technology use.

Conclusion

We have shown through a variety of examples some ways that attention to ethical issues has been expressed in Participatory Design. But the lesson from these examples is that the ethical commitments of Participatory Design fundamentally shape it and will always need to be addressed, extended, shifted, re-expressed and revisited in any specific design situation. In the future, these issues will continue to exist though they will always align themselves to each other and the situation in different ways; for example, privacy issues may be paramount in designing and using social technologies. This means that the basic ethical principles of Participatory Design can be used to ground reflection on how to 'act well' in new situations involving new technologies, new objects of design and new contexts. It is never trivial to negotiate these issues in actual projects and design practice. We close this chapter with some consideration of the ways that Participatory Design's basic ethical commitments can support designers and researchers who are engaging in Participatory Design in the future, irrespective of what is being designed.

The headings that we have used to structure much of the discussion in this chapter can themselves be used as guides to design reflection and planning of future actions. So too can the basic commitments of Participatory Design, such as: recognising that those who do a particular activity know most about how it gets done; recognising the importance of mutual learning and the development of shared understandings between designers and other participants; recognising the need to involve multiple voices and equalise their expression, to ensure active and emancipatory participation, to take a stand, working with participants to represent their own actions – both current and desired future actions – and recognising that design will always be completed in use.

These principles can also be used to explicitly formulate questions to guide ongoing reflection and iteration during a design process. For example, designers might find the following questions useful in critical reflection of the Participatory Design methods, tools and techniques they are using in their projects.[1]

- Do users actually have decision power? If so what kind?
- Does a design method, tool or process recognise and encourage participants' abilities to learn?
- Does a design method, tool or process guide designers and researchers to analyse and develop their interests and attitude towards participants?
- Does a design method, tool or process include participants' evaluations not just of what is being designed but of the design process itself, including the opportunities for and process of participation?
- Does a design method, tool or process deal with a justified loss or change of design focus, for example when participants identify problems that require non-information technology solutions while the process was initiated to design information technology)?

While these simple ethical design tools can be used to orient Participatory Design decision-making and planning, they are complex to interpret within actual design projects. They are offered here as a place to start the process of reflection on the ethics issues that might need to be addressed within particular Participatory Design projects.

Participatory Design, as a community of researchers and designers, can also work to develop resources to support reflection and deliberation on how to act ethically when seeking participatory solutions to complex issues, such as health and community planning or the design of new services and other situations where design will be increasingly completed in use. We suggest that a renewed focus on ethics can offer new tools that can help resolve ethical issues/conflicts that may arise in current use and, most importantly, in future use. One of these tools, much used in ethics in general, is ethical case discussion. As Participatory Design is deeply committed to understanding practice it generates its own cases for such a discussion. We suggest that this is an activity that could be expanded and done more 'knowingly' so that a corpus of cases to be used in design planning and design thinking could be developed. As we described earlier, it is essential to ethical case discussion that case descriptions are rich in detail and that many different voices contribute.

Finally, Participatory Design can recognise an ethical responsibility to make all we have learned about participation in the design of future practices available to other areas where complex problems arise that can only be solved by the ongoing active participation of those who are affected by them. We believe that Participatory Design needs to continue to broaden its strong focus on technology design so it can drive the human-centred design of social change. This process needs to include, within its core, reflection on what makes a 'good life' and how people's living and working conditions can be improved and sustained.

Note

1 We are grateful to Volmar Pipek for suggesting, in an early review of this chapter, that we include a list such as this and some of these questions.

References

Abelson, R. and M.-L. Friquegnon (eds) (1995) *Ethics for Modern Life*, fifth edition, New York: St Martin's Press.
Altman, I. (1977) 'Privacy regulation: culturally universal or culturally specific?' *Journal of Social Issues*, 33: 66–84.
Ambrosino, N. and A. Vianello (2002) 'Where to perform long-term ventilation', *Respiratory Care Clinics of North America,* 8: 463–78.
Austrian Federal Chancellery (2009) 'Ethical aspects of the development and use of assistive technologies', *Opinion of the Bioethics Commission at the Federal Chancellery*, Opinion 13, Wien, Austria, July.
Balka, E., C. Reidl and I. Wagner (2007) 'Using fieldwork in analyzing ethical issues related to IT in health care', in E. Hovenga (ed.) *Proceedings of MedInfo 2007*, Brisbane, Australia: IOS Press.
Beauchamp, T. L. and J. F. Childress (1994) *Principles of Biomedical Ethics*, fourth edition, Oxford: Oxford University Press.
Beck, E. (2002) 'P for political: participation is not enough', *Scandinavian Journal of Information Systems*, 14(1): 77–92.
Berg, M. (1999) 'Accumulating and coordinating: occasions for information technologies in medical work', *Computer Supported Cooperative Work*, 8(4): 373–401.
Berg, M. and G. Bowker (1997) 'The multiple bodies of the medical record: towards a sociology of an artifact', *The Sociological Quarterly*, 38(3): 513–37.
Blomberg, J., L. Suchman and R. Trigg (1996) 'Reflections on a work-oriented design project', *Human–Computer Interaction,* 11(3): 237–66.
Bødker, S. (1998) 'Understanding representation in design', *Human–Computer Interaction,* 13(2): 107–25.
Bødker, S. (2000) 'Scenarios in user-centred design – setting the stage for reflection and action', *Interacting with Computers*, 13(1), 61–75.
Bowker, G. and S. L. Star (1999) *Sorting Things Out: Classification and Its Consequences*, Cambridge, MA: MIT Press.
Bratteteig, T. (2004) 'Making change: dealing with relations between design and use', diss., Department of Informatics, University of Oslo.
Bratteteig, T., I. Wagner, A. Morrison, D. Stuedahl and C. Mörtberg (2010) 'Research practices in digital design', in I. Wagner, T. Bratteteig and D. Stuedahl (eds) *Exploring Digital Design*, London: Springer, 17–54.
Brereton, M. and Buur, J. (2008) 'New challenges for design participation in the era of ubiquitous computing', *CoDesign*, 4(2): 101–13.
Büscher, M., D. Shapiro, M. Hartswood, R. Procter, R. Slack, A. Voß and P. Mogensen (2002) 'Promises, premises and risks: sharing responsibilities, working up trust and sustaining commitment in

Participatory Design projects', in T. Binder, J. Gregory and I. Wagner (eds) *PDC 2002, Proceedings of the Participatory Design Conference, Palo Alto, California*, New York: ACM, 183–92.

Byrne, E. and P. M. Alexander (2006) 'Questions of ethics: participatory information systems research in community settings', in J. Bishop and D. Kourie (eds) *Proceedings of SAICSIT 2006, Somerset West, South Africa*, New York: ACM, 117–26.

Chambers, T. (1999) *The Fiction of Bioethics: Cases as Literary Texts*, New York: Routledge.

Clifford, J. (1986) 'Introduction: partial truths', in J. Clifford and G. E. Marcus (eds) *Writing Culture: The Poetics and Politics of Ethnography*, Berkeley, CA: University of California Press, 1–26.

Dewey, J. (1991) *How We Think*, Buffalo, NY: Prometheus Press.

Ehn, P. (2002) 'Neither Bauhäusler nor nerd educating the interaction designer', in J. van der Schijff and G. Marsden (eds) *Proceedings of the Conference on Designing Interactive Systems, Cape Town, South Africa, February 25–27, 2008*, New York: ACM, 19–23.

Ehn, P. and R. Badham (2002) 'Participatory Design and the collective designer', in T. Binder, J. Gregory and I. Wagner (eds) *PDC 2002, Proceedings of the Participatory Design Conference, Palo Alto, California*, New York: ACM, 1–10.

Foucault, M. (1994) 'Michel Foucault: an interview by Stephen Riggins', in P. Rabinow (ed.) *Michel Foucault, Ethics: Subjectivity and Truth*, New York: The New Press, 121–33.

Frankena, W. (1973) *Ethics*, second edition, Englewood Cliffs, NJ: Prentice-Hall.

Gardiner, M. (1996) 'Foucault, ethics and dialogue'. *History of the Human Sciences*, 9: 27–46.

Gatens, M. (1996) *Imaginary Bodies*, New York: Routledge.

Gaver, B., J. Beaver and S. Benford (2003) 'Ambiguity as a resource for design', in G. Cockton and P. Korhonen (eds) *Proceedings of the ACM CHI 2003 Human Factors in Computing Systems Conference*, New York: ACM.

Gibson-Graham, K. K. (1996) *The End of Capitalism (as We Knew It)*, Boston, MA: Blackwell.

Gilligan, C. (1982) *In a Different Voice: Psychological Theory and Women's Development*, Cambridge, MA: Harvard University Press.

Greenbaum, J. (1993) 'PD: a personal statement', *Communications of the ACM*, 36(6): 47.

Hagen, P. and T. Robertson (2010) 'Social technologies: challenges and opportunities for participation', in T. Robertson, K. Bødker, T. Bratteteig and D. Loi (eds) *Proceedings of the 11th Conference on Participatory Design, PDC 2010, Sydney, Australia, November 29 – December 3, 2010*, New York: ACM, 31–40.

Hall, K. (2002) 'Medical decision-making: an argument for narrative and metaphor', *Theoretical Medicine*, 23: 55–73.

Halloran, J., E. Hornecker, S. Stringer, E. Harris and G. Fitzpatrick (2009) 'The value of values: resourcing co-design of ubiquitous computing', *CoDesign*, 5(4): 245–73.

Haraway, D. (1988) 'Situated knowledges: the science question in feminism and the privilege of partial perspective', *Feminist Studies*, 14(3): 575–99.

Held, V. (1993) *Feminist Morality*, Chicago, IL: University of Chicago Press.

Holquist, M., V. Liapunov and K. Brostrom (eds) (1990) *Art and Answerability: Early Philosophical Essays by M. M. Bakhtin*, Austin: University of Texas Press.

Johansson, M. and P. Linde (2005) 'Playful collaborative exploration: new research practice in Participatory Design', *Journal of Research Practice*, 1(1): Article M5.

Johnson, M. (1993) *Moral Imagination: Implications of Cognitive Science for Ethics*, Chicago, IL: University of Chicago Press.

Jonas, H. (1984) *The Imperative of Responsibility: In Search of an Ethics for the Technological Age*, Chicago, IL: University of Chicago Press (first published in German, 1979).

Kensing, F. and Blomberg, J. (1998) 'Participatory Design: issues and concerns', *Computer Supported Cooperative Work*, 7(3–4): 167–85.

Kohlberg, L. (1981) *The Philosophy of Moral Development: Moral Stages and the Idea of Justice*, New York: Harper and Row.

Latour, B. (1986) 'Visualisation and cognition: thinking with eyes and hands', *Knowledge and Society: Studies in the Sociology of Culture Past and Present*, 6: 1–40.

Levinas, E. (1985) *Ethics and Infinity: Conversations with Philippe Nemo*, trans. R. Cohen, Pittsburgh, PA: Duquesne University Press.

Loewy, E. (1996) *Textbook of Healthcare Ethics*, New York: Plenum.

McGuigan, J. (2005) 'The cultural public sphere', *European Journal of Cultural Studies*, 8(4): 427–45.

McNaughton, D. (1988) *Moral Vision: An Introduction to Ethics*, Oxford: Basil Blackwell.

Merkel, C. B., L. Xiao, U. Farooq, C. H. Ganoe, R. Lee, J. M. Carroll and M. B. Rosson (2004) 'Participatory design in community computing contexts: tales from the field', in A. Clement and P. van den Besselaar (eds) *Proceedings of the Eighth Conference on Participatory Design: Artful Integration: Interweaving Media, Materials and Practices, PDC 2004, Toronto, Ontario, Canada, July 27–31, 2004*, New York: ACM, 1–10.

Mörtberg, C. and P. Elovaara (2010) 'Attaching people and technology: between E and government booth', in S. Goodman and G. Kirkup (eds) *Gender Issues in Learning and Working with Information Technology: Social Constructs and Cultural Contexts*, Hershey, PA: IGI Global, 83–98.

Pedersen, J. (2007) 'Protocols of research and design: reflections on a participatory design project (sort of)', PhD thesis, IT University of Copenhagen.

Puri, S., E. Byrne, J. Nhampossa and Z. Quraishi (2004) 'Contextuality of participation in IS design: a developing country perspective', in A. Clement and P. van den Besselaar (eds) *Proceedings of the Eighth Conference on Participatory Design: Artful Integration: Interweaving Media, Materials and Practices, PDC 2004, Toronto, Ontario, Canada, July 27–31, 2004*, New York: ACM, 42–52.

Rauhala, M. (2011) 'When ethical guidance is missing and do-it-yourself is required: the shaping of ethical peer review in the FRR project', in J. F. M. Molenbroek, J. Mantas and R. de Bruin (eds) *A Friendly Rest Room: Developing Toilets of the Future for Disabled and Elderly People*, Assistive Technology Research Series Vol. 27, Amsterdam: IOS Press, 49–59.

Reidl, C., I. Wagner and M. Rauhala (2007) 'Examining ethical issues of IT in health care', *Action for Health Project*, final report, Vancouver, September 2007.

Reidl, C., M. Tolar and I. Wagner (2008) 'Impediments to change: the case of implementing an electronic patient record in three oncology clinics', in D. Hakken, J. Simonsen and T. Robertson (eds) *Proceedings of the Tenth Conference on Participatory Design, PDC 2008, Bloomington, Indiana, October 1–4, 2008*, New York: ACM, 21–30.

Robertson, T. (2006) 'Ethical issues in interaction design', *Ethics and Information Technology*, 8(1): 49–59.

Schmidt, K. (2011) 'Reflections on the visibility and invisibility of work' presented at 'Celebration of Leigh Star: Her Work and Intellectual Legacy', NSF-funded workshop, San Francisco, 9–10 September.

Schmidt, K., I. Wagner and M. Tolar (2007) 'Permutations of cooperative work practices: a study of two oncology clinics', in T. Gross and K. Inkpen (eds) *Proceedings of the 2007 International ACM Conference on Supporting Group Work*, New York: ACM, 1–10.

Schön, D. (1987) *Educating the Reflective Practitioner – Towards a New Design for Teaching and Learning in the Professions*, San Francisco, CA: Jossey-Bass.

Shapiro, D. (2005) 'Participatory design: the will to succeed', in O. W. Bertelsen, N. O. Bouvin, P. G. Krogh and M. Kyng (eds) Proceedings of the 4th Decennial Conference on Critical Computing: Between Sense and Sensibility *(CC'05), Aarhus, Denmark*, New York: ACM, 29–38.

Simonsen, J. and F. Kensing (1997) 'Using ethnography in contextual design', *Communications of the ACM*, 40(7): 82–8.

Singer, P. (1993) *Practical Ethics*, second edition, Cambridge: Cambridge University Press.

Star, S. L. and G. Bowker (2007) 'Enacting silence: residual categories as a challenge for ethics, information systems, and communication', *Ethics and Information Technology*, 9: 273–80.

Star, S. L. and A. Strauss (1999) 'Layers of silence, arenas of voice: the ecology of visible and invisible work', *Computer Supported Cooperative Work*, 8(1–2): 9–30.

Steinkamp, N. and B. Gordijn (2003) 'Ethical case deliberation on the ward: a comparison of four methods', *Medicine, Health Care and Philosophy*, 6: 235–46.

Suchman, L. (1993) 'Do categories have politics? The language/action perspective reconsidered', in G. de Michelis, C. Simone and K. Schmidt (eds) *Proceedings of the Third European Conference of Computer Supported Cooperative Work (ECSCW93), Milan, Italy*, New York: Kluwer Academic Publishers.

Wagner, I., Basile, M., Ehrenstrasser, L., Maquil, V., Terrin, J. and Wagner, M. (2009) 'Supporting community engagement in the city: urban planning in the MR-tent', in *C&T '09, Proceedings of the Fourth International Conference on Communities and Technologies*, New York: ACM, 185–94.

Willems, D. (2004) 'Advanced home care technology: moral questions associated with an ethical ideal', *Ethics and Health Monitoring Report 2004 no. 4*, The Hague: Health Council of the Netherlands.

Winschiers-Theophilus, H., S. Chivuno-Kuria, G. Kapuire, N. Bidwell and E. Blake (2010) 'Being participated – a community approach', T. Robertson, K. Bødker, T. Bratteteig and D. Loi (eds) *Proceedings of the 11th Conference on Participatory Design, PDC 2010, Sydney, Australia, November 29 – December 3, 2010*, New York: ACM, 1–10.

Wittgenstein, L. (1965) 'A lecture on ethics', *The Philosophical Review*, 74(1): 3–12.

5

Ethnography

Positioning ethnography within Participatory Design

Jeanette Blomberg and Helena Karasti

This chapter explores the history of ethnography in Participatory Design, the varied approaches that have been developed to connect ethnography and cooperative design, and the association this particular history has with the more general question of the relation between the sensibilities, commitments and requirements of design and of ethnography. As part of this exploration we discuss the practical limits and philosophical synergies between ethnography and design with attention to the similarities and incongruities between Participatory Design and ethnography. We conclude by reimagining ethnography within Participatory Design, pointing to the opportunities and challenges for a new generation of participatory designers.

The commitments and guiding principles of ethnography and Participatory Design are examined, followed by a presentation of the foundational research on the application of ethnography to Participatory Design. Then the (re)positioning of ethnography and design are explored, including discussion of the role of reflexivity in Participatory Design. Finally, new opportunities and challenges are presented.

This chapter re-examines the relationship between ethnography and Participatory Design, suggesting that researchers continue to interrogate and reflect on the role of ethnography in Participatory Design. It notes that a dichotomy has emerged in how ethnography is positioned in relation to Participatory Design; on the one hand normalised, accepted as part of Participatory Design practice, and on the other 'backgrounded', secondary to those activities that directly engage participants in design. It argues that the analytic purchase of ethnography as more than method is just as important today as it was earlier and that Participatory Design could learn from ethnography's reflexivity.

Positioning ethnography within Participatory Design is taking us beyond familiar terrains, confronting the challenges of designing for large-scale systems and the socio-technical infrastructures that enable global connections, and doing so with the participation of people from different knowledge traditions and socio-economic circumstances. Given these challenges, the sensibilities of ethnography continue to provide an important guide to Participatory Design.

Introduction

Ethnography as a resource for design has been a topic of debate within Participatory Design since the late 1980s when a group of anthropologically trained social scientists began interacting with computer scientists who were developing new approaches to cooperative design of information technology systems. While ethnographers participated in Participatory Design projects as early as 1984 (cf. Florence project, Bjerknes and Bratteteig 1995), the question of the appropriate relation between *studying the work practices of the workers* for whom new technologies are being developed and *directly engaging workers in design* became a central concern within Participatory Design when US-trained anthropologists began interacting with Scandinavian Participatory Design researchers (Blomberg et al. 1993). What emerged from these interactions was a general consensus that it was useful to combine the study of work practice with the iterative design of workplace interventions and that both of these activities required the investment and direct participation of workers. More recently this view has been extended to include the design of interventions for domestic and community spaces. The challenge for those working within the cooperative design tradition has been to develop ways of integrating ethnography in Participatory Design (Bødker and Kensing 1994), while ethnographically trained researchers have looked for ways of incorporating iterative design into their field studies (Blomberg et al. 1997; Suchman et al. 1999). In the ensuing years the boundary between ethnographic research and design has continued to be explored and (re)defined, and throughout ethnography has remained an important component of Participatory Design.

This chapter explores the history of ethnography in Participatory Design, the varied approaches that have been developed to connect ethnography and cooperative design, and the association this particular history has with the more general question of the relation between the sensibilities, commitments and requirements of design and of ethnography.

Ethnography and Ethnomethodology

Ethnography has its historical roots in anthropology where it emerged as an approach for gaining insights into the everyday 'realities' of people living in small-scale, non-Western societies (Agar 1996) and as a means to enable communication across cultural distance. The approach and analytic sensibilities rely on the ability of all humans to figure out what's going on through participation in social life. As such the techniques of ethnography bear a close resemblance to the routine ways people make sense of the world in everyday settings (e.g. by observing what others do, participating in activities, and talking with people). Today, the ethnographic approach is not limited to investigating small-scale societies, but has been adopted and adapted by many traditional and applied social science and interdisciplinary fields (Hammersley 1992).

Ethnomethodology also has contributed to the exploration and practice of aligning studies of work and design (Button 1992; Button and Harper 1996; Hughes et al. 1992; 1993; 1994). Ethnomethodology is a particular approach to characterising human action and interaction which developed within sociology as a counter to prevailing ways of describing social life and institutions. Ethnomethodology and ethnography share a commitment to describing phenomena from the inside, from the perspective of those involved. Unlike traditional sociology where *sociological categories* (e.g. gender, class, power, religion) are used to describe and explain phenomena, ethnomethodology makes visible participants' situated *methods* for creating the coherence of phenomena, while ethnography seeks to describe phenomena using *participants' categories* and *organising frameworks*.

As part of this exploration we discuss the practical limits and philosophical synergies between ethnography and design with attention to the similarities and incongruities between Participatory Design and ethnography. We conclude by reimagining ethnography within Participatory Design, pointing to the opportunities and challenges for a new generation of participatory designers.

Commitments and guiding principles of ethnography and Participatory Design

Both ethnography and Participatory Design have been characterised as guided by a core set of principles and commitments. This is not to say that these are without controversy and subject to interpretation within ethnography and Participatory Design. But nonetheless they can help us identify important elements that have defined and shaped the relationship between ethnography and Participatory Design and led to challenges of combining these two approaches.

Ethnography

At its foundation a handful of principles define ethnography (Table 5.1). These include studying phenomena in their *everyday settings*, taking a *holistic* view, providing a *descriptive understanding,* and taking a *members' perspective* (Blomberg et al. 1993). While a commitment to change is not often cited as among these core principles, ethnographic research has been occupied with and implicated in change and change initiatives from the start (Willigen 2002). That said, there is a strong commitment in ethnography to describe the 'here and now' before prescribing or even recommending future states. This sometimes has been confused with a belief that ethnography is non-interventionist and that ethnographers have a commitment to things staying the same. To respond to this misunderstanding, one of the early groups combining ethnography with Participatory Design (Suchman et al. 1999) developed the saying 'Innovation is an imagination of what could be based in knowledge of what is', arguing that awareness of the current context is a resource for proposing meaningful change.

Ethnography's focus on *everyday settings* follows from the view that to understand the world you must encounter it first-hand, gathering information in the settings in which the activities of interest occur. Conducting research in everyday settings also allows study participants to have access to the people and artefacts that define the activities in which they are engaged as they respond to requests by researchers to describe those activities (note how this contrasts with laboratory settings or interviews conducted away from the locations where the activities of interest occur). *Holism* points to the importance of understanding activities with reference to the larger setting and array of related activities. Ethnographers have a commitment to *describe* events and activities as they happen, withholding judgement of the efficacy of people's everyday practices. This compels the ethnographer to confront the particular logic of people's practices from the *perspective of members* (Blomberg et al. 1993). Every account is shaped by a myriad of things, such

Table 5.1 Principles of ethnography and participatory design

Ethnography	Participatory Design
• Everyday settings	• Respect for different knowledge
• Holistic view	• Opportunities for mutual learning
• Descriptive understanding	• Joint negotiation of project goals
• Member's point of view	• Tools and processes to facilitate design

things as characteristics of the researcher, the goals of the project, and the dynamics of the relationship between the researcher and study participants (see discussion of reflexivity below). Acknowledging this does not diminish the efficacy of describing activities in terms relevant and meaningful to study participants and paying attention to the ways people talk about and categorise activities in an effort to increase the likelihood that the research reflects an insider's view.

Participatory Design

Participatory Design likewise has articulated a few guiding principles such as the importance of *mutual respect for different knowledge* (workers[1] and designers), the need to create *opportunities to learn* about the other's domain of knowledge (workplace[2] and technical), a commitment to *joint negotiation of project goals* (not driven solely by a technology or workplace agenda), and a dedication to develop *tools and processes* to facilitate participation (Table 5.1). Woven throughout each of these principles is a commitment to workplace democracy and empowering people to define and direct the technologies that affect their lives. Participatory Design has been defined by its insistence that workers' knowledge is available to shape design directions by providing places and spaces for interaction between designers and practitioners that do not privilege one kind of knowledge over another. In this sense the tools and processes of Participatory Design are a means to an end of active worker involvement in design to ensure their interests are taken into account. Over the years there has been criticism that Participatory Design has lost its commitment to workplace democracy and worker empowerment, instead emphasising technology efficacy (Beck 2002) where workers (users) are simply participating to provide input to design. This has been a particular concern as researchers not familiar with the history of Participatory Design have adopted some of its methods, without the principles that motivated their development.

Participatory Design has long recognised the importance of *mutual respect for different knowledge* that participants bring to the design effort. Those who take part in Participatory Design projects (e.g. developers, users, managers, researchers, customers) bring unique experiences and perspectives to their interactions with each other. Acknowledging these differences and the value they provide helps ensure that everyone is heard. This is particularly important when disparity in authority or organisational position among participants might weaken the contributions of some who are critical to the success of the project. Mutual respect for knowledge differences must be coupled with the *opportunities to learn about others' domain of knowledge*. Allocating time and identifying contexts in which participants can interact, so each can learn from the other and help shape the project and its outcomes, has been recognised as important for Participatory Design projects. The quality and degree of participation in Participatory Design projects is shaped by whether *project goals are jointly negotiated*. Participants are more likely to buy into the project and feel a sense of shared commitment if they help define the goals and have a voice in the outcomes. Joint negotiation of project goals also improves the likelihood that all participants benefit in some way from participation. Lacking this willingness, sustaining the level of commitment needed for effective participation is difficult. Finally, Participatory Design has *developed tools and processes to facilitate participation*, including future workshops, design games, prompted reflections, cardboard mock-ups and case-based prototypes (Blomberg et al. 1996; Ehn 1988; Greenbaum and Kyng 1991; Grønbæk et al. 1997; Kensing 1987; Trigg et al. 1991). As Kensing and Blomberg (1998, p. 176) state: 'These tools and technologies avoid the overly abstract representations of traditional design approaches and allow workers and designers to more easily experiment with various design possibilities in cost effective ways.'

Synergies, alignments and incongruities

There are synergies among the core principles of ethnography and Participatory Design and at the same time some of their differences (sometimes misunderstandings and stereotypes) have led to debates about whether the two traditions can productively inform and enhance each other.

Ethnography's commitment to a members' perspective which focuses on gaining an insider's view and using terms relevant and meaningful to the people studied resonates with the Participatory Design principle of respect for the different knowledge that workers and designers bring to Participatory Design projects. The workers as 'experts' in their domain of knowledge must have a strong voice in design. Likewise, the emphasis in ethnography on studying activities in their 'natural settings', which is anchored in the underlying assumption that one of the best (only) ways to grasp a situation is to encounter it first-hand, connects with the commitment in Participatory Design to creating opportunities for designers and workers to learn about each other's domain through direct interaction. Ethnographic studies typically include gathering information in settings in which the activities of interest occur, where Participatory Design projects often include providing designers with the opportunity to spent time in the work setting as well as creating situations where workers can experience the design possibilities and encounter first-hand their constraints.

Ethnography's notion of holism or the view that activities must be understood within the larger context in which they occur is a reminder to participatory designers that while the design space may be limited and constrained in many ways, the outcome of the design can have effects well beyond those experienced by the direct users of the designed artefact. For example, changes in a technology that is used by employees may also have an impact on the customers they serve or on the management systems that are enabled.

Ethnography's commitment to describing the current situation before prescribing a change has been viewed by some as slowing down innovation by anchoring change in the past or present and thus limiting future imagination. One proposal to address this concern is to develop ways to disrupt the staged, sequential approach of first describing the 'as is' state and then proposing a 'to be' state by interleaving studies of current practice with interventions of various kinds (mock-ups, provocations, cultural probes, prototypes, etc.). These intermediate interventions can also serve to make more visible the requirements of the work (or other activity) that a new design would/should take into account.

Those involved in early co-design and cooperative prototyping (Bødker et al. 1987; Kensing 1987; Sandberg 1979a, 1979b) relied on the participation of workers with their own knowledge and experience to provide a perspective on their everyday work practices, often in the context of envisioning new artefacts and ways of working. The commitment to worker participation has led some Participatory Design researchers to be sceptical of the value of any 'outside' perspective. Instead they argue that the people engaged in those activities are best positioned to understand their requirements in relation to the designed artefacts (e.g. Kyng 1995).

As discussed by Karasti (2001b), the very notion of participation is understood differently in ethnography and design. In design, the participation of designers (in joint activities with practitioners) is taken for granted and participation only becomes an issue with regard to user involvement in design (e.g. how best to involve the user in design). In ethnography, on the other hand, the researcher's participation in activities of the field site is often carefully reflected upon and rarely taken as self-evident (ibid.). The question of participation or how the field-worker finds ways to engage in the life of the studied community is an essential concern because the research relies on the personal involvement of the researcher with members of the community. To some degree in Participatory Design, particularly when the roles of researcher and designer are blurred, the designer is faced with a similar situation.

Mutual learning means that the designer must have opportunities to see first-hand, participate in, the life of the user participants. Equally important, although not always realised in practice, is the ability and commitment of the designer to set aside, at least temporarily, their focus on design and intervention so they can see the work as it is and not through the lens of intervention. The designer in some sense must be willing to engage in a continuum of 'roles' with the ability to cycle between participation in the life of user practitioners and looking for new possibilities for change. This issue of reflexivity will be further explored in later sections.

To return to the question of intervention and its place within the traditions of ethnography and Participatory Design, the starting point for Participatory Design is to bring about change that is defined by the interests of workers, the requirements of their work, and the jointly negotiated path to change. For ethnography, change is neither the starting point nor a necessary goal. While ethnographic research has been part of many change agendas, the research is defined by the driving commitment to 'see the world' (and describe it) from the point of view of those studied. Change is something that can be informed by this understanding and may even be the reason for the ethnography, but it should not interfere with developing a descriptive appreciation and awareness.

Through extended dialogue among researchers from these different traditions there has emerged an appreciation for different kinds of expertise, including expertise that derives from ethnographic research. Bødker et al. (2004, pp. 140–41) remarked,

> Good IT design requires knowledge of work practices in order to determine which company traditions are fundamental and sustainable, and which are outdated. Put in a different way, only when a design team has fundamental knowledge of existing work practices can it arrive at what we call a 'sustainable design'.

Exploring the ethnographic perspective in (participatory) design

This section describes three early influential research programmes that explored the connections between ethnography and (participatory) design and proposed strategies for integrating the two agendas. We have labelled these programmes *Ethnography and Participatory Design in reflexive relation*, *Ethnography as a component of Participatory Design methodology*, and *Ethnography to inform design*. These approaches are exemplified by the work of researchers at Xerox PARC, Roskilde University and Lancaster University respectively.

The turn to ethnography in design

In the late 1980s there was a turn to ethnography as a resource for design which occurred not only within PD but also within the fields of Human–Computer Interaction (HCI), Computer Supported Cooperative Work (CSCW), and even more broadly in Information Systems (IS) (for reviews and discussions see Anderson 1997; Blomberg 1995; Harvey and Mayers 1995; Plowman et al. 1995; Pors et al. 2002; Rogers and Bellotti 1997; Schmidt 2000). The interest in ethnography was connected to expanding possibilities for how new computer technologies might be used – in for example office settings, call centres, manufacturing floors, and educational institutions. Designers and developers of new technologies were looking for ways of gaining deeper understandings of the everyday experiences of people working in these varied environments (Blomberg et al. 1993). With the growth of networked devices aided by the availability of local area networks (LANs) and early Internet implementations, designers increasingly were focusing their attention beyond the activities of single, isolated users interacting with information technologies to the information and communication practices of people interacting with one another, both face-to-face and through mediating technologies. Interest in the ethnographic continued to grow as the result of Internet expansion, accelerating the move of information technologies out of the workplace and into homes, recreational environments, and other non-work settings. Designers were faced with new challenges as they were asked to design and build applications that leveraged powerful, digital technologies for use by people of all ages, engaged in a myriad of work- and non-work-related activities.

Ethnography and Participatory Design in reflexive relation

A group of anthropologists and computer scientists working in the area of Work Practice and Technology at Xerox PARC were engaged for nearly two decades in exploring the integration of ethnography and Participatory Design as part of, and embedded in, a more comprehensive research programme. Their research agenda aimed at reconstructing technologies as social practice and was undertaken through two interrelated projects: one based on the anthropological tradition that called for 'making sense of what we have' and the other, more reformist, with an agenda of 'remaking what we have into something new' (Suchman et al. 1999, p. 393). Through three lines of research: critical analyses of existing technical discourses and practices (Blomberg 1987, 1988; Orr 1990; Suchman 1987, 1994, 1997), studies of work and technologies-in-use (Blomberg 1987; Blomberg et al. 1996, 1997; Suchman 1983, 1993, 1996, 1997; Suchman and Trigg 1991; Suchman and Wynn 1984; Trigg et al. 1999) and new strategies for relating work practice studies and technology design (Blomberg et al. 1993; Blomberg 1995), they developed alternative, work-oriented and cooperative ways to intervene into the processes of professional technology production (Blomberg et al. 1996).

Their work-oriented design projects integrated studies of specific worksites with cooperative development of prototype systems. Detailed understandings of today's workplaces, i.e. how people work using both existing and prototype technologies, informed an exploration of future technologies and practices. Their programme involved close collaboration with individuals from particular worksites and sought proactive ways of conducting fieldwork, for instance by creating possibilities for practitioners' involvement in using case-based prototypes to evaluate new technology potentials within actual use environments (Blomberg et al. 1996; Trigg et al. 1999). A central challenge for their work was to develop innovative ways of making insights from research projects available to product development (Blomberg et al. 1996) in a context where it was difficult to bring practitioners and designers into direct collaboration (Blomberg and Henderson 1990; Blomberg et al. 1997). This required that they find ways to engage the designers directly in exploring the implications of their field studies and prototypes for product development projects (Blomberg et al. 1996; Blomberg and Trigg 2000).

Ethnography as a component of Participatory Design methodology

Researchers working at Roskilde University developed an approach that integrated ethnographic research methods into the collaborative design of new technologies and that attended to diverse stakeholder interests, including workers, managers and system developers (Bødker et al. 2004;

Kensing et al. 1998a; Simonsen and Kensing 1994). In order to conduct Participatory Design that combined ethnography and intervention in organisational contexts in a systematic manner, they developed 'a conceptual framework and a coherent method' called MUST (Kensing et al. 1998a), which was informed by experiences with several information technology design projects, including an airline (Kensing and Winograd 1991), two universities (Bødker et al. 2004), a film institute (Simonsen and Kensing 1994, 1997), a broadcasting corporation (Kensing et al. 1997, 1998b) and a pharmaceutical company (Bødker et al. 2004). The MUST methodology focused on the early activities in systems development, offered guidelines for both project management and design, and considered the relations between the design project and an organisation's business and information technology strategies. MUST lays out a design process structured into the phases of initiation, in-line analysis, in-depth analysis and innovation (ibid., pp. 81–193) that considers three domains of discourse: users' present work as ascertained through first-hand experience with working practices, new systems of work based on genuine user participation (of both users and managers), and technological options anchored in coherent visions of future possibilities.

Ethnographic fieldwork is an important component of the MUST methodology and provides the context for learning about the users' present work in particular work settings with a special emphasis on gaining an understanding of practitioners' concrete experiences. Designers are directly involved in the fieldwork as part of their cooperation with users, with special attention directed to combining observation with interviews to address the well-known 'say–do distinction' where researchers are cautioned not to rely solely on what people say they do (Blomberg and Burrell 2007; Blomberg et al. 1993). In a practical sense, cycling between ethnography and intervention allows for refining understandings about work practice in a manner that is relevant for design:

> While ethnography and intervention contrast in terms of their basic approaches and intended results, we have experienced that at a practical level, combining the two approaches and iterating between them has been an effective way in learning about the organisation and has been an important resource in generating realistic visions of future use of technology.
>
> *(Kensing et al. 1998b, p. 266)*

Ethnography to inform design

Another set of pioneering studies aimed at bringing ethnography into a productive relation to design was carried out by a group of researchers at Lancaster University. The group explored ways in which insights from ethnomethodological ethnography could be used in software engineering. Rather than aiming at a transformative take on design, their project was incremental, focusing on how ethnographic studies of work could be used in specific contexts to inform the design of specific information systems. The series of research projects that informed their approach included the domains of air traffic (Harper and Hughes 1993; Hughes et al. 1993), system design (Hughes et al. 1994), law enforcement (Shapiro et al. 1991) and the financial services (Blythin et al. 1997; Rouncefield et al. 1994).

The Lancaster group adopted a practical approach to address the problematics of connecting ethnography and system design, including reconciling the different traditions and practices of communication and representation (e.g. the incommensurability of the rich descriptions of ethnography and the formal notations of design), managing real-world restrictions on resources in design projects, and positioning the ethnographer in design as an issue that is defined by project management. Ethnography was seen to contribute to design in four ways: concurrent ethnography (i.e. in parallel with design), quick and dirty ethnography (i.e. short-term studies), evaluative ethnography (i.e. assessing design in context) and re-examination of previous ethnographic studies (i.e. for how they can contribute to the current design effort) (Hughes et al. 1994).

Integration of ethnography and design for the Lancaster group relied on professional ethnographers taking responsibility for work analysis and mediations between the workplace and the system design community, while designers were left to make design decisions based on requirements analysis informed by the ethnographers' explications of work. Because user participation was not an option for a host of practical reasons (Bentley et al. 1992; Hughes et al. 1993), it became important to secure ways for effective communication between ethnographers and designers often involving 'debriefing meetings' where the designers asked questions of the ethnographers, who acted as user representatives (Hughes et al. 1993). The dissemination of ethnographic information was further facilitated by the explicit structuring of fieldwork observations and records (e.g. as a 'presentation framework' and through software tools) so ethnographic analysis was presented in a more designer-friendly form (Hughes et al. 1997; Twidale et al. 1993). See Table 5.2.

Joining ethnography and (participatory) design

Having reviewed three of the early research programmes exploring relations between ethnography and design, we now focus on different proposals that have been made for positioning ethnography within design. Here we adopt interdisciplinarity as a lens through which to consider the possibilities (Frodeman et al. 2010). The early approaches discussed above differ in their understandings of the interdisciplinary relations between ethnography and design, each having been influenced by such things as the histories of the research groups, how closely they were aligned with system design, the background of those conducting the ethnography, and the organisational context of the research. This section draws on literature in Computer Supported Cooperative Work (CSCW), Human–Computer Interaction (HCI) and Participatory Design in discussing alternative ways of joining ethnography and (participatory) design as interdisciplinary research.

The discussion is organised into two major sections. The first, *ethnographically informed design as interdisciplinary research*, deals with issues that are widely shared in ethnographically informed design and the second, *ethnography and Participatory Design as multi-perspectival collaboration*, focuses

Table 5.2 Ethnographer's institutional and disciplinary affiliation for the three formative research programmes

Programme	Ethnographers' Institutional Affiliation
Ethnography and Participatory Design in reflexive relation	Academically trained anthropologists (and computer scientists) working at Xerox PARC, a corporate research centre
Ethnography as a component of Participatory Design methodology	Academic system designers (primarily computer scientists and information system designers) working at Roskilde University
Ethnography to inform design	Academic social scientists (primarily ethnomethodologists) working at Lancaster University

on Participatory Design with its explicit commitment to direct user participation. We are concerned with the purpose, value and extent of interdisciplinary collaboration that defines the position of ethnography in relation to design. We also consider whether the interdisciplinarity is defined by methodological or theoretical concerns and is intended to direct instrumental or critical goals (Klein 2010).

Ethnographically informed design as interdisciplinary research

Ethnography as a way of providing socially enriched understandings of current work practices that go beyond formal representations of work is generally perceived as valuable in design. Debates on interdisciplinarity in the fields of HCI and CSCW, and to a lesser extent in Participatory Design, often focus around how much emphasis should be on workplace studies or on (technology) design (Crabtree 1998; Crabtree et al. 2009; Dourish 2006).

Ethnographic workplace studies unencumbered by design

Ethnography unencumbered by design is primarily concerned with understanding social phenomena via detailed analytic descriptions of work practice and with exploring conceptual and theoretical issues in the social sciences (e.g. Bucciarelli 1995; Henderson 1991; Luff et al. 1992, 2000; Sharrock and Anderson 1994; Star and Ruhleder 1996; Suchman 1983; Suchman and Wynn 1984; Wynn 1979). The findings of these studies are positioned as relevant to ongoing debates within or between the social sciences, with potential relevance sited in theoretical debates in design. These studies proceed relatively unfettered with the problems of design (Anderson 1997) and as such have been termed 'innocent' ethnographies (Hughes et al. 1991). While the studies are designed and undertaken without a specific design agenda, they later lay the groundwork for design-oriented projects, for example the study of air traffic controllers (Harper et al. 1991), the study of ground operations at an airport (Brun-Cottan et al. 1991; Suchman 1993) and the study of the use of workflow technologies in the production printing industry (Bowers et al. 1995).

The influence of these types of studies on system design has been significant, making important theoretical contributions (Anderson 1997; Plowman et al. 1995; Schmidt 2000). Some of these studies have played an important role in shaping the agenda, concerns and central questions of CSCW and HCI, most recognisably Suchman (1987). Others have contributed to the conceptual foundation of the field, for example articulation work (Gerson and Star 1986), peripheral awareness (Heath and Luff 1992), working division of labour (Hughes et al. 1992; Hutchins 1990). Over time these studies have incited and inspired design professionals to explore ways in which to take into consideration these theoretical concepts in the development of new technologies.

Ethnography as input to design

Ethnography is considered valuable in making visible 'real-world' aspects of a work setting, but studies stop short of determining the design direction or specification, leaving that task to designers and system developers (although often in collaboration with those conducting the ethnographic studies). It is argued that the production and integration of ethnographic materials into design can best be achieved by professional specialists working in parallel areas of expertise because the practices of design and fieldwork differ markedly (Hughes et al. 1997, p. 157; Sommerville et al. 1993). Consequently, the collaboration of ethnographers and designers relies on disciplinary division of labour, the differing expertise complementing one another. In this instrumental view (Klein 2010, pp. 22–4), interdisciplinarity is seen as a functional activity where the existing disciplinary categories remain unchallenged, fundamental questions can be avoided and specialisation is championed (Salter and Hearn 1996). This instrumental stance can also be viewed as 'methodological' interdisciplinarity (Klein 2010, p. 19) where, for example, ethnography is contracted to the role of informational input to design, and the analytic aspirations of 'innocent' ethnography have made room for an enquiry conscious of the design problematics (Hughes et al. 1992). The objectives of these studies are set chiefly by the needs of the design orientation, and the role of workplace studies is seen in terms of a method for data collection feeding into the requirements engineering process (Sommerville et al. 1993). 'Quick and dirty' ethnography (Hughes et al. 1994) and rapid ethnography (Millen 2000) name two methods that epitomise this mode of joining ethnography and design. The Lancaster group offers a good example of how interdisciplinary collaboration of the instrumental kind increasingly demands high levels of interaction as collaborating parties (ethnographers, system designers and developers) must learn from each other over time.

This particular interdisciplinary arrangement can be argued to be the most popular way to position ethnography in relation to design. However, there is an increasing critical awareness of the limitations of treating ethnography as an observational method for requirements engineering (e.g. Anderson 1994, 1997; Button and Harper 1996; Nyce and Löwgren 1995). On this view ethnography is limited to providing informational input for design with less emphasis in exploring conceptual and theoretical issues in the social sciences.

Reconciling (inter)disciplinary difference

In addition to the above lines of research that largely conform to their respective disciplines, interdisciplinary collaboration has provocatively been addressed through attempts to bring together and reconcile the theoretical perspectives and core precepts of the involved disciplines. These discussions have pointed to differences between the two disciplines (e.g. Bader and Nyce 1998; Button and Harper 1996; Grudin and Grinter 1995; Simonsen and Kensing 1998) and revealed certain disciplinary dichotomies, such as being descriptive versus prescriptive, providing rich descriptions versus notational formalism, focusing on the particular versus seeking generalisations, identifying concrete examples versus abstract representations, orienting to the present versus pointing to the future, and understanding the here and now versus intervening to bring about change. Some of the debate has been insightful and stimulating, but the level of theoretical stipulation has made the incongruities between disciplines seem most intractable (Shapiro 1994). In general the discussion has resulted in misdirected and inadequate characterisations of what is at stake in the integration of ethnography and system design (Anderson 1994). Nonetheless these debates have continued to stimulate experimentation on the practical requirements of joining the perspectives of ethnographers and designers.

From the point of view of joining ethnography and Participatory Design, two topic lines are particularly interesting in the early debates. One has roots in the critical awareness for treating ethnography as mere observational (fieldwork) method for informing design and the other is sometimes expressed as need 'to "channel" access to users'. Regarding the first, critics argue that positioning ethnography as another method for data collection is a severe misconception, stressing that this neglects the explicitly analytical and interpretive relation ethnography has to the subject matter and the representational traditions in ethnography (e.g. R. J. Anderson 1994; B. Anderson 1997; Button 2000; Button and Harper 1996; Nyce and Löwgren 1995). Some see the analytic quality of ethnographies compromised if carried out by others than trained ethnographers fully utilising their analytic devices. For example, reservations have been expressed about 'insider' or 'native' ethnographies (Forsythe 1999; Kindermann 1996) and 'designer' ethnographies (Button 2000). This has raised the question within Participatory Design, with its tradition of promoting multiple voices, of whose ethnographies are relevant.

In some approaches that join ethnography and design, such as in 'lay Participatory Design', the 'lay' participants are 'insiders' combining the roles of ethnographer and designer (Syrjänen 2007), while in others there are explicit efforts to teach user participants, designers, developers and even project sponsors the theoretical and analytical precepts of ethnography (Jordan 2011; Karasti 2001b; Simonsen and Kensing 1998). These multiple positionings raise issues regarding how ethnographic understandings are informed by the subject positions of the researcher.

The second topic of interest with regard to linking ethnography and Participatory Design represented in these early debates relates to the expressed need 'to "channel" access to users' (e.g. Mambrey et al. 1998). In this channelling effort the adopted role of the ethnographer is characterised as an intermediary one, positioned between the work site and system development activities. Names for such a role include 'user advocate', 'user champion', 'proxy user' and 'user surrogate' (e.g. Bentley et al. 1992; Hughes et al. 1993; Mambrey et al. 1998). The idea of proxies or champions for user participants contradicts one of the guiding principles of Participatory Design. In fact, there remains a notable distrust in Participatory Design that user surrogates or advocates could ever provide the skilled craftsmanship and tacit knowledge embodied in workers and worksites, and as such this intermediary role is seen to compromise the essence of work and workers' experience (Ehn 1988; Kyng 1991, 1995).

Ethnography and Participatory Design as multi-perspectival collaboration

In contrast to the above characterisations of interdisciplinary relations in joining ethnography and design where direct user participation is not necessarily an issue, in Participatory Design users (workers, practitioners) are a central element affecting the possibilities for integrating ethnography and design. It has been argued that this calls for multi-perspectival collaboration that extends beyond traditional forms of interdisciplinarity. Here a different kind of 'intermediation' (Shapiro 1994) is needed, where hybrid, interdisciplinary, multi-perspectival explorations of work-oriented design are interleaved with analysis, evaluation and envisionment (Karasti 2001a, 2001b).

Suchman and Trigg (1991) describe a joint enterprise where the three perspectives of research, design and practice are linked and where the recognition of workers', researchers' and designers' situated locations and partial knowledges require ongoing collaborations. They stress that the perspectives are not absolute, fixed positions but are relative to each other, and participants are often required to move between the perspectives (ibid., pp. 85–6).

The dynamic shifting among perspectives raises a host of issues including concerns with the role of the ethnographer as mediator between the social (workplace) and the technical (design intervention), the limitations on mutual learning across experiential and epistemological divides, and the practitioner contributions to analysis and understanding of work practice and to envisioning future design scenarios.

Ethnographer as mediator

To the extent that the ethnographer acts as a mediator between the social world of users and the project of design, the boundary between the sites of change and the designers of change is reinforced. This critique has been made more generally of ethnography as it distances us (as the reader of ethnographic accounts) and them (as the subject of those accounts: Clifford 1988; Clifford and Marcus 1986). Many Participatory Design practices have attempted to lessen the need for the ethnographer as a mediator by bringing designers into direct interaction with practitioners in the context of both fieldwork and design activities. However, to the degree that analytic ethnography adds value to the design goals, the ethnographer as interpreter (*qua* mediator) continues to have a place in design even when those conducting the ethnography are not academically trained ethnographers.

Mutual learning

Mutual learning is one of the principles of Participatory Design, and yet there are limits to the extent practitioners, designers and ethnographers are able to participate in each other's domains of knowledge. The idea of 'mutual learning' in its traditional sense, where design professionals learn about the actual use context and workers about possible technological options, often does not create the opportunity for the seen but unnoticed features of work to be revealed.[3] The problem of mutual learning also stretches to the design realm where users struggle to have the opportunity to drive design even when their input is actively and iteratively sought. The expertise of designers is often privileged, with users having few opportunities to become deeply conversant with the technical requirements of design and limited authorisation to define the project's technical outcomes (Hartswood et al. 2002). The critical question is whether and in what ways the goals of mutual learning (knowing enough about each other's worlds to enable the collaborative and cooperative design of workplace changes) are achieved in Participatory Design projects.

Foregrounding user/practitioner

In most of the early Participatory Design projects, designers relied on users as the ultimate experts of the work context who provided knowledge of relevant workplace skills, experiences and interests to the design processes. However, the collaborative sessions were often focused on technology and future orientation (e.g. prototyping, future workshops), and as such focused less on understanding the details or the workers' current practices.

Moreover, while users know things performatively, they may not be inclined to provide discursive accounts of the worlds in which they engage (Shapiro 1994), particularly in the context of a workshop setting away from the everyday environment in which they work. Some ethnographers have also questioned whether 'native' accounts provide enough analytic distance to be useful or at least equivalent to what an analytic ethnography provides. On the other hand, Karasti (2001a, 2001b) points out that practitioners often gain 'analytic sensibilities' towards their work when it is reflected back to them through an ethnographic account.

While ethnography aims to describe the details of what goes on in a particular setting and there are examples of valuable descriptions of complex work (e.g. Hughes et al. 1992 for air traffic control and Karasti 2001a for diagnostic image interpretation in radiology), as Shapiro (1994) notes it is not possible to ever 'complete' an analysis of a setting, and as others have noted all ethnographies are partial and perspectival (Suchman 2002). Karasti (2001b) adds that in complex work settings no ethnographer has the experiential knowledge of how the work has evolved in the past or the ability to project to an imagined future of how the work could evolve that compares to that of an experienced practitioner, thus arguing for the need for opportunities for these differently positioned actors to engage with each other and with the goals of the collaborative project.

(Re)positioning ethnography within Participatory Design

While much of the literature on the relation between ethnography and design positions ethnography in the role of informing design or serving a design agenda, strategies have been explored for aligning ethnography and design that radically reposition ethnography not as a tool for design but as deeply integrated into the doing of design. In the following section we review some of these strategies.

Case-based prototypes

The Work Practice and Technology research programme (Suchman et al. 1999) introduced case-based prototypes to support their efforts at reconceptualising and restructuring how work and technology design were undertaken (Blomberg et al. 1996; Trigg et al. 1999). They developed alternative, work-oriented and cooperative ways to intervene in the processes of professional technology production that involved integrating studies of specific worksites with cooperative development of prototype systems. Understanding how people work, using both existing and prototype technologies, enabled an exploration of future technologies and practices. By creating possibilities for practitioners' involvement in using and otherwise engaging with increasingly realistic and robust case-based prototypes to evaluate new technology potentials within actual use environments, the approach embeds design within use and positions ethnography as the analytic lens through which to understand design in use.

Case-based prototypes themselves are artefacts that incorporate actual materials from the sites of technology's intended use and are positioned to support the imagination of future work practices in cooperative prototyping. Importantly, they convey design ideas while maintaining their relation to work practices. In addition to providing for the possibility to iteratively gain user input throughout implementation, assessment and redesign; the prototypes also offer the context for discussion and mutual learning. The case-based prototypes allow potential future directions to be assessed in relation to other technologies-in-use, as individual technologies are seen to 'add value' to the extent they work together in effective configurations (Blomberg et al. 1996; Trigg et al. 1999).

Case-based prototypes are also useful in engaging product developers in understanding requirements of the work, as these are reflected in the prototypes themselves and often in a way that is easily communicated to developers more focused on technical requirements than work requirements (Blomberg et al. 1996; Blomberg and Trigg 2000; Trigg et al. 1999). In this way case-based prototypes help overcome an often-cited obstacle, where there is little or no opportunity to bring work practitioners and developers into direct collaboration (Blomberg and Henderson 1990; Blomberg et al. 1997).

Co-realisation

Co-realisation, drawing on earlier work on 'bricolage as a design approach' (Shapiro et al. 1996; Büscher et al. 2001) and 'designing technologies in use' (Grønbæk et al. 1997), is an orientation to technology production that developed out of 'a principled synthesis of ethnomethodology and Participatory Design' (Hartswood et al. 2002, p. 9). Co-realisation integrates ethnomethodology's analytic mentality with a practical, Participatory Design orientation in order to achieve 'design-in-use' (Voss 2006, p. 108). It involves a respecification of the working division of labour in systems development (Voss 2006, p. 3) that was earlier configured in the collaborations taking place between ethnomethodologists and system developers at Lancaster University (Hughes et al. 1992,

1993, 1994, 1995; Randall et al. 1995).

Co-realisation starts from the observation that has been identified in ethnographically informed design, namely that the full implications of a new system for work practices cannot be grasped by studying the work as it is now, but will only be revealed in and through the system's subsequent use. Hartswood et al. (2002) point out that Participatory Design projects often do not move beyond the design phase including construction of early prototypes, and thus do not provide the opportunity to see the new system in use. This raises the issue of how to position ethnography in order to have an ongoing relation to changes brought about by the new design.

Co-realisation has tackled this in two ways. First, it is committed to *long-term*, direct engagement between design(ers) and use(rs) that distinguishes it from most of the 'ethnography to inform design' approaches and Participatory Design methods that rely on mediation or punctuated user participation in workshops or focus groups. Second, co-realisation moves the locus of design and development activities into workplace settings where the new technologies will be used, and promotes long-term immersion in the field site. It aims to create a shared practice between users and designers that is grounded in the experiences of users, and where users drive the process. The key issue for a respecified information technology design and development practice is supporting 'design-in-use' (first introduced by Henderson and Kyng 1991), recognising that the information technologies and work practices co-evolve over time and that new technical artefacts require effective configuration and integration with work practices.

Co-realisation holds that the insights of ethnomethodological workplace studies are consonant with the partnership elements of Participatory Design. With the ethnomethodological call for 'becoming a member' (Garfinkel 1967) and being accountable, it is argued that designers can deliver 'uniquely adequate, "work-affording" artifacts' and 'solutions to the problems of IT-organizational integration' (Hartswood et al. 2002, pp. 9, 13). With its stress on 'design-in-use' and the longitudinal involvement by designers in the 'lived work' of users, co-realisation shifts the debate about how to bring ethnographic accounts back from the field by embedding them in the design process itself.

Co-realisation insists on maintaining a dialogue between users and designers which requires designers 'being there' in the workplace, becoming a member of the setting, and acquiring familiarity with members' knowledge and mundane competencies. The aim of 'being there' is to create a situation where spontaneous interactions and shifts in attention are afforded and where designers are able to help users realise their objectives, in some cases by playing the role of 'facilitator', which involves acting as design consultant, developer, technician, trouble-shooter and handy-person (Hartswood et al. 2002; Voss 2006). The hybridity of the facilitator role, the crossing of traditional domains and boundaries, necessitates reflection on how the role evolves within the setting. The aim of co-realisation is to erase the boundaries between 'design' and 'use' by fostering a longitudinal partnership between technology and non-technology professionals where there is an orientation to 'the work of and with information technology systems' as a whole rather than as a separate process. The challenge for co-realisation is in establishing the organisational working relations that can enable and sustain long-term partnerships between the interests of designers, worker practitioners and other organisational actors.

Design ethnography

Design anthropology (ethnography) aspires to create new ways of integrating ethnography with design. Proponents advocate that we '[f]orget about sending anthropologists to the field to collect data. And forget about stand-alone ideas and individual inventors' (Halse et al. 2010, p. 15). Innovation, they argue, will emerge by creating 'new connections in the networks of people and things' (ibid., p. 15). While these are provocative statements, arguments for reconceptualising the boundaries between ethnography and design are not new to Participatory Design.

Blomberg et al. (1996, p. 240) developed an approach that 'involve[d] cycling among studies of work, codesign, and user experience with mock-ups and prototypes of new technologies ... [where] work practice studies [are] embedded in design activities, whereas design efforts contribute to work analysis'. Karasti's (2001a, 2001b) multi-party workshops that employed video collages of radiologists using both traditional film-based and new digital imaging systems, enabled 'co-constructed' and shared understandings of *both* work practices and design possibilities. Kensing et al. (1998b) similarly advocated cycling between ethnography and design as part of the MUST method. In these examples studies of work are interleaved and integrated with design and analysis.

Another strategy used within the context of Participatory Design to fuse ethnography and design has been to use artefacts to 'provoke' responses from work practitioners (Mogensen 1992; Mogensen and Robinson 1995; Mogensen and Trigg 1992). The aim of these provocative artefacts is not to 'understand' the work per se, but to expose both the possibilities and constraints on future design directions. The provoking artefacts are purposefully introduced and the responses to these artefacts enable design collaborators (users and system designers) to endorse future possibilities and correct misconceptions.

More recently Gaver et al. (1999, 2004) and others have been exploring the use of what they call 'cultural probes' to animate the design space. Probes are 'collections of evocative tasks meant to elicit inspirational responses from people' (Gaver et al. 2004, p. 53). The use of cultural probes is meant to inspire ideas for designs that would engage people and enrich their lives. Gaver stresses that probes are not analytic devices meant to provide comprehensive understanding of people's lives, but instead are used to provide small clues about those things that make people's lives meaningful and pleasurable. Our interest here is in the role of cultural probes as provocative artefacts that elicit connections and alignments between design agendas and the experiences of user participants. Crabtree et al. (2003, p. 8) appropriated the notion of cultural probe for the purpose of 'supplying information to inform and shape design'. What they termed informational probes are thought to be particularly useful in settings where a more traditional ethnographic engagement (e.g. through interviews and observations of daily life) would have been difficult (e.g. in their case, with psychiatric patients). They argue that informational probes promote collaboration between users and designers, as users are more actively involved in generating materials for design and not 'docile victims of research and passive recipients of design' (ibid., p. 10).

While the use of probes repositions the practitioner or user with respect to both the ethnographic study and the design goals, probes do not explicitly embody the sensibilities and commitments of Participatory Design, namely *opportunities for mutual learning*: they are one-way communication and *joint negotiation of project goals* as the researchers' goals are not open for input or contestation.

Today a new generation of participatory designers is finding resonance with these earlier explorations. Halse et al. (2010, p. 14) have outlined their DAIM (Design Anthropological Innovation Model) approach for 'how ethnographic observations can be transformed into actionable insights for design' and for 'how design interventions can be transformed into interesting ethnographic questions'. Starting with the premise that user-centred design too often separates the activities of ethnographic enquiry and design, they show through a series of case studies how the design and research impulses can co-exist in the same Participatory Design activities. They argue that we need to 'abandon the idea that the field of use is a place to visit and to be known, and that the design studio is a privileged place for invention' so we can 'unleash a greater potential of combining anthropology and design' (ibid., p. 15).

The DAIM approach builds on earlier work by Buur and collaborators (Buur et al. 2000; Buur and Bødker 2000) who have been developing the theoretical foundation for what they call 'Participatory Innovation', which is a cross-disciplinary approach to user-driven innovation bringing together the traditions of anthropology and interaction design and analysis. Their approach involves using ethnographic 'video as design material', that can be used in the design process as representing the user experience and perspective in that the video is co-authored in the field not as ethnographic data, but as a vehicle for design imagination (ibid.; Buur et al. 2010).

In a similar vein a group of researchers at the University of Copenhagen are developing a strategy 'wherein assemblages of patients, health professionals, diseases, information technology, prototypes, and design researchers together perform shifts between *promoting new practical design solutions* and *raising novel questions on the socio-material complexities of healthcare*' (Andersen et al. 2011, p. 1, italics added). They argue for an interventionist approach that integrates Participatory Design with a critical mode of enquiry. Following Halse (2008) they argue that interventions 'open new ways of conceiving the world' and enable a deeper integration of design and anthropology. Here, unlike Mogensen (1992), their interests are in both furthering their design agenda and advancing understandings of new socio-material configurations.

Critical reflection – reflexivity in design and ethnography

In recent years there have been calls encouraging Participatory Design researchers to become more critically reflective (e.g. Balka 2006, 2010; Dearden and Rizvi 2008; Finken 2003; Karasti 2010b; Wagner et al. 2010) in addressing current and future challenges of Participatory Design. Dearden and Rizvi (2008, p. 88) note that 'participatory methods have been adopted by the mainstream to highlight issues of technique at the expense of concerns with relationships' and maintain that participatory designers should reflect on their motivations and priorities. Balka (2010, p. 80), emphasising the need for a reflexivity that entails more attention to the users' perspectives on the Participatory Design projects in which they participate, writes, 'we seldom discuss the outcomes our projects achieve in relation to the ideals we hold dear, and even less frequently do we seek input from our participants about the views of our processes and the outcomes that result'. Joining the call for critical reflection, Mörtberg et al. argue,

> It is necessary for researchers and designers … to be able to reflect upon not only activities in the design process, but also upon the multiple intentions and interpretations that build the analytic lens of the research or design project.
>
> *(Mörtberg et al. 2010, p. 107)*

The traditions of design and of ethnography have developed reflexive practices that both shape project and research processes and outcomes and contribute to the development of these disciplines. We discuss differences and alignments between reflexivity in design and ethnography.

In the Participatory Design world, Schön's notion of 'reflective practitioner' (Schön 1983) has been consistently used to gain understanding of what designers artfully do and how different domains of knowledge figure in the design process. 'Reflection-in-action' entails building new understandings, typically by experimenting within the situations, to inform actions in unfolding situations. 'Reflection-on-action' takes place after the activity and enables the exploration of what happened and why in order to develop questions, ideas and examples about the activities and practices in focus. These reflections have yielded insights about how the designer's own tacit understandings have affected the design work.

The question of reflexivity in ethnography (and similarly in many other social sciences) is concerned with how the researcher is never independent from the object/subject of his or her research. Reflexivity is 'particularly central to the practice of ethnographic research where the relationship between researcher and researched is typically … intimate, long-term and multi-stranded, and the complexities introduced by the self-consciousness of the objects of research have even greater scope' (Davies 1999, pp. 3–4). Incorporating reflexivity into ethnographic research is clear in the participant observer role which is based on both involvement and detachment. In Jordan's words:

> [the participant observer's] primary attitude is that of a novice who tries to become a part of the life of the community; at the same time she needs to maintain enough distance to record her observations and reflect on her evolving understanding of the situations she encounters.
>
> *(Jordan 1996a, p. 27)*

Maintaining an appropriate relationship to the study participants involves reflecting on one's role in the situation at any given time and how it is affecting the scene and one's interpretation of it. Thus reflexivity requires that we acknowledge how such things as personal histories, particular relations between ethnographer and study participants, debates within academia, and broad sociocultural circumstances affect the outcomes of the research.

Reflection in Participatory Design as inspired by Schön and reflexivity in ethnography differ somewhat in that Participatory Design emphasises consideration of the relation between users, technologies and settings, whereas ethnography specifically directs attention to the researcher's location vis-à-vis study participants, considering such things as status relationships, personal expectations and commitments. As such, in ethnography '[r]eflection focuses on understanding the assumptions, biases, and perspectives that underlie the research' through self-inspection (Stuedahl et al. 2010, p. 10). Some have argued that Participatory Design researchers, while focusing on technology and users, have missed the opportunity to make visible the 'self' or their particular knowledge, agency and responsibilities, in addition to their relationship to the study participants and the overall project outcomes (cf. Finken 2003).

With the influence of ethnography's commitment to reflexivity as exemplified by accounts of the ethnographer's changing role in design settings (e.g. Jordan 1996b; Plowman et al. 1996; Rogers 1997), some reflexive accounts by researchers with design backgrounds have emerged (e.g. Karasti (2001b) on becoming participant observer and turning into participant interventionist, and Voss (2006) on creating the role of a co-realiser). In addition, some participatory designers have been very open and explicit about their commitments outside the specific design project, not only in reporting on their research but also in their relations with worker participants. For example, the Work Practice and Technology group at PARC were clear that their interest in co-designing a document management system for a governmental department of transportation was motivated by the importance to Xerox, the organisation for whom they worked, in understanding how new networked devices with optical character recognition (OCR) capabilities might change how documents were created, shared, modified and stored (Suchman 2000a, 2000b; Suchman et al. 2000). While these 'outside' entailments in part defined and constrained their project in many ways, they also maintained a strong commitment to allowing the interests of the workers and the requirements of the work to shape the design.

In some situations, however, Participatory Design researchers may find it difficult to identify or be explicit about their commitments and entanglements. Markussen (1994) in response to Kyng's keynote address at the 1994 biennial Participatory Design conference questioned whether it was really just coincidence that so many of the technology designs (designed with worker participation) had a client-server technical architecture. Could it be, she asked, that this particular design choice was influenced by the popularity of client-server architectures in technology circles at the time. She noted that even in Participatory Design projects where user practitioners are 'equal' partners in defining project goals and shaping outcomes, the old adage that 'when you have a hammer everything looks like a nail' may still apply (ibid.). Furthermore, the commitments of academic Participatory Design researchers to publishing, students and career advancement, not to mention the need to compete for funding (Balka 2006; Mathiassen and Nielsen 2008; Simonsen 2009), undoubtedly influence possibilities for both project scoping and technology design.

New opportunities and challenges

As Participatory Design and ethnography have been adopted and adapted by researchers with interests different from the ones initially motivating efforts to align the two disciplines, new issues have emerged that challenge the efficacy of an ethnographically informed Participatory Design, while at the same time creating opportunities for broader influence on the *making of* and *theorising about* change through design interventions. Participatory Design continues to expand into new contexts, including e-government (Dittrich et al. 2003; Oostveen and van den Besselaar 2004), developing countries (Braa et al. 2004; Korpela et al. 1998; Mursu et al. 2000; Verran 2010; Winschiers-Theophilus et al. 2010), commercial settings (Cefkin 2009; Kyng 2010) and community Participatory Design (Karasti and Baker 2008; Karasti and Syrjänen 2004; Merkel et al. 2004) to name a few. These shifts have raised questions about how ethnographically informed Participatory Design projects are able to scale temporally (from single projects taking place at one point in time to connected projects that occur over years) and spatially (both geographically and organisationally), and how a commitment to workplace democracy and user empowerment can be maintained, while serving broader agendas (e.g. commercial and governmental). In the following section we discuss some of the efforts to extend the scope of Participatory Design and how these have complicated the alliance of ethnography and Participatory Design.

Temporal scaling

There is a growing awareness of the benefits of developing more longitudinal approaches for Participatory Design projects where the processes of design-in-use can be observed and harnessed for Participatory Design aims. Our earlier discussion of co-realisation (Hartswood et al. 2002; Voss 2006) pointed to the importance of long-term involvement in the sites of technology design and implementation. In a related way, Karasti and Baker (2008) and Karasti et al. (2010) argue for enabling communities to evolve technologies over time for their specific purposes. Similarly, Simonsen and Hertzum (2010) argue for an 'iterative Participatory Design', stressing the value of ethnographically informed Participatory Design for later stages of technology implementation and integration, in, for example, technology assessments where emergent change can be studied and evaluated. Bossen et al. (2010) have assessed how participants of a previous Participatory Design project have been able to integrate what they gained and learned into activities in other settings over time. These more longitudinal and iterative approaches suggest that it is not useful to position ethnography as something that precedes design, as both ethnography and design are ongoing achievements of participants over time.

As noted by Kyng (2010) and Pollock and Williams (2010), extending research and design projects temporally can create many challenges, not the least of which is the way research is funded, in discrete time-bounded ways. This often prevents ethnographic longitudinal studies taking place over multiple funding cycles. An approach that is somewhat commonplace in anthropology and that addresses this issue is returning to the 'same' field site in successive years to provide a longer-term perspective. Although this has not been the practice in Participatory Design research, it might align with Participatory Design goals of empowering the sites of technology use to drive the change agenda. While these longer-term strategies have advantages, they require establishing continuing relationships with the sites of change and securing funding that recognises the value of continuity and long-term commitments to change.

Alternatively, more emphasis might be placed on learning from past projects (cf. Bossen et al. 2010 above) and not starting anew with each new Participatory Design project, including taking advantage of the ethnographically derived insights from earlier projects. In addition, Participatory Design researchers might adopt new strategies and methods to grasp and explore, via 'here and now' materials and conceptual tools, processes that occur in longer temporal horizons. Karasti's workshops (2001a, 2001b) drawing on Change Laboratory's use of temporal contexts of past, now and future (Engeström et al. 1996) offer an example of extending the temporal horizon of the 'here and now' collaborative activities. Through the analysis and juxtaposition of work with traditional and new digital imaging systems, the evaluation of new and the (re)design of future systems was enabled. Co-creating shared understandings of these work contexts with different system versions allowed the participants to move along an extended temporal continuum and make use of its temporal qualities for ongoing work and system analysis, evaluation and redesign.

Spatial scaling

Locating the sites for Participatory Design and identifying the particular focus of intervention can be challenging in situations where people are interacting with others who are geographically distributed, for example in the context of their work or leisure, and family activities. In particular the question is raised as to whether and in what ways ethnography, with its traditional reliance on the 'field site', is well suited for the study of the contemporary experiences of people in a globalising world (Marcus 1995). The proposal of a multi-sited approach that addresses the theoretical and practical concerns of studying the contemporary condition of migrations, diasporas and technologically interconnected (virtual) communities suggests the need for strategies to study geographically distributed groups and activities (Coleman and von Hellermann 2011; Falzon 2009; Hannerz 2003; Hine 2007). Multi-sited ethnography emphasises a focus on the connections between people, places and things independent of their geographic proximity. Geographic locale alone does not delimit the span of an ethnographic study; instead, the research questions establish the scope of the study. On this view the boundaries of the study are always 'constructed' and not defined by place alone.

While geographic scaling presents challenges for Participatory Design, the fluidity and permeability of organisational boundaries (e.g. supply chains, customer supplier relations, outsourcing), along with the cross-organisational reach of information and communication infrastructures, opens new terrains for Participatory Design, and specifically ethnography, that go beyond the single site. Strategies are required for research and participatory engagement with user practitioners who come from different organisations, with differing incentive structures and spans of control. Communication and collaboration among these organisational entities may benefit from standard technology infrastructures and agreed-upon ways of interacting. The design of these interstitial socio-technical systems suggests Participatory Design projects that engage across organisational boundaries. As with issues with temporal scaling, these projects can be difficult to undertake given funding realities and the locus of decision-making authority.

In response to these challenges some have proposed a 'distributed Participatory Design' where the project locales are multiple and extend as appropriate throughout the life of a project. For example, Obendorf et al. (2009) describe a project where the technology design evolved as new groups of users became involved, shifting the site of design. In response to the demands of conducting Participatory Design in the 'Global South', Titlestad et al. (2009) developed strategies to pool resources, skills and tools across country boundaries so that the overall capability of the region grows in terms of both design strategies and the systems that result. They emphasise the benefits of circulating people (with knowledge and experience), artefacts (to be integrated into the local settings) and technology and process standards (which provide the benefits of systems that can connect people and integrate information across country boundaries).

Large-scale information systems

Shapiro (2005; 2010) and Kyng (2010) advocate a reformist Participatory Design agenda that places Participatory Design at the centre of the design (procurement and development) of large-scale information systems, noting that Participatory Design projects for the most part have had a rather narrow scope, with a few exceptions (e.g. projects with Mærsk in Denmark). They observe that many technologies introduced into workplaces today are based on packaged systems (e.g. SAP, Oracle) and involve the adoption and adaptation of systems by different groups and departments within an organisation, increasingly crossing organisational boundaries (e.g. supply chains, customer–provider interactions, outsourcing). Shapiro (2005, 2010) argues strongly for finding a way to help shape the design and implementation of public sector information systems, where critical issues of citizen, student, teacher, not to mention worker, interests are being shaped by the possibilities afforded by these large-scale systems.

Large-scale information system design also raises the issue of who should participate in such projects. These systems touch many people throughout an organisation who have differing relations to the system. This presents challenges not only logistically, but also in terms of empowerment and located accountability. Often, conflicting and competing interests cannot be ignored if the political commitments of Participatory Design are to be recognised and acted upon. These same issues come up in the design of e-government systems where the citizenry are the user practitioners, who are highly distributed with many different and sometimes competing interests (Dittrich et al. 2003; Oostveen and van den Besselaar 2004).

Developing countries

While Participatory Design has its roots in Scandinavia with a majority of scholarly and applied efforts focused in Europe and North America, there has been interest for many years in applying Participatory Design frameworks and practices more broadly to developing countries and emerging markets, particularly in health informatics projects (Braa et al. 2004; Korpela et al. 1998; Puri et al. 2004). Participatory Design has been seen as appropriate for these contexts 'because of its democratic origins and contextual approach' (Mursu et al. 2000, p. 1). Many challenges have been noted in applying Participatory Design in these contexts, including the need to broaden the range of people who participate in Participatory Design projects, to develop the capacity of people to participate in design projects (Byrne and Sahay 2007) and to redefine what participation means in contexts where there is little previous experience with participatory involvement. Some of these issues are explored in Chapter 10 of this volume, and our focus here is on the implications of these challenges for positioning ethnography in Participatory Design.

Participatory Design has been faulted for accepting overly simplistic notions of power and hierarchy, sometimes assuming more homogeneity and less conflict among participants than is warranted. The egalitarian values that characterise Scandinavian countries (perhaps uncritically) have resulted in design practices that assume an ethic celebrating participation and open dialogue. This criticism has been particularly pointed in relation to the appropriation of Participatory Design in non-Western contexts, where participation can be fraught and expectations of appropriate and proper behaviour may interfere with the ability and willingness of relevant stakeholders to participate (Elovaara et al. 2006; Puri et al. 2004; Robertson et al. 2002; Winschiers-Theophilus et al. 2010). Helen Verran notes, '[in] situations where practitioners of disparate knowledge traditions with differing ways of seeing, of thinking, and of working in the world struggle to work together … the design knowledge community needs to take different logics of thinking, seeing and feeling seriously' (Verran 2010, p. 13).

Participatory Design researchers can benefit from reflecting critically on the positionality of those who participate in Participatory Design projects, developing an awareness of the potentially unfamiliar constraints they may confront. In addition, there is value in Participatory Design researchers turning the mirror on themselves and asking what motivates their participation in these projects. Participatory designers perhaps have something to learn from anthropology's past, where there was not enough reflection on the relation ethnographic projects had to Western colonial agendas (Asad 1991; Pink 2006).

Although ethnography is not frequently positioned in Participatory Design to inform the design of the participatory project itself (for an exception see Winschiers-Theophilus et al. 2010), in contexts where there are different knowledge traditions and ways of being in the world, ethnography could be useful for enabling an explicit reflection on the implication of these differences for the joint project (e.g. who should be involved, in what activities, where should they occur, etc.). We should not assume that the tools and techniques of Participatory Design developed for Scandinavian (and other European and North American) audiences will enable multiple voices to define and inform the design when transported to very different traditions. Here ethnography's commitment to studying the everyday 'realities' of people living in non-Western societies can become as asset for Participatory Design.

Commercial settings

Ethnographic research, sometimes with an explicit Participatory Design methodology, has been adopted by large and small enterprises (from multinational companies to boutique design firms) for primarily instrumental aims of increasing revenues and reducing costs and inefficiencies. As Cefkin (2009, p. 2) writes in the introduction to *Ethnography and the Corporate Encounter,* corporations increasingly are 'actively engag[ing] ethnographic work as a part of their strategic and operational efforts'. Ethnographic research in its myriad of incarnations is being used to inform the design of new products and services, to develop marketing strategies to increase sales, to improve the internal organisational operations, and more. As part of these efforts users or consumers or practitioners are sometimes actively sought to participate in research, providing their perspectives and guidance in shaping products and services and in defining and bringing about change within the organisations in which they work. Intel ethnographers Salvador, Bell and Anderson describe ethnography in the corporate context as

> a way of understanding the particulars of daily life in such a way as to increase the success probability of a new product or service or, more appropriately, to reduce the probability of failure specifically due to a lack of understanding of the basic behaviors and frameworks of consumers.
>
> *(Salvador et al. 1999, p. 37)*

Similarly, in a commentary article in *Ethnography and the Corporate Encounter* Blomberg writes, 'A central, although sometimes just-under-the-surface, assumption that underpins much, if not all, of the work of corporate ethnographers is that ethnography is good for something or at least has to be argued to be good for something' (Blomberg 2009, p. 217).

The instrumental focus of commercially oriented Participatory Design is shared by many Participatory Design projects where, as Noble (2007, p. 340) articulates, 'resources (human, tangible, intangible, technical and so forth) … are mobilize[d] and enroll[ed] to produce effects'. While in principle what differentiates Participatory Design projects from those with an explicitly commercial agenda is their explicit aim of strengthening workplace democracy and furthering the interests of practitioners, it behoves Participatory Design researchers to reflect on the ways their projects achieve these objectives and to ask in what ways they too are serving the goals of the funders and sponsors of their research, be they companies or not-for-profit granting agencies.

In these commercial settings, what participation means varies widely, from being respondents to structured and open-ended surveys to the co-designers of new offerings or ways of working. While at the one extreme we might not consider this participation, at the other the ways users are involved in design projects can look very similar to those of more conventional or traditional Participatory Design projects. However, what is often absent in these commercial contexts is a commitment to participant empowerment and enabling users to define and shape the project and its goals. Participants are enlisted in these projects to contribute to the instrumental aims of the project's sponsors. While on occasion the project outcomes do benefit participants directly, this is difficult for the ethnographers (and designers) to promise, since they too are often not 'in control' of the project definition or outcomes.

Conclusion

We hope this discussion will rekindle researchers' interest in examining the relationship between ethnography and design and in becoming more reflective about the role of ethnography in Participatory Design, especially with regard to the new directions and challenges. A dichotomy seems to have emerged in how ethnography is positioned in relation to Participatory Design. On the one hand ethnography seems to have been normalised, accepted as part of Participatory Design practice. On the other hand ethnography is being 'backgrounded', secondary to those activities that directly engage participants in design. What seems to have been lost is the analytic purchase of ethnography as more than method, providing insights that point to future possibilities and ground those possibilities in the realities of the 'here and now'. As we look back on the last two decades, during which ethnography has become somewhat commonplace in Participatory Design, it may be time to reimagine the relation of ethnography to design, not as having a singular relation to Participatory Design, but as a varied contribution including connecting to the everyday 'realities' of the sites of design and intervention, informing the possibilities for participation given local contingencies, being iteratively allied to reflection and intervention, and constituting the source and outcome of design.

Positioning ethnography within Participatory Design is taking us beyond familiar terrain, confronting the challenges of designing large-scale systems over longer time periods and the socio-technical infrastructures that enable global connections, and doing so with people from different knowledge traditions, economic circumstances and disciplinary backgrounds. At the same time ethnography is being interleaved with design in more complex and varied ways, raising new questions about how to support interdisciplinary learning. These challenges suggest that reflexivity is as important, if not more so, today as we look toward the future of Participatory Design and its relation to ethnography.

Acknowledgments

Karasti's work has been supported by Academy of Finland.

Notes

1 Participatory Design developed to enable workers to define how their futures would be shaped by new technologies; however, today Participatory Design is also concerned with giving voice to other groups such as citizens, families, consumers and students. Throughout this chapter we will refer to workers, but the arguments we are making could as easily be applied to these other groups. Where this is not the case we will make note.
2 We refer to the workplace as the site of Participatory Design; however, today Participatory Design is not limited to the workplace, but also includes domestic and community sites.
3 This was one of the early motivations for exploring ways of linking ethnography and Participatory Design.

References

Agar, M. (1996) *The Professional Stranger*, second edition, San Diego, CA: Academic Press.
Andersen, T., J. Halse and J. Moll (2011) 'Design interventions as multiple becomings of healthcare', in I. Koskinen, T. Härkäsalmi, R. Mazé, B. Matthews and J.-J. Lee (eds) *Proceedings of the Nordes'11: The 4th Nordic Design Research Conference*, Helsinki: Aalto University, 1–10.
Anderson, B. (1997) 'Work, ethnography and system design', in A. Kent and J. G. Williams (eds) *The Encyclopedia of Microcomputing*, New York: Marcel Dekker, 20: 159–83.
Anderson, R. J. (1994) 'Representations and requirements: the value of ethnography in system design', *Human–Computer Interaction*, 9(2): 151–82.
Asad, T. (1991) 'Afterword: from the history of colonial anthropology to the anthropology of Western hegemony', in G. Stocking (ed.) *Colonial Situations: Essays on the Contextualization of Ethnographic Knowledge*, Madison: University of Wisconsin Press, 314–24.
Bader, G. and J. M. Nyce (1998) 'When only the self is real: theory and practice in the development community', *Journal of Computer Documentation*, 22(1): 5–10.
Balka, E. (2006) 'Inside the belly of the beast: the challenges and successes of a reformist participatory agenda', in G. Jacucci and F. Kensing (eds) *Proceedings of the Ninth Conference on Participatory Design – PDC 2006*, New York: ACM, 134–43.
Balka, E. (2010) 'Broadening discussion about Participatory Design: a response to Kyng', *Scandinavian Journal of Information Systems*, 22(1): 77–84.
Beck, E. (2002) 'P for political: participation is not enough', *Scandinavian Journal of Information Systems*, 14(1): 77–92.
Bentley, R., J. A. Hughes, D. Randall, T. Rodden, P. Sawyer, D. Shapiro and I. Sommerville (1992) 'Ethnographically-informed system design for air traffic control', in J. Turner and R. Kraut (eds) *Proceedings of Computer Supported Cooperative Work*, New York: ACM, 123–9.
Bjerknes, G. and T. Bratteteig (1995) 'User participation and democracy: a discussion of Scandinavian research on systems development', *Scandinavian Journal of Information Systems*, 7(1): 73–98.
Blomberg, J. (1987) 'Social interaction and office communication: effects on user's evaluation of new technologies', in R. Kraut (ed.) *Technology and the Transformation of White Collar Work*, Hillsdale, NJ: Lawrence Erlbaum Associates, 195–210.
Blomberg, J. (1988) 'The variable impact of computer technologies on the organization of work activities', in I. Greif (ed.) *Computer-Supported Cooperative Work: A Book of Readings*, San Mateo, CA: Morgan Kaufmann, 771–82.
Blomberg, J. (1995) 'Ethnography: aligning field studies of work and system design', in A. F. Monk and N. Gilbert (eds) *Perspectives on HCI: Diverse Approaches*, London: Academic Press, 175–97.
Blomberg, J. (2009) 'Insider trading: engaging and valuing corporate ethnography', in M. Cefkin (ed.) *Ethnography and the Corporate Encounter: Reflections on Research in and of Corporations*, New York: Berghahn Books, 213–26.
Blomberg, J. and M. Burrell (2007) 'An ethnographic approach to design', in J. Jacko and A. Sears (eds) *Human–Computer Interaction Handbook: Fundamental, Evolving Technologies and Emerging Applications*, Hillsdale, NJ: Lawrence Erlbaum Associates, 965–88.

Blomberg, J. and H. Henderson (1990) 'Reflections on Participatory Design: reflections from the Trillium Project', in J. Carrasco Chew and J. Whiteside (eds) *Proceedings of the ACM CHI 90 Human Factors in Computing Systems Conference*, New York: ACM, 353–59.

Blomberg, J. and R. Trigg (2000) 'Co-constructing the relevance of work practice for CSCW design: a case study of translation and mediation', *Occasional Papers from the Work Practice Laboratory*, Blekinge Institute of Technology, 1(2): 1–23.

Blomberg, J., J. Giacomi, A. Mosher and P. Swenton-Wall (1993) 'Ethnographic field methods and their relation to design', in D. Schuler and A. Namioka (eds) *Participatory Design: Perspectives on Systems Design*, Hillsdale, NJ: Lawrence Erlbaum Associates, 123–55.

Blomberg, J., L. Suchman and R. Trigg (1996) 'Reflections on a work-oriented design project', *Human–Computer Interaction*, 11(3): 237–65.

Blomberg, J., L. Suchman and R. Trigg (1997) 'Back to work: renewing old agendas for cooperative design', in M. Kyng and L. Mathiassen (eds) *Computers and Design in Context*, Cambridge, MA: MIT Press, 267–87.

Blythin, S., J. Hughes and M. Rouncefield (1997) 'Never mind all that ethno stuff: what does it mean and what do we do now? Ethnography in a commercial context', *Interactions*, 4(3): 38–47.

Bødker, K. and F. Kensing (1994) 'Design in an organizational context – an experiment', *Scandinavian Journal of Information Systems,* 6(1): 47–68.

Bødker, K., F. Kensing and J. Simonsen (2004) *Participatory IT Design: Designing for Business and Workplace Realities*, Cambridge, MA: MIT Press.

Bødker, S., P. Ehn, M. Kyng, J. Kammersgaard and Y. Sundblad (1987) 'A UTOPIAN experience', in G. Bjerknes, P. Ehn and M. Kyng (eds) *Computers and Democracy – A Scandinavian Challenge,* Aldershot, UK: Avebury, 251–78.

Bossen, C., C. Dindler and O. Iversen (2010) 'User gains and PD aims', in T. Robertson, K. Bødker, T. Bratteteig and D. Loi (eds) *Proceedings of the 11th Conference on Participatory Design – PDC 2010*, New York: ACM, 141–50.

Bowers, J., G. Button and W. Sharrock (1995) 'Workflow from within and without: technology and cooperative work on the print industry shopfloor', in H. Marmolin, Y. Sundblad and K. Schmidt (eds) *Proceedings of the Fourth European Conference on Computer-Supported Cooperative Work*, Dordrecht: Kluwer Academic Publishers, 51–66.

Braa, J., E. Monteiro and S. Sahay (2004) 'Networks of action: sustainable health information systems across developing countries', *MIS Quarterly,* 28(3): 337–62.

Brun-Cottan, F., K. Forbes, C. Goodwin, M. H. Goodwin, B. Jordan, L. Suchman and R. Trigg (1991) *Workplace Project: Designing for Diversity and Change*, Palo Alto, Xerox PARC Video Production, Xerox Palo Alto Research Center, video.

Bucciarelli, L. (1995) *Designing Engineers*, Cambridge, MA: MIT Press.

Büscher, M., S. Gill, P. Mogensen and D. Shapiro (2001) 'Landscapes of practice: bricolage as a method for situated design', *Computer–Supported Cooperative Work (CSCW) The Journal of Collaborative Computing*, 10(1): 1–28.

Button, G. (ed.) (1992) *Technology and Working Order: Studies of Work, Interaction and Technology*, London: Routledge.

Button, G. (2000) 'The ethnographic tradition and design', *Design Studies*, 21(4): 319–32.

Button, G. and R. Harper (1996) 'The relevance of "work-practice" for design', *Computer–Supported Cooperative Work (CSCW) The Journal of Collaborative Computing*, 5(4): 263–80.

Buur, J. and S. Bødker (2000) 'From usability lab to "design collaboratorium": reframing usability practice', in D. Boyarski and W. A. Kellogg (eds) *Proceedings of the 3rd Conference on Designing Interactive Systems: Processes, Practices, Methods, and Techniques – DIS'00*, New York: ACM, 297–307.

Buur, J., T. Binder and E. Brandt (2000) 'Taking video beyond "hard data" in user-centred design', in T. Cherkasky, J. Greenbaum, P. Mambrey and J. K. Pors (eds) *Proceedings of the Participatory Design Conference – PDC 2000, Palo Alto, CA*, New York: ACM, 21–9.

Buur, J., E. Fraser, S. Oinonen and M. Rolfstam (2010) 'Ethnographic video as design specs', in M. Brereton, S. Viller and B. Kraal (eds) *Proceedings of the 22nd Australasian Computer–Human Interaction Conference – OZCHI 2010, Brisbane, Australia*, New York: ACM, 49–56.

Byrne, E. and S. Sahay (2007) 'Generalizations from an interpretative study: the case from a South African community-based health information system', *South African Computer Journal*, 38: 8–20.

Cefkin, M. (ed.) (2009) *Ethnography and the Corporate Encounter: Reflections on Research in and of Corporations*, New York: Berghahn Books.

Clifford, J. (1988) *The Predicament of Culture: Twentieth-Century Ethnography, Literature, and Art*, Cambridge, MA: Harvard University Press.

Clifford, J. and G. Marcus (eds) (1986) *Writing Culture: The Poetics and Politics of Ethnography*, Berkeley: University of California Press.

Coleman, S. and P. von Hellermann (eds) (2011) *Multi-Sited Ethnography: Problems and Possibilities in the Translocation of Research Methods*, London: Routledge.

Crabtree, A. (1998) 'Ethnography in Participatory Design', in R. Henderson Chatfield, S. Kuhn and M. Muller (eds) *Proceedings of PDC 98: 5th Biennial Participatory Design Conference, Palo Alto, CA*, New York: ACM, 93–105.

Crabtree, A., T. Hemmings, T. Rodden, K. Cheverst, K. Clarke, G. Dewsbury, J. Hughes and M. Rouncefield (2003) 'Designing with care: adapting cultural probes to inform design in sensitive settings', in S. Viller and P. Wyeth (eds) *Proceedings of 2003 Australasian Computer Human Interaction Conference – OzCHI 2003*, Brisbane: Ergonomics Society of Australia, 4–13.

Crabtree, A., T. Rodden, P. Tolmie and G. Button (2009) 'Ethnography considered harmful', in D. R. Olsen, Jr, R. B. Arthur, K. Hinckley, M. R. Morris, S. E. Hudson and S. Greenberg (eds) *Proceedings of the 27th International Conference on Human Factors in Computing Systems – CHI 2009, Boston, Massachusetts, USA*, New York: ACM, 879–88.

Davies, C. A. (1999) *Reflexive Ethnography: A Guide to Researching Selves and Others*, London: Routledge.

Dearden, A. and H. Rizvi (2008) 'Participatory IT design and participatory development: a comparative review', in J. Simonsen, T. Robertson and D. Hakken (eds) *Proceedings of the Tenth Conference on Participatory Design, PDC 2008*, New York: ACM, 81–91.

Dittrich, Y., A. Ekelin, P. Elovaara, S. Eriksén and C. Hansson (2003) 'Making e-Government happen: everyday co-development of services, citizenship and technology', in *Proceedings of the 36th Hawaii International Conference on System Sciences*, Hawaii: Computer Society Press, 1–12.

Dourish, P. (2006) 'Implications for design', in R. Grinter, T. Rodden, P. Aoki, E. Cutrell, R. Jeffries and G. Olson (eds) *Proceedings of ACM CHI 2006 Conference on Human Factors in Computing Systems, Montreal, Canada*, New York: ACM, 541–50.

Ehn, P. (1988) *Work-Oriented Design of Computer Artefacts*, Stockholm: Arbetslivscentrum.

Elovaara, P., F. T. Igira and C. Mörtberg (2006) 'Whose participation? Whose knowledge?', in G. Jacucci and F. Kensing (eds) *Proceedings of the Ninth Conference on Participatory Design – PDC 2006*, New York: ACM, 105–14.

Engeström, Y., J. Virkkunen, M. Helle, J. Pihlaja and R. Poikela (1996) 'Change Laboratory as a tool for transforming work', *Lifelong Learning in Europe*, 1(2): 10–17.

Falzon, M.-A. (ed.) (2009) *Multi-Sited Ethnography: Theory, Praxis and Locality in Contemporary Research*, Aldershot, UK: Ashgate.

Finken, S. (2003) 'Discursive conditions of knowledge production within cooperative design', *Scandinavian Journal of Information Systems*, 15: 57–72.

Forsythe, D. E. (1999) '"It's just a matter of common sense": ethnography as invisible work', *Computer Supported Cooperative Work (CSCW) The Journal of Collaborative Computing*, 8(1–2): 127–45.

Frodeman, R., J. T. Klein and C. Mitcham (eds) (2010) *The Oxford Handbook of Interdisciplinarity*, Oxford: Oxford University Press.

Garfinkel, H. (1967) *Studies in Ethnomethodology*, Englewood Cliffs, NJ: Prentice-Hall.

Gaver, W., A. Dunne and E. Pacenti (1999) 'Cultural probes', *Interactions*, 6(1): 21–9.

Gaver, W., A. Boucher, S. Pennington and B. Walker (2004) 'Cultural probes and the value of uncertainty', *Interactions*, 11(5): 53–6.

Gerson, E. M. and S. L. Star (1986) 'Analyzing due process in the workplace', *ACM Transactions on Office Information Systems*, 4(3): 257–70.

Greenbaum, J. and M. Kyng (1991) *Design at Work: Cooperative Design of Computer Systems*, Hillsdale, NJ: Lawrence Erlbaum Associates.

Grønbæk, K., M. Kyng and P. Mogensen (1997) 'Toward a cooperative experimental system development approach', in M. Kyng and L. Mathiassen (eds) *Computers and Design in Context*, Cambridge, MA: MIT Press, 201–38.

Grudin, J. and R. E. Grinter (1995) 'Ethnography and design', *Computer Supported Cooperative Work (CSCW) The Journal of Collaborative Computing*, 3(1): 55–9.

Halse, J. (2008) 'Design anthropology: borderland experiments with participation, performance and situated intervention', unpublished doctoral dissertation, IT University of Copenhagen. Online. Available at: http://www.dasts.dk/wp-content/uploads/2008/05/joachim-halse-2008.pdf (accessed 15 November 2011).

Halse, J., E. Brandt, B. Clark and T. Binder (2010) *Rehearsing the Future*, Copenhagen: Danish Design School Press.

Hammersley, M. (1992) *What's Wrong with Ethnography? – Methodological Explorations*, London: Routledge.

Hannerz, U. (2003) 'Several sites in one', in T. Eriksen (ed.) *Globalization*, London: Pluto Press.

Harper, R. and J. A. Hughes (1993) 'What a f-ing system! Send 'em all to the same place and then expect us to stop 'em hitting. Managing technology work in air traffic control', in G. Button (ed.) *Technology in Working Order: Studies of Work, Interaction, and Technology*, London: Routledge, 127–44.

Harper, R., J. A. Hughes and D. Shapiro (1991) 'Harmonious working and CSCW: computer technology and air traffic control', in J. M. Bowers and S. D. Benford (eds) *Studies in Computer Supported Cooperative Work*, Amsterdam: Elsevier Science Publishers (North-Holland), 225–34.

Hartswood, M., R. Procter, R. Slack, A. Voss, M. Büscher, M. Rouncefield and P. Rouchy (2002) 'Co-realisation: towards a principled synthesis of ethnomethodology and Participatory Design', *Scandinavian Journal of Information Systems*, 14(2): 9–30.

Harvey, L. J. and M. D. Myers (1995) 'Scholarship and practice: the contribution of ethnographic research methods to bridging the gap', *Information Technology and People*, 8(3): 3–12.

Heath, C. and P. Luff (1992) 'Collaboration and control: crisis management and multimedia technology in London Underground line control rooms', *Computer-Supported Cooperative Work: The Journal of Collaborative Computing* 1(1–2): 69–94.

Heath, C., J. Hindmarsh and P. Luff (eds) (n.d.) *Workplace Studies: Rediscovering Work Practice and Informing Design*, Cambridge: Cambridge University Press.

Henderson, A. and M. Kyng (1991) 'There's no place like home: continuing design in use', in J. Greenbaum and M. Kyng (eds) *Design at Work*, London: Lawrence Erlbaum Associates, 219–40.

Henderson, K. (1991) 'Flexible sketches and inflexible databases', *Science, Technology and Human Values*, 6(4): 448–73.

Hine, C. (2007) 'Connective ethnography for the exploration of e-science', *Journal of Computer-Mediated Communication*, 12(2): 618–34.

Hughes, J., D. Randall and D. Shapiro (1991) 'CSCW: discipline or paradigm? A sociological perspective', in L. Bannon, M. Robinson and K. Schmidt (eds) *Proceedings of the Second European Conference on Computer-Supported Cooperative Work – ECSCW '91*, Amsterdam: Kluwer Academic Publishers, 309–23.

Hughes, J., D. Randall and D. Shapiro (1992) 'Faltering from ethnography to design', in J. Turner and R. Kraut (eds) *Proceedings of the Conference on Computer Supported Cooperative Work – CSCW '92, Toronto, Canada*, New York: ACM, 115–22.

Hughes, J., D. Randall and D. Shapiro (1993) 'From ethnographic record to system design', *Computer-Supported Cooperative Work: The Journal of Collaborative Computing*, 1(3): 123–41.

Hughes, J., V. King, T. Rodden and H. Anderson (1994) 'Moving out of the control room: ethnography in system design', in J. B. Smith, F. D. Smith and T. W. Malone (eds) *Proceedings of the 1994 ACM Conference on Computer Supported Cooperative Work*, New York: ACM, 429–39.

Hughes, J., T. Rodden and H. Anderson (1995) 'The role of ethnography in interactive system design', *Interactions*, 2(2): 56–65.

Hughes, J., J. O'Brien, T. Rodden, M. Rouncefield and S. Blythin (1997) 'Designing with ethnography: a presentation framework for design', in S. Coles (ed.) *Proceedings of Designing Interactive Systems Conference: Processes, Practices, Methods, and Techniques (DIS'97)*, New York: ACM, 147–58.

Hutchins, E. (1990) 'The technology of team navigation', in J. Galegher, R. Kraut and C. Egido (eds) *Intellectual Teamwork: Social and Technological Foundations of Cooperative Work*, Hillsdale, NJ: Lawrence Erlbaum Associates, 191–220.

Jordan, B. (1996a) 'Ethnographic workplace studies and CSCW', in D. Shapiro, M. Tauber and R. Traunmuller (eds) *The Design of Computer Supported Cooperative Work and Groupware Systems*, Amsterdam: Elsevier Science, 17–42.

Jordan, B. (1996b) 'Transforming ethnography – reinventing research', in J. Schlestl and H. Schelle (eds) *Groupware – Software für die Teamarbeit der Zukunft: Grundlegende Konzepte und Fallstudien*, Marburg, Germany: Tectun Verlag, 200–12.

Jordan, B. (2011) 'Transferring ethnographic competence: personal reflections on the past and future of work practice analysis', in M. H. Szymanski and J. Whalen (eds) *Making Work Visible: Ethnographically Grounded Case Studies of Work Practice*, New York: Cambridge University Press, 344–58.

Karasti, H. (2001a) 'Bridging work practice and system design: integrating systemic analysis, appreciative intervention, and practitioner participation', *Computer Supported Cooperative Work (CSCW) The Journal of Collaborative Computing*, 10(2): 167–98.

Karasti, H. (2001b) 'Increasing sensitivity towards everyday work practice in system design', unpublished doctoral dissertation, University of Oulu. Online. Available at: http://urn.fi/urn:isbn:9514259556 (accessed 1 June 2012).

Karasti, H. (2010a) 'Participant interventionist: researcher role integrating ethnography and Participatory Design', in H. Hakala (ed.) *Proceedings of the 3rd Qualitative Research Conference, 1–3. June 2010,* Vaasa: University of Vaasa, Finland, 1–12.

Karasti, H. (2010b) 'Taking PD to multiple contexts: a response to Kyng', *Scandinavian Journal of Information Systems,* 22(1): 85–92.

Karasti, H. and K. S. Baker (2008) 'Community design: growing one's own information infrastructure', in D. Hakken, J. Simonsen and T. Robertson (eds) *Proceedings of the Tenth Conference on Participatory Design – PDC 2008,* New York: ACM, 217–20.

Karasti, H. and Syrjänen, A.-L. (2004) 'Artful infrastructuring in two cases of community PD', in A. Clement and P. van den Besselaar (eds) *Proceedings of the Eighth Conference on Participatory Design – PDC 2004,* New York: ACM, 20–30.

Karasti, H., K. S. Baker and F. Millerand (2010) 'Infrastructure time: long-term matters in collaborative development', *Computer Supported Cooperative Work (CSCW) The Journal of Collaborative Computing,* 19(3–4): 377–415.

Kensing, F. (1987) 'Generating visions in system development', in P. Docherty, K. Fuchs-Kittowski, P. Kolm and L. Mathiassen (eds) *Proceedings of the IFIP TC 9/WG 9.1 Working Conference on System Design for Human Development and Productivity: Participation and Beyond,* Amsterdam: North-Holland, 285–301.

Kensing, F. and J. Blomberg (1998) 'Participatory Design: issues and concerns', *Computer Supported Cooperative Work (CSCW) The Journal of Collaborative Computing,* 7(3–4): 163–85.

Kensing, F. and T. Winograd (1991) 'Operationalizing the language/action approach to design of computer-support for cooperative work: collaborative work, social communications and information systems', in R. Stamper, P. Kerola, R. Lee and K. Lyytinen (eds) *Proceedings of the IFIP TC 8 Working Conference COSCIS'91,* Amsterdam: North-Holland, 311–31.

Kensing, F., J. Simonsen and K. Bødker (1997) 'Designing for cooperation at a radio station', in J. Hughes, W. Prinz, T. Rodden and K. Schmidt (eds) *Proceedings of the Fifth European Conference on Computer-Supported Cooperative Work,* Dordrecht: Kluwer Academic Publishers, 329–44.

Kensing, F., J. Simonsen and K. Bødker (1998a) 'MUST: a method for Participatory Design', *Human–Computer Interaction,* 13(2): 167–98.

Kensing, F., J. Simonsen and K. Bødker (1998b) 'Participatory Design at a radio station', *Computer-Supported Cooperative Work: The Journal of Collaborative Computing,* 7(3–4): 243–71.

Kindermann, A. (1996) 'Applied ethnography in work systems design', Cognitive Science Research Paper, University of Sussex, CSRP 1350–3162.

Klein, J. T. (2010) 'A taxonomy of interdisciplinarity', in R. Frodeman, J. T. Klein and C. Mitcham (eds) *The Oxford Handbook of Interdisciplinarity,* Oxford: Oxford University Press, 15–30.

Korpela, M., H. A. Soriyan, K. C. Olufokunbi, A. A. Onayade, A. Davies-Adetugbo and D. Adesanmi (1998) 'Community participation in health informatics in Africa: an experiment in tripartite partnership in Ile-Ife, Nigeria', *Computer Supported Cooperative Work (CSCW) The Journal of Collaborative Computing,* 7: 339–58.

Kyng, M. (1991) 'Designing for cooperation: cooperating in design', *Communications of the ACM,* 34(12): 65–73.

Kyng, M. (1995) 'Making representation work', *Communications of the ACM,* 38(9): 46–55.

Kyng, M. (2010) 'Bridging the gap between politics and techniques: on the next practices of Participatory Design', *Scandinavian Journal of Information Systems,* 22(1): 49–68.

Luff, P., C. Heath and D. Greatbatch (1992) 'Tasks-in-interaction: paper and screen based documentation in collaborative activity', in J. Turner and R. Kraut (eds) *Proceedings of the Conference on Computer-Supported Cooperative Work – CSCW'92,* New York: ACM, 163–70.

Luff, P., J. Hindmarsh and C. Heath (2000) *Workplace Studies: Recovering Work Practice and Informing System Design,* Cambridge: Cambridge University Press.

Mambrey, P., G. Mark and U. Pankoke-Babatz (1998) 'User advocacy in Participatory Design: designers' experiences with a new communication channel', *Computer Supported Cooperative Work (CSCW) The Journal of Collaborative Computing,* 7(3–4): 291–313.

Marcus, G. E. (1995) 'Ethnography in/of the world system: the emergence of multi-sited ethnography', *Annual Review of Anthropology,* 24: 95–117.

Markussen, R. (1994) 'A historical perspective on work practices and technology', in B. P. Anderson, B. Holmqvist and J. Jensen (eds) *The Computer as a Medium,* New York: Cambridge University Press, 457–76.

Mathiassen, L. and P. A. Nielsen (2008) 'Engaged scholarship in IS research: the Scandinavian case', *Scandinavian Journal of Information Systems,* 20(2), 3–20.

Merkel, C. B., L. Xiao, U. Farooq, C. H. Ganoe, R. Lee, J. M. Carroll and M. B. Rosson (2004) 'Participatory Design in community computing contexts: tales from the field', in A. Clement and P. van den Besselaar (eds) *Proceedings of the Eighth Conference on Participatory Design – PDC 2004*, New York: ACM, 1–10.

Millen, D. R. (2000) 'Rapid ethnography: time deepening strategies for HCI field research', in D. Boyarski and W. A. Kellogg (eds) *DIS'00 – Proceedings of the 3rd Conference on Designing Interactive Systems: Processes, Practices, Methods, and Techniques*, New York: ACM, 280–86.

Mogensen, P. (1992) 'Towards a provotyping approach in systems development', *Scandinavian Journal of Information Systems*, 3: 31–53.

Mogensen, P. and M. Robinson (1995) 'Triggering artefacts', *AI & Society*, 9: 373–88.

Mogensen, P. and R. Trigg (1992) 'Artefacts as triggers for participatory analysis', in M. J. Muller, S. Kuhn and J. A. Meskill (eds) *Proceedings of the 2nd Biennial Conference on Participatory Design – PDC '92*, New York: CPSR, 55–71.

Mörtberg, C., T. Bratteteig, I. Wagner, D. Stuedahl and A. Morrison (2010) 'Methods that matter in digital design research', in I. Wagner, T. Bratteteig and D. Stuedahl (eds) *Exploring Digital Design: Multi-Disciplinary Design Practices*, London: Springer-Verlag, 105–46.

Mursu, A., H. A. Soriyan, K. Olufokunbi and M. Korpela (2000) 'Information system development in a developing country: theoretical analysis of special requirements in Nigeria and Africa', in *Proceedings of the 33rd Hawaii International Conference on System Sciences – HICSS*, Hawaii: Computer Society Press, 7, 1–10.

Noble, B. (2007) 'Justice, transaction, translation: Blackfoot Tipi transfers and WIPO's search for the facts of traditional knowledge exchange', *American Anthropologist*, 109(2): 338–49.

Nyce, J. M. and J. Löwgren (1995) 'Toward foundational analysis in human–computer interaction', in P. J. Thomas (ed.) *The Social and Interactional Dimensions of Human–Computer Interfaces*, Cambridge: Cambridge University Press, 37–47.

Obendorf, H., M. Janneck and M. Finck (2009) 'Inter-contextual distributed Participatory Design', *Scandinavian Journal of Information Systems*, 21(1): 51–76.

Oostveen, A.-M. and P. van den Besselaar (2004) 'From small scale to large scale user participation: a case study of Participatory Design in e-government systems', in A. Clement and P. van den Besselaar (eds) *Proceedings of the Eighth Conference on Participatory Design – PDC 2004*, New York: ACM, 173–82.

Orr, J. E. (1990) 'Sharing knowledge, celebrating identity: war stories and community memory in a service culture', in D. Middleton and D. Edwards (eds) *Collective Remembering: Memory in Society*, Newbury Park: Sage, 169–89.

Pink, S. (ed.) (2006) *Applications of Anthropology: Professional Anthropology in the Twenty-First Century*, New York/Oxford: Berghahn Books.

Plowman, L., Y. Rogers and M. Ramage (1995) 'What are workplace studies for?', in H. Marmolin, Y. Sundblad and K. Schmidt (eds) *Proceedings of the Fourth European Conference on Computer-Supported Cooperative Work – ECSCW'95, Sweden*, Dordrecht: Kluwer, 309–24.

Plowman, L., R. Harper and Y. Rogers (1996) 'Representing ourselves and representing the users: the role of the fieldworker in workplace studies for CSCW', University of Sussex, Cognitive Science Research Paper, CSRP 1350–3162.

Pollock, N. and R. Williams (2010) 'e-Infrastructures: how do we know and understand them? Strategic ethnography and the biography of artefacts', *Computer Supported Cooperative Work (CSCW) The Journal of Collaborative Computing*, 19: 521–56.

Pors, J. K., D. Henriksen, B. R. Winthereik and M. Berg (2002) 'Challenging divisions: exploring the intersections of ethnography and intervention in IS research', *Scandinavian Journal of Information Systems*, 14(2): 3–7.

Puri, S. K., E. Byrne, J. L. Nhampossa and Z. B. Quraishi (2004) 'Contextuality of participation in IS design: a developing country perspective', in A. Clement and P. van den Besselaar (eds) *Proceedings of the Eighth Conference on Participatory Design – PDC 2004*, New York: ACM, 42–52.

Randall, D., M. Rouncefield and J. Hughes (1995) 'Chalk and cheese: BPR and ethnomethodologically informed ethnography in CSCW', in H. Marmolin, Y. Sundblad and K. Schmidt (eds) *Proceedings of the Fourth European Conference on Computer-Supported Cooperative Work*, Dordrecht: Kluwer Academic Publishers, 325–40.

Robertson, T., L. Dyson, H. Norman and B. Buckley (2002) 'Increasing the participation of Indigenous Australians in the information technology industries', in T. Binder, J. Gregory and I. Wagner (eds) *Proceedings of the 7th Biennial Participatory Design Conference – PDC 2002, Palo Alto*, New York: CPRS, 288–94.

Rogers, Y. (1997) 'Reconfiguring the social scientist: shifting from telling designers what to do to getting more involved', in G. C. Bowker, S. L. Star, W. Turner and L. Gasser (eds) *Social Science, Technical Systems, and Cooperative Work: Beyond the Great Divide*, London: Erlbaum, 57–77.

Rogers, Y. and V. Bellotti (1997) 'How can ethnography help?', *Interactions*, 4: 58–63.

Rouncefield, M., J. A. Hughes, T. Rodden and S. Viller (1994) 'CSCW and the small office', in J. B. Smith, F. D. Smith and T. W. Malone (eds) *Proceedings of the 1994 ACM Conference on Computer Supported Cooperative Work*, New York: ACM, 275–86.

Salter, L. and A. Hearn (eds) (1996) *Outside the Lines: Issues in Interdisciplinary Research*, Montreal: McGill-Queen's University Press.

Salvador, T., G. Bell and K. Anderson (1999) 'Design ethnography', *Design Management Journal*, 10(4): 35–41.

Sandberg, A. (1979a) *The DEMOS Project*, Swedish Centre for Working Life: Malmö.

Sandberg, A. (1979b) *Project DUE*, Swedish Centre for Working Life: Malmö.

Schmidt, K. (2000) 'The critical role of workplace studies in CSCW', in C. Heath, J. Hindmarsh and P. Luff (eds) *Workplace Studies: Rediscovering Work Practice and Informing Design*. Cambridge: Cambridge University Press, 141–9.

Schön, D. A. (1983) *The Reflective Practitioner – How Professionals Think in Action*, New York: Basic Books.

Shapiro, D. (1994) 'The limits of ethnography: combining social sciences for CSCW', in J. B. Smith, F. D. Smith and T. W. Malone (eds) *Proceedings of the 1994 ACM Conference on Computer Supported Cooperative Work*, New York: ACM, 417–28.

Shapiro, D. (2005) 'Participatory Design: the will to succeed', in O. W. Bertelsen, N. O. Bouvin, P. G. Krogh and M. Kyng (eds.) *Proceedings of the 4th Decennial Conference on Critical Computing: Between Sense and Sensibility*, New York: ACM: 29–38.

Shapiro, D. (2010) 'A modernised Participatory Design? A response to Kyng', *Scandinavian Journal of Information Systems,* 22(1): 69–76.

Shapiro, D., J. Hughes, R. Harper, S. Ackroyd and K. Soothill (1991) 'Policing information systems: the social context of success and failure in introducing information systems in the police service', *Proceedings of the 2nd Conference on Government and Municipal Information Systems*, Amsterdam: North-Holland, 183–97.

Shapiro, D., P. Mogensen and M. Büscher (1996) 'Bricolage as software culture and practice', in *Proceedings of the COST4 Workshop on Software Cultures*, December, Vienna: Technical University of Vienna.

Sharrock, W. and B. Anderson (1994) 'The user as scenic feature of the design space', *Design Studies,* 15(1): 5–18.

Simonsen, J. (2009) 'A concern for engaged scholarship' *Scandinavian Journal of Information Systems,* 21(2): 111–28.

Simonsen, J. and M. Hertzum (2010) 'Iterative Participatory Design', in J. Simonsen, J. O. Bærenholdt, M. Büscher and J. D. Scheuer (eds) *Design Research: Synergies from Interdisciplinary Perspectives*, New York: Routledge, 16–32.

Simonsen, J. and F. Kensing (1994) 'Take users seriously, but take a deeper look', in R. Trigg, S. I. Anderson and E. Dykstra-Erickson (eds) *Proceedings of the 3rd Biennial Conference on Participatory Design – PDC 1994, Palo Alto*, New York: CPSR.

Simonsen, J. and F. Kensing (1997) 'Using ethnography in contextual design', *Communications of the ACM,* 40(7): 82–88.

Simonsen, J. and F. Kensing (1998) 'Make room for ethnography in design!', *Journal of Computer Documentation*, ACM-SIGDOC 22(1): 20–30.

Simonsen, J., J. O. Bærenholdt, M. Büscher and J. D. Scheuer (eds) (n.d.) *Design Research: Synergies from Interdisciplinary Perspectives*, New York: Routledge.

Sommerville, I., T. Rodden, P. Sawyer and R. Bentley (1993) 'Sociologists can be surprisingly useful in interactive systems design', *Proceedings of the Conference on People and Computers VII (1993)*, New York: Cambridge University Press, 342–54.

Star, S. L. and K. Ruhleder (1996) 'Steps toward an ecology of infrastructure: borderlands of design and access for large information spaces', *Information Systems Research*, 7(1): 111–34.

Stuedahl, D., A. Morrison, C. Mörtberg and T. Bratteteig (2010) 'Researching digital design', in I. Wagner, T. Bratteteig and D. Stuedahl (eds) *Exploring Digital Design: Multi-Disciplinary Design Practices*, London: Springer-Verlag, 3–16.

Suchman, L. (1983) 'Office procedures as practical action: models of work and system design', *ACM Transactions on Office Information Systems*, 1(4): 320–28.

Suchman, L. (1987) *Plans and Situated Actions: The Problem of Human–Machine Communication*, Cambridge: Cambridge University Press.

Suchman, L. (1993) 'Technologies of accountability: of lizards and aeroplanes', in G. Button (ed.) *Technology in Working Order: Studies of Work, Interaction and Technology*. London: Routledge, 113–26.

Suchman, L. (1994) 'Working relations of technology production and use', *Computer Supported Cooperative Work (CSCW) The Journal of Collaborative Computing*, 2: 21–39.

Suchman, L. (1996) 'Constituting shared workspaces', in Y. Engeström and D. Middleton (eds) *Cognition and Communication at Work,* Cambridge: Cambridge University Press, 35–60.

Suchman, L. (1997) 'Centers for coordination: a case and some themes', in L. B. Resnick, R. Säljö, C. Pontecorvo and B. Burge (eds) *Discourse, Tools, and Reasoning: Essays on Situated Cognition,* Berlin: Springer-Verlag, 41–62.

Suchman, L. (2000a) 'Making a case: "knowledge" and "routine" work in document production', in P. Luff, J. Hindmarsh and C. Heath (eds) *Workplace Studies: Recovering Work Practice and Informing System Design,* Cambridge: Cambridge University Press, 29–45.

Suchman, L. (2000b) 'Organizing alignment: a case of bridge-building', *Organization,* 7(2): 311–27.

Suchman, L. (2002) 'Located accountabilities in technology production', *Scandinavian Journal of Information Systems,* 14(2): 91–105.

Suchman, L., and Trigg, R. (1991) 'Understanding practice: video as a medium for reflection and design', in J. Greenbaum and M. Kyng (eds) *Design at Work: Cooperative Design of Computer Systems,* Hillsdale, NJ: Lawrence Erlbaum Associates, 65–89.

Suchman, L. and E. Wynn (1984) 'Procedures and problems in the office', *Technology and People,* 2: 133–54.

Suchman, L., J. Blomberg and R. Trigg (1999) 'Reconstructing technologies as social practice', *American Scientist,* 43(3): 392–408.

Suchman, L., R. Trigg and J. Blomberg (2000) 'Working artifacts: ethnomethods of the prototype', *British Journal of Sociology,* 53(2): 163–79.

Syrjänen, A.-L. (2007) 'Lay Participatory Design: a way to develop information technology and activity together', unpublished doctoral dissertation, University of Oulu. Online. Available at: http://urn.fi/urn:isbn:9789514285912 (accessed 1 June 2012).

Titlestad, O. H., K. Staring and J. Braa (2009) 'Distributed development to enable user participation: multilevel design in the HISP network', *Scandinavian Journal of Information Systems,* 21(1): 27–50.

Trigg, R., S. Bødker and K. Grønbæk (1991) 'Open-ended interaction in cooperative prototyping: a video-based analysis', *Scandinavian Journal of Information Systems,* 3: 63–86.

Trigg, R., J. Blomberg and L. Suchman (1999) 'Moving document collections online: the evolution of a shared repository', in S. Bødker, M. Kyng and K. Schmidt (eds) *Proceedings of the Sixth European Conference on Computer-Supported Cooperative Work,* Norwell: Kluwer Academic Publishers, 331–50.

Twidale, M., T. Rodden and I. Sommerville (1993) 'The designers' notepad: supporting and understanding cooperative design', in G. D. Michelis, C. Simone and K. Schmidt (eds) *Proceedings of the Third European Conference on Computer-Supported Cooperative Work,* London: Kluwer Academic Publishers, 93–124.

Verran, H. (2010) 'Design as knowledge/knowledge as designed: different logics of seeing and thinking', *Cumulus Working Papers,* Publication Series G, Aalto University, School of Art and Design, 13–16.

Voss, A. (2006) 'Corealisation: a radical respecification of the working division of labour in systems development', unpublished doctoral dissertation, University of Edinburgh. Online. Available at: www.era.lib.ed.ac.uk/handle/1842/1764 (accessed 15 November 2011).

Wagner, I., T. Bratteteig and D. Stuedahl (eds) (2010) *Exploring Digital Design: Multi-Disciplinary Design Practices,* London: Springer-Verlag.

Willigen, J. V. (2002) *Applied Anthropology: An Introduction,* Westport: Greenwood Publishing Group.

Winschiers-Theophilus, H., S. Chivuno-Kuria, G. K. Kapuire, N. J. Bidwell and E. Blake (2010) 'Being participated – a community approach', in T. Robertson, K. Bødker, T. Bratteteig and D. Loi (eds) *Proceedings of the 11th Biennial Participatory Design Conference,* New York: ACM, 1–10.

Wynn, E. H. (1979) *Office Conversation as an Information Medium,* Berkeley, CA: University of California.

6

Methods

Organising principles and general guidelines for Participatory Design projects

Tone Bratteteig, Keld Bødker, Yvonne Dittrich,
Preben Holst Mogensen and Jesper Simonsen

Much of the research in Participatory Design has been concerned with developing new methods, techniques and tools. Methods are 'recipes' for how to do Participatory Design and include – in addition to tools and techniques – organising principles and general guidelines for the process, all based on a particular worldview or perspective. This chapter departs from some of the fundamental perspectives of Participatory Design described in earlier chapters, and discusses how these perspectives have been translated into ways of organising and carrying out Participatory Design.

The chapter starts with a definition of a method that makes a useful distinction between methods and tools and techniques. The chapter presents STEPS, MUST, CESD and use-oriented design as four genuine examples of Participatory Design methods. Then three fundamental perspectives relevant for all Participatory Design methods are discussed in terms of 'having a say', mutual learning and co-realisation. Finally, the chapter discusses some of the challenges concerning the methods and method development in Participatory Design.

The chapter gives an overview of recognised Participatory Design methods and explains how the perspectives of Participatory Design can be realised in concrete organising principles and guidelines that constitute a context for the tools and techniques described in Chapter 7. Several core perspectives of Participatory Design are discussed as to how one can organise and carry out a Participatory Design process to support these perspectives.

Current specialisations of information technology design challenge how and when users can have a say. Technological developments challenge how Participatory Design addresses design that occurs after design. Contemporary work life and the organisation of work challenge Participatory Design with respect to the scope and effect of user participation. We end this chapter by discussing these challenges and point to how Participatory Design might address them.

Introduction

Participatory Design is about engaging users in the design of new information technology. Much of the research within Participatory Design has been concerned with developing and improving methods, techniques and tools supporting *how* Participatory Design can be done in practice. Methods are 'recipes' for Participatory Design. Methods are prescriptions (i.e. normative descriptions) of how Participatory Design projects can be set up so that users are enabled to take an active part in the activities and decisions throughout which new information technology is designed and built. Participatory Design methods include tools and techniques, as well as organising principles and general guidelines for the process. These are all based on a particular Participatory Design worldview or perspective. This chapter departs from some of the fundamental perspectives of Participatory Design – as described in previous chapters – and aims to show how they can be translated to ways of conducting, organising and carrying out Participatory Design.

Participatory Design methods have traditionally all been concerned with information technology development projects – also referred to as 'system development' and 'system development projects' (Andersen et al. 1990). Information technology is a highly complex technical artefact. As its functionality depends on a computer program, which is a description of the technology's behaviour, it is extremely malleable. At the same time this provides a challenge. The program does not resemble the final product that the user will experience. The program has to be executed for the user to experience its interaction and its behaviour. The challenge for the design process, in the context of Participatory Design, is therefore how to develop a highly complex piece of technology and at the same time be flexible for learning processes resulting in changes to both the interface and the functionality of the technology throughout the design process – and even beyond.

What is a method?

Method, as a general concept, is often interpreted as a 'recipe' for how to carry out a set of activities – like a cookbook recipe. The method concept in Participatory Design refers to a coherent set of organising principles and general guidelines for how to carry out a design process from start to finish – within a Participatory Design perspective. Methods are generalisations from a vast amount of empirically based *experiences* on how to conduct Participatory Design. A Participatory Design method cannot be applied like a cookbook recipe, but provides general guidelines that must be carefully selected, adapted and appropriated to the specific project and situation at hand. Thus, the Participatory Design method concept should be interpreted broadly as a 'methodology' or 'meta-method', i.e. as a 'set of principles of method which in any particular situation has to be reduced to a method uniquely suitable to that particular situation' (Checkland 1981, pp. 161f).

We define a Participatory Design method by using a definition provided by Andersen et al. (1990) who argue that any description of a coherent method should include the following elements:

- Application area
- Perspective
- Guidelines:
    - Techniques
    - Tools
    - Principles for organisation

Application area refers to what type of development activities the method is intended for, i.e. the scope of the method. The design of one type of system, e.g. a website, may require a different method than the design of a very different system, e.g. an enterprise-wide information system (Andersen et al. 1990). Grudin (1991) suggests a similar distinction in his framework of types of system development activities related to in-house, contract or product development projects, as well as the range of coverage of the development activities for this type.

A method is built on some basic assumptions about technology design – and the world in general, e.g. that design should be carried out close to the user so that the user can participate in design decisions. This *perspective* makes the basis for guiding principles that constitute the backbone of the method. Participatory Design methods typically include perspectives on design and information technology that favour user participation.

The *guidelines* are recommendations for how to carry out the design process. For Participatory Design methods this typically includes which type of users (and stakeholders in general) to include; how to involve users in core activities; how to resolve conflicting views on the functionality and/or form of the products. The *techniques* typically explain how to go about carrying out specific activities, while the *tools* are concrete instruments supporting the techniques. Participatory Design includes techniques for investigating current practices, with tools for creating descriptions (and other intermediary products) or for facilitating creative workshops where users collaborate with designers on envisioning future work systems and future information technology support. The third type of guideline is *principles for organisation*: how to distribute and coordinate work tasks in the design process, how to organise the planned set of interrelated activities, and who to involve in the design.

Based on this description of a method, this chapter primarily discusses this perspective and the way a Participatory Design perspective influences how the design is planned and carried out. The perspective constitutes, in other words, whether you are doing Participatory Design or not, while the guidelines describe how to conduct and carry out a Participatory Design process. Methods include guidelines in terms of tools, techniques and principles for organisation, but this chapter only briefly mentions these since tools and techniques are the subject for the next chapter. The application area will be discussed in particular as part of the challenges at the end of the chapter. Using Grudin's (1991) concepts we can say that Participatory Design methods traditionally were developed for in-house and custom development 'in which the developers and users work under the same corporate roof' (ibid., p. 62), and (to some degree) for contract development where the use context is known and access to users lasts over some time. The target of Participatory Design methods typically is socially embedded systems, rather than technical embedded systems steering a technical device which in turn is socially embedded. As shown in previous chapters, the subject area of Participatory Design methods has typically been professional work, be it nurses, graphic workers or landscape architects; while in the new millennium there has been a movement to also include application areas outside of work, like public services, leisure, sports and community-based organisations (see Chapter 8).

Concepts and models

Information technology design is a process where both the design result and the design process are designed. Andersen et al. (1990) suggested dimensions of the work that need to be addressed in the process, covering the dimensions of process–product, current situation–future situation and managing–performing. Figure 6.1 illustrates the different activities that need to be planned and how they influence each other.

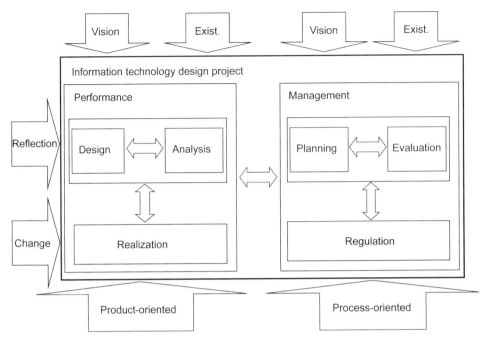

Figure 6.1 Dimensions of information technology design (based on Andersen et al. 1990)

Information technology design includes two types of work: developing an information technology system – performing systems design – and managing the process. Both performance and management include activities oriented towards the current state of affairs as well as the future: performance includes analysing the current situation and designing the future situation, while management involves evaluation of the current situation and planning the future. Analysis and design are reflective activities, as are planning and evaluation. Information technology design also includes change-oriented activities: realisation of the design in a concrete, running system and, in management, regulating the plans according to the situation at hand. The three dimensions – product–process, existing situation–future, and reflection–change – characterise information technology design as a work process and hence the knowledge and skills that designers need and utilise in their work. We can see that Participatory Design influences all of the mentioned dimensions and all the activities in the process. Participatory Design methods address how these dimensions are handled when users are to be involved.

Participatory Design methods: examples

There is a vast number of techniques and tools for Participatory Design, but few methods. In a historical overview of methods and approaches within Participatory Design, Kensing (2003) concludes that there are few full-blown methods proposed within the Participatory Design tradition, whereas there are many techniques and tools. The early Participatory Design projects (see Chapter 2) had a strong political nature and developed approaches aimed at ways of helping various groups (re-)gain rights or influence decisions regarding the introduction of new technology in the workplace. In relation to Participatory Design methods, some researchers in Scandinavia would emphasise the political roots of the trade union projects (e.g. Bansler 1989), while others emphasise the focus on people (e.g. Nurminen 1988). However, only a few studies discuss the historical links between Participatory Design method development and deeper sociocultural perspectives (see e.g. Boland 1998; Bratteteig 2004).

Many of the Participatory Design projects in the early or mid-1980s were aimed at developing tools, techniques and methods for design approaches where all participants, including future users, could participate on equal terms in the design of technical solutions. According to Kensing (2003), Participatory Design methods originate from this type of project, and they embed a distinct set of Participatory Design principles and perspectives in contrast to other acknowledged methods that might include Participatory Design techniques and tools, like ETHICS developed earlier by Mumford (1983) or Multiview (Wood-Harper et al. 1985; Avison and Wood-Harper 1990).

In this section we present four Participatory Design methods providing guidelines for carrying out a Participatory Design project. They have all been widely recognised in the literature and they illustrate important perspectives in Participatory Design as such and in a historical perspective.

STEPS

One of the early conceptual contributions to Participatory Design methods was the work of Christiane Floyd and her group at Hamburg University and their STEPS process model. STEPS – Software Technology for Evolutionary Participatory Systems Development (cf. Floyd, Reisin and Schmidt 1989) – was based on empirical studies of systems development practices and can be regarded as a methodological frame combining Participatory Design and software engineering with a focus on custom development of new software made 'from scratch'. The STEPS process model is based on the insight that technical construction of software cannot be separated from its quality-in-use. Information technology design is understood as a design process shaping both the technical artefact and its context of use. See Figure 6.2.

The *application area* is software development for socially embedded systems with a special emphasis on co-development of usage and technology. STEPS provides a methodological framework that needs to be complemented by specific tools and techniques to facilitate the collaborative design.

The central *perspective* is to facilitate the co-development of usage and software as a joint design and exploratory learning process. Programs are tools for people, and both the technical system and the work system need to be considered during development. Software quality is determined in use. The development process is designed as an iterative one, where evolutionary prototypes of the software are the central design artefact mediating a mutual learning process. The emphasis is on adapting the process according to the evolving requirements. This design perspective was prepared by proposing a paradigm change in software engineering from a 'product-oriented paradigm' to a 'process-oriented paradigm' (Floyd 1987, 1992).

STEPS was intentionally designed to be further refined to fit a specific project: the basic feature is a software development cycle, which is established under the joint responsibility of users and designers. Each cycle combines development and application of the software. It acknowledges activities of users and activities of designers, as well as joint activities. The basic cyclic strategy needs to be adapted to the situation at hand. Likewise, the model only defines a minimum of intermediary products to be complemented with what is deemed suitable for a specific project. The design process is subject to design as well. Designers and users together decide on the scope of the revision, and on the specific tools and techniques applied for the collaborative design resulting in additional intermediary products. Basically any method,

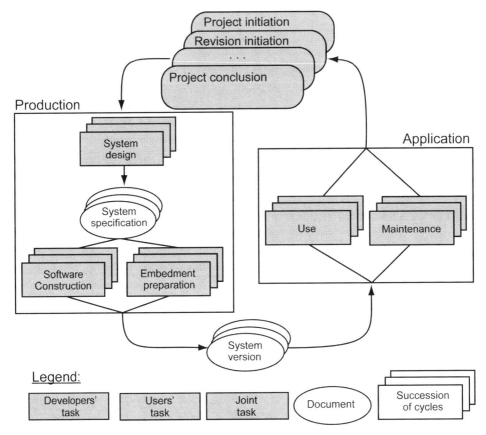

Figure 6.2 The STEPS model (Floyd, Reisin and Schmidt 1989). With kind permission from Christiane Floyd and Springer Science+Business Media

technique or tool can be applied together with the STEPS framework as long as it allows for evolutionary modelling (Floyd, Reisin and Schmidt 1989).

The system design is also specified as a joint activity of users and designers. The design result informs, on the one hand, the implementation of the software by designers. On the other hand, it provides input for the preparation of the use context in which the system will be deployed. The concrete usage of the system and the maintenance informs the next design cycle.

By specifying joint responsibilities as well as role-specific responsibilities, STEPS recognises the need to bring heterogeneous perspectives from users and designers to bear on the design. This is even more important because the design perspective on software development takes requirements not as a given but as a subject for analysis. Rather, requirements need to be gradually established in anticipative, constructive and evaluative steps carried out by designers and users in interaction (Floyd, Reisin and Schmidt 1989). Likewise, design is not understood as the achievement of predefined goals, but 'is guided by insights emerging in the actual process' (ibid., p. 54). The collaborative design process allows the designers to build a theory (Naur 1985) that enables them to relate the implementation of the software to its use context, as users develop an understanding of how the software can support their work practices. The different activities are seen as different domains of discourse that carry logical dependencies, but that are all relevant throughout the development cycle. In the 1980s, STEPS was already challenging the temporal order of activities as defined earlier by the waterfall model (Royce 1970).

Summing up, STEPS is designed as a methodological framework emphasising not only the Participatory Design of the software artefact, but also the co-determination of the software development process. Its basic structure emphasises mutual learning between users and designers, and both work context and technology are seen as subject to the evolutionary design. The framework does not define what specific tools and techniques to use but provides criteria to select and deploy whichever the participants find necessary.

MUST

MUST (a Danish acronym for theories and methods of initial analysis and design activities) is a Participatory Design method that was developed by researchers from Roskilde University based on 13 projects with Danish, American and multinational companies over a time span of a decade (Bødker et al. 2004). The method encourages a business-oriented and socially sensitive approach that takes into consideration the specific organisational context as well as first-hand knowledge of users' work practices, and it allows all stakeholders – users, management and other staff – to participate in the process. The method has been commercially applied by a large number of private companies and public organisations (Kensing 2000; Bødker et al. 2011).

The core idea behind the research that resulted in the MUST method was to develop a Participatory Design approach responding to contemporary business needs and conditions for information technology projects. New information technology has moved from the 'back office' (accounting, inventory control, payroll) to the 'front office', supporting knowledgeable and often also quite powerful users like caseworkers or clinicians, who are in direct contact with citizens. In-house development (Grudin 1991) has to a large extent become history: today information technology is procured by a user organisation from a vendor that typically develops the information technology systems by engaging in global outsourcing and off-shoring arrangements. Information technology projects involve building systems – no longer from scratch – but more as assemblages of commercial off-the-shelf, ready-made products, or by applying highly configurable enterprise-wide systems or tailorable generic packages. Furthermore, an information technology project may often include investigating and providing the background information for organisational decision-making concerning a suite of future information technology projects established through contractual bids and subsequent implementations projects.

MUST includes a conceptual framework for the Participatory Design process, emphasising the need for a thorough problem setting during the early stages of design 'that reveals goals, defines problems, and indicates solutions' (Bødker et al., 2004, p. 13). Ethnographic studies of use practices are included, and formal or technical descriptions are deferred to a succeeding implementation. MUST is – similar to STEPS – presented as a 'meta-method', i.e. in every design project the participants have to design the project using MUST as a resource for action (Suchman 2007). MUST provides four types of resources for this: (a) well-defined concepts to help designers understand and frame the situation; (b) a particular perspective formulated as four Participatory Design principles forming the backbone of the method; (c) suggestions for how to organise the design project in four phases; and (d) a set of techniques and tools for specific activities, including meta-guidelines to help in selecting and tailoring techniques or tools to specific purposes; see Figure 6.3. In the following the four core Participatory Design principles are highlighted.

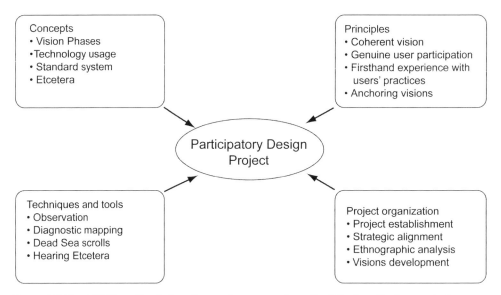

Figure 6.3 The MUST method's four types of resources for a Participatory Design project

Coherent visions for change

According to MUST, the objective of a design project is to achieve sustainable change by introducing new information technology systems. 'Visions' play a central role in describing future information technology systems and their use. The result of a design project is one or more coherent visions for change in the company in question and in relation to its environment. 'Coherenc' refers to a call for developing each vision to strike a balance between information technology system(s), organisation of work, and the qualifications users need to perform their job with the help of the proposed information technology systems in the proposed work organisation. The method systematically relates its overall activities and results to such coherent visions for change.

Genuine user participation

This principle calls for the active participation in the design project of organisational members ('users'). In subscribing to both political and pragmatic arguments for participation (see Chapter 1), MUST acknowledges the challenges established by current business contexts: in large companies, not all employees can be involved in the design project – a design project thus has to rely on representation of users; experienced users are hard to involve because they are needed in daily operations. In such circumstances, open criteria for participation are essential, as is anchoring the intermediary and end results from the design project. Further, mutual learning as a principle is applied to ensure that all participants and their knowledge are genuinely accounted for. MUST applies a framework for mutual learning (see Table 6.1) as a guide to support different kinds of mutual learning situations.

First-hand experience with work practices

As discussed in Chapter 5, ethnographic techniques have come to play an important role in Participatory Design in getting access to concrete experience and other elements of tacit knowledge involved in work and use of information technology. Trying to overcome the classic say/do problem and its many dimensions in design projects by applying ethnographically inspired techniques is a vital part of the MUST method. The method suggests that designers observe and participate in users' in situ practices as part of understanding current practices or experience from using early prototypes in work-like settings. Seeing how work – or another practice – as a social activity is different from descriptions, prescriptions or visions is basically a major tenet from first-hand encounters that brings a rich body of knowledge to any design project. Such insights can be used to challenge current understandings or early design visions as well as for deriving new designs.

Anchoring visions

This principle involves ensuring that stakeholders understand and support the design project's goals, visions and plans. The idea is that when the domain of the design project is large and complex, the project needs to communicate and solidify findings and proposals among the larger group encompassing the organisation's employees as well as top management (Simonsen 2007). The various representations of the existing situation and visions of desired change are perceived and interpreted individually and differently by the people to whom they are presented. Thus, it is suggested to communicate representations that provide the most coherent image, as interpreted by the participants in the Participatory Design project, to the stakeholders that are not directly involved in the project. This includes (top) management, future users, and internal and external groups that at a later stage become involved in the technical and organisational implementation of the proposed visions.

CESD

The Cooperative Experimental System Development (CESD) approach is built on the results of several Participatory Design projects conducted by researchers from Aarhus University, where both theoretical and practical results have been developed (Grønbæk et al. 1997). The basis for this approach is the 'tool perspective' (Ehn and Kyng 1987), developed as a vision: to make systems that act as good tools for skilled workers (Ehn 1989). CESD is thus rooted in the Scandinavian tradition for Participatory Design (see Chapter 2). The tool perspective focuses on prototyping as a way to avoid making and using a technical language in communication with the users. Prototypes of varying fidelity are used as tools in analysis as well as in design.

CESD features cooperative and experimental techniques throughout the life cycle of an information technology system, from initial ideas to tailoring of the system for specific use contexts. The *cooperative* aspect of CESD covers workshop techniques that enable actors such as end-users, analysts, designers and programmers with quite different competencies to actively contribute to the development process. The *experimental* aspect of CESD covers the iterative approach where alternative futures are explored and compared through experiments with embodied design visions such as mock-ups and prototypes in work-like situations. Compared to previous Participatory Design approaches, CESD stands out with regard to three aspects: (1) it actively pursues a strategy of utilising experimental approaches in the analysis of existing practices (Mogensen 1994); (2) it applies the cooperative and experimental techniques also in the parts of the project where the main concern is technical design and implementation, i.e. designers with Participatory Design competencies and technical skilled designers cooperate throughout a project; (3) it pays explicit attention to the transformation of loosely specified design artefacts, such as mock-ups and prototypes, into properly engineered and documented computer systems.

125

Concerns

CESD suggests seeing activities as separate from concerns. At an abstract level, the category of concerns captures what a system development project is all about. *Management* is directed towards the project itself as a cooperative process concerning how it is established and sustained as work progresses and conditions change. *Analysis* focuses on the need to understand constraints and potentials in the user's practice with respect to technological possibilities. *Design* focuses on the creation and shaping of visions of technology in use; and *realisation* focuses on the realisation of the visions in technological artefacts and organisational changes. Finally the category of *computer supported work* focuses on the ongoing use and adaptation of computer systems and the work they support.

Activities

Activities are what goes on in a project, the concrete actions and situations: meetings, workshops, implementation of a prototype, etc. In various papers regarding Participatory Design, the focus has often been on activities and their abstract representation as techniques, such as future workshops, mock-up techniques and cooperative prototyping (Bødker et al. 1993; Grønbæk and Mogensen 1994; Kyng 1994). Activities and techniques are well suited for presentations of cases, for describing what has been done, as well as 'how to'. However, they are less useful in conveying an understanding of 'why and when'.

Conceptual model

In the centre of the top layer of Figure 6.4 are the project *activities*. The important and distinct CESD activities are workshop-based cooperative experiments and interventions. The activities unfold in the context of the involved domains: the practice of the designers and of the users, and the technology and the visions of technology in use.

In the middle layer, the *concerns* are shown. As indicated by the grey cone, concerns are realised through activities. One activity typically contributes to more than one concern, but usually an activity has one concern as its main focus.

Figure 6.4 also illustrates that project management is mainly – but only mainly – oriented towards the designer's practice, analysis towards user's practice, design towards visions of technology in use and realisation towards technology.

Finally, the project *assignment* – the task as it is understood by the project participants – gives direction to the concerns.

In 1997–8, the CESD approach was used in a large project designing and implementing (parts of) a comprehensive global customer service system for a large shipping company (Christensen et al. 1998), and has subsequently been deployed in a number of research and development projects.

Use-oriented design

In the Florence project (see Chapter 2), researchers from Oslo University developed an 'application perspective' emphasising the use context as the overall context of the information technology design – including the evaluation of the quality of the system (Bjerknes and Bratteteig 1988b). The approach is grounded in the future use – use before use – and differs from user-oriented approaches by being concerned with the activities and logic of the activities – the use – rather than the users. However, use is only accessible through users.

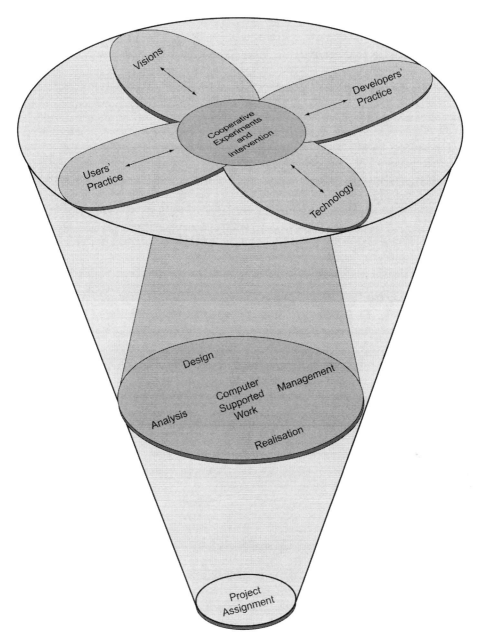

Figure 6.4 CESD conceptual model

The basic claim of this approach is that users may expand the space of design ideas because their imagination will be based on their experiences, which will be different from the designers' experiences (cf. e.g. Robinson 1993; Grudin 1994). The approach is explorative, aiming to postpone the decision about the design problem so that users and designers can collaborate (or negotiate) on the problem setting after they have got to know each other. The main emphasis in this approach is thus the early phases of design, and ends up with a stepwise refining of a prototype to an unambiguous specification for a system.

The guidelines for this approach include a range of techniques and tools for mutual learning, where the users learn enough about technical possibilities to develop a technical imagination (Bjerknes and Bratteteig 1987; Mörtberg and Elovaara 2010). Sketching and prototyping are ways to concretise ideas and visions as a way to explore them and as a way to communicate them. A basic perspective in this approach (as with the MUST and CESD approaches) is that users should not be forced to apply a technical-oriented language when describing their work (cf. e.g. Bjerknes and Bratteteig 1987; Ehn 1989). The process is organised so that the users and designers discuss (and negotiate) the problem setting and the solution, both being aware that they have interests in the future solution. The 'users' may actually include several different user groups, in which the process towards an agreed problem and solution is more complex (Bjerknes and Bratteteig 1995).

Figure 6.5 describes the iterative cycle of development, including the set of Participatory Design activities involved. Each activity can be carried out differently, utilising a set of techniques and tools fit for the aim of the activity and at the specific stage of design. The core characteristic of the approach is the way in which needs are identified and how the understanding of practice and the ability to concretise and materialise technical solutions interplay.

Participatory Design perspectives

We have now established what we mean by 'method' and we have provided short introductions to recognised Participatory Design methods. In this section we turn to discuss essential characteristics of Participatory Design methods. The Participatory Design worldview is basically

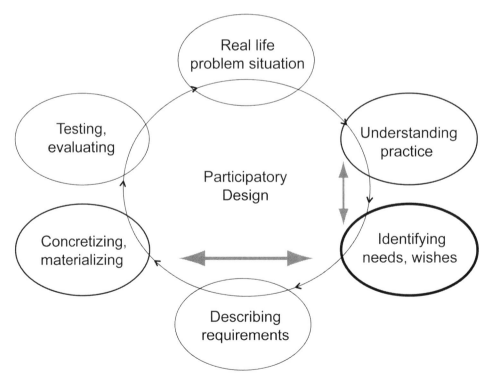

Figure 6.5 The use-oriented design cycle

concerned with the fact that information technology is never neutral. A technical solution is developed by someone for someone, and answers to a particular problem, which is defined by someone. The solution thus implements a particular worldview, and for pragmatic as well as for democratic reasons (see Chapter 1) the discussion of both what the problem is and what the solutions could be should be discussed where all stakeholders are invited. This basic worldview leads us to the three core perspectives: having a say, mutual learning and co-realisation. All three perspectives have been grounded in earlier chapters, and we discuss them here in relation to Participatory Design methods.

Having a say

The basic perspective in Participatory Design is that users are 'having a say' in design, and many chapters in this book discuss this, see e.g. Chapters 1, 2, 3 and 4. Having a say means having something to say as well as affecting the outcome of an activity with what you say – i.e. having an influence. To enable users to have an influence implies that the users need to be informed, they need to be given the chance to form and express their opinion, and they need to be given the power to influence the decisions in design. The right to be informed in due time before decisions about new technology are made and to express one's opinion was in focus in early Participatory Design projects and became part of Scandinavian work life legislation; see Mathiassen et al. (1983). The aim to enable users to have a say has consequences for how the design process is organised and which methods, techniques and tools are used. The design process includes a number of decisions, and of particular importance is the decision about what problems should be solved and how to solve them. The users need to be involved in the design process so that they can voice their opinion. Participatory designers share the rights to make these decisions among the whole team: a fundamental principle in Participatory Design is the sharing of decision-making power between all participants in the design process. Having a say therefore addresses power and participation in the decision-making in design.

Having a voice does not mean having a say

Taking part in decision-making involves more than having a voice: it means having a say. It is a challenge for Participatory Design participants to recognise that decision-making regarding new information technology in a particular context (e.g. a work setting) needs to involve a range of competencies: about the technical solution, about the context, and about the ways in which the technical solution can support the users in their activities. The Participatory Design process allows all types of competencies and expert arguments to have weight and respect. Both technical and use-oriented knowledge are needed.

Giving equal voice to different types of knowledge and at the same time respecting the different views – and worldviews – is not easy. In his theory about 'model power', Bråten (1973) argues that our worldviews and understandings are crucial for knowledge acquisition and decision-making. Our ways of understanding, i.e. our 'models' of the world, constitute the basis for how we can utilise information. Information needs to be organised, sifted and processed, and it is the processing of information into a meaningful context, just as much as the information pieces themselves, that gives us knowledge. Bråten therefore suggests that the model into which the information is interpreted or contextualised provides the originator of a model with symbolic power. Adopting somebody else's model will give the originator 'model monopoly' (ibid.). The model defines the universe of discourse and the scope of the decision-making. New information will only strengthen the model originators' position as they have a richer image of the universe of discourse than the model-weak party, who may not be able to utilise the new information to the same extent. When one model defines the discussion, the relationship between the 'model rich' and the 'model weak' is asymmetrical and continues to be so.

Model monopoly can be challenged by addressing the model power mechanisms. Changing the premises for model monopoly involves expanding the universe of discourse to also include areas outside the original model. Participatory Design methods do this by insisting on taking use practices as a basis for design, rather than any formal representation of use activities or technical matters. Inviting more stakeholders into the design process expands the universe of discourse, treating all worldviews as equally important – hence there is no one model of the world.

In a study of systems design practices, Borum and Enderud (1981) identified a set of mechanisms used to exercise power over the process as well as over the resulting system. Their conceptual model of how decision-making power can be exercised through design of the process is still valid:

- agenda control: what is discussed and who decides the themes;
- participants: who is invited in;
- scope: which solutions are possible – and hence, which problems are defined (and judged relevant) and therefore addressed;
- resources: time and people available.

To counter this kind of power, one strategy is to identify what is *not* on the agenda or which solutions (and problems) are *not* discussed, etc. – the missing elements point to power issues and make it possible to address them. Adding missing elements means widening the scope and expanding the universe of discourse. The silencing of particular issues is a well-known power strategy (Ås 1979; Star and Strauss 1999). Participatory Design therefore emphasises giving a voice to a broad variety of users and stakeholders.

Addressing power

The basic premise that Participatory Design aims to share power among all participants implies an interest to address power issues – or at least a willingness to do so. This leads a participatory designer to critically examine the established models (knowledge and perspectives) of the area of concern for the project: s/he needs to make sure that the model of the area of concern is not confused with the area itself, so that the originator of the model is given defining power and expertise of the area of concern. Participatory Design expands the area of concern in information technology design by also including use practices and several interest groups, often at several levels of society (e.g. different organisational units or levels and customers).

These principles have implications for the way the Participatory Design process is organised. Expanding the area of concern into a multidisciplinary area makes it necessary to get to know each other's expertise in order to recognise valid arguments in the shared decision-making process. Mutual learning (see below) is necessary for establishing a basis for shared decision-making about problem setting, envisioning and sketching:

- Problem setting: identifying and defining problems. Examples are future workshop (Kensing 1987), search conferences (Emery 1993), hearings and diagnostic maps (Bødker et al. 2004). The setting of the problem defines the space of possible solutions, hence Participatory Design needs to enable a discussion of what the problem is.

- Envisioning: developing ideas about possible technological designs as parts of future use practices, drawing on ideas based on technical features as well as ideas from the activity which is to be changed by the design. Various kinds of games and plays are used for generating ideas in addition to traditional techniques of brainstorming and problem-setting techniques (see Chapter 7 for examples).
- Concretising ideas through sketching or prototyping: a Participatory Design project meets more communicative challenges than a traditional project that has a more homogeneous design team, hence this is what most Participatory Design projects focus on when developing techniques and tools (see Chapter 7). Note that the concretisations of design ideas are used for exploring and mutual learning rather than for specification of a solution.

A basic principle is that the setting and solving of the problem are intertwined and cannot be separated – or put into different phases (Schön 1983). This means that Participatory Design methods are explorative – aiming for the inclusion of decisions about which problems are to be solved. In Participatory Design creative leaps and explorative moves are welcome and wanted.

Levels of influence

Participatory Design projects have sometimes been criticised for being small, local and isolated initiatives with little impact outside the project: often no other systems are involved and the initiative dies when the project stops (Kraft and Bansler 1992; Bødker 1996; Shapiro 2005). In order for a Participatory Design project to have lasting effects, it needs to be grounded in the organisation as part of a long-term strategy or to be part of a larger strategy that addresses more than one of many societal levels. By analysing early Participatory Design projects, Bjerknes and Bratteteig (1995) identify different analytic levels of influence: the workplace (local), the organisational, the institutional and the societal levels. Similarly, Gärtner and Wagner (1994) discuss corresponding levels as different arenas for participation.

The early Participatory Design projects typically made alliances with institutions like trade unions in order to ground the project in larger strategies, utilising the institutionalised structures to prolong and disseminate the results of the single project initiative. Historically (see Chapter 2) the Iron and Metal project included several small or local projects, as well as a national initiative using the local projects as input to develop new legislation to regulate the design and introduction of information technology. The UTOPIA project collaborated with the graphical workers' union in the Nordic countries to develop professional tools for graphical workers, while the Florence project collaborated with a hospital and developed a pilot system that worked as a blueprint for later information technology systems.

Several Participatory Design projects link the local initiative to a global strategy so the local project becomes a resource and an example of and for the global strategy (Bjerknes and Bratteteig 1995). Addressing several societal levels at the same time is, however, challenging and time demanding. The principles for organisation need to take into account how the single project can influence beyond the project borders. A local workplace has very different problems and perspectives from its contextual institution, whether it is a trade union or a work organisation. The Participatory Design project that manages to connect across arenas will have a larger and longer lasting impact.

Methodological guidelines for Participatory Design often address how to communicate with users, how to investigate and discuss their needs, how to involve them in developing design ideas, and how to iteratively test and redesign a solution together (see also Chapter 7). These are all necessary for users to be able to form and voice their opinions. However, the most difficult part for designers is to give some of the decision-making power to the users – and for the users to take that power (Bjerknes and Bratteteig 1988a; Nygaard 1996). To let users make design decisions during design requires that both technical and contextual aspects are part of the design discourse – opening up for technical decisions grounded in the use context. The basis for evaluation of the design result is widened. Similarly, technical decisions that affect and even change the use context will be part of the design-with-users. Hence the users find themselves responsible for design of a technical solution that will change people's work conditions. Having power implies having responsibility. The sharing of power to make decisions in design presupposes mutual trust and respect.

Mutual learning

Mutual learning is a core part of Participatory Design (see Chapter 1). The only way to gain mutual respect between different groups of people (like designers and users of technology) is to have them learn about each other so that they understand the different ways of reasoning. Mutual learning is the guiding principle for achieving this. The notion of 'mutual learning' is grounded in the fact that users know most about the activities into which the system will be embedded (they constitute the 'domain' experts). In order for designers to learn about the users' domain and activities, they need to familiarise themselves with the use practices in situ that have led to emphasising ethnographic studies as an important part of Participatory Design (see Chapter 5). Commitment to mutual learning, and guidance on how to achieve this, is one of the distinguishing elements of Participatory Design methods.

In any design process designers need to develop a relationship with the client so that they are trusted – and so that their envisioning of the future is trusted. Building trust includes several processes. Many of them have to do with getting to know and respect each other across differences in position, perspective, knowledge and skills (Bjerknes and Bratteteig 1988a). A basic element of this is seeing the other participants as skilled practitioners in their professional context. Planning for a longer period of mutual learning and shared knowledge building as a multidisciplinary team normally provides the necessary basis for trusting the co-participants to have relevant opinions, even though they are different and based on a different logic. Seeing the reason for the different logic is fundamental to respecting each other. Mutual respect opens up into sharing the power of making decisions concerning problem setting and solving.

Two-way learning

A Participatory Design process addresses an area in which no participant normally knows everything: the 'designers' know about technical issues and design processes, while the 'users' know the domain and use context, i.e. the activities and practices into which the new technology will be introduced. The focus area is the intertwining of technology and human activity, where knowing about technology and design does not give (enough) understanding of the effects of technical choices, and knowing the practices does not give (enough) imagination for possible other ways of doing things. This multi- and inter-disciplinarity makes a process of 'mutual learning' necessary: all participants need to know enough about the whole area in order to recognise and respect each other's expertise. Understanding other people's knowledge and perspective paves the way for discussion on equal terms and hence for making equally valid arguments in the decision-making processes.

The mutual learning implies that designers learn about the use context from the users, but also that the users learn about the technical possibilities from the designers: the mutuality here makes

Participatory Design different from other design methods. As knowledge and ideas develop continuously throughout the design process, designers are committed to work closely with users in ways where all involved – groups and individuals – contribute to the knowledge and hence the basis for making decisions in the design project. Users do not do what they say – and they do not say what they do.

Kensing and Munk-Madsen (1993) provide a framework that identifies three knowledge domains to be established in a design project: current work practice, technological options (the design space) and the new information technology applications. The framework suggests that knowledge must be developed at two levels: at an abstract level and through concrete experience (see Table 6.1).

The framework captures the principles in mutual learning. Users join the design project with knowledge and experience from their current practices (be they work or other activities), while the professional designers have knowledge of technological options and concrete experience with (some of) these. Through learning from each other, the design team develop the potential to generate ideas and visions about new information technology applications and possible new ways of working. In the beginning of a design process these are merely ideas about possibilities for new practices and how information technology can support them. Later in the process, the ideas are further developed, made more concrete and tested. The distinction between the two levels of knowledge captures what has been discussed above regarding theories-in-use, espoused theory and the need for ethnographic studies: users do not do what they say, and they do not say what they do (Argyris and Sohön 1974). Hence, an overview of technological options is not enough, we also need concrete experiences. Both levels are important, and in the design activities we have to consciously move between the two types, as they are interrelated. The emphasis on mutual learning influences how the project is organised and carried out, which techniques and tools to use, and how the design object is given its form and function (Bødker et al. 2004).

Co-realisation

The third basic perspective is involvement in design, or co-realisation. Because of the fact that it is difficult for users to imagine technical possibilities, Participatory Design emphasises different ways of visualising possible solutions, with prototyping as the most important technique. Using prototypes – tangible artefacts – to enable co-construction and learning through sharing concrete experiences of a new imagined artefact became an early 'branding' of Participatory Design methods. Pretending to be in a work-like context and utilising the work knowledge enables the users to better evaluate the adequacy of the functionality and form of a suggested design solution. A tangible artefact makes it easier to imagine the consequences of a design suggestion than would an abstract description. Users can utilise their professional competence and experience in the evaluation of a design suggestion, both as an artefact in their work and as a possibility for doing their work differently.

Table 6.1 Knowledge domains for mutual learning (adapted from Kensing and Munk-Madsen 1993)

	Current practices	Practices with new technology	Technological options
Abstract knowledge	Relevant descriptions	Visions and design proposals	Overview of technological options
Concrete experience	Concrete experience with current practices	Concrete experience using new technology	Concrete experience with technological options

Speaking their own language

Design-oriented Participatory Design projects from the 1980s developed a range of techniques and tools for Participatory Design. The perspective underlying these techniques was that users should be able to express themselves in their own ways and not adopt any abstract formal language – even if this meant showing instead of telling. The concept of 'tacit knowing', i.e. personal, experienced knowledge (Polanyi 1966), was introduced as a concept in Participatory Design (Ehn 1989). Both the UTOPIA and the Florence projects originally introduced paper mock-ups or 'cardboard computing' as ways to facilitate the feeling for a solution-in-the-making.

An early concern of Participatory Design was that classic design techniques and tools forced users into using a design language when describing their work, hence adopting the perspective implemented in the language (Ehn 1989; Nygaard 1996). As a consequence of this view, it became important to let the users maintain their language – or even enable them to communicate without speaking, by doing. Participatory Design projects developed techniques and tools in which the language to describe use practice was based on concepts and language from the use context, advocating 'home-made' description techniques aimed at understanding the use context, rather than descriptions aimed at specifying the system. It became important to have techniques and tools for de-scribing rather than pre-scribing processes, for analysis rather than design (Nygaard 1986). Language is power, thus being able to speak one's own language becomes a way to avoid 'model monopoly' and to expand the universe of discourse (see Ehn 1989; Dittrich 1997). The emphasis on user knowledge 'in the doing', mainly referring to non-verbal and not explicable knowledge (Polanyi 1966), suggested that mutual learning of that knowledge also had to be 'a doing action' rather than a description. This led to two characteristics of Participatory Design: a strong emphasis on observation of user practices in the field, and the development of techniques and tools for ways of communicating about existing and future work situations through games, demonstrations and walkthroughs (see Chapter 7). In this way users could use their own language to communicate with designers about the future of their work.

Intertwining analysis and design

It is often difficult to tell the difference between analysis and design in Participatory Design: demonstrations and prototypes can also be used as tools for analysis, for exploring the use context. Furthermore, analysis and design are more intertwined when design is carried out stepwise, when analysis and design are integrated into each step: we understand the situation, we make a design suggestion, and we analyse and evaluate – understand the new situation – and then make this a basis for a new design suggestion (Schön and Wiggins 1992). A closer connection between analysis and design makes it possible for all participants to engage in the moves between understanding and exploring new possibilities: the understanding develops during the design process, and all participants should be able to take part in this development. In this way, users 'who do not know what they want before they see it' can see various possibilities open up and hence develop a sense and an opinion of what they really want.

Iterative prototyping approaches are most often described as an iterative process reflecting a hermeneutic circle, as in the task–artefact cycle (Carroll et al. 1991). This occurs when the new system (artefact) and the task it is developed to support interact and mutually define each other: 'A task implicitly sets the requirements for the development of artefacts to support it; an artefact suggests possibilities and introduces constraints that often radically redefine the task for which the artefact was originally developed' (ibid., p. 97).

Participatory Design uses prototypes both as techniques for analysis – understanding the use context and the technical possibilities better – and for design – trying out ideas for new technical solutions. This differs from the normal conception of analysis as a reflective activity without experimenting or intervention involved in the analysed practice. Participatory Design aims to actively involve users in the analysis as active subjects, and the analysis becomes not only a joint activity of understanding the contextual conditions for the design, but also an activity of exploring opportunities for change. When we become more aware of the taken-for-granted aspects of current practice, it is easier to investigate constraints and potentials with respect to possibilities for change, and in particular identifying durable structures and structures that most likely will change. In this sense, mutual learning also provides a basis for learning about one's own practice. Reflecting on the work as a part of a mutual learning process can make procedures, skills, assumptions, etc., that are involved in the work, come to the foreground and hence be subject for evaluation and change (Mogensen 1992). Questioning the taken-for-granted – and in essence challenging it – can lead to new understandings of current practices as well as to new opportunities for change.

Participatory Design methods hence emphasise using both concrete experience and abstract descriptions of knowledge: the concrete experiences are necessary for concrete discussions about future (work) activities and for judging the relevance of abstract descriptions, and the abstract descriptions are necessary for discussing the larger picture and how a new technical solution will affect the organisation as a whole (Bødker et al. 2004).

Challenges to Participatory Design methods

The challenges discussed in this section address how to carry out Participatory Design in the light of recent technological and societal developments – while maintaining its overall perspectives and ambitions. In doing so, we point to a number of challenges and identify work within Participatory Design that addresses these challenges. Today information technology has entered almost all sociocultural practices, meaning that Participatory Design methods have new arenas to cover. There is a need for addressing new *application areas*, like service design, infrastructural design and design for leisure and the home. The *principles for organising* Participatory Design shift when conditions for accessing users change. Establishing cooperation with users who are constantly 'on the move', or where the place where they 'work' is inaccessible (such as in their home), presents different challenges from a group of employers and management in an organisation and at a particular workplace. Participatory Design also needs to be *organised* differently when the work context or the design context is distributed: when the users are permanently in different places or the design process is distributed among several different design contexts. Finally, the perspective changes as technology develops and the world changes. Transferring the Participatory Design perspective more into design of consumer products challenges existing Participatory Design methods. Participatory Design has traditionally ended when the design result is handed over to the use context, but today it makes sense to widen the Participatory Design perspective to also include design in use – design-after-design – in which Participatory Design practitioners need to refine their approach and refine the visions resulting from the Participatory Design process.

Addressing new application areas

Many of the early Participatory Design projects were part of a larger work environment movement (based in Scandinavia and Europe), addressing work conditions and work tools for and with workers and their unions (see Chapter 2). Computers were used mainly in work organisations, and the users were skilled, knowledgeable people interested in improving their work conditions. They took the time to engage and participate in design projects. They were stable and able to maintain a long-term cooperation with designers.

Today, information technology is used everywhere, in a variety of forms and in all kinds of activities. The technical development has gone hand in hand with societal development, changing the range of contexts in which information technologies are used – and hence changing the range of application areas for Participatory Design methods. Many information technologies are used outside of the work setting: in the school and other educational settings like museums, in leisure activities (games, music, movies, social media, entertainment) and in the home. In contrast to workplaces, these use contexts present challenges for establishing access to users and their use context.

Mixed realities, migrating users and transitory commitments

A major feature of the early Participatory Design projects with workers as users was that the workers were located in the workplace: they show up every day for work, you get to know them and they know you, and they are interested and committed to improving their work conditions. Designing for public places (urban design) or public services (like e-government services) involves large, varied and potentially unstable user populations. The users are everywhere and nowhere, they vary in numbers, and they may have very little commitment to the place – or to a design project. Participatory Design methods that presuppose that designers and (the same) users meet over a time period for mutual learning and mutual respect are not easily applicable when the users have to be recruited from the public for a short time slot for each design session and with little or no commitment to the design project.

Many of today's application areas are complex mixes of very different elements, human as well as technical. Several projects have explored how Participatory Design can be used in designing digital parts or layers in an originally non-digital environment, like the museum, involving users – adults and children – in designing new digitally enhanced experiences (Samis 2001; Ciolfi and Bannon 2002; Taxén et al. 2004; Bannon et al. 2005; Hall and Bannon 2006; Hornecker and Stifter 2006; Dindler et al. 2010). The museum projects are aimed at exhibitions or exhibited artefacts, and involve museum employees in the Participatory Design process (curators, historians, etc.). On the audience side, many of the museum projects address children and therefore build on Participatory Design methods for involving children (Druin and Fast 2002; Lee and Bichard 2008). These projects are developing the experience base on which Participatory Design method development can be founded.

Participatory Design has also addressed mixed reality environments, i.e. environments where physical and digital artefacts co-exist and interact in real time, both as an approach and as a result. The Atelier project, for example, developed a mixed reality tool to facilitate participatory urban design with architects, inhabitants, the public and researchers (Maquil et al. 2007; Wagner et al. 2009). The mixed reality tool constituted a basis for a set of design approaches combining abstract and concrete reasoning utilising images, sound and text in the communication. The project in this way continues the Participatory Design research tradition of developing tools that support a greater range of communication forms between participants by removing particular obstacles or limitations for the communication. Participants with different communication styles can participate in the discussion using their preferred communication mode and influence the design result (Bratteteig and Wagner 2010).

Within service design, members of the public as well as municipal employees constitute the users (Dittrich et al. 2003). Projects developing e-government and public services have used

Participatory Design approaches mainly in collaboration with the employees (Dittrich and Lindeberg 2002; Borchorst et al. 2009; Sefyrin and Mörtberg 2009; Mörtberg and Elovaara 2010). Participatory Design has also been applied widely in the design of health services. Health services can be developed within a hospital context – for employees and patients – with Participatory Design approaches utilising the fact that both these user groups are present and committed (e.g. Bratteteig et al. 2010). A number of Participatory Design projects have explored how Participatory Design can contribute to the design of health services outside hospitals, in general practitioners' clinics and in the patients' homes, supported by electronic communication or with digital artefacts monitoring patients. Participatory Design methods are being developed to design such services, to design the service itself as well as the artefact (product) where the service is accessed (Bødker and Granlien 2008; Kanstrup et al. 2010).

A particular difficult application area for Participatory Design methods is infrastructure development (see Chapter 8): they are large and standardised, hence development of standards and following standards is necessary. Today the development of technology and standards make Participatory Design approaches only parts of a system, to configure a large-scale system to a concrete work environment, but using real data. Participatory Design shifts as the frame and scope of influence is only partly controlled by any local context: infrastructures by definition intersect several use contexts. Today a particularly interesting infrastructure development occurs when sensors are embedded in the physical environment, constituting an invisible infrastructure to be operated by users' movements (e.g. smart home solutions; see Lainer and Wagner 1998; Jansson et al. 2008).

Accessing private spaces

An interesting challenge for Participatory Design is designing systems for the home. The home as a place for home practices is challenging for outsiders to access, and methods, tools and techniques relying on mutual learning through observations and participation in the use context need to be adjusted. The difficulties of getting access to users in the home are more comprehensive than the difficulties of getting access to companies and organisations.

When mutual learning activities cannot be based on designers observing users, other ways of learning about the use context can be applied. The most commonly used approach is self-reporting methods (Hagen et al. 2006). Cultural probes (Gaver et al. 1999) can be used as a basis for interviews, with users aimed at learning about their practices and identifying their needs (Loi et al. 2004; Bratteteig and Wagner 2010). Various kinds of diaries and logging done by the users or automatic logging of user behaviour can be a means for establishing mutual learning. Involving people in Participatory Design in and about their homes and the selection of users are both challenging aspects and of vital importance (Kanstrup and Christiansen 2005). Mutual learning and mutual respect can be developed also in home contexts in a similar way to the early small-scale Participatory Design projects: developing an example of a system with users, to be used in that context.

Changes in the Participatory Design contexts

The conditions for Participatory Design change as the world evolves into global work organisations. Global work organisations have distributed teams as well as work units and work processes that are divided between different people and places. This poses challenges to Participatory Design methods that typically depend on collaborative techniques and tools based on proximity.

When the work context is distributed and the users are permanently located in different places, all sorts of collaborative work are affected (Hinds and Mortensen 2005). Permanently distributed teams in global work organisations can 'work around the clock', like a relay taking over work tasks as work hours end in one time zone and start in the next (Herbsleb et al. 2000). Global work organisations sometimes also distribute work tasks between units according to a predefined division of labour – organising sub-contractors in a large production system. Participatory Design methods have to address how to select representative users, and how to establish teams of users who know and trust each other. In projects crossing organisational units – or even organisations and countries – Participatory Design has to be conducted on different organisational levels and translated between levels as well as between units.

In their editorial for a special issue on Distributed Participatory Design, Öberg et al. (2009) acknowledge these challenges for participation 'originally developed with a focus on co-located design activities. This view of activity was developed to allow users and designers to collaborate face-to-face, building on mutual learning through the design process' (ibid., p. 23). Titlestad et al. (2009) report from experience in the HISP project, where information technology developed for one context with a specific user group has been adapted to other use contexts (see also Chapter 10). They suggest concepts such as scaffolding and boundary spanners for dealing with issues of diversity in terms of geography, organisation and roles. Networking of projects, allowing for the pooling of resources and exchanging best practices and tools while still maintaining local ownership of projects, is also a part of the suggestions for how to deal with these recent challenges (Titlestad et al. 2009).

Expanding the Participatory Design perspective

While early Participatory Design projects developed information systems in an organisational setting aiming at tools for skilled workers, the design of a consumer product has a different aim: to 'seduce' the consumer into buying the product through its first impression (Silverstone and Haddon 1996). A focus on the first meeting with a system typically emphasises the interface, the presentation and qualities like being easy to learn and easy to start using (to be achieved by classic usability guidelines, e.g. Nielsen 1993; Shneiderman 1997). In addition, Participatory Design traditionally stops when the design result is handed over to the use context, but today's information technologies can also be modified and customised by the users. Several researchers discuss how Participatory Design should expand to also include design in use – or design-after-design.

Design-after-design

Researchers working with Participatory Design have always been involved with and fascinated by the idea to provide users with the tools to develop or refine their tools themselves (Henderson and Kyng 1991). Few non-information-technology professionals develop their tools from scratch today. Now they use standardised tools that are highly 'configurable': the technologies increasingly allow for changes and modifications after having been implemented and taken into use. Information technologies design is 'industrialised' and we live in the 'era of configurability' (Balka et al. 2005). For example, the software products that are used as building blocks of information technology infrastructures are not developed as custom applications but procured as standard systems that are configured and customised to fit a specific organisation. Part of the design is deferred to the context of use (Patel 2003), where the user has the possibility to change and adjust the software. Such 'end-user development' (Lieberman et al. 2006) can range from simple programming of mail filters to the design of complex spreadsheet applications, and to the configuration of large-scale electronic patient record systems to fit a specific type of ward. In a Participatory Design perspective, configuration and end-user tailoring might have to be combined with an evolution of the base system, as the dynamics of the use context often necessitate changes beyond the predefined tailoring possibilities (Costabile et al. 2006; Eriksson and Dittrich 2007).

A supplementary strategy is to postpone some design issues to the use phase, suggesting that the users should 'finish off' the design. End-user development (Mørch and Andersen 2010) and meta-design (Fischer 2010) are conceptualisations of this approach to users 'designing after design' (A.Telier 2011). If we cannot imagine how the future practices will be, we need to postpone the finalising of the system.

Continuing design in use depends on the technology being a platform open for further development and not a finished or 'closed' system. Technically this is increasingly the case, through more and more flexible and configurable platforms. Such platforms utilise the growing penetration of industry standards, the embedded organisational and domain specific business logic (e.g. the Health Level Seven International standard (HL7) within the healthcare domain), as well as the world-wide flexible de facto standards for presenting information in the user interface (e.g. the Extensible Markup Language (XML)). Contemporary flexible and configurable platforms provide the technical means to supplement the method development within Participatory Design in a pivotal way. Iterations within the design cycle have traditionally been concerned with relatively small-scale prototypes used in workshop settings. Future Participatory Design methods are expected to extend the iterative approach to include implementations and real use of large-scale configurable systems (Simonsen and Hertzum 2008).

Conclusion

With the backdrop of a definition of *method*, this chapter has focused on a thorough discussion of the perspectives of Participatory Design methods – leaving the next chapter to present the vast repertoire of techniques and tools for Participatory Design. We have briefly presented a few methods as an illustrative background for discussing three core issues: power, mutual learning and co-realisation.

The power issue is essential to Participatory Design. Information technology design is never neutral, and we have highlighted the importance of users having a say in problem setting, developing ideas and implementing some of the ideas through sketching or prototyping. Starting with characterizing methods by their application area, perspective and their guidelines: tools, techniques and principles for organisation, we also identified the most characteristic feature of Participatory Design methods: their explorative element. Furthermore, by addressing levels outside a specific project – workplace, institutional or societal – sustainable elements of participation is grounded in the larger context of design-and-use. Another distinctive feature of Participatory Design methods is mutual learning: the designers learn about the use context from the users, and the users learn about the technical possibilities from the designers – the learning is two-way. The design space is explored jointly and creatively to design visions. Finally, co-realisation where users take active part in visualising and prototyping ideas and in learning about their qualities in use or in use-like settings ensure that users also have a say in the forming of the artifact.

In this chapter we also addressed some of the current challenges to Participatory Design methods. Participatory Design has moved outside its original context or application area: the work place. We referred to a few of the Participatory Design projects outside work settings, i.e. projects in educational domains, in museums, urban planning or leisure activities. In such application areas, access to use settings and users is different from accessing workers in a workplace and presents new challenges to how to organize and carry out a Participatory Design process.

Global work organisations, teams and work units are distributed all over the world and 'work around the clock' also challenge Participatory Design principles in various ways. Participatory Design projects like the ones we have referred to in this chapter make up the experience base for the development of new Participatory Design methods.

References

A.Telier (Thomas Binder, Pelle Ehn, Giulio Jacucci, Giorgio De Michelis, Per Linde, Ina Wagner) (2011) *Design Things*, Cambridge, MA: MIT Press.

Andersen, N.E., F. Kensing, J. Lundin, L. Mathiassen, A. Munk-Madsen, M. Rasbech and P. Sørgaard (1990) *Professional Systems Development: Experience, Ideas and Action*, Upper Saddle River, NJ: Prentice-Hall.

Argyris, C., and D. A. Schön (1974) *Theory in Practice: Increasing Professional Effectiveness*, San Francisco, CA: Jossey Bass.

Ås, B. (1979) 'De 5 hersketeknikker', *Årbog for kvinderet*, 4: 55–88.

Avison, D. E. and A. T. Wood-Harper (1990) *Multiview: An Exploration of Information Systems Development*, Oxford: Blackwell Scientific Publications.

Balka, E., I. Wagner and C. B. Jensen (2005) 'Reconfiguring critical computing in an era of configurability', in O. W. Bertelsen, N. O. Bouvin, P. G. Krogh and M. Kyng (eds) *Proceedings of the 4th Decennial Conference on Critical Computing: Between Sense and Sensibility*, New York: ACM, 79–88.

Bannon, L., S. Benford and J. Bowers (2005) 'Hybrid design creates innovative museum experiences', *Communications of the ACM*, 48(3): 62–5.

Bansler, J. (1989) 'Systems development research in Scandinavia: three theoretical schools', *Scandinavian Journal of Information Systems*, 1: 3–20.

Bjerknes, G. and T. Bratteteig (1987) 'Florence in Wonderland', in G. Bjerknes, P. Ehn and M. Kyng (eds) *Computers and Democracy – A Scandinavian Challenge*, Aldershot: Avebury, 279–95.

Bjerknes, G. and T. Bratteteig (1988a) 'The memoirs of two survivors – or evaluation of a computer system for cooperative work', *Proceedings of CSCW'88, Portland, Oregon*, New York: ACM, 167–77.

Bjerknes, G. and T. Bratteteig (1988b) 'Computers – utensils or epaulets? The application perspective revisited', *AI and Society*, 2(3): 258–66.

Bjerknes, G. and T. Bratteteig (1995) 'User participation and democracy: a discussion of Scandinavian research on system development', *Scandinavian Journal of Information Systems*, 7(1): 73–98.

Bødker, K. and M. S. Granlien (2008) 'Participation and representation: a discussion based upon a case study in the Danish healthcare sector', in J. Simonsen, T. Robertson and D. Hakken (eds) *Proceedings of PDC 2008 Experiences and Challenges, Bloomington, Indiana*, New York: ACM, 190–93.

Bødker, K., F. Kensing and J. Simonsen (2004) *Participatory IT Design: Designing for Business and Workplace Realities*, Cambridge, MA: MIT Press.

Bødker, K., F. Kensing and J. Simonsen (2011) 'Participatory Design in information systems development', in H. Isomäki and S. Pekkola (eds) *Reframing Humans and Information Systems,* Berlin: Springer, 115–34.

Bødker, S. (1996) 'Creating conditions for participation: conflicts and resources in systems development'. *Human–Computer Interaction*, 11(3): 215–36.

Bødker, S., K. Grønbæk and M. Kyng (1993) 'Cooperative design: techniques and experiences from the Scandinavian scene', in D. Schuler and A. Namioka, A. (eds) *Participatory Design: Principles and Practices*, Hillsdale, NJ: Lawrence Erlbaum Associates, 157–75.

Boland, R. J. (1998) 'Some sources of the unity in plurality of Scandinavian research on information systems development', *Scandinavian Journal of Information Systems*, 10(1 and 2): 187–92.

Borchorst, N. G., S. Bødker and P.-O. Zander (2009) 'The boundaries of participatory citisenship', in E. Balka, L. Ciolfi, C. Simone, H. Tellioglu and I. Wagner (eds) *Proceedings of ECSCW 2009*, New York: ACM, 1–20.

Borum, F. and H. Enderud (1981) *Konflikter i organisationer: belyst ved studier af edb-systemarbejde [Conflicts in Organisations, Illustrated by Cases of Computer Systems Design]*, Copenhagen: Nyt Nordisk Forlag Arnold Busck.

Bråten, S. (1973) 'Model monopoly and communication: systems theoretical notes on democratisation', *Acta Sociologica*, 16: 98–107.

Bratteteig, T. (2004) 'Making change: dealing with relations between design and use', Dr Philos. dissertation, Department of Informatics, University of Oslo.

Bratteteig, T. and I. Wagner (2010) 'Spaces for participatory creativity', in K. Bødker, T. Bratteteig, D. Loi and T. Robertson (eds) *Proceedings of the 11th Conference on Participatory Design*, New York: ACM, 51–60.

Bratteteig, T., I. Wagner, A. Morrison, D. Stuedahl and C. Mörtberg (2010) 'Research practices in digital design', in I. Wagner, T. Bratteteig and D. Stuedahl (eds) *Exploring Digital Design*, Berlin: Springer-Verlag, 17–54.

Carroll, J. M., W. A. Kellogg and M. B. Rosson (1991) 'The task–artifact cycle', in J. M. Carroll (ed.) *Designing Interaction: Psychology at the Human–Computer Interface*, Cambridge: Cambridge University Press, 74–102.

Checkland, P. (1981) *Systems Thinking, Systems Practice*, Chichester: John Wiley.

Christensen, M., A. Crabtree, C. H. Damm, K. M. Hansen, O. L. Madsen, P. Marqvardsen, P. H. Mogensen, E. Sandvad, L. Sloth and M. Thomsen (1998) 'The M.A.D. experience: multiperspective application development in evolutionary prototyping', in E. Jul (ed.) *Proceedings of ECOOP'98 – Object-Oriented Programming: 12th European Conference Brussels, Belgium, July 20–24*, Springer Lecture Notes in Computer Science, Berlin: Springer, 13–40.

Ciolfi, L. and L. Bannon (2002) 'Designing interactive museum exhibits: enhancing visitor curiosity through augmented artifacts', in *Proceedings of the European Conference on Cognitive Ergonomics* (Catania, Italy, September 2002), ECCE, 311–17.

Costabile, M. F., D. Fogli, P. Mussio and A. Piccinno (2006) 'End-user development: the software shaping workshop approach', in H. Lieberman, F. Paternò and V. Wulf (eds) *End User Development – Empowering People to Flexibly Employ Advanced Information and Communication Technology*, Dordrecht: Kluwer Academic Publishers, 183–205.

Dindler, C., O. S. Iversen, R. C. Smith and R. Veerasawmy (2010) 'Mission from Mars: a method for exploring user requirements for children in a narrative space', *Interaction Design and Children*, New York: ACM, 40–47.

Dittrich, Y. (1997) 'Computer Anwendungen und sprachlicher Kontext. Zu den Wechselwirkungen zwischen normaler und formaler Sprache bei Einsatz und Entwicklung von Software', PhD thesis, Frankfurt/M, Europäische Hochschulschriften: Reihe 41, Informatik. Bd. 27.

Dittrich, Y. and O. Lindeberg (2002) 'Designing for changing work and business practices', in N. Patel (ed.) *Evolutionary and Adaptive Information Systems*, Hershey, PA: Idea Group Publishing.

Dittrich, Y., S. Eriksén, A. Ekelin, P. Elovaara and C. Hansson (2003) 'Making e-government happen: everyday co-development of services, citisenship and technology', *Proceedings of the 36th Hawaii International Conference on System Sciences (HICSS), January 6–9, Big Island, HI, USA*, 5, p. 147a, DOI bookmark: http://doi.ieeecomputersociety.org/10.1109/HICSS.2003.1174328.

Druin, A. and C. Fast (2002) 'The child as learner, critic, inventor, and technology design partner: an analysis of three years of Swedish student journals', *The International Journal for Technology and Design Education*, 12(3): 189–213.

Ehn, P. (1989) *Work-Oriented Design of Computer Artifacts*, Hillsdale, NJ: Lawrence Erlbaum Associates.

Ehn, P. and M. Kyng (1987): 'The collective resource approach to system design', in G. Bjerknes, P. Ehn and M. Kyng (eds) *Computers and Democracy*, Aldershot: Avebury, 17–57.

Emery, M. (ed.) (1993) *Participative Design for Participative Democracy*, Canberra: Centre for Continuing Education, Australian National University.

Eriksson, J. and Y. Dittrich (2007) 'Combining tailoring and evolutionary software development for rapidly changing business systems', *Journal of Organisational and End-User Computing*, 19: 47–64.

Fischer, G. (2010) 'End-user development and meta-design: foundations for cultures of participation', *Journal of Organisational and End User Computing*, 22(1): 52–82.

Floyd, C. (1987) 'Outline of a paradigm change in software engineering', in G. Bjerknes, P. Ehn and M. Kyng (eds) *Computers and Democracy*, Aldershot: Avebury, 191–210.

Floyd, C. (1992) 'Software development as reality construction', in C. Floyd, H. Züllighoven, R. Budde and R. Keil-Slawik (eds) *Software Development and Reality Construction*, Berlin: Springer Verlag.

Floyd, C. (1993) 'STEPS – a methodical approach to Participatory Design', *Communications of the ACM*, 36(4): 83.

Floyd, C., W.-M. Mehl, F.-M. Reisin, G. Schmidt and G. Wolf (1989) 'Out of Scandinavia: alternative approaches to software design and system development'. *Human–Computer Interaction*, 4(4): 253–350.

Floyd, C., F.-M. Reisin and G. Schmidt (1989) 'STEPS to software development with users', in G. Ghezzi and J. A. McDermid (eds) *Proceedings of the ESEC '89*, Berlin: Springer Verlag, 48–64.

Gärtner, J. and I. Wagner (1994) 'Systems as intermediaries: political frameworks of design and participation', in E. Clement, F. de Cindio, A. M. Oostveen, D. Schuler and P. van den Besselaar (eds) *Proceedings of the Third Participatory Design Conference (PDC), Chapel Hill, North Carolina*, New York: ACM, 37–46.

Gaver, B., T. Dunne and E. Pacenti (1999) 'Design: cultural probes', *Interactions*, 6(1): 21–9.

Grønbæk, K. and P. H. Mogensen (1994) 'Specific cooperative analysis and design in general hypermedia development', in E. Clement, F. de Cindio, A. M. Oostveen, D. Schuler and P. van den Besselaar (eds) *Proceedings of the Third Participatory Design Conference (PDC), Chapel Hill, North Carolina*, New York: ACM, 159–71.

Grønbæk, K., M. Kyng and P. H. Mogensen (1997) 'Toward a cooperative experimental systems development approach', in M. Kyng and L. Mathiassen (eds) *Computers and Design in Context*, Cambridge: MIT Press, 201–38.

Grudin, J. (1991) 'Interactive systems: bridging the gaps between developers and users', *IEEE Computer*, 24(4): 59–69.

Grudin, J. (1994) 'Groupware and social dynamics: eight challenges for the developer'. *Communications of the ACM*, 37(1): 92–105.

Hagen, P., T. Robertson, M. Kan and K. Sadler (2006) 'Accessing data: methods for understanding mobile technology use', *Australian Journal of Information Systems*, 13(2): 135–49.

Hall, T. and L. Bannon (2006) 'Designing ubiquitous computing to enhance children's interaction in museums', *Journal of Computer Assisted Learning*, 22(4): 231–43.

Henderson, A. and M. Kyng (1991) 'There's no place like home: continuing design in use', in J. Greenbaum and M. Kyng (eds) *Design at Work: Cooperative Design of Computer Systems*, Mahwah, NJ: Lawrence Erlbaum Associates, 219–40.

Herbsleb, J.D., A. Mockus, T. A. Finholt and R. E. Grinter (2000) 'Distance, dependencies, and delay in a global collaboration', in *Proceedings, ACM Conference on Computer-Supported Cooperative Work, Philadelphia, Pennsylvania*, New York: ACM, 319–28.

Hinds, P. and M. Mortensen (2005). 'Understanding conflict in geographically distributed teams: an empirical investigation', *Organisation Science*, 16: 290–307.

Hornecker, E. and M. Stifter (2006) 'Learning from interactive museum installations about interaction design for public settings', *CHI 2006*, New York: ACM, 437–46.

Iversen, O. S. and C. Dindler (2011) 'A matter of motivation: designing engaging interactive technologies for museums', *Proceedings of ISCAR 2011*, Rome, 5–12 September.

Jansson, M., C. M. Mörtberg and A. Miriamdotter (2008) 'Participation in e-home healthcare @ North Calotte', in K. Tollmar (ed.) *Proceedings of the 5th Nordic Conference on Human–Computer Interaction, Lund*, New York: ACM, 192–200.

Kanstrup, A. M. and E. Christiansen (2005) 'Model power: still an issue?', in O. W. Bertelsen, N. O. Bouvin, P. G. Krogh and M. Kyng (eds) *Proceedings of the 4th Decennial Conference on Critical Computing: Between Sense and Sensibility*, New York: ACM, 165–8.

Kanstrup, A. M., M. Glasemann and O. Nielsby (2010) 'IT-services for everyday life with diabetes: learning design, community design, inclusive design', in K. Halskov and M. Graves Petersen (eds) *Proceedings of the 8th ACM Conference on Designing Interactive Systems*, New York: ACM, 404–7.

Kensing, F. (1987) 'Generation of visions in systems development', in P. Docherty (ed.) *Systems Design for Human Development and Productivity, Proceedings of the IFIP TC9/WG9.1 Working Conference*, Amsterdam: North-Holland, 285–301.

Kensing, F. (2000) 'Participatory Design in a commercial context – a conceptual framework', in T. Cherkasky, J. Greenbaum, P. Mambrey and J. K. Pors (eds) *PDC 2000 Proceedings of the Participatory Design Conference, CPSR*, New York: ACM, 116–26.

Kensing, F. (2003) *Methods and Practices in Participatory Design*, Copenhagen: ITU Press.

Kensing, F. and J. Blomberg (1998) 'Participatory Design; issues and concerns', *Computer Supported Cooperative Work*, 7: 167–84.

Kensing, F. and A. Munk-Madsen (1993) 'PD: structure in the toolbox', *Communications of the ACM*, 36(6): 78–84.

Kraft, P. and J. P. Bansler (1992) 'The collective resource approach: the Scandinavian experience', in M. J. Muller, S. Kuhn and J. A. Meskill (eds) *PDC'92: Proceedings of the Participatory Design Conference, Cambridge, MA, USA*, New York: ACM, 127–35.

Kyng, M. (1994) 'Scandinavian design users in product development', in *Human Factors in Computing Systems, CHI '94, Celebrating Interdependence, Boston, MA*, New York: ACM, 3–9.

Lainer, R. and I. Wagner (1998) 'Connecting qualities of social use with spatial qualities: cooperative buildings – integrating information, organisation, and architecture', in *Proceedings of the First International Workshop on Cooperative Buildings (CoBuild'98)*, Heidelberg: Springer, 191–203.

Lee, Y. and J.-A. Bichard (2008) 'Teen-scape': designing participations for the design excluded', in J. Simonsen, T. Robertson and D. Hakken (eds) *Proceedings of PDC 2008 Experiences and Challenges*, Bloomington, IN: Indiana University, 128–37.

Lieberman, H., V. Wulf and F. Paternó (eds) (2006) *End User Development: Empowering People to Flexibly Employ Advanced Information and Communication Technology*, Berlin: Springer.

Loi, D., M. Voderberg, B. Liney, S. Marwah, P. Manrique and G. Piu (2004) '"Live like I do" – a field experience using cultural probes', in A. Clement, F. de Cindio, D. Schuler and P. van den Besselaar (eds) *PDC '2004 Artful Integration: Interweaving Media, Materials and Practices*, New York: ACM, 191–4.

Maquil, V., T. Psik, I. Wagner and M. Wagner (2007) 'Expressive interactions – supporting collaboration in urban design', in T. Gross and K. Inkpen (eds) *Group'07 Proceedings of the 2007 International ACM Conference on Supporting Group Work*, New York: ACM, 69–78.

Mathiassen, L., B. Rolskov and E. Vedel (1983) 'Regulating the use of EDP by law and agreement', in U. Briefs, C. Ciborra and L. Scheider (eds) *Systems Design for, with and by the Users*, Amsterdam: North-Holland, 251–64.

Mogensen, P. H. (1992) 'Towards a prototyping approach in systems development', *Scandinavian Journal of Information Systems,* 4(1): 31–53.

Mogensen, P. H. (1994) 'Challenging practice: an approach to cooperative analysis', PhD thesis, Aarhus University, Daimi PB–465.

Mørch, A. I. and R. Andersen (2010) 'Mutual development: the software engineering context of end-user development', *Journal of Organisational and End User Computing*, 22(2): 36–57.

Mörtberg, C. M. and P. Elovaara (2010) 'Attaching people and technology: between e and government', in S. Booth, S. Goodman and G. Kirkup (eds) *Gender Issues in Learning and Working with Information Technology: Social Constructs and Cultural Contexts*, Hershey, PA: IGI Global, 83–98.

Mumford, E. (1983) *Designing Human Systems*, Manchester: Manchester Business School.

Naur, P. (1985) 'Programming as theory building', *Microprocessing and Microprogramming*, 15(5): 253–61.

Nielsen, J. (1993) *Usability Engineering*, London: Morgan Kaufmann.

Nurminen, M. I. (1988) *People or Computers: Three Ways of Looking at Information Systems*, Lund, Sweden: Studentlitteratur.

Nygaard, K. (1986) 'Program development as a social activity', in H.-J. Kugler (ed.) *Information Processing 86,* Amsterdam: Elsevier Science Publishers (North-Holland), 189–98.

Nygaard, K. (1996) '"Those were the days"? Or "Heroic times are here again"? *Scandinavian Journal of Information Systems*, 8(2): 91–108.

Öberg, K. D., D. Gumm and A. M. Naghsh (2009) 'A special issue editorial. Distributed PD: challenges and opportunities', *Scandinavian Journal of Information Systems,* 21(1): 23–6.

Patel, N. (2003) *Adaptive Evolutionary Information Systems*, New York: Ideas Group.

Polanyi, M. (1966) *The Tacit Dimension*, Garden City, NY: Doubleday.

Robinson, M. (1993) 'Design for unanticipated use … ', in G. de Michelis, C. Simone and K. Schmidt (eds) *Proceedings of the Third European Conference on Computer-Supported Cooperative Work*, Dordrecht: Kluwer Academic Press, 187–202.

Royce, W. (1970) 'Managing the development of large software systems', *Proceedings of IEEE WESCON* 26 (August): 1–9.

Samis, P. S. (2001) 'Points of departure: curators and educators collaborate to prototype a "museum of the future"', in *Proceedings of the Sixth International Cultural Heritage Informatics Meeting* (ICHIM 2001), Milan, Italy, 623–37.

Schön, D. (1983) *The Reflective Practitioner: How Professionals Think in Action*, New York: Basic Books.

Schön, D. and G. Wiggins (1992) 'Kinds of seeing and their functions in designing', *Design Studies*, 13(2, April): 135–56.

Sefyrin, J. and C. M. Mörtberg (2009). '"We do not talk about this" – problematic silences in e-government', *Electronic Journal of e-Government*, 7(3): 259–70.

Shapiro, D. (2005). 'Participatory Design: the will to succeed', in O. W. Bertelsen, N. O. Bouvin, P. G. Krogh and M. Kyng (eds), *Proceedings of the 4th Decennial Conference on Critical Computing: Between Sense and Sensibility*, New York: ACM, 29–38.

Shneiderman, B. (1997) *Designing the User Interface*, London: Addison-Wesley.

Silverstone, R. and L. Haddon (1996) 'Design and the domestication of information and communication technologies: technical change and everyday life', in R. Silverstone and R. Mansell (eds) *Communication by Design: The Politics of Information and Communication Technologies*, Oxford: Oxford University Press, 44–74.

Simonsen, J. (2007) 'Involving top management in IT projects: aligning business needs and IT solutions with the problem mapping technique', *Communications of the ACM*, 50(8): 53–8.

Simonsen, J. and M. Hertzum (2008) 'Participatory Design and the challenges of large-scale systems: extending the iterative PD approach', in J. Simonsen, T. Robinson and D. Hakken (eds) *Proceedings of the 10th Anniversary Conference on Participatory Design*, New York: ACM, 1–10.

Star, S. L. and A. Strauss (1999) 'Layers of silence, arenas of voice: the ecology of visible and invisible work', *Journal of Computer Supported Cooperative Work*, 8(1–2): 9–30.

Suchman, L. A. (2007) *Human–Machine Reconfigurations: Plans and Situated Action*, second edition, Cambridge: Cambridge University Press.

Taxén, G., J. Bowers, S.-O. Hellström and H. Tobiasson (2004) 'Designing mixed media artefacts for public settings', in F. Darses, R. Dieng, C. Simone and M. Zacklad (eds) *Cooperative Systems Design: Scenario-Based Design of Collaborative Systems*, Amsterdam: IOS Press, 195–210.

Titlestad, O. H., K. Staring and J. Braa (2009), 'Distributed development to enable user participation', *Scandinavian Journal of Information Systems*, 21(1): 27–50.

Wagner, I., M. Basile, L. Ehrenstrasser, V. Maquil, J.-J. Terrn and M. Wagner (2009) 'Supporting community engagement in the city: urban planning in the MR-tent', *Proceedings of C&T (Communities and Technologies) 2009*, University Park, PA: Penn State University, 185–94.

Wood-Harper, A. T., L. Antill and D. E. Avison (1985) *Information Systems Definition: The Multiview Approach*, Oxford: Blackwell.

7

Tools and techniques

Ways to engage telling, making and enacting

Eva Brandt, Thomas Binder and Elizabeth B.-N. Sanders

Participatory Design is not one approach but a proliferating family of design practices that hosts many design agendas and comes with a varied set of toolboxes. In this chapter we will give examples of toolboxes with the ambition to show that there is a richness of tools and techniques available that may be combined, adapted and extended to form the basis for yet newer Participatory Design practices. The chapter shows how the making of things, the telling of stories and the enactment of possible futures together provide the basis for forming a temporary community in which the new can be envisioned.

The introduction frames tools and techniques within Participatory Design and describes Participatory Design as various practices of participation. The following sections give examples of how designers and non-designers participate in Participatory Design practices through activities focusing on telling, making and enacting. The final section reflects on present and future challenges.

We present a wide selection of tools and techniques for Participatory Design, describing how they support participants in making, telling and enacting aspects of future design. The aim is to stimulate further proliferation of formats and procedures that may bring Participatory Design to new design challenges and to new designer/user communities. Our claim is not that tools and techniques have to be applied rigorously. Instead, we suggest that sensitivity to the coherence of making, telling and enacting provides sufficient grounding for designers (and non-designers) to make the tools and techniques relevant for whatever participatory action they are involved in.

This includes being aware of what is accomplished as particular tools and techniques become part of specific Participatory Design practices, finding out how these in combination can create formats and procedures that can create engagement and a common image of the vision or Participatory Design development task, and last but not least, create ownership for the results.

Introduction

There has always been ambivalence among practitioners of Participatory Design concerning offering tools and techniques for a wider audience. On the one hand, participatory designers pioneered new approaches to designing with users, such as prototyping, future workshops and design games that have become widely accepted and used in the design community at large. On the other hand, Participatory Design grew out of critique of mainstream design and technological R&D for not accommodating the multiple voices of future users. There is still a reluctance to have the contribution of the Participatory Design community reduced to stand-alone tools and techniques if these are not accompanied by what Sanders and Stappers have called a participatory mindset (Sanders and Stappers 2008).

Despite the ambivalence, the field of Participatory Design today continues to provide a vibrant environment for the discussion and dissemination of new tools and techniques. In the early years, tools and techniques of participation were seen as essential means to remedy a professional process of systems design. Today the tools and techniques are brought forward through practices of design participation in many other and very different fields, where they form constituent parts of the activities people are involved in.

The concepts of tools and techniques were still defined along the conventional lines of the systems design tradition in the MUST approach that provided a comprehensive guideline for systems design. Based on Andersen et al. (1990), technique is here defined as 'a specific direction for performing a certain activity. It may involve activities for data gathering, processing and presentation, or project management. Techniques may be used independently of how the design project is planned' (Bødker et al. 2004, p. 21). Correspondingly, representational tools are defined as 'suggestions for graphics, figures, and models to support the processing and presentation of knowledge contributed by a technique' (ibid., p. 21). In this terminology prototyping may be the technique and, for example, the 'maketools' suggested by Sanders may be the tools.

This way of conceiving of tools and techniques is in our opinion slightly deceptive. The reason is that it indicates that techniques and tools can be applied irrespectively of, for instance, the purpose and values of a specific project. Furthermore it seems that techniques and tools can be fitted into a larger set of methods more and less at will – precisely what the Participatory Design community wanted to caution against. For the skilled practitioner this problem is, however, hardly a real one as they have experience of appropriating different techniques and tools in various projects. Nevertheless, defining tools and techniques as done in the MUST approach ensures compliance with the conventional perspective on methods in systems design (see more on methods in Chapter 6).

As evidenced throughout this book, Participatory Design is today not one approach but a proliferating family of design practices that hosts many design agendas and comes with a varied set of toolboxes. In this chapter we will look into these toolboxes with the aim of showing that there is a richness of tools and techniques available, which may actually be combined, adapted and extended to form the basis for yet newer Participatory Design practices. What is essential is that tools and techniques are appropriated in a design practice concerned with the problems at hand. This means that the concern for choosing tools and adopting mindsets is less one of doing things right and more a question of being aware of what is accomplished as particular tools and techniques become part of design practices. The emphasis on practice, which we will develop in the following section, brings us well in line with what has been suggested by, for instance, Ehn (1993) and Löwgren and Stolterman (2004).

This chapter presents and reviews a wide selection of tools and techniques for Participatory Design, describing how they contribute to supporting participants in making, telling and enacting aspects of future design. By emphasising the contexts in which they have been used, the projects they have been part of and the design communities from where they originate, we hope to give the reader a sense of the lived practices in which they participate. This is not to invite replication, but to stimulate further proliferation of formats and procedures that may bring design participation to new design challenges and to new communities of designers and users. Our claim is thus not that tools and techniques have to be applied rigorously and by the book. Instead, we suggest that sensitivity to the coherence of making, telling and enacting in design participation provides sufficient grounding for designers (and non-designers) to make the tools and techniques relevant for whatever participatory action they are involved in.

The chapter is structured as follows. In the next section we argue for the value of understanding Participatory Design as various practices of participation, and that these practices include techniques and tools for engaging people in telling, making and enacting. In the three following sections different techniques and tools are presented in relation to whether they primarily involve project participants in telling, making or enacting. Thus there is a section that focuses on telling, another on making, etc. This is a way of structuring the many different tools and techniques. Still, since our main point is that Participatory Design practices include all three activities together, we provide short case stories in the end of each section to illustrate how various tools and techniques have been combined in actual projects. Following the sections on telling, making and enacting is a section called 'From tools to games: bringing it all together'. The final section points to future directions and opportunities, and suggests a number of research areas that future PhD students in design might want to consider.

Participatory Design is the practice of participation

The heart of Participatory Design is participation. Its origin is often associated with the groundbreaking work of American and Scandinavian researchers engaged with systems design and automation in the 1980s and 1990s (well reported in Schuler and Namioki 1993 and Greenbaum and Kyng 1991). What has been less frequently acknowledged is that the issue of design and participation had already been broadly voiced in the design communities in the 1960s and 1970s. For instance, at the second conference of the Design Research Society in 1971, design and participation was the overall conference theme (Cross 1971). Several scholars, including Cross and Müllert (see e.g. Cross 1971), who continue to be active in debates on design and design research today, at that time strongly argued for new approaches to design that could contribute to the inclusion and participation of citizens at large in design and societal planning. According to Wenger, participation in communities of practice may be understood as the 'complex process that combines doing, talking, thinking, feeling, and belonging. It involves our whole person including our bodies, minds, emotions, and social relations' (Wenger 1998, p. 56). More recently Binder et al. (2011) argue that two types of values can be seen to strategically guide participation in Participatory Design projects:

> One is the social and rational idea of democracy as a value that leads to considerations for proper and legitimate user participation – the very making of things. The other value might be described as the idea of the importance of making participants' 'tacit knowledge' come into play in the design process, not only their formal and explicit competencies – skills as fundamental to the making of things as objects. We could also think about this as the value of being able to express and share 'aesthetic experiences' in the pragmatic sense of embodied experience enforced by emotion and reflection.
>
> *(Binder et al. 2011, p. 163)*

The concept of practice figures prominently in the literature on Participatory Design. For instance, Ehn argues:

147

> Through practice we produce the world, both the world of objects and our knowledge about this world. Practice is both action and reflection. But practice is also a social activity; it is produced in cooperation with others. However, this production of the world and our understanding of it takes place in an already existing world. The world is also a product of former practice. Hence, as part of practice, knowledge has to be understood socially – as producing or reproducing social processes and structures as well as being the product of them.
>
> *(Ehn 1993, p. 63)*

We will argue that the everyday practices of users, whether at work or elsewhere, are explored and put on stage in co-design dialogues through various tools and techniques, but so are the practices of the other stakeholders participating in these dialogues. What is enacted in the participatory process is not only what Ehn has called 'a meeting of language games' (Ehn 1988). Practices of the participants come together to perform what may be envisioned through design, and in this coming together something new is formed, drawing upon but still distinctively different from the everyday practices the participants come from. Muller and Druin (2012) have talked about Participatory Design as the enactment of a 'third space' belonging neither to potential users nor to the system designers. This third space may literally be the space of the participatory workshop but it may as well be the social space encompassing the players of a design game or the collaborative construction of a prototype. Following Lave and Wenger (1991), we may think of this third space as in itself a community of practice in the making. According to Lave and Wenger, communities of practice are everywhere people are collaboratively engaging with an activity and the practice is kept together by a going back and forth between what Wenger calls 'participation and reification' (Binder 1996). Wenger and Lave originally coined the term 'communities of practice' to capture the dynamics of practices long lived and well established. Here they emphasized that tangible things such as decisions, procedures or tools were constantly examined and negotiated in a similar way to Orr's (1996) illuminating examples of how communities of technicians tell and retell 'war stories' of jobs well done and challenges overcome. This storytelling holds not only much of what is remembered but also clues to what should be done in the future. In a Participatory Design practice, the telling of the community goes hand in hand with the making of things that make the community imagine and rehearse what may be accomplished in the collaboration.

There are other sources to an elaboration of the concept of practice. With these brief hints to literature, which have provided an ongoing and valuable inspiration to the Participatory Design field, we also want to suggest that tools and techniques of Participatory Design must be appropriated by the temporary practices of participation.

In a particular design project, participatory tools and techniques can be seen as the scaffolding for the temporary community of practice in the making. They support collaborative enquiry into the intertwinement of the essential questions about 'what to achieve' and 'how to achieve it'. Bringing together a network of actors with different backgrounds, competencies, experiences and interests challenges participation. Susan Leigh Star (Star 1989; Star and Greismer 1989) has suggested the notion of boundary objects as key in maintaining coherence across various social worlds. Boundary objects are to be understood as objects that can give meaning to different participants even though that they have different professional practices and professional languages – different competences. Star and Greismer describe boundary objects as follows:

> Boundary objects are objects which are both plastic enough to adapt to local needs and the constraints of the several parties employing them, yet robust enough to maintain a

common identity across sites. They are weakly structured in common use, and become strongly structured in individual-site use. These objects may be abstract or concrete. They have different meanings in different social worlds but their structure is common enough to more than one world to make them recognisable, a means of translation. The creation and management of boundary objects is a key process in developing and maintaining coherence across intersecting social worlds.

(Star and Greismer 1989, p. 393)

Boundary objects can create continuity and homogeneity by incorporating different interest groups so that they can contribute to the design process. Thus they are important in creating a common language-game within the boundaries of the project.

The successful participatory process is a community of practice in the making. Participants must be able to make things that give this practice a presence in the world. Similarly, the participatory practice must be told and enacted to become alive and generative also of that which is not yet experienced.

The simple tell–make–enact diagram illustrated in Figure 7.1 should remind us that tools and techniques do not operate in isolation. The tools and techniques we engage with and the things we enact must form a coherent Participatory Design practice in order to keep alive what is gained of insights and what is won in imagined possibilities. In what follows we will lay out in more details what this means, with the important point that the triad of making–telling–enacting opens a myriad of possibilities for participation in design projects.

Telling activities as drivers for participation

In the 1980s both systems designers and workers' unions raised the question of participation and democracy at work. Computer scientists asked why office workers were not included in specifying what would be productive new work procedures. They organised study circles where union members could tell about and participate in discussions on how computer systems were best used in the office (Kensing in Greenbaum and Kyng 1991). Other researchers turned to traditional skilled work of, for example, the print shop, and invited workers to mock-up new computer-based tools that extended the skills of the workers instead of replacing them (Sandberg and Ehn, in Greenbaum and Kyng 1991). Method was a pivotal issue. However, contrary to the aspirations of the methods movement that assumed that transparency of methods would facilitate participation (e.g. Jones 1992), the new generation of participatory designers argued that the design process had to be reworked to accommodate ongoing prototyping (Floyd 1984; Grønbæk 1988) and designing-through-the-interface (Bødker 1990).

The rethinking of systems design as an iterative and cooperative process involving both professional systems designers and equally professional skilled workers from early on raised the issue of knowledge. Participants were obviously equally knowledgeable, but bringing the knowledge of computer systems and knowledge of skilled print production into productive dialogue with one another called for tools and techniques that could span the gap between separate knowledge domains. Ehn and Sjögren, who were also drawing on earlier work on urban and rural planning, suggested game-like formats and tangible representations of design artefacts that could make sense for both the programmer and the typographer (Ehn and Sjögren 1991) and similar tools and techniques targeting white-collar workers were developed by, for example, Muller (1991, 1993). Many of these games use visual material to assist the participants in telling about experiences and dreams by, for instance, building up their own everyday setting or illustrating the flow of activities in a simplified way. The games invite discussion about problems and

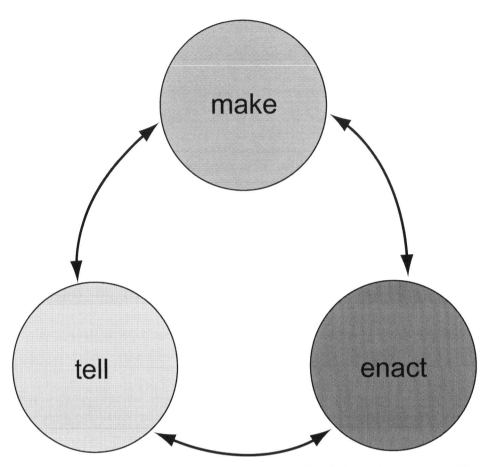

Figure 7.1 A Participatory Design practice entails tools and techniques that combine telling, making and enacting. The tell–make–enact diagram is circular with double-headed arrows to illustrate how the actions are connected, and to indicate that design process iterations go both ways round in the circle.

opportunities and provide a context that keeps the discussion grounded in everyday experiences. Still, the games typically produce an 'outcome' that visually can form the starting point for a diagramming of present and future practices that may translate into the world of systems design. See Figure 7.2.

Even though the Scandinavian tradition emphasised that design should be cooperative with an equal importance and responsibility for all stakeholders, the knowledge of system designers and, for example, skilled practitioners seemed to be of a different kind. Kensing and Munk-Madsen (1993) suggested distinguishing between abstract and concrete knowledge to draw attention to how the knowledge of practitioners was often embedded in the everyday work practice and how the transition from the present day to an envisioned future is not necessarily straightforward. Such considerations created what turned out to be a very productive link to mainly North American scholars and practitioners interested in the limits of Artificial Intelligence and the resurrection of practical knowledge (see, for example, Winograd and Flores 1986).

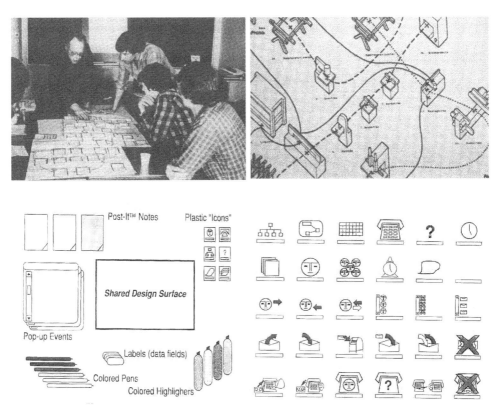

Figure 7.2 Top left: In the UTOPIA project, people involved in newspaper production played the Organisational Kit Game; a simple board game with sketches and text on small pieces of paper illustrating various tools. Top right: Production design using the Layout Kit Game (Ehn and Sjögren 1991). Bottom left: The PICTIVE design game. The design objects facilitate articulation of how the participants would like the systems interface to look. Bottom right: The PICTIVE plastic icons help the participants articulate how they imagine the new software system to work (Muller 1993).

Investigating existing (work) practices

A consequence of these insights was a growing interest in integrating ethnographically inspired fieldwork into the Participatory Design process (Kensing and Blomberg 1998). Bødker and Pedersen early suggested how to investigate workplace cultures by looking at artefacts, symbols and practice (Bødker and Pedersen 1991). Blomberg and colleagues explained the emphasis on the 'natives' point-of-view', holism and natural settings when conducting fieldwork, how to document the visits, and what to be aware of when interviewing (Blomberg et al. 1993). The purpose was, however, not to produce distant accounts of work practice, but rather to find ways for the system designer to engage in dialogues with the skilled people at work.

Julian Orr is one of the first anthropologists to make ethnography for the sake of design (Orr 1986, 1996). Orr's accounts of the role of community storytelling among office machine repair workers showed that these workers were not only highly competent, but also fully capable of innovating work procedures in order to deal with new technology. Orr finds that important 'aspects of the technicians' culture are their fondness for war stories and the eagerness with which they talk about machines (Orr 1986, p. 63). He draws the conclusion that the diagnostic process for copiers is essentially narrative, and that the diagnostic narrative is both a collection of various pieces of narration and the evolution of an understanding of the machine through talking.

Charlotte Linde (2001) has investigated the role of oral narratives in the expression and transmission of social knowledge at workplaces. She argues that stories not only recount past events but also convey the speaker's moral attitude towards these events. One of her main points is that work processes often are difficult to convey into stories. Instead, narratives are 'well suited to transmit the part of social knowledge that concerns history, values and identity' (p. 163). Linde concludes in line with Orr that the stories told at workplaces remain within the specific community of practice. They do not usually reach the communities of designers.

Several authors have suggested tools and techniques that bring the impulse from ethnography directly back into a participatory setting. For example Johansson suggests what he calls a participatory enquiry in which potential users together with designers create and produce accounts of ethnographic material from the practice of use (Johansson 2005). Together with Linde, Johansson reports on a game, which was designed to facilitate telling stories about imaginary situations that complement reflective understanding of everyday practice. The game materials are based on ethnographic video snippets from the users' everyday environments (Johansson and Linde 2005). Ylirisku and Buur (2007) give several examples of how the production of ethnographic video accounts could be done on site with a direct involvement in authoring and editing by the people studied.

Introducing change perspectives that cast new light on the well known

In a different direction other researchers have sought to enhance and expand the dialogue of participation between designers and users through introducing a change perspective casting a new light on the well known. In the 1970s Jungk and Müllert (1987) had already introduced the future workshop as an efficient technique for engaging citizens in change processes. The future workshop is a robust and relatively simple technique. At first a group of people, in a brainstorm-like format, list points of critique to their present-day situation. The list is produced collaboratively but without discussion or objections to critiques raised. In the next phase the critique is transformed to its positive opposite. In this part of the future workshop, more discussion takes place, and the participants are given the opportunity to develop a utopian perspective. The rule is still that criticism of the realism of the proposals is not allowed. In the last phase of the future workshop, the utopian vision forms the base for a plan for action, where participants discuss what can be done to move towards the vision, given the present-day circumstances.

Compared to other tools and techniques in Participatory Design, the future workshops do not engage representations or formats that point to the everyday contexts of the participants. The success of the future workshop is dependent on the participant's ability to state critique and utopian vision in a common language. Several authors within the Participatory Design tradition have used the future workshop as a structuring element in co-design dialogues, yet have added tools and techniques that facilitate a reflection on the everyday practice of participants. Kensing and Madsen (1991) have suggested introducing apparently foreign metaphors to participants, suggesting, for example, that a group of librarians evaluate their present-day work context through the lens of a factory metaphor or a storage metaphor, the point being that seeing the library as a factory or a storage facility enables the participants to become aware of how the well-known workplace is unique and different from other kinds of workplaces.

One can say that the introduction of metaphors and the rules of the future workshop share the employment of a 'what if' that produces a kind of estrangement of the familiar and that makes it easier for participants to talk about everyday experiences in a way that is also comprehensible for others. Halse et al. (Johansson et al. 2005; Halse et al. 2010) have pointed to the way this process of estrangement is relevant in both directions in the dialogue between designers and future users. The difficulty for people in a workplace or another everyday setting to describe their practice in a way that is communicative and inspirational for outsiders is not so different from the difficulties experienced by designers when attempting to open up a design space for mutual exploration. Mogensen (1992) suggested that designers might gain from making 'provotypes' rather than prototypes to prompt the dialogue with potential users but also to make designers reflect upon the design as more than a simple solution to a problem. The engagement of the 'provotype' has a clear resonance with the suggestions from Gaver, Dunne and Pacenti (1999) to learn from the art tradition of the situationists by playfully exploring and distorting images of present and future in the dialogue between designers and users.

We will end this section with a short case illustrating a specific Participatory Design practice. Tools and techniques for telling are often thought of as means for solely investigating existing practice. In contrast, in the following case, researchers from Århus University, Denmark, have combined using a fictional narrative as a telling activity in a participatory setting, together with making and enacting in order to spur innovation. It is a good example of how in new ways they have taken up and worked practically with the tension between tradition and transcendence, which Ehn pointed to as one of the core themes in Participatory Design (Ehn 1988). According to Ehn (1993), tradition and transcendence form the dialectical foundation of design in the sense that every design project has to find a balance between 'what is' and 'what could be'.

Short case: challenging tradition and transcendence through fictional narratives

Dindler, Brodersen and colleagues suggest using telling in the form of a fictional narrative as the overall frame for co-creation. The fictional enquiry technique builds on invoking a sense of suspended disbelief to fuel imagination in participatory prototyping (Brodersen et al. 2008; Dindler 2010). For instance, when collaborating with the Kattegat Marine Centre on creating new types of engaging experiences for their visitors, the authors used a fictional narrative that was inspired by the tale of the lost city of Atlantis (Iversen and Dindler 2008). A prototyping session that involved a family with two children also took place within the Centre. The first part of the fictional story related to the present. Employees at the Marine Centre had 'been noticing a strange phenomenon. In the morning, the employees would find wet footprints leading back and forth from the aquaria. A few days ago, the centre had received a message in a bottle' (ibid., p. 142). They gave the message from the bottle to the family. The letter in the bottle was from the King of Atlantis. He starts by saying that the people of Atlantis have been forgotten by humans for many years. He explains that what provides energy and life to the whole of Atlantis is stories, adventures and fantastic experiences. For years they have lived happily on the experiences at the Kattegat Marine Centre, but now it seems that the fantastic experiences are fewer and fewer. The King of Atlantis asks for help. In order to survive they need new fantastic experiences at the Kattegat Marine Centre, and they have sent a box of magic tools that can be used in whatever way the family members would like (ibid.; see Figure 7.3).

The aim of the fictional narrative was to establish a 'new universe where the normal structures of meaning and expectations are bypassed'. The narrative also includes a plot that sets the stage for action. The magic tools are meant both to inspire ideation and to be used as props for enactment. The box contained, for example, a mirror, a flute, an apple and a magnifying glass. Each family

Figure 7.3 Left: The message in the bottle was written as a letter from the King of Atlantis. In order for the people of Atlantis to survive, fantastic experiences need to take place at the Kattegat Marine Centre. Right: In the message the King of Atlantis writes that he has sent a box of magic tools. He encourages the humans to use the magic tools to create experiences that they would like to have at the Kattegat Centre (photos © Dindler).

member picked one or more magic tools and then found specific places at the Kattegat Marine Centre where they used the tools for further enquiry (see examples in Figure 7.4). As the final part in this prototyping session, scenarios of new experiences at the Kattegat Marine Centre were acted out in situ, with the family members imagining how the magic props would work. The ideas presented resulted in the functioning prototypes of the Fish Generator and the Digital Hydroscope (see Figure 7.4).

The fictional enquiry technique has a participatory prototyping design practice in the centre. The main activities in the prototyping session at the Kattagat Marine Centre are based on telling and enacting. The authors argue for using fictional narratives as the springboard and stage for change when involving people in imagining how different technologies can be designed and used for various purposes. However, in their work they stress that it has been important not to abandon existing use practices but to find ways of arranging constraints and possibilities in order

Figure 7.4 Left: The daughter of the family enacts her idea of a treasure finder to be used for finding hidden treasures beneath the floor. Middle: The mother enacts her idea of using a magnifying glass to zoom in on the details of various species. Right: Visitors explore the virtual ocean with the functioning Digital Hydroscope prototype later in the design process (Iversen and Dindler 2008).

to envision and stage a radical new place for co-creation for designers and users. They distinguish between anchoring elements that maintain a reference to current practice versus elements of transcendence. The prototyping session took place at the Kattegat Marine Centre, which anchored the participatory prototyping in the theme of the centre, and in the physical layout of the exhibition. The fictional narrative, the letter in the bottle from the King of Atlantis and the box with 'magic' items acted as concrete transcendent elements. The authors do not go into detail about the process of making the prototypes. Instead they briefly present two of the final functioning prototypes, which indicated that making is also an important part of their Participatory Design practice (for an elaboration of fictional spaces in Participatory Design see Dindler 2010).

The making of things as a means of design participation

Tools for making give people, both designers and non-designers, the ability to make 'things'. When making we use our hands for externalising and embodying thoughts and ideas in the form of (physical) artefacts. Such artefacts might describe future objects or provide views on future ways of living.

Three distinct approaches for making activities have evolved over time: participatory prototyping, probes and generative tools. Participatory prototyping has the longest history, having been introduced in the early 1980s (e.g. Bødker et al. 1987; Ehn 1988). Probes and generative tools were introduced in the same year (Gaver et al. 1999; Sanders 1999). The three approaches are distinct yet are not mutually exclusive, as the short cases at the end of this section will show.

Participatory prototyping using mock-ups and other low fidelity models is most often used in the early stages of the established design process. Making as prototyping presupposes that you have already identified the object of the design, e.g. you are designing a product or a device or an environment, etc. Thus, in the traditional design spaces, the focus has been on using prototypes to create representations of future objects to give shape to the future, i.e. to *help us see* what it could be.

In the emerging design spaces on the front end of the process, on the other hand, the focus is on using making activities to help us *make sense of the future*. In the early front end of design, making activities are used as vehicles for collectively exploring, expressing and testing hypotheses about future ways of living. Probes refers to a design-led approach that invites people to reflect on and express their experiences, feelings and attitudes in forms and formats that provide inspiration for designers (Gaver et al. 1999). Later applications of the probes concept provide information for designers, as a means for participation and for dialogue (Mattelmäki 2005). Generative tools are used in the front end of design to help non-designers to imagine and express their own ideas about how they want to live, work and play in the future (Sanders and Stappers 2008).

Participatory prototyping techniques

Making activities have a long history in Participatory Design practices where the creation of mock-ups has been an important tool in establishing a shared (concrete) language across disciplines. One of the most well-known projects from the 1980s that used prototyping is the UTOPIA project (Ehn 1993). It was a collaboration between the Nordic Graphic Workers' Union and researchers in Sweden. The goal was to introduce new computer technology into the newspaper industry. An important lesson was that when introducing and using mock-ups and other prototypes, the skilled workers could suddenly actively participate in the design process by actually doing, for instance, page make-up (Ehn 1993). Bødker and Grønbæk (1991) describe the approach taken in the UTOPIA project as one of 'cooperative prototyping'.

Christiane Floyd (1984) early stressed that the notions of prototypes and prototyping are difficult to define. The use of the terminology differs, as well as the purposes and application-oriented strategies. Floyd argues that within software development, prototypes are primarily a learning vehicle. She suggests three broad classes of prototyping: prototyping for exploration, where the emphasis is on clarifying requirements and desirable features of the system; prototyping for experimentation, where the focus is on determining the adequacy of a proposed solution; and prototyping for evolution, where emphasis is on adapting the system gradually to changing requirements (Floyd 1984).

Some more recent examples of projects that have made effective use of participatory prototyping follow. The examples have been chosen to show how broad the range of applications has become, from designing for computer-supported workplaces to city planning and architecture, to user interface design, to product design, etc. See Figure 7.5.

Within the Human–Computer Interaction (HCI) field, paper prototypes that use annotated sheets of paper to represent the screens are used to visualise user interface designs (Benyon et al. 2005). The value of 'paper-prototyping' and the use of Post-it notes as a means to quickly mock-up information architecture are now well-known design tools in the interactive domain (see e.g. Snyder 2003).

Joon-Sang Baek and Kun-Pyo Lee (2008) used two Participatory Design toolkits, Info Block and Info Tree, to explore how children would build information architectures for software services. They found that the information architectures built by the children (ages 8 to 12) differed in a number of ways from the architectures built by adults. They proposed, based on their findings, that software information architectures should be driven by the cognitive development of the children rather than the designers when children are the primary audience (for more on designing with children see, e.g., Druin 1989).

Henry Sanoff (2010) has been using participatory prototypes for many years in his work in the US on community planning and architecture. He provides participants with small-scale, paper-based representations of physical components (e.g., trees, water, existing buildings, etc.) to allow people to explore physical design options for exterior sites and internal environments.

Figure 7.5 Left: An example where the simple mock-up (the maxi-messenger) is made too large to be perceived as an actual technological product. The simple mock-ups worked as props for investigating different kind of functionalities and media for creating networks between senior people. The maxi-messenger illustrated some kind of communication device (Foverskov and Binder 2011). Right: This rough cardboard mock-up is made in a size close to what the student had in mind for creating a private space within a semi-public space (photo © Christina Lundsgaard).

Similarly Liz Sanders has been exploring the use of three-dimensional participatory prototypes in hospital planning and architecture as shown in Figure 7.6.

Sofia Hussain (Hussain and Sanders 2012) is using participatory prototyping with children and prosthetists in Cambodia to explore the design development of new prosthetic feet for the children. The children used toolkits that contained paper dolls, clothing and prosthetic options to express their ideas about the form and aesthetics of the prosthetic foot they would like to use (see Figure 7.7). The prosthetists later used a variety of materials such as wood, clay, rope and plastic wrap to create rough concepts of new prosthetic feet for the children.

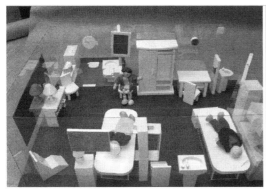

Figure 7.6 This three-dimensional 'dollhouse' toolkit has been used by health care practitioners to explore future opportunities in patient room design for new hospitals. (photo © Elizabeth B.-N. Sanders).

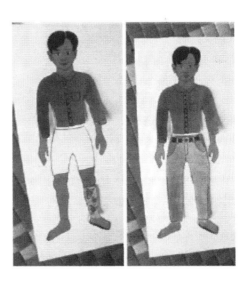

Figure 7.7 Left: These paper doll toolkits were designed to seek a deeper understanding of children's aesthetic concerns and needs related to the type of prosthetic foot they were currently using. Right: One of the children shows how he would prefer to be dressed at home and in public (Hussain and Sanders 2012).

Eva Brandt et al.

Probes as a means of exploring experience

In parallel with the extension and diffusion of participatory tools and techniques into design and innovation research at large, we also see an influx of approaches and techniques of a different origin. Gaver and his colleagues have been highly influential with their work on cultural probes (Gaver et al. 1999). Transforming questionnaires into delicately designed instruments for data collection that both expose the design agenda of the researchers and invite ambiguous and emotional responses from the informants, Gaver and his group opened a new realm for exchange and dialogue. Emphasizing the deliberately playful and insisting that what is collected is inspirational rather than factual, the cultural probes added a genuinely design-oriented approach to user research.

The use of probing kits in endless variations of Gaver's original postcards, diary book and instant cameras (see Figure 7.8) has spread rapidly in design research, and even though some of the adaptations, according to Boehner et al. (2007), may have missed the point of inviting ambiguity, the transgression of the boundaries between research and design has been strongly promoted by this work. This becomes even more obvious in the work on critical or speculative design coming out of the same research environment. Here the pioneering work of Dunne (2006) and Dunne and Raby (2001) brought design work into design research as a critical exploration of the mundane. In their Design Noir series, Dunne and Raby deliberately designed furniture that in one way or another made the user aware of the omnipresence of electromagnetic radiation, whether this was done by offering a Faraday cage couch or a table with in-built magnetic compasses.

Mazé et al. picked up on the work on critical design in their projects on awareness of energy consumption. Here they produced a number of conceptual prototypes that, like the energy curtain, collected sunlight for solar panels generating electricity for indoor lighting, but only when they were actually keeping out daylight (see Figure 7.9). This and similar prototypes were also evaluated by potential users in an everyday setting, providing new insights into how energy consumption and sustainability were reflected by people living with the prototypes (Mazé and Redström 2008).

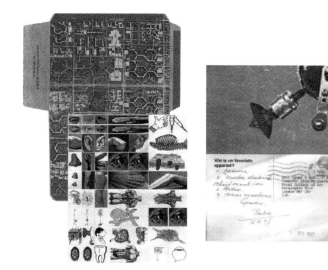

Figure 7.8 Cultural probe kits were sent home to people as a means for self-documentation. The probe kit was designed to address people's emotional, aesthetic and experiential reactions to their environments. It contained several maps and stickers to be glued on the maps, postcards with questions and a disposable camera with a list of requests for what to photograph (Gaver et al. 1999) (photo © Interaction Research Studio).

Figure 7.9 Static! Energy Curtain. The prototype from the Interactive Institute's research project 'STATIC!'. It is a window shade woven from a combination of textile, solar-collection and light-emitting materials. During the day the shade can be drawn to collect sunlight, and during the evening the collected energy is expressed as a glowing pattern on the inside of the shade (Mazé and Redström 2008) (photos © Interactive Institute, Johan Redström).

The move from research-led to design-led approaches engaging freely a broad array of tools and techniques is evident in the work reported by Westerlund. Reflecting on a decade of work of Participatory Design, Westerlund shows how probing for new technological possibilities with what he calls technology probes blends with evocative techniques of creativity to form a smooth intermingling of enquiry into ongoing practices and the prototyping of what is new (Westerlund 2009). Mattelmäki (2006), relating to what she calls empathic design (Koskinen et al. 2003), similarly explores new professional design practices as she reports on how different probing techniques and participatory workshops are brought together in innovation projects targeting public service innovation.

Generative tools for co-designing

The origin of generative tools is transdisciplinary, emerging from the intersection of design practice, applied psychology and psycholinguistics theory. The idea emerged while watching practising industrial designers communicate with each other through 'component volumetrics' (3D forms that represented core internal components of the product). Similarly, graphic designers communicated with each other through 'mood boards' containing 2D components such as photographs and other images. These observations sparked the idea to create sets of 3D and 2D visual components that non-designers could use to express their feelings, ideas and dreams about future scenarios of use.

An understanding of projective techniques (Lilienfeld et al. 2000) was useful in guiding the choice of components of the generative design language. Like projective techniques, generative tools rely on ambiguity. A good set of generative tools provides ambiguity to non-designers in order to evoke and provoke thoughts and feelings that they do not commonly talk about. Chomsky's theory of transformative generative grammar (Chomsky 1965) provided another source of inspiration. Generative grammars provide for the possibility of creating an infinite set of meaningful statements from a finite number of components. A good set of generative tools provides a limited set of components that, when used in combination, has the potential for an infinite variety of expressions about future ways of living. Today the generative tools describe a design language ideally suited for use by non-designers. It is a full palette of predominantly visual components that enable participants to explore and express playful landscapes of past, present and future experiences. These tools can be used to encourage and challenge people to express their tacit and latent needs, aspirations and dreams (Sanders 2000).

Sanders and William (2001) describe the underlying theoretical basis for the application of generative tools, Koestler's theory of creativity (Koestler 1964), and describe how to set the expression of creative ideas by non-designers in motion. They also provide descriptions and photos of some of the more commonly used generative tools and techniques, including: immersion workbooks, diaries, the day-in-the-life exercise, send-a-camera home, image collaging, cognitive mapping and Velcro-modelling. There is an overlap between some of the tools and techniques of design probes and generative tools (e.g. diaries, workbooks and cameras sent to participants). In the case of the cultural probes, these tools and techniques are the probes. In the case of the generative tools, these tools and techniques are used in priming activities to ensure that the participant is prepared for the creativity that is inherent in the subsequent generative session. See Figure 7.10.

Froukje Sleeswijk Visser et al. (2005) present a more detailed account of how to set up and conduct generative tools sessions from the initial immersion period to the session itself and then to the analysis of the data. They also describe the various ways that findings from generative research sessions can be communicated to audiences interested in the results and the insights.

Within the Participatory Design community we see a change in aim and scope for the application of participatory tools and techniques in the front end of the design process. Buur and his colleagues, who have for long been taking Participatory Design into corporate R&D, have in recent years shown that business models may also be prototyped with participatory techniques (Buur and Mitchell 2011). They provided participants with toolkits containing materials such as plastic tubes, balls, string, pulleys and toy trains and tracks for collaboratively making tangible business models. This work is still in the exploratory phases. Meanwhile, LEGO has made a business out of its LEGO Serious Play offer, which also offers a generative toolkit for business modelling (Statler et al. 2009).

Short case: improving wellbeing at work

The consequences of demographic development are one of the global challenges receiving more and more attention in this century. Growing populations and longer life expectancies provide

Figure 7.10 Examples of generative toolkits. Left: Image collaging toolkits such as this one can be used for helping non-designers to imagine and express their desires for future scenarios of use. Right: Velcro-modelling is a generative design language and toolkit that provokes imaginative explorations and embodiments of future scenarios of use (photos © Elizabeth B.-N. Sanders).

significant challenges for society and welfare. Thus, in recent years many Participatory Design projects around the world have focused on designing new ICT systems, services and/or devices to improve health care. The following short case from Helsinki addresses the challenge of keeping people in employment as long as possible so they can contribute to society.

The Aging@Work project started out from a very open design brief. The overall idea was to identify features and design technology that could improve work and wellbeing at work, with the hope that this would result in aging workers staying longer in the labour market. Tuuli Mattelmäki and colleagues write that they had no prior knowledge about the phenomenon of aging at work (Vaajakallio and Mattelmäki 2007). Thus, the first activity that the aging workers took part in combined telling and making. The researchers made probing kits that invited the workers to map and probe into their present everyday experiences. The probe kit included a map, a timetable, a task book and postcards.

The make activity that followed used a Velcro-modelling toolkit. Each study focused on one worker and took place at this person's workplace. First the workers were instructed to build (using the Velcro-modelling toolkit) a 'dream device', a tool that could help them either to work in a more focused way or to feel better while at work (see example in Figure 7.11).

After having 'completed' the making activity, the aging workers were asked to return to their usual work with the dream tool and work as normally as possible. When they thought the dream tool could change their work practice into a more desirable one, they enacted the activity using the dream tool as a prop and pretending that it worked (see example in Figure 7.12). The dream tool served as a probe to elicit future scenarios of use.

This short case shows how tell, make and enact activities in Participatory Design practices often are intertwined and take place simultaneously. Unlike the short case in the previous section, where the users at the museum used existing objects when enacting scenarios, central in the Aging@Work project is that the aging workers use the Velcro-modelling toolkit for prototyping their own personal devices. It is the participatory prototyping activity which is in the centre of this Participatory Design practice.

In the next short case, the prototype is also at the centre of the design practice, but here the users are not directly involved in the making and remaking of the prototype. It is the programmers that do this work. The case takes place during the design development of an interactive prototype. In the Nnub project, members of a community interact with an evolving prototype as their experiences with it are tracked. These data, combined with various tell activities, are the means upon which the interactive prototype develops.

Short case: applying longitudinal studies to design social technologies

Most Participatory Design projects are carried out within a relatively short timeframe, which often means that it is impossible for researchers to take part in (the final) detailed design and implementation and to follow what Dourish has called appropriation (Dourish 2003) during everyday use. Important challenges in many projects are therefore to find ways to secure that what is designed is found relevant and realistic and fits into the everyday practices of the people for whom the new design is intended. A related issue is finding ways to get knowledge beyond novelty usage.

In this example, Margot Brereton and colleagues from Queensland University of Technology present a longitudinal Participatory Design practice that addresses these challenges when designing social technologies. For some years, people in a suburb of Brisbane in Australia have used and suggested changes to a digital community noticeboard (called Nnub) located in the general store. The idea is that the gist of the neighbourhood is captured in text and images uploaded by local people to the community digital noticeboard (Redhead and Brereton 2008; Heyer and Brereton 2010). See Figure 7.13.

Figure 7.11 Top right: The worker builds her dream device using a Velcro-modelling toolkit. While building it she is encouraged to think aloud so the researchers can hear her thoughts. Top left: The resulting dream device made by the woman in the image. Bottom row: Examples of dream devices made by other aging workers using a similar Velcro-modelling toolkit (photos: © Vaajakallio and Mattelmäki 2007).

Figure 7.12 The aging worker acts out an envisioned future situation using the dream devices he has made (Vaajakallio and Mattelmäki 2007).

The main characteristic of their design practice is to integrate working exploratory prototypes into particular everyday environments and to have people interact with these in situ. In relation to the tell–make–enact framework, the main emphasis is on make and enact, with various telling activities that were set up to capture the make and the enact. They suggest a Reflective Agile Iterative Design framework to support the design process, where form and functionality of the prototype is shaped over time in response to immediate use. Thus making an initial

exploratory prototype is used as a means to invite participation and inspire new design iterations. The process is active and responsive and driven by local citizens enacting with the evolving
prototype (Redhead and Brereton 2009). Reflecting on people enacting with the exploratory
prototype is the primary means for learning. See Figure 7.14.

Heyer and Brereton suggest several tools and techniques to collect responses from using the
Nnub, upon which the reflection and new iterations of redesigning the prototype are based.
The various 'tell-techniques' included:

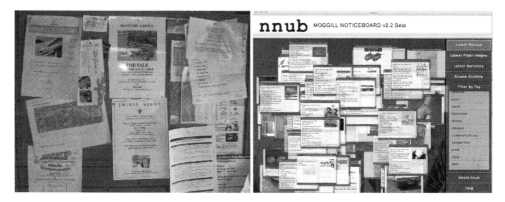

Figure 7.13 Left: Outside the Moggil general store there is a traditional noticeboard. Together
with the people living in the suburb of Brisbane, the researchers considered the
relation between the traditional and the digital noticeboard. Right: The functionality
of the working prototype was gradually developed through making based on people's responses to immediate use. For example, in the beginning it was only possible
to make notices and post photos separately. Later these could be combined. Then it
was possible to add scribbles, which the children were very fond of. Then it became
possible to tag the various contributions. Later multi-site capability changed the
Nnub from being a stand-alone screen in a specific shop to a community noticeboard
which could be reached from anywhere with Internet access (photos © Margot
Brereton and Fiona Redhead).

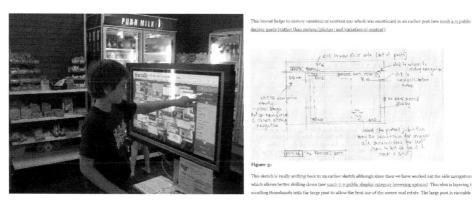

Figure 7.14 Left: Boy using the digital noticeboard in the shop. Right: hand sketch from the
'change log' that monitors the evolving design – here thoughs about the screen
layout. (images © Fiona Redhead).

- A *question log* that tells the designers about the use of the system which is used to help them to prioritise and focus design efforts. The system logs usage data automatically.
- A *notebook* that is placed in the shop for people to leave feedback.
- A *change log* monitors the evolving design and thereby tells the design team 'when bugs were fixed or features added, removed or modified'.
- A '*reflective journal* is used to record reflections on observed use, and results of data analysis' (Heyer and Brereton 2010, p. 284). The latter is yet another example of a tell-technique used to continuously inform the people involved about the project's progression.

Designing social technology that can be used by everyone in a local community is challenging, not least because it has to accommodate many different interests and various experiences with ICT technologies. The design process evolved around iterations of the making and remaking of the prototype, based on how it was being used in situ. Unlike most other Participatory Design projects, workshops were not the primary technique for participation and communication between users and designers. Instead the researchers have combined an interesting series of tools and techniques for 'telling' to support the make and enact activities.

Participation through enacting possible futures

New designs change the environments and practices of people. Essential design challenges are both to generate design proposals that create desirable changes, and to explore how possible new designs affect experiences, behaviours, rhythms, etc., in the future. The best way to find out is by working with approaches, methods, tools and techniques focusing on enacting.

With enacting we refer to activities where one or more people imagine and act out possible futures by trying things out (by use of the body) in settings that either resemble or are where future activities are likely to take place. What is enacted in the situation can, for instance, be something like a scene in a play based on a script, story or scenario made (partly) beforehand. Enacting can also be solely based on improvisation and experimentation in the situation. Thus, through enacting one can present or develop and explore ideas through embodiment, but ideas can also be evoked through acting and hence experimenting through improvisation. Even though enacting techniques can be used as a way to present a finished design, what we will focus on here is giving examples of the tools and techniques related to enacting as part of work-in-progress.

Inspiration from improvisational theatre techniques

Many Participatory Design practitioners have found inspiration from the world of drama, for instance by transforming specific drama techniques like Forum Theatre (Boal 1974) into techniques for enacting in Participatory Design sessions. In Forum Theatre actors perform a skit to which the audience members are asked to suggest changes. Based on the suggestions, the actors improvise changes to the situation at play. Thus the people in the audience are not passive spectators but are invited to take the role as authors and directors, and they can keep making changes to the play until they are satisfied with the outcome. Early on within the Participatory Design field, Ehn and Kyng (1991) and Ehn and Sjögren (1991) made informal use of this enacting technique. Brandt and Grunnet (2000) have worked with a more formal use of the Forum Theatre technique (see Figure 7.15). As a related technique, Brandt and Grunnet suggest using the technique of 'frozen images'. The frozen images are made by suddenly stopping in the middle of an action. These incidents are analysed and discussed on the spot, upon which new suggestions for enacting are made.

Figure 7.15 In the Senior Interaction Project the project team enacted scenarios using the Forum Theatre technique. Senior people and other stakeholders acted both as spectators and directors suggesting changes to the play. Suggestions were both acted out on the spot and documented on paper on the wall. Projections on the wall helped to give a sense of where the situations took place.

Another example from the world of drama is moving the 'magic if' acting technique by Stanislavskij (1940) into framing co-design activities. In drama the 'magic if' technique is used in order to create empathy for the role to be played. In Participatory Design, questions such as 'what if the user was in this or that situation?' can easily be used to enact and explore future use situations. Burns et al. (1997) were among the first to argue that by adopting the role-play technique it is possible to bridge the conceptual leap between 'what is' and 'what might be' (Burns 1994; Burns et al. 1997).

The acting-out techniques have been used to create empathy for potential users and to get to know use situations through bodily experiences. The (bodily) knowledge gained by the design team has been argued as an essential basis for generating ideas and making proposals for change (see e.g. Brandt and Grunnet 2000).

Others use professional actors to enact scenarios. For example, in the Focus Troupe approach (Sato and Salvador 1999), live performers enact scenarios that include product concepts as part of expanding traditional focus group sessions. Sato and Salvador report that live theatre as part of focus groups can create strong shared contexts with focus on interaction, and that this way of exploring seems less literal than presenting scenarios on video or presenting physical prototypes.

In the same vein Howard et al. (2002) have developed a scenario-based design approach to increase stakeholders' sense of immersion. They use professional actors for acting out scenarios with props, sometimes together with candidate users. The scenarios are staged in design contexts as well as real contexts of use. Garabet et al. (2002) have in an interesting and more experimental style done performances where they have presented wearable computing artwork in public and recorded people's reactions.

Others invite users, clients or other stakeholders to take the lead in improvising and enacting possible new future practices. We will give examples of this later in this section. The point here is that even though techniques for enacting today are widely used in Participatory Design practices, there is no consensus about who should be the ones to enact. The choices made depend on the aim of the enactment but also on the mindset that influences which activities users and other stakeholders should be part of in Participatory Design projects.

Scenarios are stories about people

Enacting is closely related to scenarios. John Carroll writes: 'Scenarios are stories – stories about people and their activities' (Carroll 2000, p. 46). Stories about the future are often conveyed through scenarios where one imagines or enacts how activities and experiences in the future could be different from today. The scenario technique has for long been recognised as a powerful means in designing. Scenarios are powerful for envisioning and simulating various future use situations. Simultaneously they are valuable means for (common) reflection and learning (see e.g., Kyng 1995; Carroll 2000). In particular, scenarios have been widely used in Participatory Design practices within Human–Computer Interaction, Computer Supported Cooperative Work and system design projects for many years. Based on Clausen (1993) and the book edited by Carroll (1995), Keld Bødker and colleagues describe the scenario technique thus:

> Developing scenarios is a technique that supports building coherent visions and thus helps in anchoring these visions. Scenarios visualize the practical application of a proposed IT system, that is, the potential effects of implementing it. Scenarios are prose-style representations exemplifying a work practice under future use of the system. Scenarios may illustrate application of the system as viewed from the different users' perspectives. Thus, they may also refer to a design sketch or prototype of a proposed system. Scenarios are based on the users' conceptualizations of their work context.
>
> *(Bødker et al. 2004, p. 216)*

In their book *Participatory IT Design: Designing for Business and Workplace Realities*, Bødker et al. (2004) give an example of a scenario from a project at a radio station. In pure text the scenario describes how the design team imagines that the editorial unit uses the new system during one week from overall planning through daily programming and broadcasting.

John Carroll's book *Making Use: Scenario-Based Design of Human–Computer Interactions* is very informative on, for instance, scenario characteristics, various aspects to consider and challenges that are involved in scenario-based design (Carroll 2000). For instance, Carroll explains that scenarios

> mention or presuppose a *setting* … Scenarios include *agents* or *actors* … each typically with *goals* and *objectives* … Scenarios have a plot; they include sequences of *actions* and *events* … Representing the use of a system or application with a set of interaction scenarios makes the *use* explicit.
>
> *(ibid., p. 47)*

Carroll argues that scenario-based techniques

> seek to *exploit* the complexity and fluidity of design by trying to learn more about the structure and dynamics of the problem domain, trying to see the situation in many different ways, and interacting intimately with the concrete elements of the situation.
>
> *(ibid., p. 45)*

An important strength is that scenarios are at once concrete and flexible.

> They are concrete in the sense that they simultaneously fix an interpretation of the design situation and offer a specific solution … At the same time, scenarios are flexible in the sense that they are deliberately incomplete and easily revised or elaborated.
>
> *(ibid., p. 54)*

Several researchers have found that stories about people and their activities are easier envisioned and more realistic when developed and explored through enacting. As an example, from the field of mobile and ubiquitous computing, Messeter and colleagues describe four scenarios that have been enacted by users and describe how a thorough analysis of these revealed important insights regarding implications for design of mobile information technology devices. The four scenarios represented both activities taking place while the users are working and activities from leisure time. The scenarios were presented with snapshots from video recordings supplemented with text about what was taking place and said in the situation (Messeter et al. 2004; see example in Figure 7.16).

There are many Participatory Design techniques that use video in various ways as a central medium and design tool. Salu Ylirisku and Jacob Buur's recent book, *Designing with Video: Focusing the User-Centered Design Process* (2007), explains the origin, history and theories behind designing with video. They give various examples of how to study what people do, with techniques for making sense of the recordings but also various techniques for envisioning the future and provoking change. When it comes to enacting scenarios this can be done in full scale, where people are enacting using their full bodies, or in small scale, where people are using

1) Helle shows her new fashion collection to a potential retailer. Helle comments on the different garments and answers questions from Elisabeth.

2) Helle takes pictures using her 'image device' of the garments Elisabeth is interested in.

3) Helle annotates the pictures with comments regarding prices, colours, etc. using her 'image editing tablet'.

4) Finally, Helle sends the annotated pictures from her 'image editing tablet' to her 'portable printer', producing a personalized catalogue.

Figure 7.16 Scenario from the COMIT project. The scenarios were enacted in Helle's fashion shop and recorded on video. Images are taken from the video recording (Messeter et al. 2004).

mainly their hands and voices in a puppet theatre fashion. In the latter, puppets and the scenery within which they are moving are important tools (see e.g. Ylirisku and Buur 2007; Foverskov and Binder 2011).

Reflecting back to the tell–make–enact diagram in Figure 7.1, the primary action involved in creating scenarios includes (story)telling. The stories are often built upon a traditional narrative structure with a clear beginning, middle and end. As exemplified, scenarios can be written as pure text but the story can also be 'told' by use of sketches, photographs or video. The activity of enacting is also closely related to scenarios. The human body is used not only to illustrate actions but also as a means for exploration through trying and acting out. Thus, through enacting, bodily and perhaps tacit knowledge is set in motion which can generate and evoke useful new knowledge about what is to be designed. Combining telling and enacting through enacting scenarios is very powerful for imagining and exploring new and possible futures.

Staging performances with props, mock-ups and/or prototypes

Enacting scenarios by interacting with props or prototypes makes future use situations explicit and hereby subject for enquiry, reflection and learning. Still, enacting needs staging. Enacting needs both to take place at a site or within a setting, and to involve various artefacts that constitute the situation. 'Constitute' is borrowed from Westerlund (2009), who recently argued that we should refrain from describing future activities and artefacts as representing the future, as they do not yet exist. Depending on where one is in the design process, the 'things' to be designed and interacted with are most often described as props and mock-ups, early and later prototypes. When the purpose is to enact use situations in Participatory Design, for instance, Bødker and Buur (2002) stress the importance of using tangible prototypes as one can interact with them and get hands-on experiences, and the prototypes can be held, placed, pointed at, etc.

Buchenau and Fulton Suri write: 'Increasingly, as designers of interactive systems (spaces, processes and products for people), we find ourselves stretching the limits of prototyping tools to explore and communicate what it will be like to interact with the things we design' (Buchenau and Fulton Suri 2000). They suggest 'Experience Prototyping' as a fruitful approach, when the subjective experience of interacting with a product, space or system is emphasised. Explorative experiments are carried out by enacting with mock-ups, prototypes or existing products. They give examples of how they prepared the enacting in situ by cutting the story up into scenes, with each scene introduced on a card explaining the goal, the rules to be followed and the roles of the players and audience. Informance or bodystorming is a technique where designers are actors and 'bodystorm' as users using simple mock-ups or prototypes. The informal improvisations are used to act out and explore design alternatives in a setting that is constructed to capture the essence of the real-use context. Another example of bodystorming is presented by Oulasvirta et al. (2003), and examples of staging-use contexts and exploring design alternatives are provided by Nilsson et al. (2000), for instance.

Enacting scenarios in real-use contexts

Having users improvising and enacting scenarios in their own environment brings the experiences as close as possible to exploring how the everyday activities could be different. With the use of very simple mock-ups, Binder shows how video-recording of enacted scenarios becomes a new and valuable common language in Participatory Design (Binder 1999). This work was followed up, for instance, by Iacucci and Kuutti (2002). In the SPES approach (Situated and Participative Enactment of Scenarios) a member of the user group is provided with a simple mock-up of a future device (the magic thing) to help imagination (Iacucci and Kuutti 2002). The designer follows the user through her daily activities and the mock-up is used to envision ideas of services and features of the product being designed (see examples in Figure 7.17).

As in the two previous sections, we will end this section with a short case that illustrates how various telling, making and enacting activities are combined into a design practice of participation.

Short case: rehearsing new roles and relations

Taking care of major societal issues often involves several stakeholders with different expertise and responsibilities. Scaling up the complexity of the development task calls for Participatory Design practices. Still, creating innovation across organisational boundaries where roles and responsibilities are often quite fixed and simultaneously involving users is challenging. In the following short case from Denmark, researchers found that it was valuable to stage Participatory Design processes that included both prototyping of future design concepts and the possibility for stakeholders to try out new roles, relationships and practices that follow with a new design.

In the DAIM project on recycling and reduction of waste, the client was a large incinerator plant owned by 19 municipalities (Halse et al. 2010). The stakeholders were both those from within various parts of the waste system and users of the system, for instance, citizens and shop owners. In the beginning the focus was on telling activities. A number of field studies were carried out. For instance, waste collectors and people operating recycling stations were followed for one day at work, and citizens were visited in their homes in order to learn about motivations and practices around recycling and waste handling. The many stories were transformed into tangible materials and formed the basis for a workshop where the participants collaboratively created dream projects about how the future could be different. The dream projects were physically gestalted (see example in Figure 7.18) and presented through storytelling. Thus the workshop combined tell and make activities. The 'new relations' design game, a simple star diagram, was used to identify different stakeholders and enquire into possible new roles and relationships in relation to specific dream situations.

Later, new roles and relations were very concretely explored through imagining and elaborating on tentative 'what if' situations identified during the previous activities. For instance: 'What if waste collectors were heroes of recycling?' 'What if shopping centres were hubs for recycling?' The stories were first created as improvised doll scenarios, where the participants staged and acted out their visions using dolls (Halse et al. 2010; see example in Figure 7.18). As part of staging, the participants made their own backdrops based on photographs from the fieldwork. Creating doll scenarios

Figure 7.17 Left: Sergey, who experiments on wood samples, uses the 'magic thing' to record details about the experiments (Iacucci et al. 2000). Middle: Matteo wanted the 'magic thing' to be hooked on the bike and to be able to check friends in the cafeteria while passing by (Iacucci and Kuutti 2002). Right: Diana, a tourist in Helsinki, uses the 'magic thing' as a shopping assistant to keep track of the type and price of trousers in different shops. The shopping assistant also remembers the location of the shops (Iacucci and Kuutti 2002).

Figure 7.18 The DAIM project. Top left: The stakeholders create a large number of dream projects using toolkits with, e.g., cardboard silhouettes. Top right: A simple star diagram
was used in the 'new relations' design game to identify different stakeholders and
enquire into possible new roles and relationships. Bottom: The workshop participants built a stage with photographs as backdrops and played out doll scenarios
where new roles and relationships were explored through improvising actions and
dialogue in front of the video camera (Halse et al. 2010).

included telling, making and enacting. Based on the doll scenarios the participants later played
themselves in full-scale video scenarios in situ, where they improvised and acted out situations using
simple props to illustrate and explore future possibilities (ibid.; see examples in Figure 7.19).

As in the other short case stories, the Participatory Design practice described here also includes
tell, make and enact activities – often in combination. In this case the centre of gravity seems to
be on storytelling and enacting. Still, one should not neglect the importance of making. It is just
as much the collaborative making of the dream projects on the boards that creates a joint focus
of attention, negotiation of experiences and interests, inspires new ways of understanding the
system, and jointly creates a vision for the future. This said, the experiences also show that it is
of vital importance in innovation projects involving many different stakeholders that new roles and
relations can be explored as part of generating concepts for new directions and future scenarios of use.

From tools to games: bringing it all together

Throughout this chapter we have pointed to the way tools and techniques in Participatory Design
amalgamate into very particular design practices of telling, making and enacting. Across differences,

Figure 7.19 The DAIM project. The shop owner, Allan, and the resident, Lillian, enact scenarios in situ assisted by the design team. Through improvisation they collaboratively explore how recycling can be combined with shopping. For instance, they develop a concept for recycling of batteries that gives a refund when buying things in the shop (Halse et al. 2010).

researchers and practitioners are concerned with the staging of a 'third space' of collaborative enquiry where different stakeholders may come together to rehearse 'the possible'. This coming together is not just an accumulation of insights, nor is it solely a negotiation of interests; rather, it is, as Ehn has called it, 'a meeting of language games'. What this entails for the emerging practice of participation is captured neither by a reference to tools and techniques as simple means of participation nor through a concern for the (often conflicting) objectives of the collaborative process. What sets Participatory Design aside from political negotiations in established political forums or from instrumental processes of achieving well-defined organisational or institutional goals is precisely the entanglement of the questions of what to achieve and how to achieve it. Design is not decision-making in a well-known space of opportunities but an exploration of what may be envisioned through the coming together of a network of actors. In this coming together, means are tentatively tried out and goals are provisionally put into play. As the exploration evolves, participants are playfully participating in a new practice that brings together means and ends in what one could call a new game of possible futures.

The notion of design games, first coined with direct reference to Wittgenstein's concept of language games by Habraken and Gross (1987) has been influential in the discussion of participation since it was first brought up by Ehn and Sjögren (1991). The basic idea of design games put forward by Habraken and Gross is that design can be modelled as a dialogical engagement with materials guided by a set of rules and taken forward through turn-taking among a number of game players. Habraken and Gross used the particular concept of design games to study different aspects of the design process, but over the years the concept of design games has attracted interest both as a metaphor for the overall process of design participation and, more importantly, as a particular way of formatting the participatory process. We will end this chapter by briefly discussing why the design game format has gained widespread attention, and how the concept of design games makes it possible to overcome the separation between tools and techniques, on the one side, and the participatory mindset, on the other side, that have so often led newcomers to misinterpret what is accomplished in Participatory Design practices.

The design game as a particular framing of design participation

At the very beginning of this chapter we discussed how early definitions of tools and techniques for participation deliberately sought to comply with the instrumental ethos of systems design, by emphasising the need to supplement conventional methodologies with a toolbox for participation. This made sense in a rhetorical dispute with the mainstream of systems design on the neglect of many stakeholders but, as we have also pointed out, it left out a concern for the playfulness and willingness to suspend conventional wisdom that is mandatory in the participatory process. Instrumentality implies a clear separation between means and ends, and as Ehn and his colleagues argue in the book *Design Things* (A. Telier 2011), design in general revolves around the making of things, where each 'thing' is at the same time an artefact and the assembly of a network of actors (much like the archaic notion of a thing as a gathering of community members to resolve issues of controversies). Without going deeply into this argument we can see that the framing of participation proposed by Ehn and others is a performative one, emphasising the openness of both process and outcome through an attention to procedure. The authors go on to suggest that design practices perform participative entangled design games on at least three levels. First, the numerous everyday interactions among users and designers in and around every design project can be seen as design games, in the sense that the meeting of language games or practices gives rise to new language games (whether this is acknowledged or not). Second, the particular staging of the design process, broadly speaking, sets the rules for design games in the sense that it provides the participants with roles and materials that in themselves define a game of interaction. Third, each particular engagement or device of what we in this chapter have called tools and techniques involves a design game, providing possibilities to tell, make and enact 'the new' in a dialogue scripted by the particular characteristics of the engagement (ibid.).

If we look back at the four cases of Participatory Design practices that we have presented in the previous sections of this chapter and compare them to the three levels of entangled design games presented above, we may see how the framing of participation as design games may help us to capture the interplay between telling, making and enacting involved in any participatory practice.

In the first case, concerning challenging tradition and transcendence through fictional narratives, we see a group of design researchers inviting museum visitors to explore a fairytale universe with magical tools in a deliberately playful manner, yet still maintaining that their participation is anchored in their specific visit to the museum. Here it is very obvious that particular rules of interaction are proposed, but still the participants are invited to wholeheartedly engage in much more than a psychological experiment. The starting point is the telling of a story, but the visitors are given means to add to and alter the story and to take part in making the universe tangible and bringing it to life through their playing out of new experiences. What is taking place is thus both a casual everyday interaction among the family members and the design researchers, a staging of the process of participation and a set of very particular engagements that gives direction to the visitors' exploration of the museum experience. The staging of the Atlantis narrative and the explicit rules of participation enable the participants not only to explore and comment but also to express and contribute to the evolving universe of new museum experiences. We can still consider the individual tools and techniques employed, but the design games perspective adds a concern for the fullness of the Participatory Design practice.

The two short cases in the section on making represent two rather different stagings of the participatory encounter. In the first case about improving wellbeing at work, the design researchers and caretakers are performing a carefully scripted set of events where the caretakers are first invited to make a dream tool for their work and immediately afterwards encouraged to act out an everyday situation with the dream tool in their well-known working environment. Already the notion of dream tool indicates that the event involves a playful exploration of imagined new technology, and the game perspective may again help us to ask if this is really a design game where all involved have the opportunity to take turns and propose and enact tools that makes sense in their everyday practice. The site of the event being the actual workplace of the caretakers similarly implies a negotiation of the 'the rules of the game' that are crucial for the maketools to make sense. Again, to ask what the design games are here makes it evident that what the participants make must be linked to what they are able to tell and experience through acting, and this must be catered for in the participatory process even though what is in the foreground are particular tools and techniques for making. The second short case in the making section, concerning applying longitudinal studies to design social technologies, reports on a Participatory Design practice evolving over a longer period of time and almost fully embedded in the everyday life of a small suburban community. Researchers are providing an infrastructure for social technologies and perform occasional interventions to have participants tell about their involvement with the technology. This does not seem much like a design game at first, but again, referring to Ehn and colleagues' three levels, the design game perspective may encourage us to look at the everyday interactions as language games and we may ask how these interactions enable turn-taking and the negotiation of rules. On the detailed level of researcher–user interaction, we may also ask how the question log, change log or reflective journal reported in the case contributes to the evolving design dialogue, for example by facilitating an interplay between emerging insights and the making of new design proposals.

In the last short case, concerning rehearsing new roles and relationships, we have an example of a Participatory Design practice that very directly addresses the second-level design games of staging the collaborative process. Here the tools and techniques of participation are brought together to mobilize stakeholders and to prompt the open negotiation of the rules and roles of participation among participants. The researchers themselves talk about the interactions as design games; for example, in the 'new relations' game the exploration of networks is governed by a strict game format. With a broader framing of the participatory practice as entangled participative design games, we may also be encouraged to consider in this case how the project draws upon and fuels the everyday meeting of language games outside the staged events of participation.

With this revisiting of the cases, we have proposed that the notion of design games both as a metaphor and as a concrete formatting of the participatory practice may give us a sensitivity to the way tools and techniques of telling, making and enacting must be brought together in a participatory mindset. We will end this section by giving a final short case in which the design researchers have deliberately pursued the design game perspective to show how it may also guide practitioners of Participatory Design to bring together tools of telling, making and enacting on a practical level.

Short case: designing (with) design games

In the mobile phone industry, successful new concept design has to be worked out with close attention to the business networks formed by service providers, telecom companies and hardware manufacturers. At the same time the need for engaging with future users is paramount, yet often difficult to establish through secrecy and internal power struggles within the business networks. At the Interactive Institute in Malmö, Sweden, a group of Participatory Design researchers were approached by a major mobile phone company and asked to propose a compact design project in which both the business network and potential future users could be engaged in concept design. The researchers chose to stage the design project through the preparation of closely linked design games that were to be played over workshops, with preparatory dialogues in between. The resulting four games combined a set of different tools and techniques ranging from creating personas (see also Grudin and Pruitt 2002), making prototypes to enacting scenarios. See Figure 7.20.

Figure 7.20 The COMIT project from the Interactive Institute was event-driven. The industrial partners and potential users participated in four workshops. Each of these was framed and organised as a design game. Top left: the User Game. Top right: the Landscape Game. Bottom left: the Technology Game. Bottom right: the Scenario Game (Brandt and Messeter 2004).

In the User Game, the aim was to create stories about people as prospective users. Through game playing the intention was to help the stakeholders develop a shared image of intended users which was firmly grounded in field data. The game material was based on video recordings from ethnographically inspired field studies. Video snippets were watched and game pieces with images from the field studies were used to create a web of interrelated stories about one (potential) user. Each story was labelled with a game piece with words on it (Brandt and Messeter 2004). The intention with the Landscape Game was to create context for the people portrayed in the User Game. This means that the focus shifted from developing stories about a person, his or her interests and relations to involving the physical surroundings. In this game it was important to identify what elements in the person's surroundings augmented various activities in that person's everyday life. The game materials included game boards and game pieces, like images illustrating parts of the environment in the field studies. The Technology Game was for projects that either aimed at developing technology or projects where technology played an important role in the activities and environments for the intended design. The intention with the game was to both introduce and investigate various technologies and the 'form factor'. The game pieces illustrated technologies or various functionalities, depending on the level of detail that was needed. Other game pieces illustrated the physical form factor and evoked discussions about shape, size, etc. The intention with the Enacted Scenario Game was that experiences from the previous games were condensed into scenarios involving persons, context, activities and, if convenient, the technology to be designed. An important feature was that these scenarios were created and acted out in situ (ibid.). In the light of the previous discussion of the different levels of design games, one may see these four games as examples of concrete engagements and devices shaped as games, but one may also see the package of games as an attempt to shape the overall project through the game metaphor (as discussed also in Brandt et al. 2008; and Brandt 2011).

Future directions and opportunities

The tools and techniques for making, telling and enacting provide a very wide range of ways for involving relevant stakeholders at points all along the design process. These tools and techniques for Participatory Design have been growing rapidly in both quantity and range in the last five to ten years. The tell-make-enact framework helps us to collect, organise and put into action all this variety. The framework also helps to reveal that opportunities for future applications of the tools and techniques can be described at three levels:

- the continued exploration and application of specific tools and techniques for participatory designing,
- investigation of the relationships between making, telling and enacting, and
- further exploration, application and refinement of the framework.

The continued exploration and application of specific tools and techniques

The number of possible tools, techniques and applications for making, telling and enacting is limitless. The challenge is to determine which tools and techniques are most effective in what types of situations and for what types of stakeholders. Successful application of specific tools and techniques demands an in-depth understanding of the design process and the ability to provide the materials, tools and techniques that are appropriate for each phase in the process. Some of the areas in need of further development at the first level are described below.

We need more research to develop a better understanding of how to apply the tools and techniques of participatory designing. For example, here are the types of questions that students and beginners pose about the specific tools and techniques of making, telling and enacting:

- How do you prepare the participants for engaging in activities of making, telling and/or enacting?
- How can you anticipate how long it will take people to engage in these activities?
- Are some types of tools and techniques better suited for people from different backgrounds/ages/gender/etc.?
- How can you improve the efficiency and effectiveness of the specific tools and toolkits?
- How do you analyse the data that is generated by making, telling and enacting activities?

Application of the probes and the generative tools is particularly challenging, since they appear easier to execute than they actually are. It takes some time and experience to master these domains. For example, the creation of a generative toolkit of components that has enough ambiguity to spark previously unconnected ideas, yet one that is not so large as to be overwhelming, is an ability that grows with practice. The best way to learn how to apply the making tools and techniques is by doing, i.e. by making, in as many different situations as possible.

In terms of new applications of the existing tools and techniques, practice is leading academia. However, the new applications in industry are rarely published. They may be described on blogs or shared through photos but rarely are the details shared, owing to confidentiality concerns. The new application of existing tools and techniques is an area ripe for design and research discovery. It is especially important that the exploration of and reflection on the use of the new tools and techniques be situated at all the phases of the design and development process. It is also important that the results of these explorations be published.

Investigation of the relationships between making, telling and enacting

Design participation is an evolving practice of making, telling and enacting. The iterative flow of events between these activities is essential, not only for participation to occur naturally, but for participation to occur with ease and with joy. When we can fully engage people's minds, hearts and bodies in imagining and expressing future situations of use, we can be assured that they have an opportunity to influence future ways of living, learning and being.

We need far more research to develop a full understanding of the relationships between the practice of making, telling and enacting. For example, here are some of the questions that students and beginners ask about the connections and relationships between making, telling and enacting:

- What are the best entry points into the iterative processes of participatory designing?
- How do you decide in what order to conduct the activities? Is it better to have participants do the making activities before enacting? Or vice versa?
- Should the participants or the researchers lead in deciding how the activities play out over time?
- Do the relationships between making, telling and enacting change at different phases of the design process? If so, how?
- Do the artefacts of the Participatory Design process change across the different stages of the design process? If so, how?

Further exploration, application and refinement of the framework

The framework for design participation is also in need of further exploration, application and refinement. For example, how can we optimise the journey among and between making, telling and enacting from the perspective of the participants? How can the game metaphor help us to better plan these journeys? What other metaphors beyond games will we find useful in the future?

The analysis and interpretation of the data that comes from design participation through making, telling and enacting poses quite another set of challenges. Each artefact that is created and the story or the enactment that goes along with it will be unique. Analysis can focus on the artefact, the story, the enactment and/or the interplay between artefact, story and enactment. The focus of the analysis also differs at different points along the design process. Analysis in the pre-design phase is more likely to focus on the story or enactment, since the artefact is a physical instantiation of a desired experience. Analysis of participatory prototyping activities that take place later in the design process is more likely to focus on the artefact itself.

There is an immediate need for publication and dissemination to keep the tools and techniques of Participatory Design open to all. The tools for making are particularly colourful and tangible. The experience of being a participant in making activities is immersive, engaging and fun and the practices of making can be done either individually or collectively. All of this is being recognised at a time when the business community is busy discovering and disseminating its own versions of what 'co-creation' and design thinking might mean. Although the business perspective on co-creation today tends to view the phenomenon from the marketing, sales and distribution end, it is only a matter of time before the business community will recognise that co-creation is even more relevant at the early front end of the design development process, where probes and generative toolkits best operate (Sanders and Simons 2009). It is important that research and practice with the tools and techniques for making be published and shared widely so that they will be open for all to use in the future. Froukje Sleeswijk Visser's dissertation (2009) is one effort that moves in this direction. But with the new tools and techniques that are emerging, this effort needs to be continually updated.

In light of all the open issues and challenges described above, it is not hard to imagine future research areas for PhD students:

- An ethnography of the design participation framework in action. How does it play out in industry versus in industry-sponsored academic projects versus in academic settings?
- How is it best to teach or to set up learning environments for the design participation framework? What is the role of theory? What is the role of hands-on learning and apprenticeships?
- What is the impact of cultural differences? How does the design participation framework work in other cultures? With hard-to-reach people?
- Can the design participation framework be used to frame and to facilitate large-scale assignments in complex social arenas where the definition is not given but part of the challenge? If so, how?

We have in this chapter proposed that a rethinking of how tools and techniques are embedded in particular design practices may be needed to ensure that tools and techniques are not used without a participatory mindset. We have suggested that the concept of design games may be of use to keep both practitioners and researchers alert regarding how the game of participation is staged and acted out. There may be other directions to go, but in any case there is today a rich repertoire of participatory toolboxes that can only gain in strength as more people become involved in design collaborations.

References

A.Telier (T. Binder, G. de Michelis, P. Ehn, G. Jacussi, P. Linde and I. Wagner (2011) *Design Things*, Cambridge, MA: MIT Press.

Andersen, N. E., F. Kensing, J. Lundin, L. Mathiassen, A. Munk-Madsen, M. Rasbech and P. Sørgaard (1990) *Professional Systems Development: Experience, Ideas and Action*, Upper Saddle River, NJ: Prentice-Hall.

Baek, J.-S. and K.-P. Lee (2008) 'A participatory design approach to information architecture design for children', *The International Journal of CoDesign in Design and the Arts*, 4(3): 173–91.

Benyon, D., P. Turner and S. Turner (2005) *Designing Interactive Systems: People, Activities, Contexts, Technologies*, Essex: Pearson Education.

Binder, T. (1996) 'Participation and reification in design of artifacts – an interview with Etienne Wenger', in T. Binder, M. Fischer and J. Nilsson (eds) *Learning with Artefacts*, special issue of *AI & Society*, 10, London: Springer.

Binder, T. (1999) 'Setting the stage for improvised video scenarios', *Proceedings of the CHI Conference 1999*, Pittsburgh, PA: Carnegie Mellon University, 230–31.

Blomberg, J., J. Giacomi, A. Mosher and P. Swenton-Wall (1993) 'Ethnographic field methods and their relation to design', in D. Schuler and A. Namioka (eds) *Participatory Design – Principles and Practices*, Hillsdale, NJ: Lawrence Erlbaum Associates, 123–55.

Boal, A. (1974) *Theater of the Oppressed*, London: Pluto Press.

Bødker, K., and J. S. Pedersen (1991) 'Workplace cultures – looking at artifacts, symbols and practice', in J. Greenbaum and M. Kyng (eds) *Design at Work: Cooperative Design of Computer Systems*, Hillsdale, NJ: Lawrence Erlbaum Associates, 121–36.

Bødker, K., F. Kensing and J. Simonsen (2004) *Participatory IT Design: Designing for Business and Workplace Realities*, Cambridge, MA: MIT Press.

Bødker, S. (1990) *Through the Interface: A Human Activity Approach to User Interface Design*, Hillsdale, NJ: Lawrence Erlbaum Associates.

Bødker, S. (1996) 'Creating conditions for participation: conflicts and resources in systems design', *Human Computer Interaction*, 11(3): 215–36.

Bødker, S. and J. Buur (2002) 'The design collaboratorium – a place for usability design'. *ACM Transactions on Computer–Human Interaction*, 9(2, June): 152–69.

Bødker, S. and K. Grønbæk (1991) 'Design in action – from prototyping by demonstration to cooperative prototyping', in J. Greenbaum and M. Kyng (eds) *Design at Work: Cooperative Design of Computer Systems*, Hillsdale, NJ: Lawrence Erlbaum Associates, 199–218.

Bødker, S., P. Ehn, J. Kammersgaard, M. Kyng and Y. Sundblad (1987) 'A UTOPIAN experience: on design of powerful computer-based tools for skilled graphical workers' in G. Bjerknes, P. Ehn and M. Kyng (eds) *Computers and Democracy – A Scandinavian Challenge*, Aldershot: Avebury, 251–78.

Boehner, K., J. Vertesi, P. Sengers and P. Dourish (2007) 'How HCI interprets the probes', *Proceedings of the CHI 2007 Conference, San Jose, California*, 1077–86.

Brandt, E. (2011) 'Participation through exploratory design games', in L. B. Rasmussen (ed.) *Facilitating Change – Using Interactive Methods in Organisations, Communities and Networks*, Copenhagen: Polyteknisk Forlag, 213–56.

Brandt, E. and C. Grunnet (2000) 'Evoking the future: drama and props in user centered design', in T. Cherkasky, J. Greenbaum and P. Mambrey (eds) *Proceedings of Participatory Design Conference*, New York: ACM, 11–20.

Brandt, E. and Messeter, J. (2004) 'Facilitating collaboration through design games', in A. Clement and P. van den Besselaar (eds) *Proceedings of the Participatory Design Conference 2004, Toronto, August*, New York: ACM, 121–31.

Brandt, E., J. Messeter and T. Binder (2008) 'Formatting design dialogues – games and participation', *International Journal of CoDesign in Design and the Arts*, 4(1, March): 51–64.

Brodersen, C., C. Dindler and O. Iversen (2008) 'Staging imaginative places of participatory prototyping', *International Journal of CoDesign in Design and the Arts*, 4(1): 19–30.

Buchenau, M. and J. Fulton Suri (2000) 'Experience prototyping', in *Proceedings of DIS 2000 Conference, Designing Interactive Systems*, New York: ACM, 424–33.

Burns, C. (1994) 'Hairdos and videotape: informance design', *Proceedings of the CHI 1994 – Conference on Computer Human Interaction, Boston*, New York: ACM, 1994, 119–20.

Burns, C., E. Dishman, B. Verplank and B. Lassiter (1997) 'Actors, hair-dos and videotape: informance design', paper presented at 'Presence Forum' (Royal College of Art), London, November.

Buur, J. and R. Mitchell (2011) 'The business modeling lab', in J. Buur (ed.) *Proceedings of the Participatory Innovation Conference*, Sønderborg, Denmark: University of Southern Denmark, 360–65.

Carroll, J. M. (ed.) (1995) *Scenario-Based Design. Envisioning Work and Technology in System Development*, New York: John Wiley.

Carroll, J. M. (2000) *Making Use: Scenario-Based Design of Human–Computer Interactions*, Cambridge, MA: MIT Press.

Chomsky, N. (1965) *Aspects of the Theory of Syntax*, Cambridge, MA: MIT Press.

Clausen, H. (1993) 'Narratives as tools for the systems designer', *Design Studies*, 14: 283–98.

Cross, Nigel (ed.) (1971) 'Design participation', *Proceedings of the Design Research Society Conference*, London: Academy Editions.

Dindler, C. (2010) 'Fictional space in participatory design of engaging interactive environments', PhD dissertation, Department of Information and Media Studies, Faculty of Humanities, Aarhus University.

Dourish, P. (2003) 'Appropriation of interaction technologies: some lessons from placeless documents', *Journal of CSCW*, 12(4): 465–90.

Druin, A. (ed.) (1989) *The Design of Children's Technology*, Hershey, PA: Morgen Kaufmann.

Dunne, A. (2006) *Hertzian Tales: Electronic Products, Aesthetic Experience, and Critical Design*, Cambridge, MA: MIT Press.

Dunne, A. and F. Raby (2001) *Design Noir: The Secret Life of Electronic Objects*, Switzerland: Birkhauser.

Ehn, P. (1988) *Work-Oriented Design of Computer Artifacts*, Falköping, Sweden: Arbetslivcentrum/Almqvist and Wiksell International.

Ehn, P. (1993) 'Scandinavian design: on participation and skill', in D. Schuler and A. Namioka (eds) *Participatory Design – Principles and Practices*, Hillsdale, NJ: Lawrence Erlbaum Associates, 41–70.

Ehn, P. and M. Kyng (1991) 'Cardboard computers: mocking-it-up or hands-on the future', in J. Greenbaum and M. Kyng (eds) *Design at Work*, Hillsdale, NJ: Lawrence Erlbaum Associates, 169–95.

Ehn, P. and D. Sjøgren (1991) 'From system descriptions to scripts for action', in J. Greenbaum and M. Kyng (eds) *Design at Work*, Hillsdale, NJ: Lawrence Erlbaum Associates, 241–68.

Floyd, C. A. (1984) 'Systematic view of prototyping', in R. Budde, K. Kuhlenkamp, L. Mathiassen and H. Zullighoven (eds) *Approaches to Prototyping*, Berlin: Springer, 1–18.

Foverskov, M. and T. Binder (2011) 'Super dots: making social media tangible for senior citizens', *Proceedings of the DPPI Conference, Designing Pleasurable Products and Interfaces*, Milan, Italy.

Garabet, A., S. Mann and J. Fung (2002) 'Exploring design through wearable computing art(ifacts)', in *Proceedings of CHI 2002, Interactive Posters. April 20–25, 2002, Minneapolis, Minnesota*, New York: ACM, 634–5.

Gaver, B., Dunne, T. and Pacenti, E. (1999) 'Cultural probes', *Interactions*, January/February: 21–9.

Greenbaum, J. and M. Kyng (eds) (1991) *Design at Work*, Hillsdale, NJ: Lawrence Erlbaum Associates.

Grudin, J. and J. Pruitt (2002). *Personas, Participatory Design and Product Development: An Infrastructure for Engagement*. Proceedings of the Participatory Design Conference. Malmö, Sweden.

Grønbæk, K. (1988) 'Rapid prototyping with fourth generation systems – an empirical study', *DAIMI PB-270*, Århus University, Denmark.

Habraken, H. J. and M. D. Gross (1987) *Concept Design Games* (Books 1 and 2). A report submitted to the National Science Foundation Engineering Directorate, Design Methodology Program, Department of Architecture, MIT, Cambridge, MA.

Halse, J., E. Brandt, B. Clark and T. Binder (2010) *Rehearsing the Future*, Copenhagen: Danish Design School Press.

Heyer, C. and M. Brereton (2010) 'Design from the everyday: continuously evolving, embedded exploratory prototypes', *Proceeding of the DIS 2010 Conference, Aarhus, Denmark*. New York: ACM, 282–91.

Howard, S., J. Carroll, J. Murphy and J. Peck (2002) 'Using "endowed props" in scenario-based design', *Proceedings of NordiCHI 2002, October 19–23, 2002, Aarhus, Denmark*, 1–10.

Hussain, S. and E. B.-N. Sanders (2012) 'Fusion of horizons: seeking the perspectives of Cambodian children using prosthetic legs through generative design tools', accepted for publication in *CoDesign*, 1: 1–37.

Iacucci, G. and K. Kuutti (2002) 'Everyday life as a stage in creating and performing scenarios for wireless devices', *Personal and Ubiquitous Computing*, 6: 299–306.

Iacucci, G., K. Kuutti and M. Renta (2000) 'On the move with a magic thing: role playing in concept design of mobile services and devices', *Proceedings of DIS Conference, Brooklyn, New York*, New York: ACM, 193–202.

Iversen, O. S. and C. Dindler (2008) 'Pursuing aesthetic inquiry in participatory design', in D. Hakken, J. Simonsen and T. Robertson (eds) *Proceedings of the Participatory Design Conference 2008*, New York: ACM, 138–45.

Johansson, M. (2005) 'Participatory inquiry – collaborative design', PhD dissertation, School of Engineering, Blekinge Institute of Technology, Sweden.

Johansson, M. and P. Linde (2005) 'Playful collaborative exploration: new research practice in participatory design', *Journal of Research Practice*, 1(1): Article M5.

Johansson, M., J. Halse and T. Binder (2005) 'Between estrangement and familarization: co-constructing images of use and user in collaborative design', in T. Binder and M. Hellström (eds) *Design Spaces*, Finland: Edita Publishing, IT Press.

Jones, J. C. (1992) *Design Methods*, second edition, New York: Van Nostrand Reinhold. (First published in 1970 under the title *Design Methods: Seeds of Human Futures*.)

Jungk, R. and N. Müllert (1987) *Future Workshops: How to Create Desirable Futures*, London: Institute for Social Inventions.

Kensing, F. and J. Blomberg (eds) (1998) *Computer Supported Cooperative Work*, Special Issue on Participatory Design, 7(3–4).

Kensing, F. and K. Madsen (1991) 'Generating visions: future workshops and metaphorical design', in J. Greenbaum and M. Kyng (eds) *Design at Work: Cooperative Design of Computer Systems*, Hillsdale, NJ: Lawrence Erlbaum Associates, 155–68.

Kensing, F. and A. Munk-Madsen (1993) 'PD: structure in the toolbox', *Communications of the ACM*, 36(6): 78–85.

Koestler, A. (1964) *The Act of Creation*, London: Hutchinson.

Koskinen, I., K. Batterbee and T. Mattelmäki (2003) *Empathic Design – User Experience in Product Design*, Finland: Edita Publishing, IT Press.

Kyng, M. (1995) 'Creating contexts for design', in J. Carroll (ed.) *Scenario-based Design*, New York: John Wiley.

Lave, J. and E. Wenger (1991) *Situated Learning: Legitimate Peripheral Participation*, Cambridge: Cambridge University Press.

Lilienfeld, S. O., J. M. Wood and H. N. Garb (2000) 'The scientific status of projective techniques', *Psychological Science in the Public Interest*, 1(2): 27–66.

Linde, C. (2001) 'Narrative and social tacit knowledge', *Journal of Knowledge Management*, Special Issue on Tacit Knowledge Exchange and Active Learning, 5(2): 160–71.

Löwgren, J. and Stolterman, E. (2004) *Thoughtful Interaction Design – A Design Perspective on Information Technology*, Cambridge, MA: MIT Press.

Mattelmäki, T. (2005) 'Applying probes – from inspirational notes to collaborative insights', *CoDesign: International Journal of CoDesign in Design and the Arts*, 1(2, June): 83–102.

Mattelmäki, T. (2006) 'Design probes', PhD dissertation, Helsinki: University of Art and Design, Helsinki.

Mazé, R. and J. Redström (2007) 'Difficult forms: critical practices in design and research', *Proceedings of the IASDR07, Conference on Emerging Trends in Design Research*, Hong Kong: Hong Kong Polytechnic University.

Messeter, J., E. Brandt, J. Halse and M. Johansson (2004) 'Contextualizing mobile IT', *Proceedings of DIS Conference 2004, Cambridge, Massachusetts, USA*, New York: ACM.

Mogensen, P. (1992) 'Towards a provotyping approach in system development', *Scandinavian Journal of Information Systems*, 3: 31–53.

Muller, M. (1991) 'PICTIVE – an exploration in participatory design'. *Proceedings of the SIGCHI Conference on Human Factors in Computing Systems – Reaching through Technology, CHI 91*, New York: ACM.

Muller, M. (1993) 'PICTIVE: democratizing the dynamics of the design session', in D. Schuler and A. Namioka (eds) *Participatory Design: Principles and Practices*, Hillsdale, NJ: Lawrence Erlbaum Associates.

Muller, M. and A. Druin (2012) 'Participatory Design: the third space in HCI', in J. Jacko (ed.) *The Human–Computer Interaction Handbook*, Hillsdale, NJ: Lawrence Erlbaum Associates.

Nilsson, J., T. Sokoler, T. Binder and N. Wetcke (2000) 'Beyond the control room – mobile devices for spatially distributed interaction on industrial process plants', *Proceedings from Second International Symposium on Handheld and Ubiquitous Computing 2000*, New York: ACM, 30–45.

Orr, J. E. (1986) 'Narratives at work – storytelling as cooperative diagnostic activity', *CSCW '86: Proceedings of the ACM Conference on Computer-Supported Cooperative Work*, New York: ACM, 62–72.

Orr, J. E. (1996) *Talking about Machines: An Ethnography of a Modern Job*, New York: Cornell University Press.

Oulasvirta, A., E. Kurvinen and T. Kankainen (2003) 'Understanding contexts by being there: case studies in bodystorming', *Personal and Ubiquitous Computing*, 7: 125–34.

Redhead, F. and M. Brereton (2008) 'Getting to the nub of neighbourhood interaction', *Proceedings of the Participatory Design Conference, Indiana, US*, New York: ACM, 270–73.

Redhead, F. and M. Brereton (2009) 'Designing interaction for local communications: an urban screen study', *Proceedings of INTERACT 2009*, New York: ACM, 457–60.

Redhead, F. and M. Brereton (2010) 'Iterative design within a local community communication fabric', *Proceedings of OZCHI2010, Brisbane, Australia*, ACM Digital Library, 388–91.

Sanders, E. B.-N. (1999) 'Post design and participatory culture', in *Proceedings of Useful and Critical: The Position of Research in Design*, Helsinki: University of Art and Design, 87–92.

Sanders, E. B.-N. (2000) 'Generative tools for codesigning', in S. Scrivener, L. Ball and A. Woodcock (eds) *Collaborative Design*, London: Springer-Verlag.

Sanders, E. B.-N. and G. Simons (2009) 'A social vision for value co-creation in design', *Open Source Business Resource*, December. Available at: www.osbr.ca/ojs/index.php/osbr/article/view/1012/973.

Sanders, E. B.-N. and P. J. Stappers (2008) 'Co-creation and the new landscapes of design', *CoDesign, International Journal of CoDesign in Design and the Arts*, 4(1, March): 5–18.

Sanders, E. B.-N. and C. T. William (2001) 'Harnessing people's creativity: ideation and expression through visual communication', in J. Langford and D. McDonagh-Philp (eds) *Focus Groups: Supporting Effective Product Development*, London: Taylor and Francis.

Sanoff, H. (2010) *Democratic Design: Participation Case Studies in Urban and Small Town Environments*, Saarbrucken: VDM Verlag Dr Muller.

Sato, S. and T. Salvador (1999) 'Playacting and focus troupes: theater techniques for creating quick, intense, immersive, and engaging focus group sessions', *Interactions – Experiences, People, Technology*, September–October: 35–41.

Schuler, D. and A. Namioka (eds) (1993) *Participatory Design: Principles and Practices*, Hillsdale, NJ: Lawrence Erlbaum Associates.

Sleeswijk Visser, F. (2009) 'Bringing the everyday life of people into design, PhD dissertation. Delft University of Technology.

Sleeswijk Visser, F., P. J. Stappers, R. van der Lugt and E. B.-N. Sanders (2005) 'Contextmapping: experiences from practice', *CoDesign, International Journal of CoDesign in Design and the Arts*, 1(2): 119–49.

Snyder, C. (2003) *Paper Prototyping: The Fast and Easy Way to Design and Refine User Interfaces*, New York: Morgan Kaufmann.

Stanislavskij, K. (1940) *An Actor's Work on Himself*, Danish version: En skuespillers arbejde med sig selv; Nyt nordisk Forlag Arnold Busck, 4. Oplag 1988.

Star, S. L. (1989) 'The structure of ill-structures solutions: heterogeneous problem-solving, boundary objects and distributed artificial intelligence', in M. N. Kuhns and L. Gasser (eds) *Distributed Artificial Intelligence, Vol. 2*, San Mateo, CA: Morgan Kaufman, 37–54.

Star, S. L. and J. R. Greismer (1989) 'Institutional ecology, "translations" and boundary objects: amateurs and professionals in Berkley's Museum of Vertebrate Zoology, 1907–39', *Social Studies of Science* (AGE, London, Newbury Park and New Delhi), 19: 387–420.

Statler, M., J. Roos and B. Victor (2009) 'Ain't misbehavin': taking play seriously in organizations', *Journal of Change Management*, 9(1): 87–107.

Vaajakallio, K. and T. Mattelmäki (2007) 'Collaborative design exploration: envisioning future practices with maketools', *Proceedings of the Designing Pleasurable Products and Interfaces Conference, 22–25 August 2007, Helsinki, Finland*, New York: ACM, 223–38.

Wenger, E. (1998) *Communities of Practice: Learning, Meaning and Identity*, Cambridge: Cambridge University Press.

Westerlund, B. (2009) 'Design space exploration: co-operative creation of proposals for desired interactions with future artefacts', PhD thesis, Human–Computer Interaction, KTH, Stockholm.

Winograd, T. and F. Flores (1986) *Understanding Computers and Cognition – A New Foundation for Design*, Norwood, NJ: Ablex.

Ylirisku, S. and J. Buur (2007) *Designing with Video: Focusing the User-Centered Design Process*, London: Springer.

8

Communities

Participatory Design for, with and by communities

Carl DiSalvo, Andrew Clement and Volkmar Pipek

Community-based Participatory Design is a distinctive field of Participatory Design research and practice that highlights the social constructs and relations of groups in settings that include, but go well beyond, the formal organisational structures commonly foregrounded in more traditional workplace studies. To provide an overview of community-based Participatory Design, we discuss the following themes: participation with and by community-based organisations; Participatory Design in activist and hobbyist communities; Participatory Design for community communications; Participatory Design as cultural production; and Participatory Design for public deliberation. We conclude by elaborating on the ideas of 'politics', 'publics' and 'infrastructuring' to further inform analytical as well as methodological perspectives on supporting community-based Participatory Design.

After a description and motivation of our perspective on Participatory Design in and for communities, we describe a series of projects from various fields of Participatory Design practice. We then elaborate three interrelated topics we believe can inform community-based Participatory Design practice.

This chapter draws together and examines a collection of previously published Participatory Design projects that cover different notions of 'community'. From this collection of projects and subsequent analysis, the chapter provides a novel articulation of community-based Participatory Design as a distinctive field within Participatory Design. It identifies and discusses the complexities, potentials and pitfalls of community-based Participatory Design and proposes a three-part framework to help capture and address recurring issues encountered in community-based Participatory Design initiatives. Finally, the chapter suggests new issues and opportunities for improving future research and practices of Participatory Design in communities.

Communities are social constructs with open, heterogeneous structures of participation that resist formulaic design strategies. In order to further community-based Participatory Design, what is needed are pluralistic approaches to employing and analysing Participatory Design practices across the diverse contexts and issues of communities. This requires inventiveness with new modes of infrastructuring, attentiveness to new forms of politics and exploration of new opportunities for community-based Participatory Design, such as social media.

Introduction

The emergence of community-based Participatory Design as a distinctive field of Participatory Design is relatively recent. In this chapter we trace major themes in Participatory Design for, with and by communities and discuss topics that are shaping the future of the field. Comparatively small as an area of research and practice, community-based Participatory Design promises to grow in importance in light of the continuing expansion of digital networking in the context of prevailing neo-liberal market globalisation forces and the publics organised against those forces. The ongoing trend of lower cost, smaller size, increased capability, tighter interconnection and deeper penetration of information technologies into everyday life presents opportunities to bring Participatory Design perspectives to bear in community contexts. Accompanying this technological trend, and indirectly related to it, is the rising importance of social services and civil society. As Carroll et al. note

> [N]on-profit community service groups … address important societal issues such as environmental protection and sustainable development, historical preservation, the arts, provision of medical services and distribution of food to the needy, housing construction for low-income people, protection of animals, aspects of public safety and security, and much more.

> *(Carroll et al 2008, p. 1)*

These issues listed by Carroll provide a glimpse of the scope of community-based Participatory Design. Still, the term 'community' is a difficult qualifier because it signals a concept that is simultaneously elusive and familiar. Given that Participatory Design is grounded historically in the workplace and work practices, we might be tempted to cast community-based Participatory Design as that which exists outside of the contexts and issues of labour; to claim that community-based Participatory Design is all that takes place outside of the factory, office, hospital or other formal organisational workplace. While this site-based distinction offers a useful starting point, it's flawed. Certainly there are communities within conventional workplaces. There are also communities of labour outside of conventional workplaces, the open source software development community being a prominent example. So, rather than counter-posing workplaces and communities as sites of Participatory Design, we instead look at the kinds of relations and interactions that distinguish communities from those associated with formal organisations, and how these affect pursuing the ideals of Participatory Design. What we mean by community-based Participatory Design, at its simplest, is work that foregrounds the social constructs and relations of groups in settings that include, but go well beyond, the formal organisational structures commonly foregrounded in more traditional workplace studies.

For instance, consider that the archetypal Participatory Design project was conducted within established enterprises in which participants are employees working mainly for wages and linked to each other through hierarchical reporting relationships. Prospective users of a system being designed would often have in common similar positions in the hierarchy, share physical work spaces as well as work schedules, and know each other from long periods of working together. These characteristics play an important but often overlooked role in Participatory Design tools and practices. For instance, brainstorming sessions, such as Future Workshops, and prototyping exercises are enabled by continuity of employment, prior mutual familiarity as well as spatial and temporal proximity. But social relations in communities outside of the workplace are generally much more fluid and ambiguous than those found in formal organisations. One key difference is that interpersonal associations and community affiliations are often largely voluntary and driven more by intrinsic rewards than by extrinsic factors such as pay. In thinking broadly about what we mean be 'community', we can consider community in three ways: in relation to geography, in relation to identity, and in relation to interests and practice.

Varieties of communities

Perhaps the most common use of community is in relation to geography, where 'community' is used as a label for a group of people defined by a bounded space or distinct locale, such as a neighbourhood, town or region. In regards to community-based Participatory Design, neighbourhoods and neighbourhood organisations can function as defining the constituents of a project, serving as a means of providing coherence and providing proximal opportunities for interaction. Neighbourhoods, though, are not the only scope of geographic communities. Many community networking initiatives with strong participatory orientations are based largely, but not exclusively, on geographic communities, of a wider scope than neighbourhoods (Schuler 1996; Gurstein 2000; Clement et al. 2012). Moreover, the designation of a geographic community alone does not necessarily constitute an internal shared sense of belongingness. As Benedict Anderson (1991) famously points out, a community requires a shared imaginary. It may be the case that the geographic construct of a community is imposed from the outside, perhaps tied to infrastructural or legislative markers such as roads or voting districts, while internal to that geographic bounding there could be a multiplicity of distinct communities, defined by identity vectors and/or shared interests and practices.

Identity is another important factor in community-based Participatory Design because it reflects back on the very question of what constitutes community. In many cases, communities form around shared identities and the work of community-based Participatory Design is qualified by these identities. Age is one of the more common identity classifications, with projects developed specifically with elders or youth (Read et al. 2002; Danielsson and Wiberg 2006; Bowen and Chamberlain 2008; Mazzone et al. 2008; Light et al. 2009). In addition to age, race, gender, sexuality, physical abilities and ethnicity are also identities that may bind a community together and form the basis of collective design initiatives.

Yet another useful way of understanding community is to focus on shared interests and practices. More than just a common interest, though, what is needed to constitute a community is an ongoing shared involvement or collective practice around a particular interest. Jean Lave and Etienne Wenger (Lave and Wenger 1991) refer to this robust form of communities of interest that lead to sustainable learning as 'communities of practice', described as 'groups of people who share a concern or a passion for something they do and learn how to do it better as they interact regularly'.[1] As an example of community-based Participatory Design, Shilton et al. (2008) report on the development of a participatory sensing and mapping programme to assist cyclists in their daily commutes in urban environments. This project illustrates how community-based Participatory Design can be organised around shared interests and practices, with the organising principle being a shared passion for an activity, and along with that, a shared desire to improve the conditions of that activity.

One important challenge for Participatory Design researchers and designers is to recognise and negotiate the plurality that exists within communities. On the one hand, it would be remiss to deny the importance of geography, identity or shared interests and practices in shaping desires, capabilities, expectations and outcomes. On the other hand, one must work with great care not to essentialise participants or communities. The issue of what constitutes a community, and keeping the notion of community open to interpretation, has been taken up in recent community-based Participatory Design scholarship. For example, Winschiers-Theophilus et al.

(2010) have explored the notion of community and participation from a perspective of African philosophy and rural practices, and Akama and Ivanka have explored the use of Participatory Design methods for articulating alternative notions of community that work to 'avoid "imagined" notions of a community that can hide social heterogeneity' (Akama and Ivanka 2010, p. 11).

Rather than arguing one definition of community or another, our goal in this chapter is to sketch the contours of community-based Participatory Design, and in doing so provide a map to this diverse domain. To do this we survey a series of projects, and through them draw out major themes in community-based Participatory Design. These themes are a reflection of our interpretation of the salient issues and activities of community-based Participatory Design. Within each of these themes the selected projects engage particular challenges or opportunities of community-based Participatory Design. We do not claim that the projects highlighted here represent the full spectrum of Participatory Design initiatives in community settings. We have relied mainly on projects reported in the Participatory Design literature, filtered through our own areas of expertise, and we expect that there are projects reported in other literatures (such as community development and community informatics) that many never appear in any Participatory Design publication. Taken together, however, the selected projects express the diversity of community-based Participatory Design. The first two themes, *Participatory Design with and by community-based organisations* and *Participatory Design in activist and hobbyist communities*, highlight new participants in the Participatory Design process. Themes three, four, and five, *Participatory Design for community communications*, *Participatory Design for creativity and cultural production*, and *Enhancing public deliberation in political and commercial environments*, highlight new purposes for Participatory Design. After presenting this map of the present and recent past, we proceed with a discussion of topics in community-based Participatory Design that we believe will be formative to the field as it develops: those of politics, publics and infrastructuring.

Participatory Design with and by community-based organisations

Projects involving community-based organisations (CBOs) provide a good starting point for a discussion of community-based Participatory Design because they share a number of characteristics with the participants and settings of archetypal Participatory Design projects. While these CBOs have a kind of organisational structure, they also often have distinctive features due to the heightened role of volunteers (rather than employees) and motivations that often come from desires for social justice or community good (rather than profit or income). Usually those projects reported in the research literature involve some kind of collaboration between external researchers/developers and pre-existing organisations that don't focus principally on information technologies, but have other mandates and consider information technologies as potentially supporting those other missions (e.g. Benston and Balka 1993; McPhail et al. 1998; Merkel et al, 2004, 2007, plus many others mentioned in this chapter). An exception to this general case is the in-house development of information management systems at the Global Fund for Women CBO, reported in Chapter 9 of this volume. Less common also are those Participatory Design initiatives that involve forming a community organisation around an information technology development in which various forms of participation play an important role. This is especially the case of community networking (CN) initiatives (see Schuler 1996).

One of the key characteristics that distinguish CBOs from the kinds of organisations where Participatory Design initiatives have been more commonly sited is that they are relatively resource poor and struggle to keep up technologically. As Carroll et al. (2008, p. 1) note, 'They often are trapped by somewhat outdated technologies and information management practices.' On the other hand, such organisations can be especially amenable to participatory approaches.

The relative lack of technological sophistication together with shared cultural values, particularly around addressing social needs inclusively, means that more conventional information technology development approaches, relying on cadres of technical staff and formalised, systems-centric methodologies, are less likely to be suitable. At the same time, the relatively greater importance placed on intrinsic rewards and having a direct say in providing services, especially among volunteers, means that members of CBOs are likely to be more familiar with participatory ideals and better able to pursue them actively than in more hierarchical organisations, where the expectation is more of financial reward for doing what one is told.

CAVEAT – a justice system reform organisation

CAVEAT was a non-profit charitable organisation, which until its closure in 2001 aimed at reforming the Canadian justice system, particularly with regard to victims' rights. In this respect it produced and served a community of interest. With its explicit political focus on an issue of public policy concern, we can see it as constituting a 'public', in the Deweyan sense discussed later in this chapter. Typical of many such small organisations, CAVEAT struggled with funding and depended heavily on volunteers. One long-time volunteer with an information technology background taking a graduate course in Participatory Design was instrumental in getting this organisation to be the field site for the major course project. Drawing directly on the textbook for the course, *Design at Work* (Greenbaum and Kyng 1991), the student team mimicked important aspects of the earlier 'classic' workplace studies. In particular, they conducted a successful Future Workshop,[2] eliciting considerable enthusiasm among the participants, and engaged in several rounds of iterative prototyping.

However, in several notable respects, their experience differed considerably from previously reported studies in more conventional workplace settings. A volunteer ethos pervaded the operation. There was a sense among members of 'working towards a common goal, but expecting in return for their contributions a degree of control over their work' (McPhail et al. 1998, p. 224). The diversity of volunteers' backgrounds can be of considerable advantage, with the organisation gaining a variety of sometimes highly talented people to draw upon, but it also makes it hard to rely on everyone reaching a given level of computer competence or experience. The variability in volunteer timetables and longevity with the organisation also had an impact on the design process. With such uneven schedules it was unfeasible to actively involve volunteers in the workshop and prototyping exercises, and hence ironically these were confined largely to the staff who were on site more regularly.

The community learning network (CLN) at St Christopher House

The case of a participatory development of a 'community learning network' by the St Christopher House community and social service agency provides an interesting contrast to CAVEAT. While volunteers were again difficult to involve, lack of resources was not a primary constraint, offering valuable insights into other strengths and challenges typical of community-based Participatory Design initiatives. St Christopher House (St Chris) is a long-standing non-profit, non-religious community organisation in Toronto, providing a broad range of services for the surrounding geographically defined community, particularly to the relatively disadvantaged (Luke et al. 2004; MacDonald and Clement 2008, 2012). Building on its experience in operating a network of public Internet access centres across its quadrant of the city, St Chris embarked in 2002 on an ambitious project to develop an open source community learning network (CLN)– content management system that would serve as 'a meeting and virtual learning/teaching facility that will test and push the horizon of the Internet's capacity to provide relevant online content for a diverse client population with a multiplicity of needs' (Luke et al. 2004, p. 13). With $300,000 (CAN) in federal government funding it contracted with a small recently formed software development company dedicated to free/open source software (FOSS) approaches, to create a flexible, multi-purpose web portal as a digital infrastructure for the organisation and the wider community it served.

In keeping with its prevailing cultural ideals, St Chris embraced a participatory approach to the system development. In testimony to this ideal, as well as the strong commitment to the CLN development, nearly all staff took part in an intensive two-day off-site needs assessment exercise with the software developers. The main outcomes were high expectations on the part of the staff and more concretely an extensive 'blueprint' document that was to serve as the specification for the construction of the CLN. However, prolonged delays in delivering the key system components led to significant frustration and disappointment all round. Overcoming substantial cost overruns and ongoing organisational tensions, the CLN was finally launched in 2005. In 2011 it still serves as the basis for the St Chris website and the participatory approach credited as a vital ingredient in its creation. See Figures 8.1 and 8.2.

From the point of view of the academic researchers who studied the project, the main difficulties stemmed on the St Chris side from a lack of prior understanding of information technology by the intended users, as well as the lack of technical management capacity in the project leadership. The development team, while sharing with St Chris many of the same ideals about openness and participation, were more familiar with conventional systems development life cycles than with Participatory Design techniques. In particular, an iterative prototyping approach would likely have fostered a more realistic understanding of system capabilities and limitations, helped align expectations among the various stakeholders and generally promoted more rapid mutual learning.

Among the lessons to be learned from this case is that it is valuable to accompany participatory enthusiasm and values with a range of effective Participatory Design techniques, such as iterative prototyping. Furthermore, the complex trade-offs in addressing the needs of disparate stakeholders can undermine a project, but these can be overcome with wider shared organisational and social commitments.

Figure 8.1 St Chris House: participants in the ASE needs assessment exercise

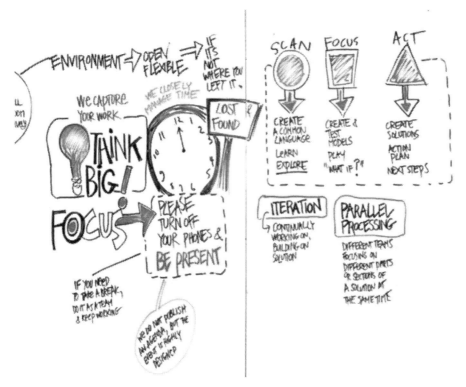

Figure 8.2 St Chris House: flipchart from the ASE needs assessment exercise

Civic Nexus

Probably the most concerted Participatory Design developments in CBOs has been within the Civic Nexus project based at the Laboratory for Computer-Supported Collaboration and Learning (CSCL) at Penn State University (Merkel et al. 2004; Farooq et al. 2007). Launched in 2003 by John Carroll and Mary Beth Rosson, building on their earlier work with the Blacksburg Electronic Village (Virginia, USA), Civic Nexus is a long-term Participatory Design project working with community partners 'to increase their ability to solve local community problems by leveraging and enhancing their capacity to use information technology' (Farooq et al. 2007, p. 7).

Over a four-year period, the research team partnered with 13 community groups active in the region around State College, Pennsylvania, focusing on environmental, conservational, historical, educational and other matters. The project team took an action research approach and sought explicitly to integrate learning with long-term Participatory Design engagements. In the early stages their fieldwork was ethnographic, 'to understand the user's work practices and identity opportunities for collaboration' (Merkel et al. 2004, p. 2). Mindful that Participatory Design initiatives tended to falter after the academic researchers left the project (Clement and van den Besselaar 1993) and wanting to 'avoid becoming yet another temporary resource taking on the role of the consultant who builds something, leaving behind a system that is difficult to use, fix, and modify' (Merkel et al. 2004, p. 2), the Civic Nexus team sought to foster sustainable innovations. They were careful to let the community organisations take the lead in deciding development priorities and after the period of direct engagement, usually a year, they sought to fade away gradually with the participants taking over the full responsibility for the immediate and future endeavours.

One of the Civic Nexus cases reported in depth is that of the Spring Creek Watershed Community developing a new website (Farooq et al. 2007). They were dissatisfied with the results of a third-party design but, like many community organisations dependent on an unresponsive vendor, lacked the capability to make changes themselves. Unlike St Chris, which tackled a similar situation by building their own content management system (CMS), Spring Creek took the considerably easier, but still daunting route of end-user development using an existing content management system. With the Civic Nexus team facilitating the decision-making process, Spring Creek settled on Mambo as the CMS in which they would build and themselves maintain their new website. This was in part because it was an open source with a lively developer community that could, and did, became an invaluable resource for problem-solving and learning about the CMS.

From this the researchers articulated several design heuristics for developing community-based technology. The one that addresses most directly Participatory Design issues in community settings deals with volunteering, which, as noted earlier, CBOs typically rely on very heavily. However, while vital, volunteers are challenging to manage. As in both the previous cases of CAVEAT and St Chris, Spring Creek deliberately excluded volunteers from the initial design processes, but in this case the organisation followed this by a cautious long-term, incremental process of developing trust in particular volunteers while allowing them to take on new roles with progressively more authority and responsibility.

One important theme that cuts across the various Civic Nexus projects is a concern for identifying the appropriate roles that Participatory Design researchers may play in assisting CBOs in taking advantage of the new capabilities offered by increasingly cheap and powerful information technologies, while helping them avoid the many pitfalls. In seeking to 'seed ownership for technology projects in the community groups themselves' (Merkel et al. 2004, p. 7), the Civic Nexus researchers came to see their design role as not simply to elicit project requirements or provide technology solutions, but as calling for a wider range of less directly interventionist roles, including as 'lurkers, facilitators, consultants and bards' (Merkel et al. 2004, p. 7). In at least one case, this meant resisting the desires of an over-stretched community organisation to pass the entire design project over to the research team. Drawing on Bødker and her colleagues (e.g. Bødker and Iverson 2002), they note that 'the focus should not just be on design skills but on the designer's ability to create conditions that encourage a collaborative design process and active reflection' (Merkel et al. 2004, p. 7). This calls for participatory designers working with CBOs to be highly reflective themselves and sensitive to the varied circumstances of the organisations they work with.

Learning is another important theme that characterises the community-based Participatory Design in the Civic Nexus as well as other projects. Participatory Design researchers have viewed the ideal of 'mutual learning', between 'users' and 'developers' through common experiences, as intrinsic to a Participatory Design approach, and this term appears prominently in Participatory Design reports from the earliest Scandinavian experiments (Floyd et al. 1989). This contrasts sharply with the conventional norms of formal learning, implying a more unidirectional flow of knowledge and asymmetric relation between the parties.

Learning often takes place in the course of everyday activities, in overcoming impediments to action producing immediately appreciable practical rewards, with knowledge accumulating continuously throughout one's lifetime as part of becoming a competent member of a community or society (Dewey 1966). The Civic Nexus project, following Piaget and Inhelder (1969) and Vygotsky (1978), adopted such a 'developmental' view of learning in which users would 'develop qualitatively different roles through the course of long-term collaborative design process with designers' (Farooq et al. 2007, p. 7). They see this as vital to achieving the goal of sustainability of community-based innovation, enabling the members to take over full 'ownership' and effective control of their information technology operations. This also suggests a strong connection to the formation of 'communities of practice' – through a process of legitimate peripheral participation (Lave and Wenger 1991) volunteers and other newcomers can simultaneously grow in knowledge while becoming integral to the community and its ongoing viability.

Participatory Design in activist and hobbyist communities

Activist and hobbyist communities are examples of communities organised by a commitment to an issue, interest or practice, which comprise another new and novel set of participants in Participatory Design. They overlap with CBOs as they too are kinds of organisations, though they are usually less formally structured.

Oftentimes, within these hobbyist communities few or no external stakeholders have been involved in the development of the information infrastructures they rely upon, and rather than being planned these information infrastructures tend to emerge along with the competencies, qualifications and experience that is available in a community. For instance, Syrjänen (2007; Karasti and Syrjänen 2004; Pipek and Syrjänen 2006) described the evolving infrastructure of a dog-breeding community in Finland that emerged over 15 years. The community was interested in breeding the Karelian Bear Dog, a species that had become almost extinct during World War II. Special breeding strategies were necessary to avoid inbreeding and to maintain the typical features of a Karelian Bear Dog. Up to the late 1980s, the bureaucracy connected with the organisation of the breeding processes (deciding on good breeding pairs, judging breeding results at dog shows) operated purely on paper documents, but then community members decided to transfer the information on breeding results into a database. Starting from that database, community members began to learn about the use of computers and relevant applications, and later started to learn programming to develop specific applications that allowed them to manage more sophisticated breeding strategies (that were developed in parallel), and to include more community-related functionalities (membership management, organisation of dog shows).

Groups of technology aficionados are another example of hobbyist communities. As Bogdan and Bowers (2007) point out in their description of radio amateurs, having an ongoing, emergent technological challenge actually may help community dynamics. In their example, the triplet of further developing radio technologies, further developing communication strategies to cope with the shortcomings of the medium, and furthering social interaction in a community distributed worldwide actually allows for people growing into the community. For example, radio amateurs often make innovations and usages available to others (listeners), as by nature their hobby is also a public articulation space.

Other community-based Participatory Design projects, in the spirit of advancing the interests of the marginal or resource-weak, have taken to working directly with activists. This work often intertwines research and practice in community planning and community informatics in regards to issues of public and environmental health and access to information technology. In discussing the processes of designing with activists, Hirsch (2009b) outlines a series of challenges this presents to the designer. Central among these are the need to establish trust among a group that is often subjugated and often sees itself as outside of the mainstream, and moreover at times may be engaging in activities that are illegal or otherwise under the scrutiny of law enforcement. In regards to activist communities as participants in Participatory Design, it is notable that these communities are particularly hybrid, consisting of CBOs, NGOs and individuals with a range of commitments (Hirsch 2009a). Perhaps most significantly, in describing a practice of contestational design Hirsch calls attention to the distinctive character of designing with activists and how their values affect the process of design:

> Indeed, significant energy is directed at creating discursive modalities within activist circles that challenge implicit beliefs held by the broader culture. Hence the never-ending discussions about 'process' among anti-authoritarians and the rise of such innovations as 'spokescouncils', 'affinity groups' and consensus-based decision making, all of which are aimed at ensuring a full airing of ideas and guaranteeing the ability of all participants to be heard. By their very definition, activist groups often find increased participation among socially marginalized groups.
>
> *(Hirsch 2008, p. 108)*

CBOs, hobbyist communities and communities of activists overlap in their motivations and even structures, while differentiated by their interests and practices. No one of these new categories of participants in Participatory Design is homogeneous, but neither are they the familiar participants of Participatory Design. They bring with them new contexts and values, and, too, require new methods for engagement and new themes for analysis and assessment.

Participatory Design for community communications

Along with new participants in community-based Participatory Design come new purposes. Participatory Design projects aimed at supporting communications in geographic communities were among the first applications of information technologies outside of workplaces. Because they aimed to serve a range of individuals living in proximity, they generally did not work primarily with pre-existing CBOs. The earliest of these experiments was the Berkeley Community Memory project in the early 1970s (Farrington and Pine 1996), which created an online community bulletin board service accessed by a network of computer terminals in various Berkeley stores. Users found messages of interest via keyword search and were free to post their own publicly searchable items. Later similar 'free net' experiments such as in Cleveland laid the basis for community networks (notably the Seattle Community Network (SCN) and Blacksburg Electronic Village (BEV)) and the burgeoning field of community informatics more generally (Schuler 1996). While there are strong resonances between the democratic ideals of Participatory Design and community informatics (Carroll and Rosson 2007), it has been only recently that the design implications of such community settings have been explored from the perspective of Participatory Design methodology.

An example of this is the work of Brereton, Redhead and their colleagues at the Queensland University of Technology, in a multi-year community engagement in Moggill, a commuter suburb of Brisbane. Growing out of involvement as neighbourhood residents, parents and shoppers, they began by developing a website for neighbourly information-sharing at the request of the local community organisation. Subsequently they studied local communication patterns and found that while the website and email lists functioned well among a group of active members during a period of intense organising, their use waned considerably once the crisis passed. (Redhead and Brereton 2006). In order to support a more inclusive mode of communication sustainable over the longer term they experimented with a large format (40 inch) interactive noticeboard installed in a well-frequented local meeting place. This operated very similarly to the Community Memory bulletin board mentioned earlier, but took advantage of a touch-sensitive, graphical interface and web-integration for remote access.

As researchers they struggled with two contending approaches to the design process: (1) consultation with community organisations, and (2) 'technology push' using lightweight but readily adaptable prototypes. The former approach was more in keeping with conventional Participatory Design, in which prototypes are developed and refined through workshop sessions before field deployment. But they found it hard to find participants willing to put in the time required. As an alternative, they placed an exploratory prototype in the Moggill general store, and then iteratively refined it over a period of more than 18 months through direct observation, feedback provided by users and the analysis of usage logs. This allowed the evolving design to be responsive to a wide range of users without burdening them with more formal workshop and survey methodologies (Redhead and Brereton 2010).

Participatory Design for enabling creativity and fostering cultural production

As Participatory Design moves into spaces other than the workplace it takes on new purposes as well as engaging new participants. One such purpose is fostering creativity, and there is a cluster of community-based Participatory Design work that engages with communities through practices of cultural production. Here the social structure varies, in some cases involving community-based organisations, in others working with looser affiliations of community members. What is novel throughout this work is the use of Participatory Design methods to support the processes of creative and critical discovery and expression through the arts. In addition, it is important to recognise that these forms of cultural production involve learning and are often politicised acts.

Malmö Living Labs

In Malmö, Sweden, designers and researchers have been investigating new forms of community-based Participatory Design through the Living Labs – spaces developed to foster and support community-driven innovation (Ehn 2008; Björgvinsson et al. 2010). To be sure, the approach to Living Labs in Malmö is not representative of all Living Labs, but it is representative of the contours and possibilities of community-based Participatory Design. The setting of Malmö itself presents a unique sociocultural context as it has become one of the most demographically diverse cities in all of Sweden: since the late 1990s, immigration from Africa and the Middle East has drastically changed the ethnic and religious composition of the city. Those designers involved with the Malmö Living Labs are taking advantage of this scenario, explicitly situating their work within this dynamic and at times contestational setting, as they state 'exploring innovation as a historically and geographically located phenomenon (rather than as a universal and ahistorical one)'. (Björgvinsson et al. 2010, p. 44).

The Malmö Living Labs are spread across three sites, known as the Stage, the Neighbourhood and the Factory, each of which provides distinct opportunities for community participation in and through design. So, for example, the Stage is located in a music club and focuses on various forms of cultural production, primarily with youth who are first- and second-generation immigrants. Through this space and programme the designers have worked together with a grass-roots community-based hip-hop organisation to develop new forms of community journalism and public performance. Both of these endeavours speak to larger issues within that community and within community-based Participatory Design more generally. Through collaboratively designing and implementing these new forms of community journalism and public performance, the youth and designers – together – were able to surface and address issues of cultural visibility and legitimacy in dramatic ways.

The purpose of such community-based Participatory Design projects is to foster and support imaginative ability, and the outcomes take the form of dramatic, affective artefacts, systems and events. As an example, at one of the Malmö Living Labs projects (mostly) Arab immigrant youth designed and produced a system called Barcode Beats (Björgvinsson et al. 2010). Using this system, the youth could scan products in a market and the barcode data would trigger different percussive sounds and loops, enabling the making of ad hoc hip-hop compositions. While on the one hand this project is an arts project, it is also a community-based Participatory Design project through which the youth used design to develop a means of public expression. This creativity and creative expression, as Björgvinsson, Ehn and Hillgren note, should be contextualised within a social milieu in which these youths are often surveyed and 'feel that they have to behave more exemplarily in public spaces than native Swedes do' (Björgvinsson et al. 2010, p. 45). That is, this creativity and creative expression, facilitated through community-based Participatory Design, should be considered as a manner of engaging in meaningful public acts related to identity and politics.

Neighbourhood Networks

Another example of community-based Participatory Design that was developed to foster creativity was the Neighbourhood Networks project (DiSalvo et al. 2008, 2009). The Neighbourhood Networks project was a series of public Participatory Design workshops in Pittsburgh, PA, USA, that provided opportunities for neighbourhood residents to engage in the creative exploration and application of robotics and sensing technologies in the context of neighbourhood activism and identity expression. Over the course of three years, the researchers held workshops in two neighbourhoods, engaging over 100 participants across the workshops. As part of this effort, designers and engineers on the research team also created affordable technology platforms suited to these public programmes, an example of which is the Canary, a low-cost, simple-to-use platform for constructing environmentally reactive works of art and design. These platforms enable novices to engage with emerging technologies in the context of their own communities. For example, in Figure 8.3 a neighbourhood resident is measuring air quality in a neighbourhood park. In Figure 8.4, participants are working together with maps to document and share the findings from their neighbourhood-sensing activities.

Although each Neighbourhood Networks programme was distinctive in terms of the specific technologies, time span, constituents and issues, they all followed a similar trajectory. The first phase of each workshop series was designed to familiarise participants with the basic capabilities and limitations of sensing and robotics. The second phase concentrated on the discovery and invention of possible uses of the technology in the context of the neighbourhood and its issues. The objective of this phase was twofold: for participants to imagine what might be technologically plausible and to facilitate the development of their design concepts. Phase three focused on iterative design and production of a final prototype and documentation for public presentation. The final phase of each workshop series was a public presentation of their concepts, in the form of interactive prototypes and exhibition-like displays, back to the communities in which they resided, in order to share their ideas and prompt discussion of the issues that lay underneath their concepts and designs.

Throughout this process, the research team developed numerous tools and activities to scaffold Participatory Design with unfamiliar technologies, to enable a kind of informed

Figure 8.3 The Neighbourhood Networks project: measuring air quality in a neighbourhood park

speculation. More than applied solutions, or directives for future products or services, the goal of this endeavour was to foster critical engagement, creative expression and technological fluency among the participants. Moreover, these goals were seen as being a continuation of a tradition of political computing in Participatory Design, set in a community context. As such, the project provides a salient example of community-based Participatory Design through cultural production, and begins more generally to highlight the informal learning experiences and new modes of political expression that are common in community-based Participatory Design.

Figure 8.4 The Neighbourhood Networks project: collaborative mapping of air quality in the neighbourhood

How to foster imaginative ability, document the process and support the making of expressive media and events in community contexts are key questions for Participatory Design practice and research. Most often, within Participatory Design, tools and techniques for eliciting creativity are used as part of a process towards the development of a good or service. These tools and techniques still have value when the goal is not so defined and is instead a more ambiguous pursuit of creativity and creative expression. So, for example, Büscher et al. describe 'ways of grounding imagination': a triangulation of bricolage, prototyping in situ, and future laboratories as techniques that allow for shifting, balancing and negotiating between blue-sky conceptualising and pragmatic issues of development and implementation (Büscher et al. 2004). Although these techniques were initially developed for use with a team of architects and computer scientists envisioning a future workspace, there is no reason why such techniques cannot be extended to community contexts. This is, in fact, the case for many tools and techniques, from design games (see Brandt 2006) to drama (see Iacucci et al. 2002). The question for Participatory Design research is less what tools and techniques need to be developed to elicit creativity, but instead: how and towards what ends does creativity as purpose and creative expression as product work within a community context?

DemTech

The Democratising Technology (DemTech) project in the UK is exemplary of this notion of creativity as purpose and creative expression as product (Light et al. 2009). The project was born from a broad goal of increasing inclusion in the public conversations concerning technology. It sought to engage a community often marginalised in technology discussions – elders – in an exploration of possible futures for sustainable power. One aspect of the project's novelty was the choice to structure the engagement through the arts, and in particular by working with socially engaged artists. This took multiple forms, including a workshop intervention developed with a performance artist and commissioning other artists to work in partnership with participants to develop artworks for an exhibition titled *The Not Quite Yet: On the Margins of Technology*. In this project, then, the purpose was not to contribute to the invention or configuration of a specific operational good or service. Rather, the purpose was, working with and through the arts, to enliven and celebrate the creativity within the participants, in order to enable a collaborative imagination of the future and include the community's particular knowledge and desires. According to Light et al. (2009, p. 45) the project had a transformative effect on the participants, as they 'came to feel differently about themselves as well as the technology'. This feeling of difference was the very purpose of this engagement, following from a general belief that creativity and creative expression can work to impart 'a sense of agency and confidence in participating [that] leads to an interest in the tools structuring society' (2009, p. 46). Put another way, the project was founded on a belief that by fostering and supporting the imaginative abilities of community members, that community might be opened to novel resources and opportunities to reconsider their environment and their role in shaping that environment.

For some, a project such as DemTech might bear little resemblance to Participatory Design, because those involved are not immediately participating in the design of a good or service. But we maintain this is still very much Participatory Design, and it prompts us to continue to consider what the purposes and practices of community-based Participatory Design are and might become. In projects such as DemTech, design, or creativity broadly construed, becomes a means of participation in society. Perhaps one could say that those involved were participating, through design, in the discourses and practices of the shaping of techno-science.

In developing community-based Participatory Design programmes to foster and support imaginative ability and making use of dramatic, affective artefacts, systems and events, the challenge and opportunity is to rethink what constitutes participation in contemporary society and what are the means by which that participation is enabled and exercised. Moreover, while acknowledging that creativity as purpose and creative expression as product are worthy in and of themselves, we can also see them as part of a new perspective on capacity-building, where creativity is recognised as a key capacity in contemporary culture.

These programmes also served as reflexive experiments into community-based Participatory Design, allowing for the articulation of new theories concerning the processes, products and politics of Participatory Design. In particular, from the experiences of those at the Malmö Living Labs have emerged new conceptualisations of infrastructuring and the idea of 'thinging' or participation in design things: making and making experiential the assemblages of people, objects, agendas and attachments that constitute the contemporary political condition (Ehn 2008; Björgvinsson et al, 2010). In no small part, it is the community context itself that gives rise to such new ideas, as researchers struggle to understand, describe and analyse what is occurring in these programmes and practices.

Participatory Design for enhancing public deliberation in political and commercial environments

Community-based Participatory Design meets additional challenges and opportunities when addressing larger and/or distributed communities. These are further amplified when the Participatory Design process is used to enhance public deliberation in formal political or economic processes, such as urban planning or product development.

Blacksburg Electronic Village

A number of projects have generated experiences in how more or less informal Participatory Design processes interacted with established democratic structures like parliaments, city councils and governments. For the Blacksburg Electronic Village (BEV), Kavanaugh et al. (2005) describe several examples of connecting the existing community network with public deliberation processes for formal democratic procedures. They address two modes of improving this connection: making the ongoing democratic process more visible by offering more and more immediate information (e.g. by posting video recordings of town council meetings in the online community) and using tools to support citizen involvement in governmental design processes. The most prominent examples evolved around urban and land use planning processes, which in many communities require a formal participation of the citizens affected.

The mutual influence of an informal information technology-supported community and the formal democratic system is illustrated nicely by the initiatives and decisions around the development of a new sewer system for parts of Blacksburg. The plans for the new sewer systems were part of a city development plan ('Comprehensive Plan') for the county that was developed with citizen participation between 2000 and 2003. The level of participation in that initiative was very low until city staff members started significant marketing efforts to encourage participation, and also started using the information technology infrastructure of BEV for deliberation. After the town council started actively considering an alternative, more expensive sewer concept (that was thought to satisfy the interest of real estate developers who may have felt disadvantaged by the Comprehensive Plan), community members began using the deliberation infrastructure to raise awareness of the pending decision. The town council then tried to rush the decision for the expensive sewer concept, but there was only a 4:3 majority for it. The debt to be incurred in building the more expensive sewer system required a 5:2 majority (a regulation intended to guarantee fiscal responsibility). So the existing majority tried to change the town charter to weaken the council's voting requirements for large debts, which again stimulated a campaign against this change that used the information technology infrastructure of BEV for campaign coordination. As a consequence, three candidates opposing the sewer project were elected in the next council elections, and the project was stopped.

This example highlights the specifics of the relation between a community network (and its potentials for Participatory Design) and the formal political system. While typically a community has only a weak governance structure where levels of participation vary widely, parliaments, governments and authorities have formal structures with defined roles, resources that are reliable and plannable, and operate within given procedures (decision processes with respect to legislation) and timeframes (e.g. election periods). When the participation with regard to the Comprehensive Plan was low, the community network could provide a basis for marketing and deliberation of larger numbers of people. Instead of having a series of participation events, the BEV became a place to go to when citizens were interested in this development effort. Activity levels in the community network followed the schedule of the political system, e.g. with regard to the sewer project, campaigning to raise awareness, first of the sewer plans and later of the planned changes to the town charter, became time-critical activities that also required a temporal self-organisation of the community (e.g. individuals taking responsibility for leafleting, posting signs, organising rallies, etc., as well as for the necessary coordination responsibility).

Media Centre Software

Another example of a community Participatory Design process oriented towards formal structures for community deliberation and decision-making was given in Hess et. al. (2008). In this case of 'Community-Driven Development' (CDD), a 'community of interest' formed around the use of a Media Centre Software (MCS) for Windows-based PCs, and was enrolled by the software producer in the design of a new version of the software. The software producer had established a web-based online forum three years before the Participatory Design process started, with more then 5,000 registered members who were discussing issues around the use of the software (e.g. how to configure it to work with specific hardware, or how to set up complex TV show recording patterns). There, the community always had generated hints about technological shortcomings and difficulties in using the software, and the customer relationship department of the software producer often reacted to these issues, either by commenting on use problems or by providing bug-fixing updates. Under the pressure of heavy competition the software producer decided to initiate a structured Participatory Design process to develop the next version of the software product. The software producer established an online 'User Parliament' (open to all community members) as an institution where representatives of the community could give feedback on issues and ideas for improving the software, and a 'Central Committee' (same number of community members as software developers) where decisions about issue prioritisation and implementation details were taken. The results of the Central Committee's meetings were summarised in a public space (a wiki system) to create a central requirements specification that formed the basis for the software development process. An initial prototype was built and given to all interested users as soon as possible, so that they could further test and improve it in a second development cycle.

The project became a success in terms of producing an outcome that in general satisfied the community but, looking at the details, the process produced some issues that reflect important concerns with regard to Participatory Design in communities. The defined structures (User Parliament, Central Committee, requirements wiki) helped in driving and focusing the process, but also established different spheres of visibility and responsibility. Engagement changed significantly over time, although of 70 users (out of thousands of registered 'community members', i.e. software purchasers) enrolled in the User Parliament, only 15 participated regularly throughout the process. The Central Committee lost one third of its community members over time. Having access to the material produced did not necessarily mean that community members felt involved. In taking the Participatory Design process seriously, for some of the community members a leisure activity (communicating in a discussion forum of a product one is interested in) almost turned into a work chore (being a responsible member of the Central Committee). As a consequence of the drop-out rate, some community members called the legitimacy of the decision structures into question.

The results reflected in the requirements wiki, which manifested the transition to the economic product development process, also showed that different levels of qualification and experience can lead to an imbalance of Participatory Design outcomes. Many suggestions, particularly of new software functionalities, came not from the community but from product managers of the software producer. Although the decisions to include these functionalities were taken unanimously, it could be observed that actors with a stronger background knowledge about possible design alternatives could better articulate their ideas, and that the professionals were able to invest more time than the users.

A number of different ideas have been explored to support deliberation processes online. Potential benefits are a selective anonymity of participants, an ordering and simplification of contributions as it has been explored by the IBIS method (Kunz and Rittel 1970) and implemented in tools like gIBIS (Conklin and Begemann 1988) and ZENO (Gordon and Karacapilidis 1997), an integration of representations of the discourse and representations of the designed artefact (Pipek 2005; Sidlar and Rinner 2007), the use of simulations to illustrate the outcomes of possible alternatives (Metadesign – Fischer and Scharff 2000; UrbanSim – Borning et al. 2005). Coming back to Hess et al. (2008), it is also interesting to see that additional options exist if the deliberation process targets a digital artefact. To support the feedback from the community to the User Parliament, a feedback module has been integrated into the first prototype of the software that allowed for in-use feedback on functionalities into the User Parliament. Along similar lines, Pipek's (2005) integrated discourse environments allowed user communities to negotiate groupware tool configurations within the tool itself, and Stevens and Wiedenhöfer's 'Community Help in Context' (2006) supported a community-driven localisation of descriptions within a tools help system that allowed new requirements to emerge. The developments around social networks allow further forms of online deliberation support, but as a consequence of the increasing opportunities, tools and environments for online deliberation need to be considered as implicitly being subject to a secondary Participatory Design process on their own behalf. Similar to architectural or cultural public goods, they form a class of technological public goods, a 'Societyware', that needs frequent, ongoing community maintenance.

The ideas showed a significant potential for supporting participation in online communities, and also for supporting participation in the design of information technology or information technology-enhanced products. But the studies also showed that for community-driven processes a compromise is necessary to find organisational structures that are strong enough to lead to a satisfactory process convergence, and yet are not so strong that community members feel excluded. And it showed that in communities of interest, participation is not always seen as a strong necessity and may significantly add to the workload of the participants, and that any professional structures within such a community process have a potential to dominate design outcomes. While this community interacted largely online, these participatory challenges around inclusion/exclusion, workload/reward balancing, and strictures and affordances of formal structures will be familiar to anyone involved in community-based initiatives conducted exclusively through face-to-face encounters.

Topics shaping the development of community-based Participatory Design

With these projects and clusterings in mind, we discuss three topics formative to the future of the field of community-based Participatory Design: new forms of politics, publics and infrastructuring. Although each of these is presented distinctly, they are interrelated and build on each other.

New forms of politics

In her paper 'P for political' Beck (2002, p. 77) asks: 'What constitutes political action through computing?' This is an important question for Participatory Design generally, and it's worthwhile to explore the question specifically in the context of community-based Participatory Design. There is a range of political actions in community-based Participatory Design. Some of these are overtly political such as Hirsch's work with activists (2008, 2009a, 2009b). When working to support protests and demonstrations or provide spaces for the debate of water rights, the political qualities of the design work are clear. Moreover, in such cases, both the participants and the designers are unequivocally implicated as political actors. Projects such as Civic Nexus are similar in their overtly political nature, but without necessarily the contestational character. With Civic Nexus, and many other community computing and community informatics projects, the work strives to support political organisations or improve the mechanisms of politics, such as through access to information, voting and deliberation more generally.

In some cases, community-based Participatory Design echoes, with very little distortion, the inherent but not always explicit politics of workplace Participatory Design. For example, Le Dantec's work on providing resources to the homeless, as well as the social workers and service providers who work with them, engages all manner of politics and political issues (Le Dantec and Edwards 2008a, 2008b, 2010; Le Dantec et al, 2010). These span from the level of the social system to the individual, from the structures of accounting and authority between the various service providers, law enforcement and the homeless, to the stigma, social status and the presentation of self among the homeless. The Participatory Design activities of that project expressed inherent political relations, which then had to be taken into account in the technical implementation of the system. This, of course, is a common theme in Participatory Design, for instance recounted in Carstensen, Schmidt and Wiil's (1999) work on designing systems with and for labourers. Community-based Participatory Design can and should learn much from the political endeavours of workplace and work-practice Participatory Design.

Within community-based Participatory Design we also witness a form of politics in which the design and use of computation is itself a politicised act or meant to evoke political issues. For example, in the Neighbourhood Networks project, DiSalvo et al, make the claim that one outcome of the project is a politicised public argument, a kind of public rhetoric, about how the community wants to shape its environment (2008). A similar case is made by Light et al. (2009) in the DemTech project, through which a community of elders engages in designing as a way to give material voice to their interests as they intersect with the city, large-scale infra-structure and energy. Likewise, Björgvinsson et al. (2010) claims some of the Malmö Living Labs projects provide opportunities for the expression of marginalised voices and novel media-based expressions of identities. In each of these cases, design and the use of computational media become a form of political action through which the desires and agendas of a community are explored and instantiated.

Both DiSalvo and Ehn have employed the concept of agonistic democracy to frame some contemporary design projects. The notion of agonistic democracy comes from political theory and has been most clearly articulated through the works of Chantal Mouffe (2000). The basic conception of agonism is that contestation, *not consensus*, is the basis for democracy; that is, democracy is founded upon a radical pluralism and the ability to dispute, not a homogeneous field and the requirement for agreement. As such, one challenge and opportunity for Partici-patory Design is to create the constructs and situations through which this pluralism and dis-putation can manifest itself constructively. Cultural production and learning are key to developing and challenging contestation, and this then becomes one more of the possible forms of politics supported by and enacted through community-based Participatory Design. More-over, these constructs and situations for enabling pluralism and disputation can be seen as intersecting with notions of publics and infrastructuring, the two other themes we maintain are formative to the future of community-based Participatory Design.

Publics

Within Participatory Design the notion of publics has gained attention as a way of providing an issue-oriented focus of relevance to community-based work. This notion of 'publics' draws from the work of American pragmatist philosopher John Dewey and his book *The Public and Its Problems* (1927) as a way of framing groups of people and their motivation for undertaking action and pursing change. For Dewey, the idea of the public as a generic, undifferentiated mass was off the mark. Rather than a singular public, there is a multiplicity of publics. These publics are groups of people brought together around and through an issue, in order to address that issue and its consequences. As he describes, 'Those indirectly and seriously affected for good or for evil form a group distinctive enough to require recognition and a name. The name selected is "The Public"' (Dewey 1927, p. 7).

Within the context of community-based Participatory Design, a public is a kind of community that is identified with and constituted by an issue. Thus, the notion of a public provides some focus to the notion of community. There are multiple ways this notion of publics could affect Participatory Design practice and research. First, we can imagine a kind of Participatory Design aimed at the articulation of issues and their mutually constituted publics. Second, in the analysis of Participatory Design projects, the notion of publics could be used to frame and understand the multiplicity of perspectives and courses of action around a given topic (e.g., Le Dantec, 2010).

This notion of a Deweyan public is of interest beyond just Participatory Design. It has also been a significant topic of research in the field of Science and Technology Studies (STS) (e.g., Le Dantec, 2010). Indeed, as a theme, publics provide a rich site of overlap between Science and Technology Studies and Design more generally. Much of this can be traced to the work of science studies scholar Bruno Latour. In the catalogue essay accompanying the 2005 exhibition 'Making Things Public', Latour (Latour and Weibel 2005) invokes Dewey and the notions of publics, and combines this with an exploration of the notion of 'things' as socio-material–political assemblages. By this combining of publics and things, Latour proposes and through both the catalogue essay and exhibition probes the question of what an object-oriented democracy might be like: that is, a democracy that is acted out of and through the artefacts and systems, the products of design. From the perspective of design, then, we can interpret this as reinvigorating the interplay of artefacts and politics, but with a greater attention to the role of design in the production of those artefacts.

Notably, in 'Participation in design things', Ehn draws together Dewey and Latour to consider how the notion of publics might inform Participatory Design practice (Ehn 2008). Specifically, Ehn points out that one of the needs of publics is the provision of platforms for coordinating, facilitating the expression of multiple voices, planning and, importantly, for dealing constructively with the disagreements that inevitably occur while in pursuit of issue-oriented action or change. This development of platforms constitutes a kind of infrastructuring by design, or the development of support tools, techniques and processes for participatory approaches to contending with issues. This notion of infrastructuring, then, is the third theme to be addressed in regards to the future of community-based Participatory Design.

Infrastructuring

We are in the midst of a formative period. The information and communication infrastructures that underpin everyday life, at the personal, organisational and societal scales, are undergoing historically rapid transformation as digital networking is increasingly woven into the fabric of our contemporary economic, social, political and cultural practices. Contributing to the development of information and communication infrastructures, especially in articulating and serving broad public interests, represents community-based Participatory Design's potentially most rewarding challenge. An infrastructuring approach to community-based Participatory Design emerges out of community information technology development projects as information technology application becomes more familiar and intensifies in scope and depth, and especially as it plays an increasingly communicative, interconnecting role.

Leigh Star and her collaborators offer some valuable insights into how to think about community-based participatory information technology developments as infrastructuring, rather more conventionally as creating 'applications'. In their analysis of a distributed information system that served a scientific community as a platform for archiving and exchanging data, Star and Ruhleder (1996, later rephrased in Star 1999 and Star and Bowker 2002) describe eight salient characteristics of infrastructure (see Table 8.1, column 1). Their definition stresses socio-technical relations, in the sense that infrastructure should always be seen as a relation between organised human 'doing' in social systems and technologies that enable and support these ways of 'doing'. Unlike other more technically focused frameworks and terminologies of 'infra-structure', it covers aspects that relate to activities of users as groups and communities.

Star and Bowker's (2002) interpretation of the term 'infrastructure' carries notions of com-munity in it when they write about infrastructures being 'learned as part of membership', or about infrastructures 'shaping and being shaped by conventions of practice'. Their choice of title, 'How to infrastructure', focuses on doing and leads to the exploration of 'infrastructur-ing' as a more comprehensive term for the creative design activities of professional designers and users (Karasti and Syrjänen 2004; Pipek and Syrjänen 2006; Karasti and Baker 2008). Pipek and Wulf (2009), in particular, highlight the activities that change or maintain specific infrastructural characteristics (see Table 8.1, column 2). Such a framework opens the opportunity to create a common ground (Carroll et al. 2006) for addressing all actors and interests relevant for a suc-cessful establishment of an information technology usage without privileging the activities of the 'designer' over the activities of the 'user'. Many of these aspects of infrastructuring are also

Table 8.1 Adapted from 'How to infrastructure' (Star and Bowker 2002) and 'Infrastructur-ing' (Pipek and Wulf 2009)

Characteristics of Infrastructure (Star and Bowker 2002)	Activities of Infrastructuring (Pipek and Wulf 2009)
1. Infrastructures are embedded in other social and technological structures	Activities that connect different technological and social structures, activities that change standards, routines, or traditions involved in mediating between different technological and social structures;
2. Infrastructures are transparent in invisibly supporting tasks	Activities that change the visibility of an infrastructure;
3. Infrastructures have a spatial and temporal reach or scope	Activities that increase the longevity of an infrastructure, or that add new members, elements, or application areas;
4. Infrastructures comprise taken-for-granted artefacts and organisational arrangements learned as part of membership in a community	Activities that change, or reflect changes in, the community or communities being supported;
5. Infrastructures shape and are shaped by conventions of practice	Activities that aim at changing conventional practices, or that impose existing practice on new technologies;
6. Infrastructures are plugged into other infrastructures and tools in a standardised fashion, though they are also modified by scope and conflicting (local) conventions	Activities that change standards that mediate between infrastructures (may also include activities that aim at local specialisations of standards); activities that change the scope to which standards apply; activities that articulate or mediate conflicts;
7. Infrastructures do not grow de novo, but wrestle with the inertia of the installed base and inherit strengths and limitations from that base	Activities that interface and align new applications with existing information technology infrastructures: activities that challenge and develop existing practices;
8. Infrastructures are invisible but become visible upon breakdown	Activities that help in articulating reasons for a breakdown; recovery activities after a breakdown.

captured by Suchman's phrase of 'artful integration', with its attention to contextual situation, ongoing design-in-use and exemplary designing coming not so much through singular achievements as in the ongoing alignment of disparate actors (Suchman 1999).

The challenge described also has a methodological dimension. In many of the examples of community-oriented Participatory Design discussed in this chapter, we found that (professional) designers were not being the initiators of Participatory Design processes, nor were they fully in charge of organising a Participatory Design process (some 'designers' grow into this role during the process while starting 'just' as a practitioner). In many community settings, design emerges from and integrates with an ongoing practice. In comparison with more 'professional' environments, it becomes obvious in community settings, with their less standardised, less discrete and more interwoven practices, that needs emerge, design objects change, designers morph and the design process is continuously reconstructed by all interested publics (which also may change depending on the emergence of the other process aspects). The classical distinction between (professional) 'designers' and 'users' does not make sense any more, neither does it make sense to view 'design' activities as separate from an ongoing practice (also of technology use).

The integration of creative design and use activities also encourages embedding participation tools into the infrastructure itself. Pipek (2005) describes a range of functionalities addressing the collaborative sense-making activities a community may engage in to (re-)define infrastructure usages. In particular, appropriation support functionalities may serve as a starting point for a methodological or a tool support of infrastructuring activities, but they require a further specification about their scope within communities. Dewey's notion of publics is helpful here, to capture, define and extend the scope that infrastructuring activities may have. With regard to community-based Participatory Design, a dual understanding of the relation between infrastructure and publics needs to be maintained: infrastructures, particularly information technology infrastructures, may support the emergence and maintenance of publics on the one hand; on the other hand, by their nature (taken-for-grantedness, dependability), they create publics around issues such as access, reliability, ownership and usage.

We can see other forms of participatory infrastructuring in several of the projects discussed in this chapter. For instance, when St Christopher House launched its ambitious community learning network project, it sought to develop an information and communication infrastructure that could serve not just the organisation but also the wider community. While it had to scale back the scope in the face of daunting organisational and technical challenges, it can be seen as ahead of its time in what it attempted. Nearly a decade later, many other community organisations have similar goals, and fortunately many of the tools (e.g. content management system, blogging platform, wiki) that St Chris had to build itself are now, thanks greatly to the FOSS movement, widely and cheaply available. The Civic Nexus projects likewise offer a harbinger, as well as useful insights, into what will likely be more widespread attempts by local organisations to preserve and promote what is valuable to their constituents, especially as economic conditions are at risk of worsening. Local cooperative self-reliance will need to fill the gaps when government or private sector initiatives fail to maintain vital, universally needed infrastructures.

Participatory infrastructuring is also a latent theme in two chapters of this volume devoted to initiatives that have received Artful Integrators awards at Participatory Design Conferences. The first Artful Integrators Award recipient was the Global Fund for Women (GFW). Chapter 9 discusses how the decade-long development of an organisation-wide shared information space to support the core activities of fundraising and grantmaking (i.e. infrastructuring) sought to reflect core values of the non-profit and its respect for the knowledge and expertise of all project stakeholders. While there were strong shared values across the organisation which provided a unity of overall purpose, the principle of inclusion resulted in internal tensions, the working out of which constitutes a central Participatory Design challenge in any infrastructuring effort (see also Trigg 2000).

Another Artful Integrator awardee is the Health Information Systems Programme (HISP). Chapter 10 charts the remarkable 15-year trajectory of 'design, development, implementation and scaling of the DHIS (District Health Information Software) within an action research framework in the context of the public health sector in various developing countries'. While not using the language of infrastructuring and publics, this project exemplifies many of their most salient features as we have used them here. As HISP grew from small information systems among the interstices of larger initiatives through processes of local learning and software development to become an established, self-sustaining and vital health information infrastructure in many developing countries, it created and successfully (for the most part) aligned an ever larger and more diverse public. An important part of this has been the emergence of the role of 'HISP facilitator or boundary spanner' who can mediate relations across the increasingly disparate network of actors typical of infrastructural publics. Also important in recent years has been the adoption of free/open source software (FOSS) development, which offers a means for engaging with a wider range of technical collaborators (see also Braa and Hedberg 2002; Braa et al. 2004, 2007).

Conclusion

In exploring community-based Participatory Design, this chapter has considered one of the principal ways in which Participatory Design has developed as a field from its formative Scandinavian experiments. In retaining the original democratic ideals but focusing on a wider range of social relations than are normally foregrounded in studies of formal organisations, we have sought to enrich the scope and depth of Participatory Design understandings and thereby provide a basis for more ambitious ventures that can wrestle with contemporary socio-political challenges. The projects and perspectives we have discussed here, while far from offering a comprehensive survey, do point in significant respects to a promising future of Participatory Design as it takes a broadening range of social relations into account. This will especially be the case as the locus of innovative development increasingly shifts from creating relatively isolated organisational information systems or applications to developing digital, social media that play infrastructural roles in everyday life.

One area which we have touched on only in passing, but which will likely reward greater attention in the future, is the potentially mutually fruitful connections between Participatory Design and the free/open source software (FOSS) and open access movements. Several of the projects mentioned above have adopted FOSS packages and platforms, or promoted open access approaches, both for expediency and on principle. However, there have so far been few Participatory Design initiatives that have taken on FOSS or open access media as a primary focus of attention. This appears to be a gap worth addressing, since open source/access approaches are revolutionising information technology applications and use, but largely without the benefit of a reflective or collaborative practice of taking users' experiences and interests directly into account when developing new systems and services. This is where Participatory Design has much to offer, especially with the FOSS movement, with its tendencies to meritocratic, 'geek' cultures prone to clash with growing demands for easier-to-use and customised platforms and infrastructures.

The distinctions between workplace/work practice Participatory Design and community-based Participatory Design from which it has arisen have implications for how Participatory Design activities are structured and performed. Most obviously the basis and motivation for participation in community-based design initiatives changes, calling for greater emphasis on addressing people's values and interpersonal preferences. Design activities will often have to be brought to the varied sites and locales, whether physical or online, where community members are in the habit of finding each other and conducting the activities that are central to the maintenance of community ties. Furthermore, roles such as designer and user are less pre-defined, hence subject to negotiation and likely to shift over time and across different spaces. While this presents some difficult challenges, Participatory Design in community settings can elicit and help focus the creative talents and energies of many people in productive and rewarding ways.

Notes

1 Wenger later (1998) developed a theory of social learning under the same label.
2 While the Future Workshop was modelled mainly on that described in *Design at Work,* the principal student facilitator, with a background in organisational development in the non-profit sector, modified it based on her prior experience with a closely related 'workshop' method for brainstorming. This indicates the close connections between Participatory Design and the long-standing community development field. Indeed, as Kensing and Madsen (1991) note, they drew this technique from political organising around opposition in Europe to the installation of Pershing missiles in the 1980s.

References

Akama, Y. and T. Ivanka (2010) 'What community? Facilitating awareness of "community" through playful triggers', in K. Bødker, T. Bratteteig, D. Loi and T. Robertson (eds) *Proceedings of the 11th Biennial Participatory Design Conference*, New York: ACM, 11–20.

Anderson, B. (1991) *Imagined Communities: Reflections on the Origin and Spread of Nationalism*, New York: Verso.

Beck, E. (2002) 'P for political – participation not enough', *Scandinavian Journal of Information Systems,* 14: 77–92.

Benston, M. and E. Balka (1993) 'Participatory design by non-profit groups', *Canadian Woman Studies/Les Cahiers de La Femme*, 13: 100–103.

Björgvinsson, E., P. Ehn and P. A. Hillgren (2010) 'Participatory design and "democratizing innovation"', in K. Bødker, T. Bratteteig, D. Loi and T. Robertson (eds) *Proceedings of the 11th Biennial Participatory Design Conference*, New York: ACM, 41–50. Online. Available at: http://dx.doi.org/10.1145/1900441.1900448 (accessed 10 November 2011).

Bødker, S. and O. S. Iverson (2002) 'Staging a professional participatory design practice: moving PD beyond the initial fascination of user involvement', in O. W. Bertelsen (ed.) *Proceedings of the Second Nordic Conference on Human–Computer Interaction*, New York: ACM, 11–18. Online. Available at: http://dx.doi.org/10.1145/572020.572023 (accessed 10 November 2011).

Bogdan, C. and J. Bowers (2007) 'Tuning in: challenging design for communities through a field study of radio amateurs', in C. Steinfield, B. T. Pentland, M. Ackerman and N. Contractor (eds) *Communities and Technologies 2007: Proceedings of the Third Communities and Technologies Conference, Michigan State University, 2007*, New York: Springer, 439–61.

Borning, A., B. Friedman, J. Davis and P. Lin (2005) 'Informing public deliberation: value sensitive design of indicators for a large-scale urban simulation', in H. Gellersen, K. Schmidt, M. Beaudouin-Lafon and W. Mackay (eds) *Proceedings of the Ninth European Conference on Computer-Supported Cooperative Work*, New York: Springer, 449–68.

Bowen, S. J. and P. J. Chamberlain (2008) 'Engaging the ageing: designing artefacts to provoke dialogue', in P. Langdon, J. Clarkson and P. Robinson (eds) *Designing Inclusive Futures*, London: Springer, 35–44.

Braa, J. and C. Hedberg (2002) 'The struggle for district-based health information systems in South Africa', *The Information Society*, 18: 113–27.

Braa, J., E. Monteiro and S. Sahay (2004) 'Networks of action: sustainable health information systems across developing countries', *MIS Quarterly*, 28(3): 337–62.

Braa J., E. Monteiro, S. Sahay, K. Staring and O. H. Titlestad (2007) 'Scaling up local learning – experiences from south–south–north networks of shared software development', in *Proceedings of the 9th International Conference on Social Implications of Computers in Developing Countries, São Paulo, Brazil, May 2007*. Online. Available at: www.ifipwg94.org.br/fullpapers/R0112–1.pdf (accessed 13 November 2011).

Brandt, E. (2006) 'Designing exploratory design games: a framework for participation in participatory design?' in I. Wagner, J. Blomberg, G. Jacucci and F. Kensing (eds) *Proceedings of the Ninth Conference on Participatory Design: Expanding Boundaries in Design*, New York: ACM, 57–66. Online. Available at: http://dx.doi.org/10.1145/1147261.1147271 (accessed 10 November 2011).

Büscher, M., M. E. Eriksen, J. F. Kristensen and P. H. Mogensen (2004) 'Ways of grounding imagination', in A. Clement, F. de Cindio, A. M. Oostveen, D. Schuler and P. van den Besselaar (eds.) *Proceedings of the Eighth Conference on Participatory Design: Artful Integration: Interweaving Media, Materials and Practices*, New York: ACM, 193–203. Online. Available at: http://dx.doi.org/10.1145/1011870.1011893 (accessed 10 November 2011).

Carroll, J. M. and M. B. Rosson (2007) 'Participatory design in community informatics', *Design Studies*, 28: 243–61.

Carroll, J. M., M. B. Rosson, G. Convertino and C. H. Ganoe (2006) 'Awareness and teamwork in computer-supported collaborations', *Interacting with Computers*, 18(1): 21–46. Online. Available at: http://dx.doi.org/10.1016/j.intcom.2005.05.005 (accessed 13 November 2011).

Carroll, J. M., P. M. Bach, M. B. Rosson, C. Merkel, U. Farooq and L. Xiao (2008) 'Community IT workshops as a strategy for community learning', *First Monday*, 13(4). Online. Available at: www.uic.edu/htbin/cgiwrap/bin/ojs/index.php/fm/article/viewArticle/2052/1955 (accessed 13 November 2011).

Carstensen, P., K. Schmidt and U. K. Wiil (1999) 'Supporting shop floor intelligence: a CSCW approach to production planning and control in flexible manufacturing', in S. C. Hayne (ed.) *Proceedings of the International ACM SIGGROUP Conference on Supporting Group Work*, New York: ACM, 111–20.

Clement, A. and P. van den Besselaar (1993) 'A retrospective look at PD projects', *Communications of the ACM*, 36(4): 29–37.

Clement, A., M. Gurstein, G. Longford, M. Moll and L. R. Shade (eds) (2012) *Connecting Canadians: Investigations in Community Informatics*, Edmonton: Athabasca University Press.

Conklin, J. and M. L. Begemann (1988) 'gIBIS: a hypertext tool for exploratory policy discussion', in I. Greif (ed.) *Proceedings of the 1988 ACM Conference on Computer Supported Cooperative Work*, New York: ACM, 140–52.

Danielsson, K. and C. Wiberg (2006) 'Participatory Design of learning media: designing educational computer games with and for teenagers', *Interactive Technology and Smart Education* special issue: Computer Game-based Learning, 3(4): 259–74.

Dewey, J. (1927/1966) *Democracy and Education*, New York: Macmillan/Free Press.

DiSalvo, C., I. Nourbakhsh, D. Holstius, A. Akin and M. Louw (2008) 'The Neighborhood Networks Project: a case study of critical engagement and creative expression through participatory design', in J. Simonsen, T. Robertson and D. Hakken (eds) *Proceedings of the Tenth Anniversary Conference on Participatory Design 2008*, Indianapolis: Indiana University Press, 41–50.

DiSalvo, C., M. Louw, J. Coupland and M. Steiner (2009) 'Local issues, local uses: tools for robotics and sensing in community contexts', in N. Bryan-Kinn (ed.) *Proceeding of the Seventh ACM Conference on Creativity and Cognition*, New York: ACM, 245–54.

Ehn, P. (2008) 'Participation in design things', in J. Simonsen, T. Robertson and D. Hakken (eds) *Proceedings of the Tenth Anniversary Conference on Participatory Design 2008*, Indianapolis: Indiana University Press, 92–101.

Farooq, U., C. Ganoe, L. Xiao, C. Merkel, M. Rosson and J. Carroll (2007) 'Supporting community-based learning: case study of a geographical community organization designing its website', *Behaviour and Information Technology*, 26(1): 5–21.

Farrington, C. and E. Pine (1996) 'Community memory: a case study in community communication', in P. E. Agre and D. Schuler (eds) *Reinventing Technology, Rediscovering Community*, Norwood, NJ: Ablex.

Fischer, G. and E. Scharff (2000) 'Meta-design: design for designers', in D. Boyarski and W. A. Kellogg (eds) *Proceedings of the 3rd Conference on Designing Interactive Systems: Processes, Practices, Methods, and Techniques*, New York: ACM, 396–405.

Floyd, C., W. Mehl, F. Reisen, G. Schmidt and G. Wolf (1989) 'Out of Scandinavia: alternative approaches to software design and system development', *Human–Computer Interaction*, 4(4): 253–350.

Gordon, T. F. and N. Karacapilidis (1997) 'The ZENO argumentation framework', in J. Zeleznikow, D. Hunter and L. K. Branting (eds) *Proceedings of the 6th International Conference on Artificial Intelligence and Law*, New York: ACM, 10–18.

Greenbaum, J. and M. Kyng (eds) (1991) *Design at Work: Cooperative Design of Computer Systems*, Chichester, UK: Lawrence Erlbaum Associates.

Gurstein, M. (ed.) (2000) *Community Informatics: Enabling Communities with Information and Communication Technologies*, Hershey, PA: Idea Group Publishing.

Hess, J., S. Offenberg and V. Pipek (2008) 'Community-driven development as participation? Involving user communities in a software design process', in J. Simonsen, T. Robertson and D. Hakken (eds) *Proceedings of the Tenth Anniversary Conference on Participatory Design 2008*, Indianapolis: Indiana University Press, 31–40.

Hirsch, T. (2008) 'Contestational design: innovation for political activism', PhD dissertation, Massachusetts Institute of Technology. Online. Available at: http://hdl.handle.net/1721.1/46594 (accessed 13 November 2011).

Hirsch, T. (2009a) 'Communities real and imagined: designing a communication system for Zimbabwean activists', in J. M. Carroll (ed.) *Proceedings of the Fourth International Conference on Communities and Technologies*, New York: ACM, 71–6.

Hirsch, T. (2009b) 'Learning from activists: lessons for designers', *Interactions*, 16(3): 31–3.

Hughes, T. P. (1983) *Networks of Power: Electrification in Western Society, 1880–1930*, Baltimore, MD: Johns Hopkins University Press.

Iacucci, G., C. Iacucci and K. Kuutti (2002) 'Imagining and experiencing in design, the role of performances', in O. W. Bertelsen (ed.) *Proceedings of the Second Nordic Conference on Human–Computer Interaction*, New York: ACM, 167–76.

Karasti, H. and K. Baker (2008) 'Community design: growing one's own information infrastructure', in J. Simonsen, T. Robertson and D. Hakken (eds) *Proceedings of the Tenth Anniversary Conference on Participatory Design 2008*, Indianapolis: Indiana University Press, 217–20.

Karasti, H. and A. L. Syrjänen (2004) 'Artful infrastructuring in two cases of community PD', in A. Clement, F. de Cindio, A. M. Oostveen, D. Schuler and P. van den Besselaar (eds) *Proceedings of the Eighth Conference on Participatory Design: Artful Integration: Interweaving Media, Materials and Practices*, New York: ACM, 20–30.

Kavanaugh, A. L., P. L. Isenhour, M. Cooper, J. M. Carroll, M. B. Rosson and J. Schmitz (2005) 'Information technology in support of public deliberation', in P. van den Besselaar, G. de Michelis, J. Preece and C. Simone (eds) *Communities and Technologies 2005*, Dordrecht: Springer, 19–40.

Kensing, F. and K. H. Madsen (1991) 'Generating visions: future workshops and metaphorical design', in J. Greenbaum and M. Kyng (eds) *Design at Work: Cooperative Design of Computer Systems*, Hillsdale, NJ: Lawrence Erlbaum Associates, 155–68.

Kunz, W. and H. W. J. Rittel (1970) 'Issues as elements of information systems', Working Paper No. 131, Institut für Grundlagen der Planung, University of Stuttgart. Online. Available at: www.cc.gatech.edu/~ellendo/rittel/rittel-issues.pdf (accessed 14 November 2011).

Latour, B. and P. Weibel (2005) *Making Things Public: Atmospheres of Democracy*, Cambridge, MA: MIT Press.

Lave, J. and E. Wenger (1991) *Situated Learning: Legitimate Peripheral Participation*, Cambridge: University of Cambridge Press.

Le Dantec, C. A. and W. K. Edwards (2008a) 'Designs on dignity: perceptions of technology among the homeless', in M. Burnett, M. F. Costabile, T. Catarci, B. de Ruyter, D. Tan, M. Czerwinski and A. Lund (eds) *Proceedings of the Twenty-Sixth Annual SIGCHI Conference on Human Factors in Computing Systems*, New York: ACM, 627–36.

Le Dantec, C. A. and W. K. Edwards (2008b) 'The view from the trenches: organization, power, and technology at two nonprofit homeless outreach centers', in D. W. McDonald and B. Begole (eds) *Proceedings of the 2008 ACM Conference on Computer Supported Cooperative Work*, New York: ACM, 589–98.

Le Dantec, C. A. and W. K. Edwards (2010) 'Across boundaries of influence and accountability: the multiple scales of public sector information systems', in E. Mynatt, K. Edwards, T. Rodden, S. E. Hudson and G. Fitzpatrick (eds) *Proceedings of the 28th International Conference on Human Factors in Computing Systems*, New York: ACM, 113–22.

Le Dantec, C. A., J. E. Christensen, M. Bailey, R. G. Farrell, J. B. Ellis, C. M. Danis, W. A. Kellogg and W. K. Edwards (2010) 'A tale of two publics: democratizing design at the margins', in K. Halskov and G. Petersen (eds) *Proceedings of the 8th ACM Conference on Designing Interactive Systems*, New York: ACM, 11–20.

Light, A., G. Simpson, L. Weaver and P. G. T. Healey (2009) 'Geezers, turbines, fantasy personas: making the everyday into the future', in N. Bryan-Kinn (ed.) *Proceeding of the Seventh ACM Conference on Creativity and Cognition*, New York: ACM, 39–48.

Luke, R., A. Clement, R. Terada, D. Bortolussi, C. Booth, D. Brooks and D. Christ (2004) 'The promise and perils of a participatory approach to developing an open source community learning network', in A. Clement, F. de Cindio, A. M. Oostveen, D. Schuler and, P. van den Besselaar (eds) *Proceedings of the Eighth Conference on Participatory Design: Artful Integration: Interweaving Media, Materials and Practices*, New York: ACM, 11–19.

MacDonald, S. and A. Clement (2008) 'Participatory tensions in developing a community learning network', in J. Simonsen, T. Robertson and D. Hakken (eds) *Proceedings of the Tenth Anniversary Conference on Participatory Design 2008*, Indianapolis: Indiana University Press, 234–7.

MacDonald, S. and A. Clement (2012) 'Systems development in a community-based organization: lessons from the St Christopher House community learning network', in A. Clement, M. Gurstein, G. Longford, M. Moll and L. R. Shade (eds*) Connecting Canadians: Investigations in Community Informatics*, Edmonton: Athabasca University Press.

McPhail, B., R. Barclay, D. Bruckmann, T. Costantino and A. Clement (1998) 'CAVEAT exemplar: participatory design in a volunteer organisation', *Computer Supported Cooperative Work*, 7(3): 223–41.

Marres, N. (2007) 'The issues deserve more credit: pragmatist contributions to the study of public involvement in controversy', *Social Studies of Science*, 37(5): 759–80.

Mazzone, E., J. Read and R. Beale (2008) 'Design with and for disaffected teenagers', in A. Gulz, C. Magnusson, L. Malmborg, H. Eftring, B. Jönsson and K. Tollmar (eds) *Proceedings of the 5th Nordic Conference on Human–Computer Interaction: Building Bridges*, New York: ACM, 290–97.

Merkel, C., L. Xiao, U. Farooq, C. H. Ganoe, R. Lee, J. M. Carroll and M. B. Rosson (2004) 'Participatory design in community computing contexts: tales from the field', in A. Clement, F. de Cindio, A. M. Oostveen, D. Schuler and P. van den Besselaar (eds) *Proceedings of the Eighth Conference on Participatory Design: Artful Integration: Interweaving Media, Materials and Practices*, New York: ACM, 1–10.

Merkel, C., U. Farooq, L. Xiao, C. H. Ganoe, M. B. Rosson and J. M. Carroll (2007) 'Managing technology use and learning in nonprofit community organizations: methodological challenges and opportunities', in E. Kandogan and P. M. Jones (eds) *Proceedings of the 2007 Symposium on Computer Human Interaction for the Management of Information Technology*, New York: ACM.

Mouffe, C. (2000) *The Democratic Paradox*, London: Verso.

Nonnecke, B. and J. Preece (2000) 'Lurker demographics: counting the silent', in T. Turner and G. Szwillus (eds) *Proceedings of the SIGCHI Conference on Human Factors in Computing Systems*, New York: ACM, 73–80.

Piaget, J. and B. Inhelder. (1969) *The Psychology of the Child*, New York: Basic Books.

Pipek, V. (2005) 'From tailoring to appropriation support: negotiating groupware usage', PhD dissertation, University of Oulu. Online. Available at: http://herkules.oulu.fi/isbn9514276302/isbn9514276302.pdf (accessed 14 November 2011).

Pipek, V. and A.-L. Syrjänen (2006) '"Infrastructuring" as capturing in-situ design', in *Proceedings of the 7th Mediterranean Conference on Information Systems, San Servolo, Italy, October 5–9, 2006*, MCIS.

Pipek, V. and V. Wulf (2009) 'Infrastructuring: towards an integrated perspective on the design and use of information technology', *Journal of the Association for Information Systems*, 10(5): 447–73.

Read, J. C., P. Gregory, S. J. MacFarlane, B. McManus, P. Gray and R. Patel (2002) *An Investigation of Participatory Design with Children – Informant, Balanced and Facilitated Design. Interaction Design and Children*, Eindhoven: Shaker Publishing.

Redhead, F. and M. Brereton (2006) 'A qualitative analysis of local community communications', in J. Kjeldskov and J. Paay (eds) *Proceedings of the 18th Australia Conference on Computer–Human Interaction: Design: Activities, Artefacts and Environments*, New York: ACM, 361–4.

Redhead, F. and M. Brereton (2010) 'Iterative design within a local community communication fabric', in S. Viller and B. Kraal (eds) *Proceedings of the 22nd Conference of the Computer–Human Interaction Special Interest Group of Australia on Computer–Human Interaction*, New York: ACM, 388–91.

Schuler, D. (1996) *New Community Networks: Wired for Change*, Reading, MA: Addison-Wesley.

Shilton, K., N. Ramanathan, S. Reddy, V. Samanta, J. Burke, D. Estrin and M. Hansen (2008) 'Participatory Design of sensing networks', in *Proceedings of the 10th Conference on Participatory Design*, Bloomington, IN: ACM.

Sidlar, C. L. and C. Rinner (2007) 'Analyzing the usability of an argumentation map as a participatory spatial decision support tool', *URISA Journal*, 19(2): 47–55.

Star, S. L. (1999) 'Ethnography of infrastructure', *American Behavioral Scientist*, 43(3): 377–91.

Star, S. L. and G. C. Bowker (2002) 'How to infrastructure', in L. A. Lievrouw and S. Livingstone (eds) *Handbook of New Media: Social Shaping and Consequences of ICTs*, London: Sage.

Star, S. L. and K. Ruhleder (1996) 'Steps toward an ecology of infrastructure: design and access for large information spaces', *Information Systems Research*, 7: 111–33.

Stevens, G. and T. Wiedenhöfer (2006) 'CHIC – a pluggable solution for community help in context', in A. I. Mørch, K. Morgan, T. Bratteteig, G. Ghosh and D. Svanæs (eds) *Proceedings of the 4th Nordic Conference on Human–Computer Interaction: Changing Roles*, New York: ACM, 212–21.

Suchman, L. (1999) 'Working relations of technology production and use', in D. Mackenzie and J. Wajcman (eds) *The Social Shaping of Technology,* second edition, Buckingham, PA: Open University Press.

Suchman, L. (2002) 'Located accountabilities in technology production', *Scandinavian Journal of Information Systems*, 14(2): 91–105.

Syrjänen, A.-L. (2007) 'Lay participatory design: a way to develop information technology and activity together', *Acta Universitatis Ouluensis A* 494. Available at: http://herkules.oulu.fi/isbn9789514285912/.

Trigg, R. H. (2000) 'From sandbox to "fundbox": weaving participatory design into the fabric of a busy nonprofit', in T. Cherkasky, J. Greenbaum, P. Mambrey and J. K. Pors (eds) *PDC 2000: Proceedings of the Participatory Design Conference, New York, NY, USA, 28 November – 1 December 2000*, Palo Alto, CA: Computer Professionals for Social Responsibility, 174–83.

Twidale, M. B. and Floyd, I. (2008) 'Infrastructures from the bottom-up and the top-down: can they meet in the middle?' in J. Simonsen, T. Robertson and D. Hakken (eds) *Proceedings of the Tenth Anniversary Conference on Participatory Design 2008*, Indianapolis: Indiana University Press, 238–41.

Vygotsky, L. S. (1978) *Mind in Society: The Development of Higher Psychological Processes*, Cambridge, MA: Harvard University Press.

Wenger, E. (1998) *Communities of Practice: Learning, Meaning, and Identity*, Cambridge: Cambridge University Press.

Winschiers-Theophilus, H., S. Chivuno-Kuria, G. K. Kapuire, N. J. Bidwell and E. Blake (2010) 'Being participated: a community approach', in K. Bødker, T. Bratteteig, D. Loi and T. Robertson (eds) *Proceedings of the 11th Biennial Participatory Design Conference*, New York: ACM, 1–10.

Section II
Outstanding applications of Participatory Design

9

Integrating Participatory Design into everyday work at the Global Fund for Women

Randy Trigg and Karen Ishimaru

In this case study, the authors reflect on a decade of Participatory Design experience in a single workplace.

As in-house staff at the Global Fund for Women, a non-profit foundation making grants to support women's human rights around the world, we've utilised a Participatory Design approach in the design and development of grantmaking and fundraising databases for the last 11+ years. This chapter reviews our work in and across the organisation, and discusses the challenges we have encountered in conducting Participatory Design and in realising a shared information space for the Global Fund's work.

Following an introduction to the Global Fund and our Participatory Design work, we reflect on the *process* of doing in-house Participatory Design and the information space that represents the *product* of our efforts. In the Process section, the reader learns how classic Participatory Design questions, like 'Who has time to participate?' and 'Who is at the decision-making table?' play out in the case of a well-established non-profit. The challenge is to sustain an organisational culture supportive of Participatory Design in the face of evolving priorities, staff turnover and diverging goals across departments and levels. The Product section explores issues of shared ownership, access and information. Maintaining the organisation-wide shared information space is especially challenging in the context of decentralization, off-the-shelf products and cloud-based services. Finally, we consider when, why and how one might move from concerns with information management to questions of workplace democracy.

Introduction

The Global Fund for Women is a non-profit organisation that makes grants to support women's rights around the world. As in-house staff at the Global Fund, we've utilised a Participatory

Design approach in the design and development of databases for the last 11+ years. This chapter reviews our work in and across the organisation, and discusses the challenges we have encountered in conducting Participatory Design and in realising a shared information space for the Global Fund's work.

We begin with a brief introduction to the Global Fund for Women and the context it provides for Participatory Design. Our reflections are framed both in terms of the *process* of doing in-house Participatory Design and the information space that represents the *product* of our efforts. We discuss our successes and challenges, the implications they have for our future work and lessons learned. We end with a brief discussion of workplace democracy and concluding reflections.

The Global Fund for Women

The Global Fund for Women was founded in 1987 out of the belief that women's human rights and the full participation of women at all levels of society are essential to the advancement of global agendas for social, economic and political change.[1] Twenty-five years later, the Global Fund is the largest US-based grantmaking organisation exclusively funding women's rights globally. Since its founding, the organisation has given $100 million in core funding to more than 4,500 women-led organisations in 174 countries. These groups work on a range of issues including gender-based violence, economic justice and sexuality rights, often within marginalised communities and in remote areas of the world. We are publically funded and our donors include individuals, foundations, corporations and other institutions. Also crucial to our work is the Global Fund's extensive network of regional and global advisors, which provides staff with context, perspectives and guidance related to the issues and groups we support. In partnership with our grantees, donors and advisors, the Global Fund is working to build women-led social movements that are vital to strong civil societies.

As important as *what* we do, is *how* we do it. This is one of the Global Fund's earliest principles, referring to the manner in which our fundraising and grantmaking is done. We believe that women on the ground can and should articulate the problems that affect them and identify their own solutions. Whereas US grantmaking is often focused on project-based support, the Global Fund gives general funding to women's groups, enabling them to focus on their highest priorities and build capacity for their organisations. Likewise, the questions we ask grantees on reporting forms reveal outcomes they deem important, in addition to traditional measures of impact like numbers served. We believe this grantmaking strategy is empowering and effective. As one grantee from Armenia writes,

> GFW's grantmaking process is flexible and built on trust. On the one hand, this funding model gives [us] freedom in prioritizing the grant money. On the other hand, it raises the level of [our] organizational and management responsibility for the optimal and most efficient resource distribution. The practice of flexible funding for general support indicates that GFW is truly concerned about sustainability of women's groups and the development of women's movements in the countries of our region.

The same values of respect and trust apply to our fundraising. Our fundraising philosophy is one that values every donor and every gift, no matter the size. The focus is on cultivating relationships and involving donors in ways that celebrate their participation in the movement, through donor trips, social media and events featuring Global Fund grantee partners, advisors and board members. These principles infuse all aspects of the organisation, including the information systems and design processes for building these systems as we discuss below.

Staff members lie at the heart of the work and mission of the organisation. The Global Fund has grown significantly over the years, from a few people working out of a shared office space in Palo Alto, California, to more than 50 staff members working in offices in San Francisco and New York. Although the organisation has developed more formal systems and hierarchical structures in response to the growth, our work and strategies continue to be informed from the bottom up even as they are guided from above. Staff throughout the organisation remain committed to its mission and ultimately realise its goals and values through their day-to-day activities and interactions with donors and grantees.

Participatory Design at the Global Fund for Women

At the Global Fund, we have adopted a user-centred, flexible approach to system development in which staff are equal partners and active participants. At least since Randy first began volunteering at the Global Fund in 1999, development and maintenance of the internal databases has involved a Participatory Design approach.[2] In a paper at the Participatory Design Conference in 2000, he observed that making a pitch for Participatory Design at the Global Fund was like 'preaching to the choir' – staff saw the approach as not only preferable but obvious, especially given how well it fit with the feminist ethos of the workplace (Trigg 2000).

In 2008, Karen joined Randy in forming a new department, the Information Management sub-team (IM). We are positioned within Finance & Admin, one of the five organisational 'teams' at the Global Fund. Finance & Admin is responsible for the main support functions of the organisation and works in conjunction with the other teams: Development (fundraising), Programs (grantmaking), Communications, and Human Resources. In addition to outlining responsibilities around the databases, IM's charter identifies Participatory Design as fundamental to our work process. By employing Participatory Design in our co-design projects with staff, we start from a place of respect for the knowledge and expertise of all project stakeholders.

The Global Fund's approach to grantmaking and fundraising requires that our systems respond to the changing contexts, complex realities and diverse needs of both international women's groups and donors. Moreover, grantmaking and fundraising efforts, as well as other aspects of our work, have always been fundamentally linked, leading the organisation to look for customised solutions that seamlessly integrate the various activities of the organisation.

Central to the Global Fund's information systems are two interconnected databases. The *grantmaking database* contains information about groups that have applied to the Global Fund for funding, and supports the work of Program team members in reviewing proposals, requesting endorsements and approving grants. The Grants Administration team uses the database to build contracts and make payments once grants are approved, and to track payment history. The *development database* holds information about the Global Fund's supporters and their gifts, dating back to those of the organisation's original founders. A critical point of intersection between the two databases occurs during the 'releasing' process, when incoming donations restricted to certain regions or issues are matched with outgoing grants to women's groups. That matching process helps coordinate and streamline the work of the teams, goals that are important across the databases, from generating contracts with grantees, to creating donor thank-you letters and reconciling gift information with Finance. The databases also enable us to track not only our ongoing activities, but the nature and degree of the impact of our work.

An example of information management: classifying the Global Fund's grants

The system of classifying the Global Fund's grants within the databases is the result of a proto-typical Participatory Design project. It exemplifies many of the rewarding as well as challenging aspects of our Participatory Design work as in-house developers. The classification system is also an illustration of how Participatory Design has been instrumental in connecting the design and functionality of the databases to the organisation's mission and values.

The classification system represents the Global Fund's worldview – what we care about, what we support and what we hope to achieve. Staff members apply these classifications to grants to analyse and communicate our grantmaking strategies internally and externally. Each grant is classified by selecting a subset of the categories that best characterise the concerns, strategies and beneficiaries underlying the group's proposed work (Figure 9.1).

The classification categories are derived from the Program team's analysis of materials and reports written by grantees themselves. As a result, the classification system reflects the complex nature of the issues as well as grantees' frequent use of multiple strategies and approaches for effecting real and lasting change. While there is clear understanding of the value and importance of having a classification system, the processes of distinguishing among categories (e.g. what age range does 'youth' represent?) and boiling down comprehensive strategies to fit into a broader framework are challenging. Nonetheless, because of the collective process through which the categories have been designed and redesigned, the classification system is a tool in active use throughout the organisation, and reflects the Global Fund's priorities for funding international women's rights.

Figure 9.1 The Global Fund for Women's classification categories as of October 2011, divided into Populations, Strategies and Issues, and sub-groups within these. The text area to the right shows in-line documentation of a selected sub-group ('Expanding political participation' within Issues).

The classification system has been revised four times in the last 11 years, evolving from a set of checkboxes in one corner of the grantmaking database to a multi-tiered system spanning both development and grantmaking databases. (Table 9.2 shows the set of classifications as of 2001 before the split into Populations, Strategies and Issues.) After more than a year, the latest classifications revamp hasn't quite reached completion. This is partly owing to the intense work required by many staff in reviewing past proposals – as well as the nature of the work they are doing. The initial phases of the classification project, envisioning new categories and thinking through the transition, had a fairly high profile throughout the organisation, while the later phases had less visibility and lower impact on people's work, leading to less urgency around their completion.

The classifications revamp is a great example of a project that we didn't lead. Partnering with Randy, a few individuals on the Program team led the effort, working with other regional sub-teams – and with other teams across the organisation – to develop new categories and structures, reach a common understanding of how to apply the categories consistently, and determine how to map old categories to newly created ones. For example, the earlier category 'gender-based violence' was split into more specific categories like 'domestic violence', 'female genital mutilation', 'femicide and attempted assault' and 'political violence'.

Program team leadership was crucial when it came to mobilising the efforts of grantmaking staff – we on IM were able to make the necessary database changes, but on our own could never have marshalled the input of so many staff members, including those on other teams. The project lead got the project approved by leadership before starting, as well as the buy-in of other important groups throughout the organisation. We were able to do our work without taking much of the Program team's time or attending Program team meetings because we worked with the project lead as our liaison. On the flip side, we didn't really know

Table 9.2 The 'flat' list of the Global Fund for Women classifications as of March 2001

Arts/Theater/Culture/Sports	H Environmental Health	Population
Conflict resolution	H Health & Human Rights	P Girls/Youth/Adolescents (up
Disability	H HIV/STDs/AIDS - Health	to 17) - Population
Economic Opportunity	H Mental Health	P Indigenous Women -
Education/Formal School	H Reproductive Health	Population
(i.e. Preston)	H Respectful Treatment of	P Migrant/Refugee Women -
Education/Non-formal	Women - Health	Population
School/Literacy	Labor/Worker Rights	P Rural Women - Population
Emergencies	Leadership	Prostitution/Sex Workers
E Albania - Emergency	Dev/Training/Capacity Bldg	Reproductive Rights
E Hurricane Mitch - Emergency	Legal Rights	Research/Info/Documentation
E Kosova Crisis - Emergency	Legislative Advocacy	Center
E Turkey - Emergency	Lesbian Rights	Sexuality
Environment	Media/Technology/	Spirituality
Female Genital Mutilation	Communication	Trafficking
(FGM)	Political Participation	Violence Against Women
Female Human Rights Within	Populations	V Domestic Violence
Religions	P Adult (18 and older) -	V Sexual Assault/Harassment -
Gender FHR Awareness/Public	Population	Violence
Ed	P Domestic Workers -	V Violence in Conflict/Wars
Health	Population	Population
H Access to Health	P Ethnic & Cultural Minorities -	

how participatory the project was. We've since learned that input from all levels of the Programme team was solicited. As we'll see in other contexts, however, this isn't always the case.

While originating with the Programme team, the project had cross-team implications. Collaborating with other teams meant a shared development, understanding and use of an organisation-wide classification system. In the past, parts of the database had their own classification systems that only particular teams or sub-groups understood. Having a single unified system that other teams were also involved in developing has helped create a common language between teams and – perhaps the driving factor of each revamp – provided a broader way of communicating about and analysing our grantmaking.

Reflections on in-house Participatory Design

The evolution of the Global Fund's classifications system is an example of the kind of long-term redesign for which our in-house presence is vital. Because so many of the published examples of Participatory Design are written from the perspectives of researchers or consultants coming from outside the context of use, it's worth reflecting on some of the characteristics of our work that can be traced to being in-house.

- Our relationships with people are based not on single projects or even series of projects, rather we have ongoing relationships with them as fellow staff members and colleagues.
- Our in-house presence as members of staff enables the mutual learning process so important to Participatory Design to unfold over successive projects and work relationships. On the one hand, we've developed an understanding of grantmaking and fundraising concepts over years of working with our colleagues. Likewise, staff members who work with us also begin to think like designers, say, by coming to us when they notice a process that could be automated in the database.
- Since we work regular hours in the office, we can listen for and act on recurring themes arising in different corners of the organisation, including those not made explicit in project plans.
- We have found that interest in certain projects ebbs and flows. Momentum can be lost because of workloads, staff transitions, changes in direction and priorities, and the like. More often than not, the issues and ideas re-emerge at a later time. Being in-house lets us 'ride the wave' when it starts to build momentum by conveying the earlier history to new staff, informing them about existing infrastructure and information in the database, and engaging with them around their current vision and context.
- Just as projects are set aside and picked up again over time, certain functions in the database have rotated between different teams and seen various divisions of labour. We have helped to transfer information and ensure continuity.
- Our 'purview' and authority are largely defined by the team and hierarchical structures that we are a part of, and by extension, those of the staff members with whom we work.
- With an insider's understanding of structures and politics within the organisation, we have been able to try alternative approaches and insert ourselves in different spaces when one approach isn't working.

These characteristics of in-house Participatory Design inform the work we discuss in the next sections. Yet as in-house staff members, we're sometimes viewed as having vested interests and a limited range of experience and expertise compared to that of an external consultant. We do indeed favour certain values and ways of working, as we'll see in the remainder of this chapter. At the same time, we have the interests of the organisation and mission in mind, as well as first-hand experience with, knowledge of and insights into the Global Fund's systems, organisational culture and history. It is for these reasons that we work to engage staff members in the design and practices around the databases, and to continue to lobby for the importance of this work.

Participatory Design process and product

Our work at the Global Fund is based on two fundamental premises that have remained largely unchanged over the course of 11 years. The first, a focus on participation, underlies *how* we do our work. The second, regarding the value of shared information spaces, characterises *what* we've been doing. For us, participation starts from the traditional Participatory Design concerns with involving and empowering end-users of technology. As we'll see, this is increasingly tied to our ability to engage users at higher levels in the organisational hierarchy whose influence and understanding of informational technologies impacts both the degree of interest in being involved and the sense of empowerment among those they supervise.

The second premise involves the kinds of systems we've been building. The Global Fund's databases are a tangible product of the Participatory Design approach employed from the very beginning of the organisation's history (before our arrival). Designed in close collaboration with staff throughout the organisation and spanning many different tenures, the architecture, fields and functionality of the databases uniquely reflect the philosophy and work of the Global Fund, as has the choice to employ in-house developers who value Participatory Design and customisable systems.

We have found the process and content premises to be intertwined. Naturally, the more limited access becomes, either as a result of 'unbundling' our information spaces across external vendors or by individuals claiming ownership over select pieces, the harder it is to enable participation by our staff in the design process. Likewise, the more we can engage our colleagues in design discussions, especially across teams, the more the information spaces become truly the Global Fund's in a way that enhances cohesion and coordination throughout the organisation and makes shared access essential.

In the next two sections, we explore these two premises from the perspective of the challenges they've entailed. Finding ways to address these challenges is an ongoing effort, as they often return months or years later with new twists and in different contexts. We close with a discussion of our experience advocating for workplace democracy beyond our normal design and maintenance work.

Participatory process

Some of the biggest challenges to effective Participatory Design at the Global Fund involve the ins and outs of access: our access to our colleagues, as well as their access to us and to the systems we build. Over the years, we've tackled problems of access using structured interactions such as team meetings, all-staff meetings, new hire orientations and team-wide trainings. We've also partly addressed these challenges through organisational structures of participation: informal and formal liaisons, formal committees, working groups formed around specific projects, and our own incorporation into a department of Information Management. These structures raise challenges of their own, particularly around questions of accountability and recognition, with which we still grapple today. In this section, we start by outlining our 'normal' Participatory Design process and then review these challenges to effective participation as they've arisen over the years, and note how they've led to our current advocacy efforts around workplace democracy.

How we work

Our Participatory Design process can be described as a series of high-level steps. Exactly whether and how each step is carried out depends on the context of the given project or request from staff. Nonetheless, the overall structure suffices to frame the challenges we discuss in this section. See Chapter 6 of this book for more on Participatory Design methods.

- *Origin and approval*. Our work usually starts with a project proposal or a request from staff. The distinction between more demanding 'projects' and less complex feature requests or bug reports is important. Ideally, projects have more lead time, are approved by management, and appear in our annual/quarterly plans. If we and the requestors determine that a new request exceeds the 'project' threshold in terms of complexity and resource demands, then we pause the Participatory Design process to discuss the request with our respective managers to gain official approval and possibly reprioritise other projects. As we'll see, the approval process can be challenging even for simpler requests if the proposed change impacts the work of staff members other than the requestor. We'll also discuss challenges that arise when there is no clear proposal or request made to IM, even when we may be heavily implicated.
- *Planning and scheduling*. Regardless of the size of the request, we agree on a timeframe by which the work should be complete. We also discuss with the requestor(s) who else needs to be involved in the design and implementation, and who should be informed when the work is complete. For small requests, we can usually commit immediately to a completion date. For more complex requests, we arrange a next meeting to develop a schedule and an initial design.
- *Design, prototyping and testing*. The duration of this stage depends on the complexity of the request. We sometimes prototype simple solutions together with the requestor in a single session at a computer, while more complex requests can take weeks or even months. The latter generally involve a series of sessions where we work with project stakeholders on the latest prototypes. When outstanding issues involve only the look of an interface rather than its behaviour, we sometimes obtain stakeholder feedback by emailing screen snaps of the prototype interface.
- *Documentation and training*. At a minimum, when the final version is 'delivered' to the stakeholders we include instructions for its use. Sometimes, these instructions are revised by team members for understandability and to reflect the context of their work processes. When accompanying changes to staff work processes are required, we try to schedule training for the relevant team members. We strive to integrate the change into our overall documentation, though this sometimes lags when our plates are full.
- *Follow-up and monitoring*. At some time after completion of the work, we check back with the requestors to see how things are going. Our primary interest is in whether and how the new facility is being used and whether we need to make changes. For larger projects, we want to learn the stakeholders' reactions to the product of our work as well as to the process we conducted with them. It is in this way that we can learn lessons that inform our subsequent work.

In the rest of this section, we discuss the kinds of challenges we encounter carrying out this Participatory Design process in our workplace. Because our relationships with fellow staff members are crucial to the challenges as well as to the overall process, the following sub-sections focus on questions related to who is involved and how they impact our process.

Who has time to participate?

In autumn 1999, when Randy started volunteering at the Global Fund, he worked directly with one member of the Program team on revamping the grantmaking database. She had herself just arrived at the Global Fund and was concerned about several aspects of that database, including its 'flat file' nature.[3]

Together, they planned a revamped database that would be relational in nature, have a new interface that was more accessible and legible for Program team members, and include features that supported integration and centralisation. For example, letters to applicants and grantees were built and stored in Microsoft Word; to find correspondence for a particular grantee, you had to know who had written the letter and have access to their hard drive. In the revamped database, each letter was generated and stored within the database from which it could be printed or emailed. This was an early example of our efforts to build a single shared information space.

Process-wise, the strategy was to prototype the new database in such a way that all staff would have access to it throughout its development. The prototype included a subset of the real grantmaking data and so felt familiar in spite of its new features and interfaces. After six months of development that included one-on-one and group meetings and trainings with Program team members, the new database was adopted and formally launched, although development continued for several more months in the now live database. That story is recounted in more detail in a conference paper written a few months after the launch of the new database (Trigg 2000).

Our primary challenge was access to the Program team, the future users of our revamped grantmaking database. As with most non-profits, staff members at the Global Fund were swamped with work. (For more on Participatory Design in the non-profit sector, see McPhail et al (1998) and Chapter 8 of this book.) Though interested in having a more direct role, they simply didn't have the time. Once we recognised this reality, the challenge shifted from 'How can we make them meet with us more often?' to 'How can we make do with less participation than we'd like?'

During development, Randy had a long list of features and improvements that had been suggested for the new database by staff and by him. His problem was how to prioritise this work. For example, which tasks should be done earlier, before launch, and which could wait a little longer? Once we saw that the Program team would rarely meet to discuss and prioritise their database desires, we had to find ways to proceed without that valuable input.

We employed a variety of approaches to make the most of the interactions we did have:

- Be opportunistic – when someone needs help, turn it into a training moment.
- Do cooperative prototyping sessions when possible to reduce technological mystery and show that changes are possible and sometimes even easy (Bødker and Grønbæk 1991).
- Identify a point person on the team for specific tasks – train that person to work with us, and to take on some of the customisation work around that part of the system.
- Try to schedule larger meetings during lulls in the workload – in the meantime, do work that requires less team input.
- Make the changes incremental if possible, oriented to the desires of those with the greatest urgency, but remain flexible in case the larger group second-guesses those design decisions. At the same time, try to resist 'feature creep'.

Some of the issues from that period persist today, while others have been transformed. We're still inserting training moments and cooperative prototyping whenever we can. We sometimes identify point people for particular tasks, though more often than not this is accomplished through our team liaisons or committees (see below). We still make incremental progress by working on individual needs, though we try to push back if we sense that an individual's request might need team discussion/approval.

On the other hand, the work of prioritisation has changed significantly as we balance the needs of different teams. As the Global Fund has grown and taken up more formal team-based structures within the organisation, IM's project priorities are set during our annual and quarterly planning processes. Although we meet on an (at least) annual basis with the other teams to check in on our priorities, members of the Program and Development teams don't have time to help us prioritise our work, nor is that appropriate given that IM conducts and participates in projects for multiple teams.

These days when we work with teams on specific projects, we have greater access to team meetings, especially if we keep the IM slot in their meeting short (15 to 30 minutes) and on the agenda well in advance. It's been especially heartening to see an increase in requests from the teams (rather than from us) to attend their meetings. Our presence at team meetings has helped us get team-wide buy-in and recognition for the work of our liaisons and committees, though that continues to be a struggle, as we'll see.

Who do we work with?

From the beginning, we've found it impractical to do Participatory Design with an entire Global Fund team. Instead, we work with representatives from that team, and we do so on an ongoing basis rather than just on particular projects. It's been important that these colleagues have designations that in some way formalise this organisational relationship between their team and IM. For example, there are currently two IM 'liaisons' on the Program team, and a database 'committee' of five members of the Development team.

As the designations indicate, we have used different approaches for different teams. Liaisons work well for the Program team, where functions and work in the database are fairly standardised across the sub-teams. On the Development team, sub-teams specialise in different types of donors (e.g. institutions, major donors, annual donors) who give in very different ways. As a result, the strategies and practices used by the sub-teams differ significantly. Thus the database committee includes representatives from each sub-team in order to ensure coordination and systems alignment across that team.

At the same time, getting buy-in and participation among all levels and types of users has been challenging. Some staff members are less engaged with the databases; their interests may not always be represented or even known by our liaisons. And like everyone else they are swamped with work. We attempt to reach out to these staff members in several ways. As we discuss below, we've changed our orientation process so that new hires can learn more about us. We've increased the number of database-related trainings. In the database itself, we've created 'dashboard' interfaces that provide less complex overviews of information crucial to executive staff in particular. Finally, we encourage every staff member, regardless of level, seniority or database experience, to contact us with questions and suggestions.

Who is a good Participatory Design liaison?

Originally we worked with liaisons because we couldn't involve everyone on the team owing to their workloads and our capacity. Now we realise that good liaisons can make our processes more participatory than they otherwise would be. For example, team members are sometimes more comfortable communicating with the liaisons who are on their own team, or in team meeting structures where we aren't present. Also, our liaisons are increasingly conducting focused trainings for fellow team members that are contextualised in ways that would be difficult for us to replicate.

Recently, we lost an excellent liaison on the Development team to the normal process of staff turnover. We knew we would miss the working relationship we'd built with her over the years, and also wondered how we could replace the skills that made her such a great Participatory Design partner. The week before she left, we sat in a café and over hot chocolate heard her parting wisdom on everything from Participatory Design processes and database wish lists to office politics.

At one point, our colleague described the personality qualities that she thought were essential for her work with us. This led us to think back over our liaisons over the years – have there been patterns? Is there a personality type best suited to this work? Here are some qualities we identified (no one has had all of them, but the best liaisons had most of them):

- eager to collaborate with us despite her full workload;
- easy to work with, forgiving and supportive;
- an eye for detail;
- able to snoop out bugs, and glad to report them to us;
- geeky enough to be curious about what's 'behind the curtain', and willing to follow along with our explanations;
- concerned with data integrity;
- comfortable being a resource and database expert for others on her team;
- sees the 'big picture' of how work in the databases ties into the larger goals of the organisation
- confident enough to make 'executive' decisions when necessary;
- good connections with the rest of her team;
- skilled at 'advocating up'; that is, influencing those above her hierarchically.

How do we deal with the challenge of losing such a colleague? Assuming she hasn't already identified her successor, we look for someone first and foremost who is interested in working with us. When we're lucky, such staff members seek us out. Sometimes finding a liaison on a team is quite difficult – for example, when the given team or group of colleagues haven't themselves been using the database. The result is a chicken-and-egg situation – we need a liaison to help us raise awareness of the database and address the existing (mis)perceptions on the team, but liaisons usually emerge out of groups of already intense users.

Who values participation?

The Global Fund has a culture that values participation. The organisation recruits staff members who are thoughtful and passionate about the mission, and who want to be involved in moving the organisation forward, whether it's contributing to internal systems, the website or broader organisational strategy. Yet as discussed, there is sometimes a tension between participation and time/workloads. As a result, maintaining this culture of participation is challenging; specifically, engaging with us takes time away from the 'core' work of team members and supervisees. We've found that our liaisons and committee members are sometimes given less credit for their work with us, and are perceived as doing IM's work rather than their own.

A few years ago, several members of the Development team requested that a new database administrator position be created on their team in part to offload the work of liaising with us around database design and use. We argued that we needed to work with the team members who actually do the everyday work of that team; without their expertise, Participatory Design is ineffective. The proposal didn't succeed partly because of resource limitations, though the idea is still raised from time to time.

Recently, we revamped our orientation process in part to address this sort of challenge. We now conduct two orientations with new hires so that we have an explicit chance to follow up with them a few months later. Especially for executives, we take time during the first meeting to explain the way we work, our values, and the history of Participatory Design at the Global Fund. Though we know that not every executive at the Global Fund will use the databases, we hope that they will come to appreciate the benefits of a Participatory Design approach to development for them personally, for example, in the ability to get customised interfaces and reports. By explaining from the start the Participatory Design work that members of their team are engaged in, we help them to see the rationale of our process and the possible benefits. We've found this to be an improvement over executives finding out along the way that team members work with IM on these projects without a good understanding of why.

As it turned out, the database administrator proposal was also supported by some of the database committee members; they didn't want to spend time participating in database design if that work wasn't recognised and valued. Once we understood their motivations, we began discussing with them ways to make their expertise around the database more visible. One approach that has worked well over the last year or two is for our liaisons and committee to take on some of the database training for their team. Sometimes we're present at the team meeting for technical support; sometimes we're not there at all. We've found that this helps the rest of the team understand and appreciate the Participatory Design work of our liaisons. At the end of this chapter, in the context of workplace democracy, we revisit the goal of raising the visibility of the database-related work of our colleagues.

Who is at the decision-making table?

In the sub-section, 'Who has time to participate?', we discussed the problem of getting our busy colleagues to our Participatory Design table. Here we look at the inverse challenge, getting ourselves to their decision-making tables. The first example concerns releasing restricted funds, a complex cross-team process that has been revamped at least three times in the last 11 years. The database plays an important role in the process, especially around tracking how restricted funds are distributed across the grants made by the Program team.

When issues related to the database come up for discussion, we on IM are normally brought in to the conversation. However, some years ago the releasing process was revamped in a way that included spread sheets and other tables unconnected to the database. Because our purview was seen as almost exclusively the database, we weren't engaged in discussions of the purpose and design of these artefacts living outside the database. Though aware that spread sheets were playing a role, Randy didn't realise at the time how much work was being done 'off line'. Years later, Randy and Karen learned of the nature of this work process, parts of which required calculator and pencil.

We've now streamlined this part of the releasing process significantly using interfaces designed with a Participatory Design approach; most of the releasing process is now centralised in the database and semi-automated. Going forward, we hope that such incidents are less likely. For one thing, more of our colleagues understand that 'Information Management' includes more than just the database, and thus that IM might be stakeholders in such discussions. Our colleagues are also increasingly aware of the benefits of streamlining, and often let us know when they hear about inefficient work processes.

The second example involves *Salsa*, a project to boost our online fundraising by offloading parts of our gift processing to the 'cloud'. The project was led by a manager on the Development team. Though it was clear to those doing the early planning and advocacy for the project that the databases would eventually be implicated, IM was not seen to be a stakeholder. Indeed, we first learned about the project's implementation plans when a consulting agency was preparing a proposal for the project lead and asked for a specification of the Global Fund's database schema. When that request was transmitted to IM, our response included questions as to the context of the request. Why did the consultants need to know the Global Fund's database schema? Indeed, what exactly was being asked of the consultants? When we learned that the consultants were to weigh in on how the Salsa site on the web should connect to (and possibly synchronise with) the Global Fund's internal database, we requested a bigger role in the planning process. As a result, we were present at the decision-making table and argued our case for in-house control of the data (see the sub-section called 'Salsa: an example of shared information space in the "cloud"').

Looking back, we see our absence in the initial discussions as reflecting a narrow perception of IM's roles and responsibilities. We see ourselves as not just system maintainers, but as also engaged in oversight and planning around the overall design, purpose and direction of the Global Fund's information systems. This includes interconnecting the databases with external entities like the cloud. As we'll see in the next section, the differences in perceptions of IM's work didn't end there; our Participatory Design process was also a source of contention.

Over the course of the Salsa project, our working relationship with the project leader improved markedly. By the end, we reached an understanding on roles, responsibilities and division of labour that contributed to a successful conclusion. As with the releasing example, we hope that the Salsa disconnect is less likely today. Through efforts to educate our colleagues as to our mandate and responsibilities and to include ourselves in discussions that may relate to our work, we believe that information-related cross-team projects are more likely to involve us from the start. We're also heartened that the organisation as a whole is trying to be more conscious of cross-team implications of project plans, especially during the spring annual planning process. These days, we seem more frequently to get a 'heads up' when information systems-related projects are being planned.

Who controls the process?

The Salsa project was the context for another difficult challenge. Once we officially joined the project team and the project got underway, we experienced a work style 'clash' with the project leader. According to our Participatory Design approach we needed to involve in the design process those who do the relevant gift processing work, not just their managers. The project leader was somewhat new to the Global Fund and used to a more hierarchical style from her previous job. Our challenge was how to respect her leadership role and accountability for the success of the project, while at the same time persuading her of the value of participation across levels.

Eventually, and with the support of our own manager, we negotiated a more or less happy medium. To increase transparency, we and the project leader agreed to include each other on most communications related to the project. Regarding participation, we agreed that final decisions were hers, while she agreed that we could consult with members of her team on design questions. An important lesson for us for future large projects is to clarify the ground rules related to participation from the start.

Who has knowledge of the work practice?

Another challenge related to our work process at the Global Fund involves our role in discussions of proposed changes; namely, whether and how to 'push back' when we sense that a change might be ineffective or cause more problems than it solves. Of course, we don't presume to know more than our colleagues about their work, so we've adopted a range of tactics when we have these concerns.

- Ask questions in order to learn as much as we can about the motivation for the change, whether other alternatives have been considered, and which other team members have heard about the proposal.
- Review with the person any history that might be relevant – especially times in the past when this approach was tried, or alternative approaches explored. With the high rate of turnover at the Global Fund, we find ourselves occasionally in the role of historical experts.
- If we are still concerned about the wisdom of the change, we sometimes propose that the issue be raised at a team meeting to learn whether their colleagues have concerns or know of other approaches to solve the problem. This is especially important in cases where we suspect that the proposal would cater to an individual preference rather than benefit the entire team.
- We try to keep the team members who are our liaisons informed of such requests. Often, they help us predict the rest of the team's feelings about the proposal. They also help us think about any extra database work that the proposal requires and who might take that on.

Shared information space

In the preceding section, we discussed our Participatory Design process and the challenges we've encountered along the way. In this section we reflect on the shared information space created through that process and challenges to it that in turn impact our efforts to do effective Participatory Design.

The Global Fund's grantmaking and fundraising databases are an integral part of everyday workflow and processes throughout the organisation. The underlying tools and technology, other information systems with which the databases interact and the functionality of the system comprise an information space characterised by *shared ownership*, *shared access* and *shared information* – qualities that are shaped by the Participatory Design practices we employ. We believe this shared information space is crucial to retaining institutional knowledge and helping the organisation and its staff members advance. However, in realising and maintaining such an information space we encounter challenges related to staff turnover, diverse staff member expectations and perceptions, integration with new systems, and changing needs.

Shared ownership

As discussed above, the organisation's fundraising and grantmaking databases have been built from the ground up for and by staff. As such, they are uniquely the Global Fund's in design, functionality, data, and the extent to which the individual pieces are interconnected and aligned. Shared ownership of these systems comes from the manner in which staff members regard this information space and participate in its ongoing development. Earlier, we described how IM works to maintain this quality of shared ownership. If someone wants to make a change to the database, we consult others to make sure it aligns with existing functions and infrastructure – and, at the very least, that it will not interfere with anyone's work in the database. We also try to generalise individual desires into solutions that can have broader application. Rather than making special fields, layouts or functions in response to individual requests, we work with our liaisons and committees to identify ways to meet an articulated goal that can benefit the teams. As we've discussed, there are also challenges and disconnects when major contributors to the system leave the organisation. However, as staff members have remained the primary decisions-makers on matters that affect them in the database, the Global Fund's databases have continued to evolve organically, responding to new demands, current trends in the external environment, and different perspectives and approaches of an ever-changing group of staff.

There remain a number of challenges to this sense of shared ownership. First, the FileMaker application on which these systems are built enables the degree of flexibility and customisation reflected in the databases. Yet to some, the fact that FileMaker is a proprietary application rather than open source software seems at odds with our values. Second, the home-grown nature of the databases is perceived at times as a weakness of the system. There is a sense that it is not up to par with other commercial products on the market – that the lack of 'expert' input has lowered the quality of the system.

A few years ago, the Development team was considering an off-the-shelf fundraising database to replace its existing donor database. Staff members have always had personal relationships with and a strong sense of loyalty to Global Fund supporters. They wanted to be able to respond to the increasingly complex needs and realities of individuals in an expanding donor base. There was general consensus within the team that the existing database needed fundamental changes to continue doing this. With an architecture more suited to mailings, the database made it difficult to track relationships between donor-advised funds and their donors, between employers and employees, between family members who gave gifts together. If spouses in a couple made gifts separately and wanted to be credited that way, records had to be split, making the spouse relationship difficult to see in the database. A working group composed of a few staff members on the Development team met to assess alternative fundraising systems and make a decision on how to move forward. Randy served as a member of the group and provided counsel on the various options.

At that time, the organisation's growth in assets, reputation and size had led to a greater emphasis on 'professionalisation' – seeking outside hires with extensive credentials and professional experience, as well as tools and technology that were scalable, specialised and widely used in the field. The benefits of customisation in the existing database – and of using a tool like FileMaker, with its general accessibility and broad application – were weighed against off-the-shelf fundraising products used by high-profile organisations. In one sense, it was a choice between external and internal expertise. Raiser's Edge, the leading contender at the time, represented the outside experience and knowledge of others in the field; our Participatory Design approach, like the Global Fund's grantmaking philosophy vis-à-vis our grantees, placed more value on the expertise and experience of our constituency to know what they need. The working group ultimately decided to continue using FileMaker for in-house development and to restructure the existing development database using concepts from Raiser's Edge. That decision, however, did not end the debate around customizable versus off-the-shelf databases.

Shared access

The Global Fund's databases provide a shared technological and informational workspace through which all staff can access our grantmaking and fundraising work. This shared access is justified by an organisation-wide desire for transparency, as well as a close connection between fundraising and grantmaking activities at the Global Fund. The databases represent a common tool and language that staff members on both teams understand. Programme team members meeting with donors can look up a donor's history with the Global Fund in the fundraising database. Other staff members rely heavily on the grantmaking database to share information about the Global Fund's grantees with donors and the general public. In these ways, shared access to the databases improves staff coordination and supports the organisation's partnership with donors and grantees.

At times in the organisation's history, however, there have been calls to conceal parts of the databases to protect sensitive data or maintain data integrity. This is absolutely appropriate in some situations, for example, when issues of confidentiality or legal liability arise. In most cases, however, we have pushed back and argued in favour of shared access, noting confidentiality policies that apply to all staff members. In response to data integrity concerns, we've proposed holding cross-team trainings around the database, or restricting the editing privileges for users outside of the team. Other challenges to shared access include slow or interrupted remote access to the database for our New York office, and access to integrated systems whose control and maintenance is outsourced externally, as in the Salsa case discussed below.

Perhaps the biggest challenge to accessibility is the perception that the databases are difficult to use. The Global Fund databases are largely designed for and by the most intensive, and therefore sophisticated, users in the office. As a result, we hear objections among those further removed that the systems are complicated, difficult to learn and not intuitive. We have made efforts to respond to these concerns by adding functionality for infrequent users, making special dashboard layouts, adding charts and graphs, introducing 'quick find' features, doing more extensive orientations for new hires, and attempting to engage more of these users in design. However, we haven't gone so far as to change the fundamental design or functionality of the databases in ways that work against the interests of our core users or that diverge from the Participatory Design process through which these systems have evolved.

We also haven't been willing to sacrifice flexibility and user control. For example, while FileMaker experts recommend building special layouts to control and simplify the process of doing searches, we enable staff to use FileMaker's tools themselves to do complicated searches on all the fields they normally see. It does take longer to learn the system, but the user has much more power and ability to find the exact information they need. This trade-off between the power of a tool serving its core constituencies, and accessibility – or simplicity – for all, is an example of the dilemma of sophistication versus ease of use. On this matter we're sympathetic with Doug Engelbart, the pre-eminent computer scientist and inventor, who responded to complaints about the complexity of his computer interaction systems by noting that no one expects a novice to pick up a violin and make beautiful music (Monson-Haefel 2008).

As another example, the process of building reports in the database was designed to allow for the greatest flexibility. Rather than a click of a button, or a protocol for requesting reports from a database administrator, users in the database are guided through steps to build a report based on whatever group of records they need. Staff can request our help in going through this process or in creating specialised reports. Intensive orientations and trainings have helped address confusion around the process. Yet the fact remains that staff with less need to go into the database on a daily basis tend to be less familiar with these functions. It's not surprising that the work of pulling information from the database, by way of searches or in the form of reports, is sometimes shifted to those already familiar with the system. Objections they might make relating to time and workloads can contribute to a general perception that reports are time-consuming and difficult to run.

Reports also reveal the complexity of information in the database, leading again to the perception that the databases are inherently complicated. When two people run reports and compare numbers, the resulting data can differ depending on the reports generated and the search criteria used to pull records. Some reports show figures based on strict accrual accounting practices, while others show slightly different numbers to get a real-time sense of gifts coming in. Hard- and soft-crediting is another source of confusion. Adopted by the Development team several years back, soft-crediting is a method of giving credit for a gift to a second constituent, a spouse for instance. Reports reflect when gifts have been soft-credited, yet incomplete understandings of how soft-crediting works lead to confusion about reports themselves.

The result is a chicken-and-egg dilemma. How do we involve users who feel put off by the databases, perhaps as a result of not participating in the design process, and who have little interest in co-designing a system for which they have no felt need?

Shared information

The Global Fund's information systems are based on a principle of shared information – the idea that the data residing there is *ours*. This information comes out of and feeds into people's individual work, highlighting connections between teams and activities taking place in different corners of the organisation. For example, as part of the releasing process discussed earlier, donors sometimes make gifts to support specific regions or issue areas, such as 'education in Asia'; these are known as 'restricted' gifts. Development staff members enter this gift information into the database, translating donor intentions into terms that align with our grantmaking. When Program team members review groups of proposals in light of available funds, they use information about restricted gifts to build 'suggested charges', recommendations for how to charge funds against grants in their portfolio. These in turn are used by the Finance team, along with information that the Program team enters about proposals (again translated into the Global Fund's terms), to register actual charges in the database.

While people recognise the value of this shared information, there is also a tendency to carve out pieces for private access by individuals or small teams. This occurred in the early days of tracking gift restrictions, when data was exported out of the database and work done 'off-line' in Excel spread sheets. As is often the case, individual staff didn't feel the need to share this information, and we found out about it almost by accident. Yet these isolated pockets of information often benefit others in the organisation, and work done in them needs to be reintegrated. This becomes especially difficult if the information is represented in separate systems whose control and maintenance is outsourced externally. In working on the databases, we resist these impulses by supporting and lobbying for centralised, in-house access to the information that underlies the Global Fund's work processes.

We also try to address the underlying motivations for taking information off-line. We built interfaces in the database that look and feel like Excel spread sheets so people who prefer that format don't have to divert information from the database into separate files. We have designed special workspaces in the database so staff members can play with data inside the system rather than resorting to pencil and paper notes or external spread sheets. When a tool offers functionality that is beyond the scope of the databases, our goal has been to integrate these tools with the grantmaking and development databases in a way that, as much as possible, minimises duplication of effort, protects data integrity, ensures access to information and supports the work of the organisation.

These efforts to bring information into a shared space are challenging when we are not aware of its existence (say, because individuals are maintaining personal spread sheets), we are not included in relevant conversations (see discussion above on 'Who is at the decision-making table?'), when there is insufficient organisational will for maintaining the shared spaces, or when the information lives outside the office in the 'cloud'.

At the same time, centralising information doesn't mean that it automatically becomes shared. We've found on occasion that the very act of bringing information into shared spaces leads staff members to disassociate themselves from it, as if they sense that the information now belongs to no one rather than to everyone. An example of this involves attempts to create a shared repository for informational resources. Staff members rely on resources like global statistics, research studies and the Global Fund's own Program team analyses for communication pieces and reports to funders. Several years ago, the Development and Communications teams agreed to move these resources from the spread sheets of individual staff members to a central location. Yet once the information was gathered into a single spread sheet, it slowly faded out of use and people's sense of ownership over the information grew more diffuse. Perhaps it was because the spread sheet was outside of the database, or because the maintenance of the spread sheet was made more burdensome by the fact that it benefited a larger group, or because it represented a collective tool rather than a personal file to which someone could make unilateral changes. In any case, this particular effort failed, although there is still interest in creating a shared space for this information.

At other times, challenges to centralisation may have more to do with workflow. In their article, 'Steps toward an ecology of infrastructure,' Susan Leigh Star and Karen Ruhleder discuss the concept of infrastructure, not as a thing or system by itself, but as the intersection of process and technology (Star and Ruhleder 1996; see also the discussion of infrastructure in Chapter 8 of this book). They assert that infrastructure 'occurs' when a broader technology becomes integral to an individual's or group's processes. As in the resources project above, we sometimes collaborate with others to standardise individual tools in a way that can work for groups of people rather than a single individual. Each time we make this transition, it takes time for individual practices to align with team- or organisation-wide systems. In some cases, the disconnects between local processes and organisational systems are never resolved. It may be that as Jonathan Grudin (1988) observed, unless the benefits of a process for an individual are clear, there is not strong enough motivation for that individual to do the work. It may also be that the project is important but not urgent enough to adopt processes that utilise functions we develop in the database. It tends to be these kinds of projects (important yet not urgent) that 'ebb and flow' as we described earlier. They are taken up and then drop out of sight, only to be picked up again at some later point in time.

Salsa: an example of shared information space in the 'cloud'

The Salsa project mentioned above had ramifications not only for our Participatory Design process, but for the organisation's shared information space. It represents to date the Global Fund's most significant integration with an external system and expansion to the cloud. A web-based tool for conducting online communications and fundraising,[4] Salsa offered a way to engage a largely untapped community of potential supporters and donors.

Early on, an online strategy was conceived around Salsa, relying on consultants to provide the concept and implementation. According to the original plan, the degree to which outside consultants would be deciding and controlling core aspects of our database and information was unprecedented. While we had contracted services in the past, for instance around the Development team's direct mail programme, control over the process remained in-house, especially when it came to data exports out of and imports into our system. When we became involved in the Salsa project, we lobbied to retain in-house control over the syncing process rather than outsourcing it.

At the same time, it became apparent that staff members' ability to adapt Salsa to their needs would not be the same as with the databases. Although Salsa appealed to staff both as a tool designed specifically for non-profits as well as for its open platform, our ability to influence design was limited. It was clear that Salsa would not be changed to meet the needs of one particular client. We have seen this play out in the area of tracking events at Salsa. The forms at Salsa for people to RSVP for events were so restrictive in the changes they allowed that we ended up using a different web service for managing events.

Additionally, while the original rhetoric supporting the Salsa project implied a system that would be open and accessible on the web, the reality is that very few people in the organisation have permission to access the web-based system or a good understanding of how it works. It is arguably more efficient and less prone to user error having only a few staff trained on the system; yet this prevents wider staff from benefiting from Salsa's features.

Our concerns about the shared information space went beyond outsourcing control over the syncing process. We sensed a preference for accessing donor information via Salsa rather than the development database that led to requests to push more information up to Salsa, and concomitantly less interest in reintegrating information from Salsa into the database. We worried that the project could result in a parallel system that might threaten the viability of the Global Fund's internal database.[5] Over time, through informal conversations with the project lead and collaboration with her on other projects, we were able to discuss and resolve our respective concerns. We also gained a better understanding of each other's underlying motivations and goals. The project lead came to understand our goal of a shared information space, and we recognised her desire to expose to the organisation the potential of online fundraising.

There were many lessons that we took from the Salsa project, not the least of which is that a shared information space, as we've seen at other points in our work, is not something we can take for granted. Rather, it is a continual work in progress, maintained through a combination of technical improvements and organisational negotiations. As Salsa exemplifies, this is especially true of integration projects with the cloud, where we deal with external systems and their own sets of technical considerations and stakeholders. (See Chapter 10 for another example of this kind of project.)

Shared ... by whom?

Finally, we come to the question implicit in the challenges above: *what precisely does it mean for an information space to be 'shared'?* Staff who are the most deeply involved with the database, our core constituencies, have the strongest sense of and appreciation for this shared information space because it is so central to their day-to-day work. If people's work practices don't intersect with the information spaces, they may remain outside of those spaces and distanced from the information and technology (Star and Ruhleder, 1996). This has typically been the case with staff at higher levels of the organisation and on teams whose work is not integrated with the databases. We have long recognised that not everyone at the organisation participates in the shared information space, many for good reason. Nonetheless, we believe that increased use of the shared information space leads to a higher premium placed on the information and greater concern for its quality; more recognition and active encouragement of staff members' maintenance work and participation in design (see the earlier discussions of 'Who has time to participate?' and 'Who values participation?'); use of staff knowledge and expertise to inform decisions; and invitations to staff members to contribute in ways that connect their work to the overall strategies and mission of the organisation.

In short, we believe that promoting stakeholder participation in shared information spaces strengthens the information space itself and fosters greater alignment throughout the organisation. Over time, we saw that our ability to further such a participatory process was limited by organisational attitudes and work practices. This led us to lobby for and take on greater roles in organisational efforts to promote workplace democracy.

Workplace democracy

As we've seen, we usually address Participatory Design challenges by focusing on the situation at hand, and then modifying or augmenting our own processes. In the last couple of years, we've begun to advocate for changes at a broader level, to organisation-wide attitudes and practices. In this section we look at how we got to that place and what new challenges it poses.

Johannes Gärtner and Ina Wagner (1994) conducted a landmark study of system design in which they considered not just the technical work of redesign, but also the political contexts within and external to the two European companies they studied. To analyse the forces shaping practices of design and participation, they adopted a conceptual framework of three 'arenas for participation':

- Arena A Designing work – designing systems;
- Arena B Designing organisational frameworks for action;
- Arena C Designing the industrial relations context.

Arena A covers the work of designing and redesigning work practices and technical systems. Arena B refers to the explicit and tacit norms on which organisational actors base their broader decisions. Arena C is where legal and political frameworks are negotiated that govern the relations among industrial sectors. Crucial to Gärtner and Wagner's analysis are the shifts that take place between arenas. Our recent advocacy work within the Global Fund exemplifies the shift from Arena A to Arena B.

> Often an unresolved and repeated pattern of conflict in arena A occasions action in arena B; or serves as an opportunity for taking such action. Arena B then is the location in which 'breakdowns' or violations of agreements are diagnosed and hitherto stable patterns of organisational functioning questioned and redesigned.
>
> *(Gärtner and Wagner 1994, p. 38)*

As we saw in the 'Who controls the process?' section, there have been times when participation itself, the basic premise of our Participatory Design practice, is called into question. Often this is due to a perceived dichotomy between participation and efficiency. We've responded by arguing for a longer-term view, that the systems we build are more easily adopted and adapted into everyday use when their design has involved the eventual users. We also argue that our colleagues' direct involvement leads to feelings of ownership. In short, using some of staff members' time early on leads to a more reliable and acceptable system in the long run.

Taking these arguments up a level to the organisation as a whole (Arena B) has meant lobbying for increased staff participation and transparency in decision-making overall. We were led to Arena B for several reasons.

- We believe that IM's success depends on our colleagues being able to work with us. At times, that ability is hampered by narrow definitions of the 'core work' of those lower in the hierarchy.
- If the broader organisational culture encouraged more participation, then it might be easier to bring ourselves and other stakeholders, including front-line database users, to the relevant decision-making tables. That might in turn lead to greater understanding of the implications and impact of desired changes.
- Greater participation and input by front-line staff on matters of organisational strategy and implementation might also lead to a better understanding of the shared information space and increased value of Participatory Design work.

- We are personally inclined towards what Andrew Clement (1994) refers to as the 'democratic empowerment' of workers. Indeed, in our work on the organisational assessment process, we find ourselves coming down on the side of more staff participation and autonomy, and more effective delegation of authority from executives to staff, rather than less.

Over the course of two years a staff-wide organisational assessment process created an opening for conversations about staff participation in decision-making. Both of us played roles in this process by serving on committees and councils where we advocated for increased transparency and participation in team-wide and organisation-wide decisions. We also lobbied for these causes in informal conversations with colleagues, both in the context of IM projects and more generally. Finally, we made changes to our own processes – for instance, new hire orientations now include background and justification for our participatory work practices.

Our work in Arena B poses its own challenges both practical and political. First, there is the problem of limited time. It's perhaps ironic that just as some of our colleagues worry about participation in Participatory Design coming at the cost of core work, we worry about our participation in Arena B coming at the cost of IM project work. And just as we ask others to take a long-term view, so we try to reassure ourselves (and our supervisors) that increased staff participation in decision-making will benefit IM and the organisation as a whole.

A second kind of challenge is more political than practical. What right do we on IM have to lobby for changes in another team's practices? When the context is Arena A, we argue that a staff member's work with IM leads to the outcome of a more useful system. But in Arena B, notwithstanding the organisation-wide efforts to improve transparency alluded to above, another team's particular decision-making process is arguably none of our business.

Then what *is* our business? In her rousing call for a greater focus on the political in Participatory Design, Eevi Beck (2002) states, 'PD [Participatory Design] research has shown that political and power issues are part-and-parcel of what researchers and practitioners do.' And thus, 'Rather than participation, concern with power and dominance needs to be stated as the core of the research field of PD.' Although we are Participatory Design practitioners, not researchers, we take her admonition to heart. Our 'business', then, is furthering the mission of the Global Fund through the practice of Participatory Design with its practical challenges, in its contested arenas, and in the face of its confounding politics.

Conclusion

We began the chapter describing the Global Fund and our work as in-house developers. We close with parting hopes for Participatory Design at the Global Fund in light of challenges and opportunities to come.

Practising Participatory Design over the last decade has taught us tactical and strategic lessons, and contributed to a shared information space that has advanced the mission of the organisation. As we've seen, realising that shared information space in an environment that's conducive to Participatory Design work has posed a variety of challenges over the years. Some are internal as we strive to involve staff members throughout the organisation in Participatory Design work and to incorporate information that should be shared within a collective workspace. Other challenges are external in the form of outside consultants and websites with which we must synchronise.

What does the future hold? In all likelihood, much more of the same. Rather than an information space internal to our office network and incorporating the odd web-based information store, our systems will need to encompass distributed workplaces and web-based information, *à la* the HISP system described in Chapter 10. And this is where the Participatory Design process-related challenges described earlier loom even larger. As we've seen, carrying out Participatory Design isn't easy even when our colleagues are co-located, in part because of bi-directional problems of access: getting input from our colleagues, and getting access to their decision-making spaces. It's likely that new processes, structures and communication media, perhaps more formalised, will be needed when our colleagues are thousands of miles apart, some of whom we may never meet. Somehow, we'll need to link together groups of co-located workers into a participatory whole.

Even with the new challenges that distribution and cloud computing bring, we believe that Participatory Design will be at least as crucial in such future scenarios as it is today. Indeed, the more that Participatory Design practices in the organisation are accepted and then internalised, the smoother our transition will be toward a 'cloudy' future.

Notes

1 www.globalfundforwomen.org (accessed October 2011).
2 In this chapter, we take 'database' to mean not just the relational database schema and architecture, but also the systems used to browse, update, query and generate reports over the data. This is in part because the software we use, FileMaker, covers all these aspects of database management.
3 In the grantmaking database as of 1999, organisation contact information was stored with each proposal. Given that organisations changed names and contact information over time, it was almost impossible to count unique organisations, let alone maintain up-to-date contact information for them. The development database had a similar problem; donations were stored in the same table as donors. If there was only room for 20 gifts, then the 21st required creation of a second record for the same donor.
4 www.salsacommons.org (accessed October 2011).
5 Our outlook was also coloured by experience with an earlier integration project. For a number of years, the Development team had outsourced data entry of gift information to an outside direct mail vendor charged with sending bulk mailings. We imported changes from their database into ours and vice versa. This experience resulted in a number of challenges over the years, including issues with data integrity, significant lag time and restrictions on what we could change in our own system. These ultimately led to a phasing out of that relationship – which happened to coincide with the Salsa project.

References

Beck, E. E. (2002) 'P for political: participation is not enough,' *Scandinavian Journal of Information Systems*, 14(1): Article 1.

Bødker, S. and K. Grønbæk (1991) 'Cooperative prototyping: users and designers in mutual activity,' *International Journal of Man–Machine Studies*, Special Issue on CSCW, 34(3): 453–78.

Clement, A. (1994) 'Computing at work: empowering action by "low-level Users"', *Communications of the ACM*, Special Issue on Social Computing, 37(1): 52–63. Reprinted in the anthology, R. Kling (ed.) (1991) *Computerization and Controversy*, San Diego, CA: Academic Press.

Gärtner, J. and I. Wagner (1994) 'Political frameworks of design and participation', in *Systems as Intermediaries: Proceedings of the III Participatory Design Conference (PDC 1994)*, Chapel Hill, NC: Computer Professionals for Social Responsibility (CPSR), 37–46.

Grudin, J. (1988) 'Why CSCW applications fail: problems in the design and evaluation of organizational interfaces', *Proceedings of CSCW 88*, Portland, OR: ACM, 85–93.

McPhail, B., T. Costantino, D. Bruckmann, R. Barclay and A. Clement (1998) 'CAVEAT exemplar: Participatory Design in a non-profit volunteer organisation', *Computer Supported Cooperative Work*, 7(3–4): 223–41.

Monson-Haefel, R. (2008). 'Engelbart's usability dilemma: efficiency vs ease-of-use', SYS-CON Media. Available at: http://coldfusion.sys-con.com/node/536976.

Star, S. L. and K. Ruhleder (1996) 'Steps toward an ecology of infrastructure: design and access for large information spaces.' *Information Systems Research*, 7: 111–33.

Trigg, R. H. (2000) 'From sandbox to "fundbox": weaving participatory design into the fabric of a busy non-profit' in T. Cherkasky, J. Greenbaum, P. Mambrey and J. K. Pors (eds) *Proceedings of the Participatory Design Conference (PDC 2000)*, Palo Alto, CA: Computer Professionals for Social Responsibility (CPSR), 174–83.

10

Health Information Systems Programme

Participatory Design within the HISP network

Jørn Braa and Sundeep Sahay

This chapter seeks to contribute to the ongoing debates in the domain of Participatory Design by discussing the various trends and questions within the context of the Health Information Systems Programme (HISP) initiative ongoing over nearly two decades. The focus in this chapter is to discuss issues of Participatory Design during the course of the design, development, implementation and scaling of the DHIS software within an action research framework in the context of the public health sector in various developing countries. Further, we discuss Participatory Design with respect to changes over time in technological and political contexts and the challenges following from that; from stand-alone MS Office to cloud computing and fully open source technology – enabling local Participatory Design!

In this chapter, we try to describe this rather complex HISP movement over time following three broad phases; 'traditional' Participatory Design; pilots and networking Participatory Design, and Participatory Design and web technologies. After this historical reconstruction, we describe and discuss current trends and challenges, focusing on the new area of cloud computing and the need for integration with other systems.

We elaborate on practical challenges and potentials of doing Participatory Design in the context of developing countries and in a longitudinal perspective. The reader will learn about Participatory Design in a global development perspective and about the importance of networking Participatory Design projects and to share software, lessons and resources across countries 'South–North–South' as a way to achieve sustainability and scalability. Rapid spread of communication technologies such as mobile Internet is currently changing the context for Participatory Design in developing countries. The chapter provides the reader with analysis and discussion on the potential for Participatory Design and empowerment of users in developing countries in the new area of cloud computing and in an environment where multiple systems need to be integrated.

The emerging cloud-based infrastructure represents both an opportunity and a threat. While users even in rural Kenya may now feel empowered by having instant access to own and other data, global actors are aggressively promoting their own software-based services. To counteract the latter, the challenge is to enable development of local capacity to master the new technologies, for which Participatory Design may provide both the means and the end.

Introduction

This chapter seeks to contribute to the ongoing debates in the domain of Participatory Design by discussing the various trends and questions within the context of the Health Information Systems Programme (HISP) initiative ongoing globally over the last 15 or so years (see Braa et al. 2004). The empirical basis for this chapter is provided by the efforts – technical, educational and political – in developing and evolving the HISP network with a key focus on the design, development, implementation and scaling of the DHIS (District Health Information Software) within an action research framework for the public health sector in developing countries.

HISP can be described as a global research, development and action network around health information systems (HIS) for the Global South, enabled through South–South–North collaboration. The network is by no means homogeneous and static, nor in harmony following a single goal, including how Participatory Design techniques have been and should be used. HISP was initiated through the efforts of a few as a bottom-up Participatory Design project in South Africa in 1994/5, and has today evolved into a global and thriving network spread across multiple countries and contexts. This development has been non-linear and followed different trajectories, experiencing successes and setbacks, as well as radical technological changes: the Internet and mobile network revolutions in Africa and Asia and the shift from stand-alone desktop application to networked web applications. HISP evolution has gained further impetus through increased focus on global health, including on the achievement of the Millennium Development Goals (MDGs). During times of rapid policy, technological and other changes, HISP has all along tried to be 'on top of' the changing environment, but has many times been victim to changing policies; as an example, being literally thrown out of Ethiopia after years of work as a result of political decisions at the national level. At no point in time have the HISP actors been able to foresee moves into the future, as the context of funding and politics has been constantly changing and uncertain. Maybe the only consistent element in the history of HISP has been a stubborn willingness to apply participatory approaches in designing HIS in cooperation with various levels of users in a variety of contexts.

A key focus of the application of Participatory Design techniques has been around the design and development of the DHIS software. The DHIS is a tool for collection, validation, analysis and presentation of aggregate statistical data, tailored to supporting integrated health information management activities. It is designed to serve as a district-based country data warehouse to address both local and national needs. DHIS is a generic tool rather than a pre-configured database application, with an open meta-data model and a flexible user interface that allows the user to design the contents of a specific information system without the need for programming. DHIS development has evolved over two versions. The first – DHIS v1 – has been developed since 1997 by HISP in South Africa on MS Access, a platform selected because it was at that time a de facto standard in South Africa. The second – DHIS v2 – building on the v1 data model is a modular web-based software package built with free and open source Java frameworks, developed since 2004 and coordinated by the University of Oslo.

The flexible and modular DHIS software application has all along been the pivotal element in the HISP approach; both as a tool with which to communicate design to users and as a software application suite which may provide results from day one and thereafter expand while in full production, as more functionalities, datasets and other elements are added.

This chapter attempts to describe this rather complex movement over the last 15 years of the HISP network and its associated dimensions of software development and Participatory Design processes in a multiplicity of contexts. We have interpretively developed a historical reconstruction of this movement to depict the following three broad phases of HISP development. In addressing the first phase (1995–2000), we discuss HISP in relation to 'traditional' Participatory Design based primarily on the experience in South Africa. In the second phase (2000–6), which was characterised by pilot projects and 'networking Participatory Design', we focus on how networks of action were created outside South Africa, also encompassing educational programmes. In the third phase (2006–10), development of the fully open source and web-based DHIS platform gained momentum and challenges were experienced in applying distributed Participatory Design and scaling HISP during a time of significant technological change, including rapid spread of Internet and mobile networks in developing countries. Finally, we discuss the future direction for HISP and Participatory Design in the age of cloud computing. In our coverage of HISP, we highlight the important role that context plays in each country, which we illustrate through cross-country comparisons.

Phase 1: HISP and traditional Participatory Design

The term 'traditional Participatory Design' is used to depict basic principles of the Scandinavian Participatory Design tradition as related to user participation in system design, workplace democracy and empowerment, which was the source of inspiration for the initial HISP researchers coming from Oslo. These principles found a welcome home in post-apartheid South Africa, where the focus was on 'making right the wrongs of the past', equity in health services delivery and development and empowerment of those communities and population groups that had suffered under apartheid.

HISP was initiated in South Africa at the advent of democracy in 1994 as a part of the new ANC government's reconstruction and development programme (RDP). As a legacy of apartheid, the health services were inequitable, fragmented according to race, centralised with no local decentralised management structures contributing to the marginalisation of the black majority. The restructuring plan was based on a decentralised system of health districts including their supporting HIS. HISP started out as collaboration between, on the one hand, public health researchers and activists with background from the anti-apartheid struggle, and on the other hand, informatics researchers with background from the Scandinavian Participatory Design and action research tradition. Given this background, HISP became part of the larger development process (see Braa and Hedberg 2002 for a detailed presentation of HISP in South Africa). Two key arguments underlined the HISP process in supporting health sector reform:

1 The political empowerment argument: general exclusion of deprived areas and regions from economic, social, health-wise and technological development as depicted by the quest for equity in health services delivery, or the 'digital divide' – the need for development and empowerment. This political empowerment argument was core to the ANC government's policy to uplift and empower the black majority who had suffered during apartheid.
2 The practical learning through hands-on participation argument: individual and institutional users had limited experience with practical information technology applications, requiring a participative learning approach to overcome the differences in understanding and knowledge between users and developers through a practical hands-on approach.

These two arguments reflected the decades-old dichotomy in the Participatory Design tradition between the political agenda of the early Scandinavian action research and Participatory Design projects and the subsequent more pragmatic technically oriented Participatory Design projects. Both have been important in the development of HISP. See the influential *Computers and Democracy – A Scandinavian Challenge* (Bjerknes et al. 1987), and Chapter 2 of this volume for

237

background on the Scandinavian projects. HISP started as a research project with the explicit objective to bring learning from the Scandinavian Participatory Design and action research tradition to Africa and to explore to what extent these lessons could be useful in developing African Participatory Design approaches. Two Scandinavian Participatory Design perspectives – and projects – were explicitly formulated as hypotheses for what would also be useful approaches in Africa. First, the broad political empowerment perspective of the Norwegian Iron and Metal project, which was not about design as such, but aimed at empowering workers through learning in questions regarding technological changes and threats to the workplace (Nygaard 1979). Second, the more focused design for empowerment perspective of the UTOPIA project, which developed and applied practical Participatory Design approaches as a way to empower skilled workers to participate in developing technical alternatives 'controlled' by themselves (Bødker et al. 1987). On the public health side, both HISP and the wider health information community in South Africa at that time were influenced by the concept of 'information for action' and in applying action-led, as opposed to the traditional data-led (Sandiford et al. 1992), approaches to the design and development of HIS. We now discuss the South African case.

The South African HISP case

During apartheid (1948–93), the health services were extremely fragmented according to race, type of service and the system of 'homelands'. As one consequence of this fragmentation, there were no comprehensive national standards for data collection, and each province used different datasets, definitions and flows. A cornerstone of the ANC reform strategy was the development of an HIS including a system of national standards to measure and monitor the extent to which this policy was being achieved and to pinpoint areas where more resources and efforts are needed.

The initial focus in the HISP pilot districts was on identifying information needs and supporting interim district management teams. Paper-based systems for registering patients, pregnant women for control, babies for immunisation, etc., made up the primary data sources, from which data was aggregated and reported 'upwards' using a plethora of paper forms belonging to, or defined by, different health programmes or health structures. In the absence of local governance and managerial structures, systems were centralised and fragmented and all flows of data were leading out of the district to different head offices, with no feedback. The RDP was to change this into a decentralised structure empowering the local level with new health districts as basic building blocks, as reflected in Figure 10.1 showing the proposed HIS design in Atlantis, one of the HISP pilot districts.

The information for action approach was a hot topic within the health reform process during the 1990s and was applied according to what was labelled the 'information cycle', which may be outlined as follows: set targets for the health services, for example improve immunisation coverage among infants; define information and indicators to measure achievements of your targets; collect and analyse the needed data; assess the situation and compare achievements, i.e. indicators, against targets; then act if targets are not met; then redefine targets. The approach to implement this action-led approach in the health services was to identify key indicators and to develop minimum datasets of essential data that could be used to calculate these indicators. An example of an indicator is 'Measles immunisation coverage under one year', which may be calculated based on number of measles vaccines divided by number of infants. The process of developing effective indicators and datasets was at the core of the process of developing the new HIS, and even very central in the wider health reform, as it was directly linked to the debate of what targets to prioritise. Obviously, therefore, this was not an easy process as each part and sub-part of the health services tended to have their own and often conflicting views. A rather

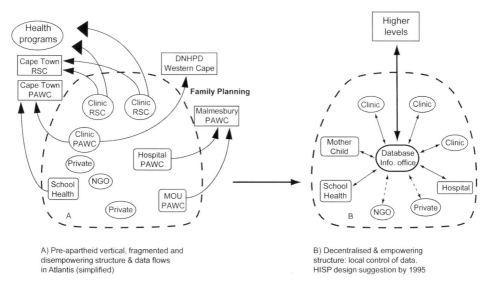

A) Pre-apartheid vertical, fragmented and
disempowering structure & data flows
in Atlantis (simplified)

B) Decentralised & empowering
structure: local control of data.
HISP design suggestion by 1995

Figure 10.1 Design for integration in South Africa, 1995

intensive process of workshops and draft proposals went on during 1995–6 without much result before, in 1997, the first version of the DHIS software was used to pilot datasets in all health facilities in the four HISP pilot districts.

At the end of 1997, after about nine months of intensive negotiations driven by local managers in collaboration with the HISP team and informed by the pilots, the first essential dataset was implemented in all local government health facilities in the Cape Metropole (including HISP pilot districts). Later, after rounds of revisions, a unified dataset was implemented in the whole of Western Cape Province which subsequently inspired the neighbouring Eastern Cape Province to do the same in 1998. The datasets being implemented in the two provinces were very different, but the fact that they were implemented, something that had never been achieved before, was widely regarded as a breakthrough. Implementing datasets using DHIS represented something new in that users now had immediate access to the data, as compared with the traditional upward reporting with no feedback apart from through annual statistics.

The first version of the DHIS software was instrumental in developing, testing and piloting the datasets and it was subsequently used to capture and analyse monthly data at all levels of first Western and then Eastern Cape Province. This application went through a series of very rapid prototype cycles over the next six months, and towards the end of 1998 the DHIS stabilised in use in the Western Cape and Eastern Cape Provinces. We see here that the Participatory Design process went on at two interconnected levels: the wider participatory process of developing the datasets and the HIS, using the DHIS as a means of engaging users and stakeholders at all levels, and the more narrow Participatory Design process of developing DHIS as a software application, engaging the 'activists'.

Results from the Eastern and Western Cape presented in a national conference in 1999 also inspired other provinces to adopt this route, leading to the DHIS and the HISP approach becoming national standards in 2002. Key to this was the HISP formulated hierarchy of standards, where each level (e.g. province) had the freedom to define their own standards as long as they aligned with the standards of the level above. This hierarchy was implemented in the DHIS and used in the Participatory Design process to prototype, negotiate and implement provincial and national datasets, which ended up being quite different from province to province. Such differences were accepted within the national system because the national standards were included as sub-sets of the provincial standards.

The development of the DHIS during these formative early years was based on rapid prototyping with new 'builds' being sometimes released on a weekly or even daily basis. The informal mechanisms for reporting bugs and requesting new functionality – all tightly integrated with user support – proved popular and encouraged users to provide feedback to the development team. This, combined with the rapid deployment of new or corrected versions, astounded many users, whose prior experience had involved long waits for responses to their requests. Requests for new functionalities were moderated by the HISP team depending on the number of users making a request and team capacity, but all relevant requests were logged in. The development process emphasised performance and progress over established prototyping models using formal and structured processes of well-established user groups, channels of communication, and mechanisms for conflict resolution. Such formal processes may not have been effective in a conflict-ridden operating environment. The methodology used was thus more informal and to a significant degree based on improvisation, whereby any interested or innovative user, regardless of his or her place in the hierarchy, had full access to the development team representing a meritocratic approach. Access was either direct or indirect via the DHIS facilitators and users were encouraged to use their preferred channels.

HISP South Africa was formed as an independent NGO in the late 1990s and has since then made a living out of supporting DHIS and related activities in the region.

Learning from the first period

The focus during this early period was on identifying information needs and supporting interim district management teams as seen in the intervened participatory processes of (a) developing datasets and data standards for primary health care and (b) developing the DHIS software application supporting the implementation and use of these datasets. Through the use of DHIS, users such as interim district management teams had immediate access to their information, processed as indicators that could be applied to measure achievements according to targets, thus making it possible to implement the 'information cycle', which until then had been difficult to try out in practice. This concrete hands-on access to own information provided by DHIS, combined with users' constant urge for better information, analytical tools and graphs, made up the engine of the Participatory Design approaches applied in HISP, which may best be characterised as 'eternal' participatory and exploratory prototyping, or evolutionary Participatory Design. There is never a 'finished' system in the HISP case. Owing to the changing environment and massive demands for improvements in the health sector, the target system and the requirements will always be changing and extended.

Phase 2: First wave of HISP extension: Participatory Design in 'network of actions' (2000–6)

This period is characterised by networking, across countries and also across educational processes. The gradual expansion of HISP has been enabled through the establishing of Participatory Design-based pilot projects in countries and linking them with educational programmes – both Master's and doctoral studies – and then the linking of these programmes across countries. The circulation of PhD and Master's students across and within countries has been the means with which learning, software and best practices have been spread in the network. This networked action was aimed at enabling the creation of capacities to carry out shared development and application of software between multiple country pilot projects. A challenge has been around adapting traditional Participatory Design to multi-country contexts, and finding the balance between education and practical action.

While, in South Africa, the HISP work continued and still continues, carried out by an independent HISP-NGO, both the PhD and Master's programmes have been based at or coordinated from the University of Oslo. Students became the major HISP advocates and developed smaller Participatory Design projects in their respective countries. This period was also characterised by efforts to build collaborative networks between countries, universities and local health authorities. While reasonable success was obtained in establishing and expanding the educational programmes, arguably far less success was obtained in country implementations of the HISP initiative. Three such examples are discussed, which also aid reflection on some of the limits of the traditional Participatory Design approach.

Cuba

In Cuba, HISP was initiated in October 2001 when Cuban delegates visited Norway in search of possible collaboration, which led to a subsequent collaboration between Ministerio de Salud Pública (MINSAP), the Cuban Ministry of Public Health, and the University of Oslo. In June 2002, one faculty member with two Master's students went to Cuba to initiate processes in collaboration with the Dirección Nacional de Estadísticas (DNE) (the national statistics office). A Norwegian donation of 11 computers in May 2002 made it possible to start, and a further donation of 60 computers contributed to the scaling process.

In two pilot provinces – Matanzas and Sanctí Spíritus – a situation study was initiated to understand the information flows, datasets and the work practices which contributed to the prototype design of local and province database applications. All existing data was paper based, and the HISP aim was to make data available locally for analysis and management. Two provincial statistical health offices, six municipal offices, two polyclinics and a municipal hospital were chosen as pilot sites within these two provinces. Subsequently, in September the two Oslo students started training the staff based on a participatory methodology aimed at empowering them by building their capacity to define and use data locally. The trainees were encouraged to participate in the design process to help tailor the system to their needs and build local ownership. This process of local empowerment, however, was in conflict with the centralised and vertical way of organising things in Cuba. The sharing and dissemination of information horizontally and locally using Excel pivot tables created a new opportunity of breaking the stranglehold of the statistical offices, creating interest and enthusiasm among other horizontal offices. However, the 'uncontrolled' horizontal interaction and data-sharing was immediately reported by somebody to Havana and all local HISP activities were closed down immediately after. In hindsight, this local focus can be seen as being in conflict with the centralised structure of Cuba, in which the national level complained of having lost control of the development process and demanded a centralised approach, expressing dislike for what they saw as the local workers becoming more skilled in the system than they were themselves. As a result, HISP had to refocus their efforts to a centralised development as the DNE in November 2002 froze all local activities.

Reflecting on the use of the Participatory Design approach in Cuba, it is obvious that the legacy of 40 years of strong central planning could not be overcome overnight. Coupled with the centralisation was a strongly compartmentalised system which impeded cooperation, for example between the statistics and information technology departments. These parallel structures at the national level were mirrored, though to a lesser extent, at the province level and below, making it relatively more possible to conduct meetings at provincial and local levels. National programmes and corresponding datasets, in line with the strong Soviet statistical legacy, were designed at the national office, unknown even to the senior directors, as decisions were made by MINSAP, Havana. Another factor stifling Participatory Design was the dominance (in numbers and power) of the statisticians in the health system, and the fact that HISP was under DNE control. The Cuban system had a large number of statisticians, even five to each polyclinic (covering about 5,000 population), who were responsible for collecting and processing data, and sending daily reports on infant and maternal mortality to Havana. The statistical structure inspired by the Soviet legacy encouraged centralisation, with data flowing to the national database for making prospective five-year national plans, impeding local and active use of information.

India

In 2000, HISP India was invited by the Chief Information Technology Advisor of the Chief Minister of Andhra Pradesh to initiate a project in one district of Chittoor. Being introduced through the political rather than the health department channel subsequently had adverse implications for HISP, and made it vulnerable to the vagaries of local politics. Initially a situation analysis was conducted aimed at understanding the organisational structure and health information flows by visiting various facilities in the district, interviewing relevant functionaries and conducting participant observations. A key aim was to rationalise the data flows and develop a 'minimum dataset' representing the least number of data items to be collected by different health facilities to satisfy all reporting needs. There were high levels of redundancy, with some data collected repeatedly to comply with different programme needs, including some that had been terminated many years earlier (Puri et al. 2004). By September 2001, the 1,200 data elements had been reduced to 400, and reports restructured to 10 (Puri et al. 2004).

Despite the obvious improvements with this new design, the Health Commissioner did not give HISP official permission to implement these changes, as formats were also being revised at the state level, accompanied by the development of a new software (called FHIMS) funded by a World Bank project (Raghavendra and Sahay 2006). After extensive persuasion enabled through HISP political allies, the Commissioner consented to sanction one computer and to send a letter to the district to permit a DHIS pilot in one health facility. However, neither the computer nor the letter ever reached the district, and staff revealed that over the phone the Commissioner had instructed that HISP should not be allowed to introduce any changes. Subsequently, HISP manoeuvred an opportunity to make a presentation to the Chief Minister and his senior advisors. The Chief Minister appreciated the HISP efforts and sanctioned 12 computers, one for each of the nine clinics in Kuppam (the electoral constituency of the Chief Minister) and the rest for the district office. DHIS implementation was initiated in these facilities.

A small window of opportunity to initiate local processes was thus given to HISP, albeit reluctantly by the Health Department, which did not want interference to its well-funded FHIMS project. In defining the datasets, HISP ensured that all data elements were included (even though some were seen to be not relevant), removing only the duplicates. HISP thus ensured there was no transgression regarding the lack of state permission to make changes, while being able to gain buy-in from the health staff, who benefited because their data-reporting load was reduced, and who also enjoyed the direct interaction with HISP in helping them learn about computers.

The HISP team continued to have a base in Kuppam for about four to five years, benefiting greatly from this experience. First, this became for them a 'deep learning' site where through engaged action they learnt about the micro-level workings and challenges of a peripheral health facility, including its HIS, and how these may be addressed. Second, this engagement led to customisation of the DHIS which was user-friendly, locally relevant and sensitive to user capacities and their sense of 'ownership' of it. This local bottom-up approach was supplemented with a top-down engagement with the politics of multiple systems, and the combined efforts over time contributed to the scaling of the system from 12 primary health centres (PHCs) to 45 in the first phase, then 82 PHCs in the entire district and then all district capitals in the state (covering about 1,300 PHCs). Seeing this success, even the state authorities (grudgingly) allowed DHIS to be integrated with FHIMS and to support its implementation, as FHIMS had not delivered the required results. However, in the end the vagaries of Indian politics took over, and with a change of the political guard with the elections in 2005, the HISP support network at the state level was lost and the initiative was terminated by the new functionaries. This demonstrated the limits of the combined top-down (for political buy-in) and bottom-up (for system learning) Participatory Design approach, which required greater top-level support in order to scale.

Mozambique

A brief example is presented regarding the attempt to adopt the 'pivot table'-based reporting approach of DHIS, used successfully in South Africa. The design assumption behind such an approach was that users should be given the flexibility to create their local reports, and that a 'learning by doing' approach would enhance user capacity and their sense of empowerment. However, this strategy led to a roadblock, as users wanted pre-designed reports which could be generated with a click of a button and sent up the reporting hierarchy. The failure of HISP to provide such functionality in DHIS contributed significantly to the limited uptake of the systems in the three provinces where HISP was piloting the project.

These different examples drove home the realisation that context matters and Participatory Design approaches need to be broad-based. The implication of context matters was that Participatory Design depends largely on the time, space and cultural conditions in which it evolves. The Scandinavian tradition of Participatory Design evolved through the 1970s found a welcome home in post-apartheid South Africa, where the focus was on local empowerment. In Cuba and India, local empowerment was largely an alien concept, as the political structures focused on centralisation due to reasons of legacies of Soviet statistics-based planning and British bureaucracy respectively. Participatory Design approaches and the evolving systems and practices in both cases could not be scaled beyond a point to be useful to the health system. The learning from South Africa about the importance of politics was reinforced, albeit with a difference. While in both Cuba and India, political buy-in was required, this was not to support user empowerment but to get permissions to try out and scale things in the field. The system design focus was found to be too limited, also requiring the building of broader education and training capacities.

HISP response to these challenges: 'networks of action'

A network, as contrasted to a hierarchy defined in terms of hierarchical relationships, refers to different people or institutions linked together with respect to specific activities or tasks. A collaborative network of action then refers to creating linkages for the purposes of collaboration through specific action around, in our case, HIS development, implementation and scaling (Braa et al. 2004). There are challenges in contextualising systems to local settings while cultivating local learning processes, institutionalising and sustaining them. The other challenge is of making one working solution spread to other sites and of ensuring its successful adaptation there. Scaling involves not only the spreading of technical systems but also the necessary learning processes, including questions of who learns and how.

In the public health system, which has a normative goal of providing equitable services to all, the problem of scale becomes a unique one of 'all or nothing', since data from only some of the sites will be useless to the district manager, who needs data on the entire catchment area under the district, including all its sub-units. And if the HIS is not at a scale to be useful, then managers will not take ownership of the system, nor will they invest resources, making the system unsustainable. This represents a vicious cycle where pilots are allowed to start, but are never used and supported because they are 'only pilots', leading to them fading away – as pilots. This implies that for interventions to be successful they need to both spread and also sustain. This is a particular challenge for HISP since the DHIS approach is about comparing and analysing statistical data which require data coverage. The 'networks of action' approach is articulated as a potential move towards addressing this challenge of scale and sustainability.

HISP conceptualised as a 'network of action' comprises various entities including universities, ministries of health, international agencies like WHO and Norad, and, in country, implementing agencies like HISP South Africa and HISP India. The network is never static and never apolitical and new partnerships are always being developed. The basic strength of a network is that it allows the possibility of learning in a collective, which is more effective than in singular units. Experience in HISP, however, is that collaboration between universities and other actors will always have a certain transaction cost, and that the perceived benefit will need to be higher than these costs or else the collaboration will die.

Reflecting on achievements during this phase, which has been largely exploratory and one emphasising learning, while there was an expansion in the scope of work to multiple countries and across different dimensions, success with respect to project implementation and scaling was limited to a few sites, e.g. India and Zanzibar. Much greater success was achieved on the education front, building a larger awareness and creating greater political visibility to HISP. A pertinent question to probe is the reason for this limited success in project implementation. This requires an analysis of the relation between the politics, technology and user needs and pull. With respect to politics, the general inference can be that HISP was not positioned 'high enough' in the hierarchy to get the support required for full-scale implementation. While local-level support was developed and cultivated through engaged and continuous participatory action, these could not be scaled and sustained, raising the paradox of how to develop local-level learning while being part of the national mainstream.

With respect to technology, the period around 2004–5 was when DHIS 2 development was initiated, the open source Java technologies being used were still new and not yet widely accepted, and so the first DHIS 2 versions started out slowly and were not triggering much interest. In South Africa, where the user base was more mature and DHIS 1 stabilised, the HISP team was reluctant to engage with DHIS 2 and new web-based technologies. At the same time, the MS Office-based DHIS 1 used in South Africa was no longer seen as representing a new paradigm, meaning that HISP was no longer seen as a technology innovator. User drive and pull is important if Participatory Design must succeed, otherwise there is little at stake for local ownership to develop. The new technological paradigm based on web and open source technologies of the next phase made DHIS 2 into an attractor, and a new area of user drive and pull developed.

Phase 3: New technological paradigm: Participatory Design in open source web-based environments (2006–10 onwards)

This phase is characterised by the explicit change from stand-alone to networked applications within health systems in developing countries. This trend is coupled with another important movement signifying the increasing momentum of open source technologies. While HISP had from the start been founded on an open source philosophy, the new situation was that these technologies had matured to such an extent that the entire web-based technology stack could be provided as Free and Open Source Software (FOSS). While, earlier, HISP spread through students and educational programmes, which are typically time and resource intensive, these new developments allowed countries to technically adopt what we call 'HISP technologies' with limited prior preparation. For example, a training and dissemination workshop in West Africa encouraged eight participating countries to decide to adopt DHIS 2. The shift in the networking dimension represents a fundamental challenge to locally focused Participatory Design approaches, as now the landscape changed to the whole country or whole region and was not limited to a pilot site. The FOSS trend introduces a new stack of technologies requiring very different capacities for participation, while changing the landscape of who participates and how.

The development of DHIS 1 involved an intensive three-year evolutionary Participatory Design with an ongoing scaling process in South Africa, where increasingly refined prototypes were tested in close collaboration with users whose capacity to use information was constantly enhanced. The ANC government's reform goals of decentralisation and local empowerment were 'inscribed' into design, for example through the hierarchy of standards and the use of Excel pivot tables which made local views of data possible. While the iterative design process produced a close fit with the reform needs, the system accumulated both rigidities and a messy architecture overall. This proved problematic when the system was introduced in Mozambique, India, Vietnam and Cuba after the turn of the millennium. In 2004 this spurred the development of a completely revised and internationalised version of DHIS 1, including a full remodelling of the database. The developer team was still in Cape Town, and employed the same technology (MS Access), but users were now in Botswana and Zanzibar, requiring Participatory Design to be enabled through extensive travelling of project staff, supplemented by e-mail communication. This contributed to the birth of DHIS 1.4, still running today in South Africa.

At the same time, however, requirements for moving to a web-based platform were mounting, triggering yet another revamp of the software. Development of DHIS 2 began in 2004 under the leadership of the University of Oslo, but aimed at distributing development activities to multiple countries in the network in order to bring software development closer to the contexts of use. A stack of 'bleeding edge' Java-based technologies was selected for DHIS 2, based on a distributed development platform typically employed by many FOSS projects. This process was challenging as it involved a radical break in technologies as well as an over-emphasis on the new online communication platform. The new flexible but complex architecture in effect hindered Participatory Design efforts, taking over a year and a half before DHIS 2 could initially be deployed, first in Kerala, India, in January 2006, when much important functionality was lacking. The system improved significantly through early use in India and Vietnam and later also in Sierra Leone, as well as through the involvement of new software developers recruited locally. While engaging with the global source code, their main task was to support local implementations, while also contributing in more limited terms to core development.

After the first pilot in Kerala in 2006, use of DHIS 2 gradually spread to other states, and was then taken up in 2008 by the National Rural Health Mission (NRHM) to support a national implementation. Simultaneously, Health Metrics Network (HMN) chose to use DHIS 2 in Sierra Leone (see below). Political support in both cases, of NRHM in India and HMN in Sierra Leone, was fundamental for the support of larger adoption of DHIS 2.

Sierra Leone

Sierra Leone, a relatively small country in West Africa, is one of the poorest countries in the world and was ravaged by civil war 1992–2002. The public health system suffered from loss of personnel and destruction of infrastructure, but was gradually being rebuilt with considerable support from a variety of international donor agencies. The rapid growth of relatively uncoordinated health initiatives created a situation of fragmented HIS, typical for most developing countries. In 2008 each facility reported data every month on 17 different paper forms, with nearly 50 per cent overlap of data across the forms.

Given this fragmented HIS, key challenges were to provide relevant information for decision-making and to diminish the workload of staff responsible for collecting and reporting data. The strategy selected was to use DHIS 2 as a tool to integrate the various data through a participatory prototyping strategy involving all 'owners' of data collection tools alongside the various levels of users. All paper forms and data elements included in these were identified and sorted out in order to identify duplications of data forms and data elements. As a result, a coherent integrated data warehouse was built, where one data element in the database could be related to a field in several data collection forms. In order to satisfy the 'form owners', each paper form was included in the data entry screen, while the duplicate data elements were integrated 'behind the scenes' in the data warehouse. Data already captured would then appear as already included in the data entry form.

In January 2008, this integration approach was implemented in 4 of the 13 districts, and in the rest of the country from six months later. Intensive training was carried out to support each district to capture their data in DHIS and export it to the national DHIS by the use of memory sticks. This process was established in all districts, and for 2008 a rather extensive national dataset became available for analysis. All stakeholders were included in this process, which convincingly documented the existing problems of overlapping data collection forms, inconsistent data definitions and poor data quality. At the same time, through actually implementing the process, it was documented that it was possible to achieve shared datasets in a national repository. This participatory learning process sparked an increased interest in revising the current collection forms, and during 2009 a series of meetings took place among the key stakeholders to negotiate a new set of harmonised data collection forms. As a result, since January 2010 a new set of completely rationalised and harmonised forms have been in use. Sierra Leone has become HMN's 'best practice' example of how even a poor African country can develop an integrated HIS.

Community-level Participatory Design – rationale and experience

As an effort to document their disadvantageous situation and thereby to better argue for improved health services, the traditional chiefdom structures in Sierra Leone were eager to use the new system. In Mayamba district, the seven different chiefdoms compete to produce the best-quality data on health services and produce tables ranking their achievements, in both their local and their national contexts.

The Sierra Leone case demonstrates the need and value for multi-level teams, including members from Oslo, West Africa, national ministries and the global HMN. Political support came both from HMN, urgently needing to show some successes, and also the Ministry, eager to reform their existing systems. This heterogeneous team and interests contributed to an intense period of Participatory Design contributing to the design of the entire HIS as well as the DHIS 2 application. While the situation of fragmentation was similar to that in South Africa, the strategy to reform was different, aiming not at a consensus-based minimum set of 'essential' data but a technologically driven shared data warehouse solution. The Participatory Design involved a three-step approach; first, implement the current system with optimally 'harmonised' datasets in order to give hands-on experience to users and to provide a platform for prototyping; second, use the prototype to demonstrate what a revised HIS could look like; and third, revise the system, including the paper forms and data standards. While DHIS 2 provided the 'plastic' and easily formable prototyping tool, political support of the HMN made it practically possible.

India

After the initiation of the first instance of DHIS 2 in a clinic in Kerala in early 2006, DHIS 2 increased to full-scale implementations in the states of Gujarat and Kerala. Following these 'best practice' state implementations, HISP was invited to the national stage by NRHM to support their efforts of reform. Examples of working in various states from 2000 were drawn upon by HISP as their empirical base to highlight the challenges in the existing systems and provide recommendations for reform. In 2008, the national HIS was redesigned, including new standards which represented, among other things, a drastic reduction of the actual data elements to be reported. DHIS 2 was then quickly customised to the revisions, and provided states with a low-cost and easy-to-use system which for the first time gave states access to their own data. Further, the flexibility of DHIS 2 to create bridges with other systems, including those at the national level, contributed to its rapid uptake in about 25 states, leading to *The Lancet* terming it the largest open source implementation in the health system in developing countries (Webster 2011).

However, this rapid scaling came at a cost, as in responding to local demands the HISP India team could not effectively coordinate with the global DHIS 2 shared core code base, leading to a 'forking' of two not fully compatible branches. For example, the HISP India team had prior experience with DHIS 1, and the DHIS 2 technologies were foreign to them. The absence of graphing facilities in the early DHIS 2, and being confronted with large volumes of data, forced the Indian team to develop workarounds and ad hoc 'hacks' to produce the needed reports. While the DHIS 2 data model was similar to that of DHIS 1, it had an additional data abstraction layer requiring the use of the Java Application Programming Interface (API) instead of directly accessing the database. The Indians found this hard to comprehend, and chose to bypass the API and access the database directly in order to get quick results, leading to 'hard-coded' but well-performing reports. Another example of forking is provided by the Indian effort to develop a dashboard module to enable graphical analysis of data and indicators in charts. While this module proved very effective in showing local users their data, the code remained incompatible and outside the global code repository, because it used too many local workarounds and hacks. Also, since the Sierra Leone implementation was simultaneously also moving at a fast pace, the global team had created an 'executive dashboard', as coordination was more problematic and time-consuming than making from new. Only in 2010, when processes were reasonably more stable, were the two code bases merged and a seemingly permanent structure for future coordination established.

While the initial objective of DHIS 2 distributed development was to bring the software closer to the users, practically this was a complex problem to overcome. This led to the refor-mulation of development strategy, based on a clearer distinction between software and system, with two sets of implications on Participatory Design processes. In-country emphasis should be on the system rather than the software, while across countries there need to be shared Partici-patory Design processes contributing to the development of the global DHIS 2. Obviously, these processes mutually feed into each other; globally distributed solutions grow out of local designs and use, and DHIS 2 as a global toolbox is utilised in local design processes. To what extent design is participatory will depend on how implementers mediate requirements between users and core developers. This raises new skill demands on implementers, requiring them to be proficient in customising the system locally in cooperation with users, and needing knowledge of the DHIS 2 to an extent that they can specify new requirements to the developers. Two levels of 'gate-keeping' are required at the national and global levels, possible through a certain level of dictatorship.

In many ways, DHIS 2 development has seen a separation of coding and system, as for example seen in Vietnam, which primarily only contributed to core development. The procedures being established now therefore aim to centralise core development and to try to outsource tasks to Vietnam, while strengthening DHIS 2 implementers globally, including processes of communication between implementers and 'coders' through DHIS 2 'gate-keepers'. For a more thorough discussion of the DHIS 2 project and challenges related to distributed Participatory Design, see Titlestad et al. (2009).

Current trends and looking forward: Participatory Design in the cloud and architecture

Various technological shifts are opening up challenging new arenas for Participatory Design in HISP. First, the rapid improvement of the mobile networks is enabling online web-based services and cloud computing in developing countries, raising the question of how Participatory Design will play out with respect to empowerment of disadvantaged communities, and enabling local control and ownership when the system is located 'far away in the cloud'. HISP is currently (in 2011) exploring these issues in Kenya and has found that, first, online easy access to own data combined with access to health data for other areas for comparison has the potential to empower local communities; and second, Participatory Design approaches are needed in order to release such an empowering potential, even in the age of cloud computing. Third, new web-based open source technologies have provided the impetus for HISP and other global actors to cooperate on developing an architecture of interoperable systems. The HMN and their framework of a national HIS architecture, have helped to identify challenges and approaches to integration, standards and interoperability. This trend further raises the challenge of changing Participatory Design approaches based on single systems to support multiple interoperable and integrated systems, or architecture. We now discuss the twin challenges of cloud computing and architecture on Participatory Design approaches.

Participatory Design in the cloud

In Africa, the Internet has not been and is still not perceived by many as sufficiently robust or reliable to support web-based data solutions for routine data reporting. The norm to date has been to capture routine data in stand-alone databases, and to report data electronically by e-mail attachments or physically to the level above. This places significant challenges on human capacity and synchronisation of multiple stand-alone databases, making the HIS fragile and complicated. Building a web-based data warehouse on a central server is simpler technically, and ironically would be more appropriate for Africa even in terms of human resources.

During 2011, DHIS 2 has been rolled out countrywide in Kenya based on a central server solution. Initially, the plan was to implement stand-alone instances in districts around the country – the traditional African way – but a field visit to Machako in October 2010, a district and hospital not far from Nairobi, changed the course of action. During a test of the DHIS 2 online server in the information office, everything went well until a power cut left the line dead. As it was a hospital, the generator started and power came back, but the Internet was gone as it would have to be restarted somewhere down the line. The team were just about to conclude that the Internet was still not available when a Japanese volunteer suggested using his 'dongle', the modem for the Internet over the mobile network. This worked fine, as mobile networks are not affected by power cuts. Immediately after this revelation, Internet modems were tested around the country. The solution worked, and the decision was taken to go for a central server solution, probably the first time for such a countrywide public sector project in Africa. However, the server in the Ministry of Health could not be used, as the connectivity was poor in the building and the server set-up not reliable. As a temporary solution, therefore, a commercial server was rented – through a London-based company, meaning cloud computing for real, although politically it was not yet acceptable to locate national health data outside the country. The Coast Province was selected as a pilot, and the system rolled out in January 2011 to all districts and hospitals, as a start. All users were provided a modem and a budget for airtime. The network was working, but the bandwidth was limited in many places, and the cost of the airtime was restrictive. In order to address a multitude of problems, the DHIS 2 lab was literally moved to Kenya; the lead developer and others took part in building a local team and engaged in rapid prototyping cycles on site with the users, first in the Coast Province to support the pilot, and later, from April 2011, to support the rollout to all eight provinces. In fact, 'rapid prototyping' changed its meaning; working on an online server meant that the system changed for all users according to their input, if possible on one day, or overnight.

A system based on Excel spreadsheets that were submitted to an FTP server was already in place. The users were thus well accustomed to computers, the data to report and the Internet. The system was initially set up based on the existing paper forms used for reporting from facilities to the district; data entry screens were made to mimic the paper forms reasonably well. A very active period of agile Participatory Design followed the implementation; standard reports were designed and GIS was set up; users' input ranged from the 'small' request for the same functionality as they had in Excel with regard to data entry, such as being able to use the arrows to navigate the data entry screen, to larger issues such as the need for online messaging enabling users to communicate with the developers and with each other. The messaging system developed following these requests have proven crucial in the countrywide deployment of DHIS 2. It was also necessary to optimise DHIS 2 for the low bandwidth in remote areas. The more serious user input, however, was the need to be able to capture data and work on it offline.

The new HTML5 standard has the potential to improve the robustness of Internet and cloud-based technologies in Africa as it allows for offline data entry, with browsers implementing this standard now including more memory or in fact a small database. The first version of such a 'semi-online' feature was implemented in DHIS in late August 2011. The user can now capture data offline by using the memory in the browser and 'flush' the data (i.e. transfer to the server) when online. This is a very useful feature in Africa since the Internet is not available everywhere and all the time. The following message was posted on the DHIS 2 message system by a user after the new feature of offline data capture had been included:

2011–09–13

Hi, this is wow! I have realised that I can now work with a lot of easy without any interruptions from network fluctuations since some of us are in the interiors where we have lots of challenges with the network. this is so good, a big Thank you.

Offline data use in a cloud-based infrastructure is the other important feature needed to optimise the system in areas with poor Internet access, which has been addressed in the following way: a small 'super lightweight DHIS 2' application installed locally is used to download data from the user's own area and other areas specified by the user, including the indicators and aggregates generated by the system, which is then used to generate Excel pivot tables used for data analysis.

Outputs are generated when online, downloaded in pdf format and archived in the offline application. As the Excel pivot tables are not easy to update or 'refresh' online regardless of bandwidth, the offline local 'datamart' represents an improvement to 'fully online' web browsing (see Figure 10.2).

The innovative approach to addressing the rather fragile Internet situation in Kenya illustrates how innovations are generated through participatory processes, implementation, use and practical problem-solving. Participatory Design and innovation may thus be seen as being an embedded part of the scaling process. Note that this is particularly enabled through a central server approach, as changes are distributed instantly and widely to all users in Kenya and all users of DHIS 2 globally. The use of open source applications within a framework of collaborative networks enables innovations in Kenya, such as the semi-online approach, to be fed back to the global community.

The project in Kenya was funded by DANIDA from 2010 and by USAID from the end of 2011, and has so far been through three phases totalling 12 months: three months' exploration and pilots in selected districts; three months' piloting in the Coast Province and gradual inclusion of other advanced user groups eager to participate; and six months' countrywide training, province by province. This rapid deployment has been made possible by the cloud-based infrastructure. Furthermore, the 'one server' deployment has made it much easier to manage the continuous participatory development of the system 'while in full production', as new features are added every day. For example, during the last part of 2011, all HIV/AIDS reporting from a USAID-funded project will be added to the system (more than 1,000 reporting units) and a

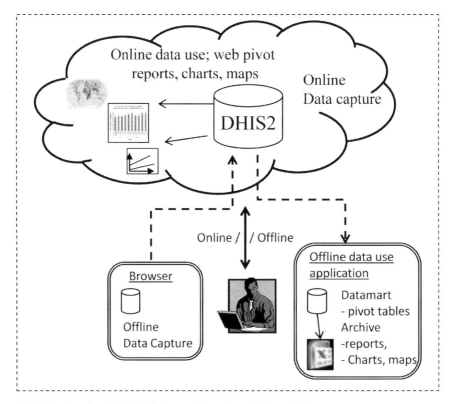

Figure 10.2 Semi-online DHIS 2 design and implementation in Kenya

new web-based module for mobile telephones is being introduced. Also the Participatory Design process in South Africa was characterised by ongoing participatory prototyping of new features on the system while in production, but it is now much easier for users and developers at multiple locations to interact when the system is implemented on one server to which all participants can connect.

Participatory Design in architectures

Discussions on how multiple systems should speak to each other and the standards of data exchange are important topics with which global (e.g. HMN and WHO) and national actors are currently engaged. The HMN and WHO have taken a strong role in defining the Public Health Information Toolkit, consisting of a suite of applications, and also the SDMX.HD standards for data exchange. With this move from individual to multiple interconnected systems, the nature and methods of Participatory Design also need to be redefined. This is illustrated through an ongoing HISP initiative in the state of Himachal Pradesh in northern India to develop an integrated health information architecture (IHIA) comprising the following five distinct HISs:

1   District and state data warehouse based on DHIS 2: DHIS 2 as a data warehouse is already in place for routine data from sub-district-level facilities. The initiative in process is to include more types of data representing different health programmes.
2   Mobile telephone reporting from sub centre level: currently the sub centres report their data monthly from multiple paper forms into the DHIS 2. Given the harsh winters, which isolate many parts of the state, the project will use the mobile telephone to report data directly to the data warehouse.
3   Name-based tracking of pregnancies and immunisation using the DHIS 2 Tracker: to enable name-based tracking of pregnant women over the life cycle of the services of antenatal, perinatal and postnatal care, and also all newborns over their period of immunisations, HISP has developed the DHIS 2 Tracker as a module in the DHIS 2. In addition to allowing for a name-based monitoring of cases, this data will be aggregated and exported using the SDMX.HD standard to the DHIS 2 to enable facility reports on various parameters such as numbers of ANC visits and numbers of immunisation. Over time, the name-based data would also be transmitted through a mobile phone application, thus enabling integration between the mobile, DHIS 2 Tracker and DHIS 2 facility reporting.
4   A comprehensive hospital information system, integrating an electronic medical record system and data warehouse for hospital management. This project is twofold: (a) to develop an electronic medical record system for district hospitals which is easy to adapt for smaller hospitals; and (b) to integrate the aggregate data from the medical record system in DHIS 2 with other data needed for hospital management, such as human resources, finances and infrastructure. This integration will allow the state to monitor key indicators such as:
    •   bed occupancy: number of patient days/nights divided by number of beds, typically provided by month; bed nights during a month divided by number of beds times 30;
    •   average length of stay: number of patient nights divided by number of discharges, typically by month;
    •   death rate: number of deaths divided by number of patients, by age, service and ward;
    •   infection rate: hospital infections divided by number of patients, by ward, age and service.

In this example, the data warehouse represents an integrated framework – an 'umbrella' – within which various systems are gradually being plugged in and subsequently scaled up. The existing HIS and routine paper-based reporting forms the backbone and point of departure. Rather than having an 'individual system'-based system approach, Participatory Design methods could be understood in terms of understanding the levels of cross-cutting information needs, and how information feeds in from the different software applications. For example, field-level nurses' information needs could be categorised into registering, tracking, reporting and analysis of pregnancy cases, which could be met through different systems and devices such as the DHIS 2 tracking mobile for individual cases and the aggregate module for reporting and data analysis, and by using mobiles in the field and desktops in the health centres.

Similarly, in the hospital setting, while doctors would need clinical patient-based information, administrators would require hospital efficiency indicators based on aggregated information. The architecture approach thus helps to provide information of a greater granularity, which also places the onus on the implementing staff to be capable of deeply understanding the nature of decision-making and information requirements, and the supporting systems that provide this. The technological domain necessarily also becomes more complex, given the multiplicity of existing systems that interconnect. Both system architects and implementers need to mediate between the users and software developers. Implementers or facilitators play a crucial role in spanning the boundaries of the different domains in shaping Participatory Design processes.

In summary, a key challenge for Participatory Design-based efforts arises from the paradox of how to address the challenge of the increasing distance of the user from the integrated software solution, which at the same time requires a more comprehensive understanding of the health system, and its communication to the developers.

Participatory Design lessons from HISP and developing countries

Comparing the HISP case with traditional Participatory Design and the early Scandinavian projects, there are some important differences.

Who are the users? And what about empowerment and politics?

While in the early Scandinavian projects Participatory Design was regarded as a tool for workers to strengthen their position in relation to management, Participatory Design in HISP is targeting users at all levels of the health systems, workers and management alike. Furthermore, HISP would always try to use Participatory Design as a 'best practice' strategy to achieve consensus and good design to the benefit of the common good (Kyng 2010). When engaging in Participatory Design in contexts characterised by diversity of users at multiple levels, as also discussed in Chapters 8 and 9, consensus and good design for all are obvious objectives, though not always possible to achieve. In the case of HISP, Participatory Design to develop better health for marginalised communities in developing countries is a highly political process. However, the nature of politics in which HISP is involved is significantly different from that in the earlier Participatory Design tradition. First, the context and relationship to technology is very different. While the democratic ideals of the Participatory Design tradition were developed in a context where workers were threatened by modern technology and feared for their jobs, communities and health services in developing countries are in an opposite situation: they are threatened by being ignored by new technologies and thereby being left out of development processes. As Castells (1996) has argued, such exclusion from the 'network society' of marginalised communities will only lead to their continued and more systematic marginalisation.

Second, HIS initiatives need to necessarily support the strengthening of the delivery and quality of public health services in developing countries. Participatory Design approaches thus need to reach out to identifying and serving the marginalised communities with respect to their health needs – 'setting the last first' (Chambers 1997) – and more strongly including the community in Participatory Design efforts. These objectives are by nature political, and not necessarily in line with the interests of health workers, managers or the political class. An improved HIS will as a principle represent transparency by providing information on how the health services are performing, thereby disclosing poor performance, mismanagement and corruption. Some officials from the health system may stand exposed. Strengthening such a focus implies that the community must necessarily be regarded as users of the information and become active participants in the Participatory Design strategy (Braa 1996; and see Chapter 8 of this volume for a general presentation of community-based Participatory Design). Only by creating a sense of community ownership to the HIS will it be possible to ensure democratic control and community participation in the running of the health services, which is the stated goal in the WHO Primary Health Approach and the policies of most countries.

The HISP experience helps to provide multiple perspectives on empowerment, which Participatory Design supports. There is first the process of empowering the users in the health services. Participatory Design has helped, as in South Africa, to foster decentralisation and empowerment of local users in terms of control, access and use of their own information. Users who previously had limited and delayed access to their own data could, with the new system, access their data on their desktops shortly after having submitted their reports. Further, this data would be organised in Excel pivot tables that enabled drill down using a variety of views and calculated indicators. More than a decade since the principles behind such empowerment were established and practised in South Africa, HISP is trying to offer the same support in the new technological paradigms offered by the web and cloud infrastructure. Technical solutions have been provided and are being constantly improved through the Participatory Design process, first, as in Kenya, to enable the data going from the community 'up to the cloud', for example by enabling offline data entry through the implementation of HTML5, and second, enabling the needed data to come 'down to the local laptop' so that local control is strengthened – faster and more 'real time' than before. In addition to the user at community level, management at county, province and national levels is also strengthened, and will for the first time have online access to all data in respective administrative areas, which can be used to direct action to areas that most need it. Third, this health information is the primary source for empowering communities, as it is the key information source on the performance of the health services at community level to support decentralised governance. This was the explicit agenda in South Africa, and today we have some (although limited) examples such as those from the Sierra Leone, where the chiefdoms are comparing their health data, and from Kerala, India, where the health information reports were also sent to the Gram Panchayat (the village-level political entity) for monitoring the health of their community, for instance as related to births, deaths and maternal deaths.

Cyclic and evolutionary Participatory Design in HISP

Participatory Design in HISP is targeting both the DHIS software application and the wider HIS, representing four different but interconnected cyclic development processes.

1 Developing the software – Participatory Design and development of the DHIS software application have involved rapid and exploratory cyclic prototyping in cooperation with users, representing a practical way both to get the requirements right and to develop the software accordingly. 'Right' in the early changing environment of South Africa, as well as later in other countries, meant to develop 'generic solutions' that could be adapted to the

ever-changing context of health sector reform, leading to a flexible meta-data structure. At present, 'right' represents integrated information from different programmes and data sources.

2   Developing the information system – the participatory and cyclic development of essential data and indicator sets is used in the DHIS application as a prototyping tool. This helped to get the generic data models right – or building the LEGO bricks – while also using the DHIS as a Participatory Design tool for prototyping to get the wider information system right, such as the datasets and the hierarchy of standards – the LEGO bricks were used to build the system.

3   Developing the information for action cycle – this represents the cyclical approach to turning the data collected into indicators which further need to be converted into action to make improvements in the health services. Such an approach will follow the planning cycle of the various health programmes and local procedures. For example, in Kenya, every province will have a quarterly assessment and planning workshops where key performance indicators are used. Using information for action will by definition help to break the earlier existing cycle of data not being used because it was of poor quality, and because it was not used it remained of poor quality.

4   Developing the action research cycle – the action research cycle enables the development of the other cycles: building the software, the information system and also that of information for action. Through collaborative action between the health system and HISP, this cycle involves identifying required interventions and their implementation and evaluation, based on the next round of iterations to be made in the cycle and thereby generating a constantly changing environment.

In this way, these four interconnected cycles provide the substance and content of Participatory Design processes within HISP. Each of these cycles involve multiple and specific techniques in use, such as agile prototyping (for development of software), workshops and stakeholder meetings (for developing the information system), carrying out database development, data analysis and capacity-building efforts with real data (for building the information for action cycle), and research and education for the action research cycle. These different Participatory Design interventions take place at multiple levels, from the national offices to province/states and districts, and also the health facilities and community levels. Further, these interventions take place over time, representing cycles which encompass the above cycles in varying rhythms and emphasis at different points of time.

  In understanding the nature of these cycles more broadly, Chambers's (1997) distinction between the 'things' and 'people' paradigms related to participation in a development context is relevant. While the things paradigm emphasises neo-Newtonian principles of a technology and top-down focus, the people paradigm represents principles of adaptive pluralism which focus on participation and a more decentralised approach. On reflection, we could say that while the South African work was more people-based, the later efforts around DHIS 2 tend to reflect more of a technology paradigm. However, as Chambers (2011) himself reflects, this distinction is rather binary and tends to reflect the primacy of the people paradigm over things. He sees this distinction as inadequate, especially as there are increasing crossovers between the two domains. The same can also be argued for the HISP efforts: for example, with DHIS 2 increasingly taking on features of messaging and social networking, it becomes more grounded in the paradigm of people, while on the other hand, as facility-level users access the cloud through mobile phones, people are becoming more grounded in technology. The challenge for HISP in the future would be to maintain a coherent balance between these two domains while being firmly grounded in the problems on hand. This is discussed in the section that follows relating to threats and opportunities.

Threats and opportunities, and concluding remarks

The case of Kenya illustrates the potentially improved opportunities for Participatory Design in Africa using the cloud-based infrastructure. Users across the country can engage in instant participation, use new features as soon as they are implemented and feed back, request new features and 'chat' using the online messaging system in DHIS 2. Compared with the case of South Africa, where new builds would have to be distributed physically on CDs and installed in each computer, the cloud infrastructure represents a tremendous improvement in the conditions for Participatory Design.

With the cloud-based infrastructure, however, comes also the threat of outsourcing software-based services from Africa to industrialised countries by providing end-to-end services. A typical example is a project by Pfizer and Vodafone in the Gambia, where Pfizer wants to monitor stock and distribution of malaria drugs in the dispensaries and Vodafone is providing the entire infrastructure – SIM cards if needed (users have their own telephones), mobile network, airtime, data management in their servers in the cloud and provision of the data to the users. DHIS 2 is running as the national HIS in the country and is including similar data, leading to duplication of both data and efforts. We have argued the need for an integrated architecture approach and suggested feeding the data reported by the Vodafone mobiles into the DHIS, i.e. the national HIS. We have also argued the need for pooling the limited resources available for HIS in the Gambia. These efforts towards integration have been in vain, since Vodafone has argued that such integration efforts could only be included 'if there is a place for them in the value chain'.

It is our general view that business models that are locating value chains derived from Africa outside Africa are of no use for Africa. But more specifically, we argue that the outsourcing of what may be labelled the 'information technology learning and innovation chain' from Africa to the West, as illustrated by the example of Vodafone and Pfizer, may even be more harmful. A key challenge, then, facing Participatory Design is how to develop country and regional capacity to be able to counter this trend, and at the same time leverage opportunities for their local good.

Open source – empowering the South

Participatory Design as a pragmatic approach in the hands of Western companies based on cloud computing in Africa is not what we would like to see happening. This would be to drain rather than to build human resources and institutional capacity. A counter strategy would be to revitalise elements of the political agenda which aims at empowering developing countries and institutions to master new technologies and take control over their information resources.

It is our strong belief that open source software is an important element in this strategy. The philosophical underpinnings of the DHIS project are based on the fact that for any developing country to develop its own HIS system from scratch, with levels of functionality equivalent to DHIS 2, would be a huge undertaking far beyond such countries' own resources. Therefore, since the development of software to support the HIS is so complex and such a huge task and since the requirements in many countries are quite similar, it makes a lot more sense to collaborate as a big virtual team in a South–South–North network than to work in isolation.

The entire web-based stack of technologies making up the DHIS 2 technology environment, from Java frameworks to GIS, are free and open source – and they are at the cutting edge of technological development. While companies such as IBM are using FOSS for competitive advantage, the DHIS 2 project has proven that these technologies are as useful for Participatory Design projects, in particular for Participatory Design projects operating in collaborative networks. Looking back at the early Scandinavian Participatory Design project, we may conclude that HISP has been lucky with timing its technological development. For example, HISP was inspired by the early Scandinavian UTOPIA project, with which it shares many approaches of participatory development of useful tools and empowerment through capacity building. The important difference is, however, that while UTOPIA was made redundant by the introduction of new commercial desktop publishing technologies, HISP is currently being 'lifted up' by current technology development.

Concluding remarks

The HISP Participatory Design experience – both historical and looking forward – is a rich and complex endeavour. It involves a diversity and multiplicity of contexts, technologies, levels, techniques and interventions. Across these multiple dimensions, it is likely that while success is obtained in some facets, less than optimal results are seen in others. The time dimension is fundamental as everything is constantly changing, redefining the relationships between technology, politics and user and health systems needs, which we have argued are the driving forces behind the design, implementation and success – or otherwise – of Participatory Design efforts.

References

Bjerknes, G., P. Ehn and M. Kyng (eds) (1987) *Computers and Democracy – A Scandinavian Challenge*, Aldershot: Avebury.

Bødker, S., P. Ehn, J. Kammersgaard, M. Kyng and Y. Sundblad (1987) 'A UTOPIAN experience: on design of powerful computer-based tools for skilled graphical workers', in G. Bjerknes, P. Ehn and M. Kyng (eds) (1987) *Computers and Democracy – A Scandinavian Challenge*, Aldershot: Avebury, 251–78.

Braa, J. (1996) 'Community-based participatory design in the Third World', in J. Blomberg, F. Kensing and E. Dykstra-Erickson (eds) *PDC '96: Proceedings of the Participatory Design Conference*, New York: Computer Professionals for Social Responsibility, 15–24.

Braa, J. and C. Hedberg (2002) 'The struggle for developing district-based health information systems in South Africa', *The Information Society*, 18(3): 113–27.

Braa, J., E. Monteiro and S. Sahay (2004) 'Networks of action: sustainable health information systems across developing countries', *Management Information Systems Quarterly*, 28(3): 337–62.

Castells, M. (1996) *The Rise of the Network Society*, Oxford: Basil Blackwell.

Chambers, R. (1997) *Whose Reality Counts? Putting the First Last*, London: Intermediate Technology Publications.

Chambers, R. (2011) 'Aid on the edge of chaos: exploring complexity and evolutionary sciences in foreign aid'. Available at: http://aidontheedge.info/2011/02/10/whose-paradigm-counts/.

Kyng, M. (2010) 'Bridging the gap between politics and techniques: on the next practices of Participatory Design', *Scandinavian Journal of Information Systems*, 22(1): 49–68.

Nygaard, K. (1979) 'The Iron and Metal project', in Å. Sandberg (ed.) *Computers Dividing Man and Work*, Demos Project Report No. 13, Malmø: Swedish Centre for Working Life, Utbildningsproduktion, 94–107.

Puri, S. K., E. Byrne, J. L. Nhampossa and Z. Quraishy (2004) 'Contextuality of participation in IS design: a developing country perspective', *Proceedings of PDC 2004*, Toronto, Canada, New York: AMC.

Raghavendra, R. C. and S. Sahay (2006) 'Computer-based health information systems – projects for computerization or health management? Empirical experiences from India', in Mila Gascó-Hernández, Fran Equiza-López and Manuel Acevedo-Ruiz (eds) *Information Communication Technologies and Human Development: Opportunities and Challenges*, Hershey, PA: Idea Group Inc.

Sandiford, P., H. Annet and R. Cibulskis (1992) 'What can information systems do for primary health care? An international perspective', *Social Science and Medicine*, 34(10): 1077–87.

Titlestad, O., K. Staring and J. Braa (2009) 'Distributing developers to enable user participation: multilevel design in the HISP network', *Scandinavian Journal of Information Systems*, 21(1): 27–50.

Webster, P. C. (2011) 'The rise of open-source electronic health records', *The Lancet*, 377(9778, 14 May): 1641–2.

11

ACTION for Health

Influencing technology design, practice and policy through Participatory Design

Ellen Balka

The Assessment of Technology in Context Design Lab's ACTION for Health project attempted to influence work practice and public policy related to technology, through participatory projects undertaken in close partnership with health sector organisations. This chapter describes the evolution of the approach that characterised projects undertaken through ACTION for Health. Descriptions of projects undertaken as part of ACTION for Health are used to illustrate important points about how we developed partnerships, our data collection methods, and the issues and challenges we faced as we participated with our partners in an effort to influence health sector information technology design.

After describing ACTION for Health, the chapter outlines how early experiences with Participatory Design led to the approach to participation adopted in ACTION for Health. Subsequent descriptions of ACTION for Health projects are used to highlight key insights about developing Participatory Design projects.

This chapter places contemporary approaches to Participatory Design strategies (including collaborating with management) within an historical context. Descriptions of projects undertaken through ACTION for Health have been selected to highlight aspects of projects which can contribute to success. These include the need to produce work which is relevant for collaborators, the need to maintain flexibility and respond to change, the ability to maintain an awareness of timing, the importance of developing low-impact means of data collection, and the importance of communicating information about technology design and implementation back to project participants.

The chapter draws attention to power relations in Participatory Design projects, and the sometimes fine line between Participatory Design, action research and consultancy. It addresses varied health sector technology customisation and implementation projects, including a hospital's move into a new building, where all technology was new.

Introduction

This chapter provides an overview of the ACTION for Health project, a four-year $3 million project, which investigated the role of technology in the production, consumption and use of health information, from work practice to policy contexts. After a brief overview of ACTION for Health, this chapter situates the ACTION for Health project within the context of the Assessment of Technology in Context Design Lab's (ATIC) work. The first section of the chapter places ACTION for Health within the broader context of Participatory Design, outlining the project's evolution in relation to earlier insights about Participatory Design. The second section of the chapter provides a detailed account of the Technology Trouble project (which marked the beginning of the ACTION for Health project), and provides insights into both the circumstances that have supported our approach to health sector research partnerships, and the methods of data collection characteristic of our group's work. Subsequent shorter synopses of research projects undertaken through the ACTION for Health project provide a backdrop through which some of the challenges we encountered in our engagement with health sector research partners are explored, and the successes we have achieved are highlighted. ACTION for Health successes and failures are discussed in relation to implications for Participatory Design practices.

The ACTION for Health Project[1]

The ACTION for Health project was a four-year, $3 million project funded by the Social Sciences and Humanities Research Council of Canada's Initiative for a New Economy funding programme's Collaborative Research Initiative (CRI) stream. The CRI programme sought to support academics, working with diverse community partners, to address issues and questions of concern to Canadians, and, as such, required and supported significant engagement of community partners. The project was organised around three themes: (1) end-user consumption of online health information in varied contexts (e.g. public libraries, community centres, doctors' offices); (2) changes to health sector work practices related to computerisation of health sector work; and (3) ethical and legal issues arising in relation to computerisation of health sector work. Much of the work concerned with end-user consumption of health information and issues arising in relation to health sector computerisation had improvements in design as its focus.

Researchers from Canada, Austria, Australia, the United Kingdom and the Netherlands carried out projects under each of the themes. Each project involved one or more community partners, who, in most cases[2] played a significant role in setting the agenda within their project. For example, in two cases (one provincial, another federal), government departments involved in provision of online health information generated questions about their websites, with an end goal of improving service provision. In another case, a hospital which was one of our research partners sought our input in evaluating a wireless paging system.

Projects related to end-user consumption of online health information included collaborations with libraries (e.g. one library wanted to know how online health information seeking would fit into patrons' broader patterns of health information-seeking trajectories), provincial and federal health agencies (which had an interest in how the online resources they had developed were being used, and how those resources could be better designed; Balka and Butt 2008; McCulloch 2007; Balka et al. 2009; Henwood and Wyatt 2009), community groups (interested in how online health information seeking would fit into broader community development goals (Bella 2009), a community clinic that put a terminal in the waiting room for patient health information seeking (Smith 2006), and patient and provider groups (Balka et al. 2010; Holmes 2005) interested in assessing the suitability of online information for their constituent groups. Other contributions addressed the roles of patients and varied providers in computer-mediated health information consumption (e.g. Bella et al. 2008; Henwood et al. 2008; Wyatt et al. 2008; Wathen, Harris and Wyatt 2008).

Projects related to how work practices were changing in relation to computerisation of the health sector addressed areas ranging from the introduction of electronic health records into the primary care sector (Boulus 2009, 2010; Boulus and Bjørn 2010) to computerisation of oncology clinics (Reidl and Tolar 2007; Schmidt et al. 2007; Reidl et al. 2008). In addition to the Technology Trouble project discussed in detail below, other projects included a study of a pilot implementation of a wireless call system (Balka, Wagner and Jensen 2005; Jensen 2007a, 2007b), a study of a failure of an electronic triage system (Balka and Whitehouse 2007) and a subsequent (more successful) effort to introduce a new system (Bjørn and Rødje 2008; Bjørn et al. 2009; Bjørn and Balka 2009), a study undertaken in an effort to gain insight about unsanctioned duplicate medical charts (called ghost charts or shadow records) (Balka et al. 2011), which was undertaken in the context of computerising the hospital's record system, and several studies which addressed the relationship between health information system design and the availability and quality of health information (Schuurman and Balka 2009; Balka and Freilich 2008; Balka 2010; Balka et al. 2006; Harris 2009; Sharman 2009; Balka 2009; Armstrong et al. 2009; Le Jeune 2009; Green et al. 2009).

Background to current approach

The Technology Impact Research Fund (TIRF),[3] aimed at addressing labour issues related to computerisation, was introduced in Canada in the 1980s. The history of a state-funded social change sector in Canada, evidenced through programmes such as the TIRF programme and other mechanisms such as Quebec's University Act, which recognises research undertaken in partnership with community organisations (Messing et al. 2005), has helped to legitimate the collaboration of academic researchers with varied 'community' partners, who work together to effect change.

Work undertaken through the Assessment of Technology in Context Design Lab (ATIC) in general and projects undertaken by ATIC Lab staff as part of the ACTION for Health project[4] in particular build on and reflect a long-standing commitment by Canadian researchers to undertaking politically engaged research, oriented towards effecting change. Throughout the history of the Assessment of Technology in Context Design Lab (as of this writing, 14 years old) and the ACTION for Health project (which ran from 2003 to 2007), an approach to conducting politically engaged research has evolved. This approach, which served as a framework for planning the ACTION for Health project, seeks to influence change in relation to technology work practices, something that has often required engagement of research team members in all aspects of research processes, through engagement with and dissemination to public policy decision-makers. While the focal point of an ATIC project may be on implications for technology design, projects are typically situated within the broader policy and political contexts in which they are occurring, as these often have significant implications for system design (Balka et al. 2008).

This approach, which characterised much of the work undertaken through ACTION for Health, grew out of much of my earlier work in Participatory Design. In the mid-1990s I undertook a project aimed at exploring the strengths and limitations of Participatory Design efforts. I felt that if we were to take seriously the claim that technology is socially biased and socially shaped, our success in guiding processes aimed at improving the lives of end-users would rest, in part, in our ability to understand the limitations of the strategies we adopted in efforts to create emancipatory ends. My work represented a friendly critique of Participatory Design, undertaken with the spirit of improving practice (Balka 2005).

This project left me puzzling over several issues. The project included a focus on the then emergent field of participatory ergonomics, and I had begun working with researchers whose work was concerned with the mitigation of occupational health issues among women workers. I was intrigued that while studies concerned with occupational health and safety, often carried out by my Francophone colleagues in a manner quite similar to work practice studies (see Messing et al. 2005), enjoyed a certain legitimacy in changing work practices, those work practice studies that sought to influence technology design in an effort to democratise work often failed to achieve long-term change.

Groundbreaking projects I had learned about during early research had not been sustainable over time. I heard about staff who became active in Participatory Design projects, who became empowered to the point of seeking new jobs with their newly acquired skills, or, worse yet, were treated with suspicion by co-workers who suspected them of colluding with management or shirking work responsibilities. Participation did not always achieve the emancipatory ends of democratic work or empowerment (Balka 2005), and Participatory Design projects were difficult to sustain over time. Projects that had support from the shop floor and upper management could be weakened by middle managers, as well as a host of other factors. These insights prompted me to search for ways to create change which could be sustained over time, which in turn led me to pursue a broader diversity of partnerships in Participatory Design projects, and approaches to intervention aimed at sustainable change. Hence, by the time we began developing the proposal for the ACTION for Health project, we were working with a broader notion of partnership than was characteristic of early Participatory Design projects (e.g. we recognised we needed to go beyond those on the shop floor to create sustainable change), and we had expanded our sense of how technology design projects were influenced by the broader contexts in which they occurred (which led us to pursue partnerships with managers and policy-making bodies as well).

Gärtner and Wagner (1996) suggested that system design could be viewed as a series of boundary crossings between different arenas in which system development occurs. They suggested that participation in system design occurs in a variety of different political arenas. In the arena of designing work and systems, new organisational forms are created; the task of redesigning work leads the agenda in this arena. In the second arena – that of organisational frameworks for action – unresolved conflicts and issues are addressed. This is the arena in which breakdowns or violations are addressed. In the third arena – that of the industrial relations context – legal and political frameworks define the relations between the different actors. Having been perplexed about how to participate in those arenas in which as an academic researcher one would normally lack influence, throughout the ACTION for Health project we sought to develop relationships with managers and decision-makers in an effort to influence change. Instead of waiting for decision-makers and those responsible for policy to come to us, we developed strategies for influencing change. These included developing policy briefs for decision-makers, and making presentations to senior members of government targeted towards their portfolios. At the local level, we made presentations to hospital committees, and often took on small projects tangential to our research foci as a strategy for building relationships.[5]

Much of the early writing about Participatory Design focused on how change occurred at one level (e.g. how new technologies contributed to changes in work practice). However, it often failed to then situate work practice changes within broader social and political contexts (e.g. within broad policy contexts, such as a push for public sector accountability combined with an emphasis on evidence-based medicine). However, it was precisely these kinds of changes which had fuelled development of electronic health records in Canada. And, when introduced, these changes – undertaken in the service of broader agendas such as evidence-based medicine – led to work practice changes. In 1999 I argued that little was known about the complex network of relationships that links workers' experiences of new health information and communication technologies (*the micro-level*) to the organisational and institutional contexts into which these technologies were introduced (*the meso-level*) and to the structure of the health information technology industry and its relation to government policies (*the macro-level*). I suggested that while several bodies of theory were useful in understanding these complex sets of interrelationships,[6] no single theoretical perspective on its own would be adequate in explaining the complexities of health technologies in workplaces (Balka 1999). My desire to overcome these earlier limitations in Participatory Design projects played a significant role in development of approaches to intervention in ACTION for Health.

Prior to the ACTION for Health project, I obtained funding to address shortcomings of single perspectives through case studies of new health information technologies, where each case study incorporated multiple theoretical perspectives (see Balka 2003 and Balka and Kahnamoui 2004 for results). While recognising that each of the theoretical approaches upon which I drew rested on a different conceptualisation of power and human agency related to technology – and some would argue that each of these theories compete with the others – I embarked on the work with the view that each of these theoretical perspectives is partial and incomplete, and that integration of micro and macro theories could strengthen our theoretical and practical comprehension of complex phenomena (Knorr-Cetina and Cicourel 1981; Turner 1991).

It can be argued that power in relation to technology is exercised neither by individuals operating outside of larger social institutions nor by social institutions, without the enrolment of individuals. In order to understand the complexities of how power is exercised in relation to technology, an approach that allows one to account for competing and partial views of technology is required. I argued that such an approach aimed to overcome the limitations inherent to any single perspective of technology by exploring the merits of what are often thought of as competing views of technology. From a theoretical standpoint, this project which preceded ACTION for Health had as its goal the development of an integrated conceptualisation of power in relation to technology. The goal from an action perspective was to improve the working conditions of health sector staff. I attempted to pursue this goal through engagement with varied stakeholders in the health sector. I built relationships with two health care unions, and began carrying out ethnographic work concerned with documenting how work was changing for nurses and clerks as electronic patient record systems were being introduced in hospitals.

Although observation of work was compelling and work practice problems were evident, our work remained quite peripheral. Our project was research driven, rather than driven by demands within the health sector or expressed through the unions, and, as such, our scope of influence was limited. I realised that projects that had their genesis in questions that I raised as an academic were not inherently interesting to health sector staff (or unions), even if addressing those questions unearthed insights of interest to particular constituencies. Answers to questions no one is asking are not likely to influence change. Our team was able to document issues that occurred within the arena of what Gärtner and Wagner (1996) called 'designing work and systems', (here used to refer to the selection and customisation of system), but we could not claim many successes in crossing boundaries into organisational frameworks for action.

Working with health sector management

A series of coincidences intensified my contact with health sector management. Amid concern that working with management might lead to pressures to compromise my change-oriented agenda, I decided to pursue a set of opportunities that lay before me as long as I could do so without compromise. A research position opened at a hospital where I had been conducting fieldwork, and, after considerable thought I accepted it and became a member of the professional practice team, a management group responsible for practice issues for all nursing and allied health groups.[7] Although offered a full-time position at the hospital, in light of recent cutbacks in the health sector I opted instead for a secondment from my university position, which offered me the continued job security of tenure.

As a member of the professional practice team I provided research guidance to other members of the professional practice team, assisted in practice issues that arose, and provided research support to members of the broader nursing and allied health communities. The ongoing research work I undertook was funded with grant funds I secured from federal funding agencies, which required that publication and other forms of dissemination of research results could not be subject to embargo or censorship.

By the time I began working in the health sector, few custom software builds were taking place.[8] In the acute care sector, systems are typically large-scale systems that often must be implemented on a large and varied base of legacy computer systems, each with their own problems and limitations. In practical terms this means that while a product a hospital purchases may not be a custom-built product, the process of getting the purchased system to work across multiple sites and multiple computing platforms in many senses resembles a custom design. Indeed, configuration is increasingly emerging as a site for participatory intervention (Balka, Wagner and Jensen' 2005; Balka and Wagner 2006), and if we take seriously the notion that the design of technology is only fully completed when in use (Suchman and Jordan 1988), processes surrounding implementation of technologies offer a site for intervention (Balka et al. 2008). Indeed, our work has shown intervention at the point of configuration and implementation can give voice to marginalised populations (Balka and Kahnamoui 2004; Balka et al. 2007; Balka, Wagner and Jensen 2005; Jensen 2007a).

Action for Health

The Tower Move project: supporting operational needs while collecting data

Once seconded into a position within a hospital setting, I began working more closely with health sector practitioners and decision-makers (see Balka 2006 for a more detailed account), which created numerous interesting – and at times challenging – opportunities for members of the ACTION for Health research team, as we struggled with the role of an action researcher/ participatory designer[9] who is engaged in activities intended to influence change at the operations level (see, for example, Jensen 2007a, 2007b; Bjørn and Boulus forthcoming; Bjørn and Balka 2009). In one of our projects, the Tower Move project (Balka and Kahnamoui 2004), work practice issues we addressed came to our attention through ethnographic field study of new technology use during and after 1,500 staff moved into a newly opened building (called the Tower) at a local hospital. Although the initial intention of our research was to study the automatic drug dispensing system (ADS), the nurse call system and the ceiling lifts used for patient handling (all technologies which we did eventually study – see Balka and Kahnamoui 2004; Balka et al. 2007; Balka, Mason and Elfring 2005; Balka, Wagner and Jensen 2005; Balka and Wagner 2006), during the course of our observations we realised that we had underestimated the problems that would arise with the implementation of less complex technologies, such as keyboard trays (Balka and Kahnamoui 2004). Consequently, we revised the scope of our enquiry in order to address problems arising with these technologies, while continuing to investigate the automated drug dispensing system.

Our focus was on identifying work practice problems staff experienced in relation to technology. The underlying logic in this approach is that new technologies engender new work procedures and as a result alter existing workflows, both those directly related to the technology and those that are seemingly irrelevant to the technology. Shortly before the move we argued that we could improve technology implementation processes through identification of problems that would arise with the introduction of new technologies in a new work environment. Situated in the research environment as a member of a team responsible for professional and work practice issues and as an independently funded researcher, I argued that the provision of research support to front-line staff and management about socio-technical challenges that arose during the move into the Tower would contribute to the identification and resolution of issues and would help with the changed workflows.

Project background

During late May and early June 2003, the first phase of the Tower Move project (which relocated most hospital units at our study site into a new building called the Tower) was completed. Planning for the Tower had begun several years earlier; construction of the building began in 1988. The first two floors of the Tower were occupied in 1996; however, monetary constraints put the remainder of the project on hold. Construction resumed in 1999 after the hospital was able to secure sufficient private and public funding. In May of 2003, the Tower was ready to house 459 patients.

During the building planning phase and much of the construction phase, the Facilities Planning and Construction Department was responsible for the new Tower. This allocation of responsibility was based on the seemingly natural fit between the jurisdiction of the Facilities Planning and Construction Department and the activities expected of contractors working on the Tower. However, during this time other departments initiated their own projects related to the Tower. For example the Capital Acquisition Department started purchasing equipment for the Tower, while the Information Management team began specifying communication technology requirements. Six months prior to the scheduled move date it became clear that an organisational body was required to coordinate these highly interrelated activities, and that moving patients had to involve the operational units. Two directors were assigned to co-lead the Tower Move project. It is worth noting that other facilities report spending up to two years in the planning phase of a move of this magnitude.

According to the Hospital's Tower Move project charter, the objective of the Tower Move project was to integrate the various independent departmental projects related to the move and 'to ensure the timely, efficient, and successful move of identified clinical areas into the Tower at the VGH site with minimal disruption in the care and workflow, while ensuring patient and staff safety' (Omnicell 2002). What set the move into the Tower apart from other moves within the facility was that the Tower was equipped with the latest technology, ranging from technology as complex as the automatic drug dispensing systems to less complex technology such as new chairs and computer keyboard trays. One of the assumptions of the Tower Move project team was that all the required equipment and information systems would be purchased, installed and properly functional prior to move dates and that construction would be completed in advance of the scheduled move dates.

Reflecting varied experiences in technology design and implementation, our project (the Technology Trouble project) was based on tenets of socio-technical research. Socio-technical research takes as its starting point the notion that 'plans differ from situated actions' and that the design of technology is not fully completed until it is in use (Suchman and Jordan 1988). Thus, the Technology Trouble research team had as one of its goals the documentation of situations where plans differed from situated actions in a manner that interrupted work practice. Articulation work[10] and work-arounds often fill the gap between plans and situated actions (Balka 1997). As such we saw the identification of articulation work and work-arounds as an important source of information about work-practice and workflow problems. The insights gained through our examination of such practices played an important role in bringing the problems staff faced to management's attention. Working with the directors responsible for the move (see below), the Technology Trouble team identified problems experienced by staff, and took those issues to the directors responsible for resolution of those problems.

Methodology

Although Participatory Design projects have typically focused on end-user involvement in technology design, as fewer companies have engaged in custom-built software, increasingly advocates of Participatory Design have turned their attention to end-user participation in system selection (Robertson 1996) and system implementation. The Technology Trouble project described here (and indeed most other projects undertaken within the ATIC Lab) was undertaken within such an action-research framework. Designed to bridge the gap between theory, research and practice (Holter and Schwartz-Barcott 1993), action research is a way of generating research about a social system while trying to change it (Hart and Bond 1995). Hart and Bond suggest that action research is particularly well suited to research that has as its goals problem-solving and improvement. In action research, researchers are experts in research methods, while practitioners are experts in the object of study (Korpela et al. 2002) – in this case, work practices on their units.

The extent to which users made constructive proposals for solutions or new designs varied from project to project within ACTION for Health projects. For example, in the Tower Move project, researchers documented issues staff identified with technology (which in the context of that project mostly related to implementation), and facilitated a process where issues were communicated to management, action plans were devised and planned actions were communicated back to staff. The point at which we became involved with that project meant that our interventions might be classified as action research (they created action), but not as Participatory Design. In contrast, in our electronic triage project (Balka and Whitehouse 2007; Balka 2010; Bjørn and Rødje 2008), our team's interventions went well beyond implementation into design of workflow and significant customisation of software. Pernille Bjørn, our lead researcher on that project, worked closely with emergency department staff and the information technology consultants to bring the ideas staff generated to fruition. Having engaged much more significantly in altering the design of the software, this project might more appropriately be termed a Participatory Design project.

Baskerville and Wood-Harper (1996) suggest that there are at least four factors which distinguish action research from consulting: more rigorous documentation; theoretical justification (rather than empirical justification); time and budgetary constraints (researchers have more time and often less money); and the nature of the process (consulting is linear and action research is cyclical). Wood-Harper et al. (1996) also raise the issue of whose perspective will dominate system development processes, and whose ethical perspective (workers or management or system designers?) will dominate system development activities.

The Technology Trouble project followed a model of action research termed the professionalising approach. 'The main aim is the improvement of professional practice at the level of organisational and cultural change, rather than in terms of a challenge to existing power relationships, or the involvement of users' (Hart and Bond 1995, p. 45). The overall research question was not generated at a grass-roots level with the input of research participants. In contrast, our research question originated as part of a pre-existing research project that had as its goal the investigation of work practice issues arising with new implementations of technology in the health sector. Once Technology Trouble team members were in the field observing and interviewing, issues identified by unit staff became the focal point of our work practice investigations. This was also true for our electronic triage project and many of our other projects, in which our concerns as researchers occurred in parallel with our participatory and action agenda, which was determined by our partners. Simply put, our partners identified issues about which they wanted insights or problems they wanted solved, and we crafted our research agenda around those issues and problems.

With the Tower Move project, the availability of research funds from the grant combined with my role at the hospital as a member of the professional practice leadership team had an impact on the design of the research project. These circumstances made it possible for the Technology Trouble team to approach the directors responsible for the move and volunteer to provide support to both the directors and staff concerning technology issues during the move, while at the same time meeting our own research needs. Although this strategy is controversial (some of these controversies are addressed in greater detail below), with this project and other projects undertaken by our group we have made a conscious effort to engage in activities that in some way support our research partners, or help them to meet a need which they articulate.

Recognising the limitations of having had only limited end-user involvement in system selection processes, the Technology Trouble project focused on the moment of use as advocated by Suchman and Jordan (1988). We conducted extensive observation and informal interviews during and after the move, which focused on documenting end-users' difficulties during system implementation processes. The research team members acted as mediators between the social and implementation team, along the lines advocated by Westrup (Wise et al. 1996). An ethnographic approach was undertaken as it often provides 'a much better means of anticipating the dynamic effects on work organization' (Randall et al. 1991, p. 21). The Technology Trouble team focused on documenting end-users' difficulties during system implementation processes, communicating documented problems to the directors responsible, facilitating resolution of problems identified, and communicating results (including the dismissal of some problems and the progress of other problems) to front-line staff.

By roaming between different units during the move our staff were able to share the knowledge we had gained in one unit with staff in other units, thereby building on the existing knowledge base and helping staff to resolve problems. The extent to which we participated in solving problems on the spot depended upon the cultural norms of each unit and the personality of individual unit staff members. For example, at the Palliative Care Unit, which is mostly made up of volunteers, the unit clerk eagerly solicited our support and participation in the set-up of the nursing station during the move, while in the Neonatal Intensive Care Unit we took on a more passive role.

Novel approaches to data collection

Various data collection methods were employed in the Tower Move project as well as other ACTION for Health projects. Observations and interviews were undertaken on all units that moved to the Tower, and these formed the basis of our understanding of micro (work practice) issues, and often provided insight into macro (or organisational) issues. During the two-week move period, considering all the activities that were taking place (and the high stress level of staff who were struggling to acquaint themselves with the new wards and the location of supplies, and to learn how to use the many new and different technologies while continuing to provide patient care), we conducted passive observations on the units that had just moved in order to prevent additional disruption. Following the move, we continued our observations. However, at this point we attempted more contact with staff and conducted informal interviews while they carried on with their work. In addition, we were also able to solicit feedback from staff as part of the daily scheduled support rounds initiated by the Professional Practice Leadership Team at the hospital. As staff settled into their new locations, our observations tapered off.

Members of the research team spent time engaged in staff rounds (typically two hours or more at a time), interviewing staff (e.g. unit clerks about keyboard trays) and conducting observations about specific technologies (such as the keyboard trays). Team members also logged 45 hours of note-taking time in the field. During this time Technology Trouble team members had contact with 411 people (which included multiple contacts with a single person).

We needed to communicate our interest in hearing about the difficulties staff were experiencing in relation to technology during the move, in a manner that made it easy for staff to identify Technology Trouble team members, and to facilitate the collection of information from staff. The four researchers who collected data wore highly visible T-shirts with a 'Technology Trouble? Talk to Us!' logo imprinted on both the front and the back of the shirt (see Figure 11.1).

techtalk@vanhosp.bc.ca

Figure 11.1 Technology Trouble logo

Although we also put other means of data collection in place (e.g. fax back sheets at nursing stations, a project e-mail address and phone number), our presence on the units with our visible T-shirts was the most effective means of data collection. These alternative means of communication were not the preferred method for reporting issues. During the research process, we received only three faxes from staff, and we received neither e-mails nor phone calls. Based on these figures, clearly face-to-face communication was the most fruitful method for micro-level data collection.

Our visibility encouraged staff facing problems to approach Technology Trouble team members for assistance. In consultation with the directors responsible for the move, it was decided that the researchers would share their skills and knowledge and provide staff with additional information about issues they were familiar with. When researchers lacked sufficient information and knowledge about a matter, they would encourage staff members to report the problem, and would supply information about the person and/or department who should receive a trouble report, if known. In addition, the researchers would record all problems observed in both their field notes and an issue log spreadsheet (discussed in greater depth below). Handwritten field notes were transcribed and subject to coding and analysis with the aid of Nvivo (qualitative data analysis software). Initial coding categories reflected the theoretical bodies of literature which informed the study (e.g. actor network theory, political economy), and were developed as part of a larger grant that explored several health technology implementations in different settings. Subsequent coding categories emerged through examination of the data collected through the Technology Trouble project.

Other data, particularly about the meso- or organisational level, were collected during meetings with various stakeholders, such as the Tower Move project team (which included representatives from numerous departments, such as operations, maintenance, facilities, information technology and pharmacy) and during the Project Support team meetings (which included the directors responsible for the move and the coordinator for the Tower Move project). During these meetings the Technology Trouble team brought an updated issues log spreadsheet for discussion. As resolutions to issues captured on the log sheet were identified, the resolutions were noted in the issues log spreadsheet (see next section). We also gathered data from e-mail communications with various people responsible for different aspects of the project. Meso-level data collection also occurred during our observations. We followed up on problems that had been raised and solution-oriented management interventions that took place.

Intervention communication strategy

Based on our initial proposal to the Tower Move project directors, we planned to provide a weekly summary report to the Technology Trouble project sponsors (the directors responsible for the move, and representatives from IT, pharmacy and occupational health). We planned to share any new problems that surfaced during data collection, and our proposed solutions. However, during the first few days of the move we realised that no centralised and structured process had been developed for collecting feedback from staff and dealing with issues directly related to the move and the new environment. The existing support structures (such as the computer help desk) were available for the duration of the move, as were the regular procedures for requesting maintenance. During the duration of the move (which occurred over two weeks) representatives from the various vendors were available on site during regular office hours and via pager during evenings, nights and weekends. A seven-page document that listed contact numbers for reporting various types of problems was also distributed to staff. However, no centralised problem resolution structure was put in place specifically for the move, and it quickly became clear both that staff lacked the time to determine to whom to direct a trouble report, and that in many cases the problems staff experienced were multi-jurisdictional, which resulted in confusion about which department should receive a trouble report. The pace of work deterred staff from clarifying such ambiguities.

To support our research and expedite the creation of our weekly summary reports we created a spreadsheet containing all the issues that we identified during data collection. The spreadsheet contained the following fields: Unique Identifier, Date Logged, Unit, Floor/Pod, Problem/Question/Issue, Possible Resolution(s), Type of Problem, Type of Technology, Status, Source of Information, Person or Group Responsible, Due Date, User Name (if available), Date Issue Communicated to Staff, Communication Vehicle, Communication Message, and Comments.

The database was then introduced to the Project Support team, and after slight modifications they assumed ownership of the database. Researchers logged issues in the database that they were informed about or observed during their data collection, and would also e-mail the database owner and inform her of the new issues. The issues were then discussed during weekly Project Support team meetings, and assigned to the appropriate people. Issues were closed upon resolution or when after further discussion it was determined the issue was either a future consideration, out of the jurisdiction of the Tower Move project team or not an issue.

While our research team provided staff feedback to management via the issues database on a daily basis, the turnaround time in resolving issues was not fast as staff would have liked. Staff at various points indicated that they felt the feedback they had provided had gone unheard and nothing had been done about the issues they had raised. For example, one staff member commented 'the first few days after the move there were people who got our feedback, but they didn't do anything about it'.

One of the key challenges that we faced in conducting a communication intervention was in upholding our ethical responsibility to staff to maintain their anonymity while at the same time ensuring that their issues were addressed. Throughout the process we had to ensure that in reporting staff issues to management we were not betraying staff trust in us. For example, during the first days after the move we were told by a staff member that the manager of their unit had provided them with access to certain narcotics from the medicine carts. This workaround was employed by the unit manager in order to reduce staff frustration that occurred as staff waited in line to use the ADS to obtain narcotics for patients who were in pain. When the Technology Trouble team communicated this intervention strategy as a short-term solution that could be employed by other units until staff felt more comfortable and at ease with the technology, the directors initially wanted to know which unit had developed this workaround so that it could be ended. We frequently commented that such strategies, though not best practice, allowed the staff to continue to deliver high-quality care under stressful circumstances, and that such practices should be allowed until greater stability was achieved on the units.

During the Tower Move project, we played a key role in identifying a myriad of problems that staff were facing in their day-to-day activities and raised those issues with management, who were responsible for finding resolutions to problems or deeming them unworthy of attention. Among our successes was the identification of defective equipment, which we were subsequently able to have removed, replaced and reinstalled. We were able to identify issues that would have remained unnoticed had we not been present on site conducting observations. Finally, in listening to staff voice their concerns, we were able to alleviate some frustration that staff were experiencing as they negotiated use of numerous new technologies.

Situating ourselves in the way that we did allowed us to learn about the complexity of technological problem-solving in a complex health organisation, and particularly the significance of meso-level support in the resolution of work practice issues that occur at the micro-level. From a research perspective, we gained considerable insight about the complexities of managing technology in a large health care organisation. After the Technology Trouble project had ended, I shared the technology trouble log we developed for tracking technology problems with others in the hospital. The spreadsheet has since been adapted for use to support project management elsewhere in the organisation.

Several factors contributed to the success of this project. As researchers, we were able to find a fit between our needs to collect data and the hospital's more action-oriented needs associated with the move. We acted primarily as intermediaries (or ombudsmen) between staff and management, able to preserve anonymity of the staff raising issues, and to encourage faster turnaround in addressing technology problems. Had we not been able to 'sell' our services in a manner that supported an operational need and at the same time did not interfere with operations, we probably would not have been successful in gaining access to the field site. These are valuable lessons for those interested in pursuing Participatory Design. As researchers, we had to define a role for ourselves within the operational activities of the move in order to gain access to the field site and build credibility for academic research within the practice-dominated worlds of the health sector. We used a similar strategy in other ACTION for Health projects, each time working to determine what role our research staff could fill or assume, which would on the one hand fill a real need for the health sector partner, and on the other hand, would meet data collection needs of research staff. Though at times an uncomfortable role for research staff (Jensen 2007a, 2007b; Boulus 2009, 2010; Boulus and Bjørn 2010), our willingness to take on practical work that contributed in concrete ways to our research partners' needs has been, and remains, a key ingredient of our success.

Mid-Main Clinic and the wireless call system: the perils of staffing changes

When we developed the proposal for the ACTION for Health project, each principal investigator brought in one or more community partners in the health sector. In Vancouver, one of our partners was a community clinic, which, at the time we applied for research funding, was in the early stages of planning for the introduction of an electronic medical record system (subsequent to ACTION for Health we held a second grant with that clinic, which has just ended; the clinic has been through a second major hardware and software upgrade and remains on the forefront of electronic record use in Canada). With our research funding in place, we developed research plans in conjunction with the clinic. With plans to introduce an electronic record system, and a clinic that has a strong commitment to patient empowerment, the clinic's executive director wanted to learn about patients' views of computerisation. Seeking to respond to research needs articulated by clinic staff, we interviewed clinic patients to learn about their views on computerisation, and sought their suggestions about how the electronic record system might be introduced. Research staff members developed an informational flyer that alerted patients to the impending change, and once the new system was in place we developed a feedback process that allowed patients to provide feedback about their experiences receiving care with the new computer system. Prior to implementation of the new computer system, responding to a request from the clinic, research staff conducted a literature review aimed at identifying best practices for electronic record implementation, and summarised results in practitioner's guidelines, designed to be accessible to non-academic audiences. Also at the request of the clinic, research staff interviewed patients in the waiting room concerning their views about the introduction of an electronic record system, and sought additional input about the implementation through a suggestions box. With the introduction of the electronic record system, while collecting data about issues and challenges associated with the new technology, one of our researchers assisted the clinic's electronic record group in tracking policy decisions made by clinic staff about electronic record use, and, based on decisions made during meetings, developed a protocol for guiding use of the electronic record system (see Boulus 2010).

After working with the clinic for in excess of a year, the executive director – with whom we had negotiated access to the clinic, and who served as our initial point of contact with medical and administrative staff – retired. Although the new executive director was sympathetic to our research interests, she was also in a demanding new job, and our access to her – and at times others in the clinic – was not initially as easy as it had been with the executive director with whom we initially developed the partnership. Over time, as the new executive director settled into her job, and as circumstances changed at the clinic, we were able to again gain unimpeded access to the clinic. Our experiences in this setting – where a staffing change interrupted the flow of research activities – was a common occurrence over the life of ACTION for Health. As researchers, we develop relationships with organisations through individuals. Organisations change (health sector organisations merge and are reorganised) and staff move on to other positions, all of which presents challenges to research partnerships and plans.

Working within an action research and Participatory Design tradition, it is essential to remain aware that staffing changes can delay or even derail researchers and designers from achieving their research and/or design goals. Staffing changes are far less likely to delay or altogether derail research and design project goals, however, if the goals of research and design activities are well aligned with the partnering organisation's goals, and fill a goal or solve a problem for the organisation. As the principal investigator of the ACTION for Health project, in the early stages of building relationships with our community partners I always tried to identify and define non-academic deliverables which would be an asset to our community partners, and which would allow members of our research team to engage in the pursuit of questions of academic interest. This often required team members to go outside their comfort zones and question their roles as researchers, as well as ponder the differences between research and consultancy and the relations of power which arise in researchers' and designers' interactions with community partners and technology users (Bjørn and Balka 2009; Jensen 2007a, 2007b; Boulus 2010; Bjørn and Boulus forthcoming).

In another case (a study of a wireless paging system), a manager we had worked with on the Technology Trouble project contacted us to conduct an evaluation of the introduction of a wireless call system, which was undertaken as a pilot project. Just as we completed the evaluation (the 'non-academic' deliverable we had agreed with the manager and wireless call system implementation team to produce), the manager who had been responsible for the pilot project and had sought our assistance in conducting the evaluation moved to another province. Although we delivered the evaluation to the manager, as she had requested, protocol dictated that she then share it with others involved with the project. In the chaos of the manager's transition to a new job, we were never sure to what extent the report had been shared with others involved with the pilot implementation. Nearly two years after the pilot implementation of the wireless call system had occurred, I received a request for a copy of the evaluation from a manager elsewhere in the organisation who was considering more widespread implementation of the wireless call system. Organisational memory was such that our research results were eventually utilised within the organisation.

Our ability to have impact through our research results in these two projects depended upon relationships with individuals and was threatened by job changes. In the case of the community clinic, we were able to re-establish our research relationship as circumstances at the clinic changed such that the clinic had a renewed need for our contributions. In the case of the wireless paging system, organisational memory kept the results of our research alive, long after the relationships that had supported the project had been altered. In another project (the electronic triage project, discussed below), a key staff member with whom we had set up a project left her position before our research was carried out. We were able to continue the initially planned research (see Balka and Whitehouse 2007 and Bjørn and Rødje 2008) which explored issues and challenges associated with the introduction of an electronic triage system in an emergency department); however, once that project was over, we had to overcome some resistance to an ongoing partnership from the new unit manager. We were able to do this by identifying research questions of interest to the unit (only of marginal interest to us) which we addressed precisely because doing something of interest to the new manager helped us build a relationship and credibility with the new manager. We were able to negotiate the complexities of what could easily have been a dead-end partnership when our initial contact left the organisation, and to transform a difficult situation into an award-winning project (see Bjørn et al. 2009). All of these cases illustrate the extent to which successful research partnerships are built on individual, personal relationships.

The perils of being frank, the need for colleagues, and simplifying complexities

After about a year and a half of working at the hospital, I learned a hard lesson. My direct boss (who had hired me) had been fired – a not uncommon event (the average tenure in a health sector management position in Canada at present is about three years). I was asked to speak about technology in health care at a conference about the future of health care, which was widely attended by senior managers. I prepared what in academic terms was an extraordinarily benign presentation, the kernel of which was that the future of technology in health care will depend upon investment in human capital (training, listening to staff concerns about technology, etc.) and developing an understanding of socio-technical aspects of systems. My presentation included a few slides from our fieldwork, including a photo of a staff member struggling with a keyboard tray, and a bag full of receipts that had been printed by an automatic drug dispensing machine, and which signalled an ambiguity in work practices.

About a month after my presentation, I went on holiday. Upon my return I learned that my acting boss had attempted to sever my relationship with the professional practice group during my absence. Eventually I left the professional practice group (under the watch of what became my third boss in 26 months). By the time this had occurred, however, I was well ensconced in the provider agency, and I was able to retain my position as a senior research scientist with my hospital-based centre even after my tenure on the professional practice team ended. Leaving the professional practice team meant I no longer held operational responsibilities at the hospital. I was able to continue to sit on a few strategic committees at the hospital, and I continued to work with senior managers on projects.

I learned several lessons from my ill-fated presentation. First, I learned that sometimes the right message can be presented the wrong way, or at the wrong time. A senior manager in the room heard my presentation as a condemnation of events that had occurred on his watch. Although ultimately I have come to conclude that he and I have considerable common ground, whatever I thought about the content of my presentation the fact remains that it threatened his interests. Second, I learned the value of allies. I have been able to repair the relationship I damaged over time through a 'loss leader'[11] and help from a colleague. Third, I have learned that size matters – I am certain that I was able to retain my position as a research scientist because I held a particularly large research grant and the health care agency stood by its commitment to honour its partnership with the state in support of that research.[12] I went on to work closely with one of my colleagues who played a pivotal role in repairing my relationship with the senior manager I offended. Working from two different positions within the organisation – my colleague as a director reporting to a vice-president – we have been working to develop sustainable structures that will institutionalise technology assessment activities and technology implementation research as a normal part of operating procedures within the health authority.

Finally, I learned about the value of tenure. Because I had remained seconded to the health provider agency and retained my position at the university, I was able to speak my mind without threat of job loss. Until I began to experience the fallout from my epic presentation to senior managers, tenure had only an intellectual meaning to me. I now see tenure as an extraordinary privilege that should be exercised in the public interest. The existence of tenure may ultimately protect academically based researchers from job loss in the face of research results that some may find unfavourable, but tenure does little to ensure that research results have impact.

Since the conclusion of the ACTION for Health project, as our group has continued to conduct ethnographic research in support of health information technology design, I have gone on to learn additional lessons about how to present design research findings to practitioner communities, so that they gain more traction and have more impact. As a social scientist, I have been trained to identify issues, problems and challenges, and to see and explain the hidden complexities of systems to others. While academic audiences may celebrate and revel in complexity, it can be overwhelming to health sector decision-makers and practitioners charged with integrating academic insights into practice environments. Simply put, outlining the complexity of contexts into which contemporary computer-based record systems are introduced can be overwhelming to practitioners, who typically live in a world where reflection takes a back seat to action. Practitioners and decision-makers need to know what to do or how to act on a problem, and do not need as much information about how complex the problem is and why it will be difficult to solve (which is often what academics are inclined to provide).

As an action researcher, I need to find ways to support the practitioner communities I work within in taking action. Increasingly I have come to believe that an important part of my role on a Participatory Design team revolves around finding simplified ways of communicating about the complexities of participants' work practices to diverse stakeholder groups. Technology users need to know that the complexities of their work are understood and will be supported with emergent designs, while technology producers need to be able to imagine product concepts that can be realised. Health sector decision-makers and practitioners need to know that proposed solutions will meet their needs. Supporting Participatory Design of information technology in the health sector requires an ability to grasp complex systems on the one hand, and the ability to break down that complexity into actionable steps on the other hand.

Finding researchable problems in unexpected places

The role of serendipity should never be underestimated in research. Upon being introduced to a friend of a friend outside of work contexts, a very brief conversation led to a research project about an electronic triage system that had interrupted work practice to such an extent that it was eventually withdrawn from use. The person I was introduced to had inherited the implementation of an electronic triage system which staff found difficult to use, and upon hearing of this predicament I volunteered to conduct research in an effort to improve the implementation and smooth work practices. By the time our ethics clearance was in place to begin collecting data, the problematic system had been removed. Our emphasis switched to documenting the underlying reasons for difficult implementation, as plans were underway to build a new system in-house.

During the early stages of the work we were able to give voice to concerns raised by nursing staff, and although negotiation of the research relationship was challenging at times (the person who had been our contact left her job, which required that we rebuild relationships with new people), our involvement with the project contributed to a decision to halt development of a home-based solution until the functions the software was to fill were better articulated. It looked for a short time as though there would be no need (from the organisation's standpoint) for our research. When circumstances changed at the hospital (the possibility of new funding for acquisition of a new electronic triage system came into view), our presence on the unit collecting ethnographic data about work practices became more desirable to the unit's management, who had figured out that our ethnographic work could be helpful to the unit in determining what a new system to support their staff members' needs could look like. The e-triage project began because a manager on the unit articulated a problem that I felt our research could help solve, and we were able to follow up with a project. When that manager left the hospital, we were able to continue the project because the new manager and staff identified a problem (the possible purchase and implementation of a new system) to which they felt we could contribute. We were able to move from a situation which seemed to be full of endings (the initial system we had planned to work on was removed; the initial manager with whom we had built our relationship left) to an award-winning collaboration which emerged in relation to the new system (Bjørn et al. 2009). From this project we have learned that research partnerships can start in unexpected places, and that receptivity of researchers in a setting has ebbs and flows that often occur in relation to external factors. Part of the success of ACTION for Health reflected our team's ability to be open to identifying and responding to researchable issues and problems in unexpected places.

Integration into senior decision-making and policy environments

With the e-triage project, our research activities expanded to a second hospital. Shortly after we began work on the e-triage project, I learned of another potential project at that hospital. Over the next few months, discussions progressed with a director of the hospital about the new project. The director gained the support of a vice-president, effectively locating the project – which ran in three units but had implications across the hospital – in a position where it was poised to have influence. The project responded to a need the hospital had to address duplicate medical charts, which had been identified by a hospital accreditation board during a previous hospital accreditation study as problematic. While our research was still ongoing, we prepared a briefing note about the project and our early results for the vice-president. The briefing note was used during the subsequent accreditation process, and the hospital administrator received accolades from the accreditation board for its research efforts related to duplicate medical charts. From our experiences with the second hospital I have learned that one enthusiastic and well-respected person on the inside of an organisation can have a huge impact on the research climate and, in particular, the uptake of research results. When working with others goes well, doors can open and the relationships with decision-makers can fall into place. This also holds true in the policy arena.

As Kyng (2010, p. 59) has pointed out,

> we are not very good at presenting and discussing the different types of projects we do. Thus we don't learn as much as we could about how to increase the chances of success outside our home ground, the 'research only' arena.

Ellen Balka

Engagement with stakeholder audiences outside what Kyng has called 'the research only arena', including policy communities, was an explicit part of the ACTION for Health research programme. Throughout the ACTION for Health programme varied activities were undertaken to disseminate information to practitioner audiences (e.g. written evaluation reports, practitioners' guidelines, briefing notes, etc.) and policy-makers (e.g. policy briefs, presentation at policy rounds and policy roundtables), both provincially and federally. Contact with decision-makers has occurred largely through contact which has evolved over time. At the same time that the ACTION for Health project was underway, our group also held funding from Health Canada (a federal ministry responsible for health) to conduct a study about the governance of health technology and patient safety. Five other research teams were funded through the same request for proposals, and at the conclusion of the projects Health Canada brought the teams to Ottawa to present results at an all-day policy roundtable, attended by senior decision-makers from several departments of the federal government. This effectively expanded the scope of my policy contacts. A well-executed presentation at the policy roundtable effectively opened doors in other contexts, and created opportunities for our research team to have an impact in what Gärtner and Wagner (1996) identified as the industrial relations context, which is the domain in which legal and political frameworks define the relations between the different actors.

Partnerships, intellectual property and intellectual autonomy

One of our partners in ACTION for Health was the Ministry of Health. Some members of the ACTION for Health team held a contract with the Ministry of Health to evaluate some tele-health and health promotion services offered by the Ministry. As part of that contract we were required to seek academic funding related to the evaluation contract, and ACTION for Health funding met that requirement. With respect to the evaluation contract, the Ministry of Health determined the questions that our evaluation team was required to address. In contrast, projects undertaken with ACTION for Health funding were researcher driven, although such questions were normally developed in close consultation with research partners. Our research conducted as part of our evaluation contract with the Ministry of Health suggested that use of the provincially sponsored health information website was considerably lower than the proportion of online health information seekers in the province, and considerably lower than the Ministry of Health had hoped. We decided to pursue the underlying reasons for the low use of the BC HealthGuide website with ACTION for Health funding. However, we had a few research costs that we were unable to cover through the ACTION for Health funding envelope, and we sought – and received – a very small sum of money from the Ministry to cover these costs. This raised issues about intellectual property and intellectual autonomy.

Although we were to receive only $2,500 from the Ministry, the Ministry initially sought the right to veto publication of our results, as is common with contractually funded work. We explained to them that a condition of use of academic funds was the requirement that we publish results, and that no restrictions be placed on publication of research findings. Ironically, the entire project that was carried out in this instance required no permission from the Ministry to conduct the work (e.g. no access to data or Ministry of Health staff was required), and the website we were conducting research about existed in the public domain (hence no permissions were required in order to access it). Had we not sought the $2,500 from the Ministry, we would have had no obligation whatsoever to even share our results with them, as the project in no way required or rested on permissions from them. Through a series of at times painful negotiations we were eventually able to negotiate an arrangement with the Ministry (we had to give them 30 days to review materials prior to publication, but they could not veto publication)

274

that allowed us to meet the norms of academic publication. Through this project, we learned about the complexities of intellectual property and freedom of expression when working with partners in the health sector (and other) settings. Issues about who has the right to publish from data, and what role community partners have in terms of potential veto of results can be challenging issues that – at least in Canada – are not always anticipated by either funding bodies or partners. We have dealt with similar issues in another context by developing an intellectual property policy, which delineates who is considered a part of the research team, whose names should go on publications under which circumstances, and who has the right to publish results from work undertaken jointly by academic researchers and community partners.

Within the Participatory Design community, work has been undertaken by those in industrial settings as well as those in academic settings. As funding norms have changed in recent years and greater emphasis has been placed in many parts of the world on university–industry and university–government partnerships, increasingly issues related to intellectual property have emerged in Participatory Design projects (Kyng 2010). Intellectual property issues have received little attention in literature concerned with Participatory Design to date, but as our experiences with the Ministry of Health during ACTION for Health have shown and as Kyng has recently argued, as funding models change and place greater emphasis on industry partnerships, the importance of addressing issues related to intellectual property is gaining importance.

Discussion

Engaging in a university–health sector partnerships is likely to be both challenging and confusing. Through ACTION for Health, many well-known insights about collaborative work (for example, that working with partnering organisations from the start in defining problems is an essential ingredient for success) were reinforced. We also gained insights we hope will be valuable for future researchers working within the Participatory Design tradition. Our commitment to making sure we did something practical for our partners – even if it was off the side of our desks (and even if not required by a research funder) – in order to create buy-in was central to the success of ACTION for Health. Our ability to be flexible allowed us to successfully navigate through staffing changes and other organisational challenges related to our partnering organisations. Our work with ACTION for Health also highlighted the importance of several aspects of communication: that timing and context of delivering messages are important, that tailoring project communications to specific audiences is critical when it comes to moving projects forward, and that maintaining an awareness of organisational needs when developing communication strategies can enhance the uptake of project information. An awareness of policy contexts and the broader environments in which Participatory Design initiatives are taking place can be essential to growing a project beyond a single workplace. Maintaining flexibility is essential, as it allows Participatory Design practitioners to navigate the ups and downs of staffing changes and to take advantage of unforeseen circumstances in setting up and moving projects forward.

When undertaking Participatory Design projects which focus on technological change in the health sector, it may prove instructive to reflect on some of the distinctions made by Baskerville and Wood-Harper (1996) and Wood-Harper et al. (1996). Along with Beck's (2002) metric (is participation used as a means through which to improve design, in the absence of a focus on understanding the manifold ways through which computerisation can contribute to dominance patterns?) we can perhaps increase our clarity about just what it is we are trying to do. Integration with management – which definitely brings challenges including intellectual property issues and other issues related to who has the right to communicate about which aspects of circumstances in which situations – was an essential ingredient in the success of many of the ACTION for Health initiatives. The approach we have taken – similar to what Shapiro (2005) has referred to as a reformist Participatory Design agenda – has the potential to succeed, but also can tempt us to lose sight of those attributes (such as an action orientation undertaken in support of marginal workers, questions of ethics and values and democracy) which brought many of us to Participatory Design in the first place. Yet an awareness of these issues as we engage in university–health sector partnerships can strengthen those partnerships.

Clearly, university–community research partnerships present numerous challenges. In addition to propelling researchers into the unknown and often uncomfortable dynamics of stakeholder politics within organisations, where work on projects can leave staff feeling as if they are walking a thin line between end-user participation in design and consultancy in academic or research-oriented projects, intellectual property issues can arise alongside debates about who is entitled to publish (and profit from) what. However, amid the challenges, messiness and discomfort that can sometimes accompany researcher engagement in Participatory Design projects, there may also be opportunities to reinstate ideas about undertaking work that is in the public interest (e.g. publicly funded research results should not be subject to embargo). As companies increasingly seek university partnerships in order to offset the costs of research, corporate and academic researchers may be able to develop new strategies that support old ideals about 'the public intellectual' whose primary goal is to represent broad public interests.

When I began working as an academic researcher in partnership with various organisations in the health sector, I seldom spoke about the challenges, contradictions and trials I encountered. Shapiro's (2005) and Beck's (2002) insights that participation in the ways we conceived of Participatory Design some years ago may not be the best ways to practise political system design now, but are helpful starting points. They offer us some language that can help us speak about new strategies as we wrestle with the limitations of what those of us in the Participatory Design community have come to think of as our practice. This signals a maturity to me: we have developed enough of a sense of security in what we are doing that we can take a more critical or self-reflective stance towards our once sacred practices.

From the odd space I inhabited as the leader of the ACTION for Health team – with the protection of tenure and external grant funding, the insider status accorded non-union staff in a major public sector agency, and support from those with whom I have worked in labour and feminist endeavours over the years – the complex partnerships described above seem more desirable than not. I am able to look back at specific projects and identify specific changes that followed from our team's endeavours, and at the same time I am able to look at our academic output, and identify contributions we have made in academic terms. I suspect, though, that over time, such partnerships will require new organisational forms, new policies within universities and among funders, as well as new forms of partnerships.

Acknowledgements

This work reported here was supported through a Social Sciences and Research Council of Canada Collaborative Research Initiative Grant titled 'The role of technology in the production, consumption and use of health information: Implications for policy and practice' (ACTION for Health – grant # 512–2003–1017). I am grateful to several colleagues including Joan Greenbaum, Ina Wagner, Karen Messing, Janet Joy, Linda Peritz and Sandy Whitehouse with whom I have spoken candidly in recent years as I have struggled to make sense of the work undertaken by the ATIC Design Lab in general and through the ACTION for Health project in particular.

Notes

1 More information about ACTION for Health (including a full list of team members, projects, publications and other project documents) can be found on the project's now archived website (www.sfu.ca/act4hlth/) as well as through Simon Fraser University's institutional data repository, where most project documents have been archived (http://summit.sfu.ca/, and then search either by author name or ACTION for Health).

2 With such a large project, the specific ways team members engaged partners and the degree to which partners set the research agenda varied from project to project. Those projects discussed here were carried out by team members located in Vancouver, in which agendas were largely set by partners.

3 This programme was replaced by the Technology Impact Programme, or TIP programme. When the TIP programme ended, the province of Ontario developed a similar funding mechanism that supported provincial programmes well into the 1990s.

4 This chapter focuses largely on projects undertaken by ACTION for Health staff located in Vancouver as this is where the greatest concentration of projects undertaken with a focus on end-user participation in design took place.

5 This was, especially for junior researchers on the project, often viewed by team members in a controversial light. See for example Jensen (2007a, 2007b); Bjorn and Bolous forthcoming; Bjorn and Balka 2009.

6 Actor network theory (ANT) highlights the need to identify a diversity of actors in the technological change process. Political economy directs attention towards structural relations of power that are overlooked by ANT. Insights from Computer Supported Cooperative Work (CSCW) and Participatory Design, and research about women and technological change, can ensure that women's experiences are not lost in meso- and macro-analyses.

7 The allied health professions consist of a range of professional groups such as physiotherapists, occupational therapists, respiratory therapists, social workers, etc.

8 One custom build that has taken place recently consisted of a shell that integrated several distinct systems – a solution that was pursued when it was determined that the cost of replacing legacy systems would be too high.

9 Some working within the Participatory Design tradition have suggested that there is no need to say Participatory Design and action research (AR), and subsequently discuss the connection between AR and Participatory Design, because Participatory Design embodies action research in its methods, motivations and commitments. A close reading of early Participatory Design work makes these links clear, which are also evidenced in the emphasis on mutual learning and a concern for ensuring that the participants completed learning cycles in early Participatory Design projects. In spite of this view, I have chosen to specifically mention both AR and Participatory Design because although there is certainly some overlap in terminology and occasionally in literature I wanted to call attention to the existence of what have, historically, been very separate literatures (and often different communities, which have addressed somewhat different issues in their respective literatures).

10 Articulation work is the often unanticipated and unplanned work that must be carried out in order to get a technology to work in situ. It is the work 'that gets things back "on track" in the face of the unexpected, that modifies action to accommodate unanticipated contingencies' (Star 1991, p. 84).

11 In retail terms, a sale that loses money but gets the buyer through the door; in research terms, anticipating that research on a particular topic was likely to be needed at some point, and underwriting the cost of conducting the research in order to demonstrate the value our team could bring to the organisation, which allowed us to rebuild a positive working relationship.

12 I owe much to colleagues around me who supported me as I negotiated new terms for my position at the health agency.

References

Armstrong, P., H. Armstrong and K. Messing (2009) 'Gendering work? Women and technologies in health care', in E. Balka, E. Green and F. Henwood (eds) *Gender, Health and Information Technology in Context*, Hampshire: Palgrave, 132–7.

Balka, E. (1997) 'Sometimes texts speak louder than users: locating invisible work through textual analysis', in A. F. Grundy, D. Kohler, V. Oechtering and U. Petersen (eds) *Women, Work and Computerization: Spinning a Web from Past to Future*, New York: Springer-Verlag, 163–76.

Balka, E. (1999) 'From work practice to public policy: case studies of the Canadian Health Information Highway', grant proposal submitted to the Social Sciences and Humanities Research Council of Canada Standard Grants competition (Committee 15), funded April 2000.

Balka, E. (2003) 'Getting the big picture: the macro-politics of information system development (and failure) in a Canadian hospital', *Methods of Information in Medicine*, 42: 324–30.

Balka, E. (2005) 'Tidying up loose ends: theoretical and practical issues related to women's participation in technological design', in H. Rohracher (ed.) *User Involvement in Technological Innovation*, Munich: Profil-Verlag, 147–73.

Balka, E. (2006) 'Inside the belly of the beast: the challenges and successes of a reformist participatory agenda', in G. Jacucci and F. Kensing (eds) *Proceedings of the Ninth Conference on Participatory Design (PDC '06): Expanding Boundaries in Design, Trento, August 2006*, New York: ACM, 134–43.

Balka, E. (2009) 'Gender, information technology, and making health work: unpacking complex relations at work', in E. Balka, E. Green and F. Henwood, (eds) *Gender, Health and Information Technology in Context*, Hampshire: Palgrave, 104–21.

Balka, E. (2010) 'From categorization to public policy: the multiple roles of electronic triage', in A. R. Sætnan, H. M. Lomell and S. Hammer (eds) *By the Very Act of Counting: The Co-construction of Statistics and Society*, New York: Routledge, 172–90.

Balka, E. and A. Butt (2008) 'Invisible logic: the role of software as an information intermediary in healthcare', in N. Wathen, S. Wyatt and R. Harris (eds) *Mediating Health Information: The Go-Betweens in a Changing Socio-Technical Landscape*, Hampshire: Palgrave, 78–93.

Balka, E. and J. Freilich (2008) 'Evaluating nurses' injury rates: challenges associated with information technology and indicator content and design', *Policy and Practice in Health and Safety*, 6(2): 83–99.

Balka, E. and N. Kahnamoui (2004) 'Technology trouble? Talk to us! Findings from an ethnographic field study', in A. Clement and P. van den Besselaar (eds) *Proceedings of Participatory Design Conference 2004, Artful Integration: Interweaving Media, Materials and Practices*, New York: ACM Press, 224–34.

Balka, E. and I. Wagner (2006) 'Making things work: dimensions of configurability as appropriation work', in *CSCW '06 Proceedings of the 2006 20th Anniversary Conference on Computer Supported Cooperative Work, Banff, November 2006*, New York: ACM, 229–38.

Balka, E. and S. Whitehouse (2007) 'Whose work practice? Situating an electronic triage system within a complex system', *Studies in Health Technology and Informatics,* 130: 59–74.

Balka, E., S. Mason and N. Elfring (2005) '"You think it is turning but it is the multiple small stuff." Gender, the division of labour and back and shoulder injury among nursing staff', *Canadian Woman Studies*, 24(1): 145–52.

Balka, E., I. Wagner and C. B. Jensen (2005) 'Reconfiguring critical computing in an era of configurability', in O. W. Bertelsen, N. O. Bouvin, P. G. Krogh and M. Kyng (eds) *Critical Computing: Between Sense and Sensibility. Proceedings of the Fourth Decennial Aarhus Conference, Aarhus, Denmark, August 20–24*, New York: ACM, 79–88.

Balka, E., K. Messing and P. Armstrong (2006) 'Indicators for all: including occupational health in indicators for a sustainable health care system', *Policy and Practice in Health and Safety*, 1: 45–61.

Balka, E., N. Kahnamoui and K. Nutland (2007) 'Who is in charge of patient safety? Work practice, work processes and utopian views of automatic drug dispensing systems', *International Journal of Medical Information*, 76(S1): 48–57.

Balka, E., P. Bjørn and I. Wagner (2008) 'Steps toward a typology for health informatics', in *Proceedings of the ACM 2008 Conference on Computer Supported Cooperative Work (CSCW 08), San Diego, November 2008*, New York: ACM, 515–24.

Balka, E., E. Green and F. Henwood (eds) (2009) *Gender, Health and Information Technology in Context*, Hampshire: Palgrave.

Balka, E., G. Krueger, B. J. Holmes and J. E. Stephen (2010) 'Situating Internet use: information-seeking among young women with breast cancer [Special Issue: Ehealth and the Delivery of Health Care]', *Journal of Computer-Mediated Communication*, 15(3): 389–411.

Balka, E., S. Whitehouse, S. T. Coates and D. Andrusiek (2011) 'Ski hill injuries and ghost charts: socio-technical issues in achieving e-health interoperability across jurisdictions', *Information Systems Frontiers*, Dordrecht: Springer, 1–24.

Baskerville, R. L. and A. T. Wood-Harper (1996) 'A critical perspective on action research as a method for information systems research', *Journal of Information Technology*, 11: 235–46.

Beck, E. (2002) 'P for political: participation is not enough', *Scandinavian Journal of Information Systems*, 14(1): 77–92.

Bella, L. (2009) 'Geeks who care: gender, caring and community access computers', in E. Balka, E. Green and F. Henwood (eds) *Gender, Health and Information Technology in Context*, Hampshire: Palgrave, 53–71.

Bella, L., R. Harris, S. Burdett and P. Gill (2008) 'Everybody's talking at me: situating the client in the info(r)mediary work of health professions', in N. Wathen, S. Wyatt and R. Harris (eds) *Mediating Health Information: The Go-Betweens in a Changing Socio-Technical Landscape*, Hampshire: Palgrave, 18–37.

Bjørn, P. and E. Balka (2009) 'Supporting the design of health information systems: action research as knowledge translation', in *Proceedings of the 42nd Hawaii International Conference on System Sciences (HICSS), Big Island, January 2009*, Washington, DC: IEEE Computer Society, 1–10.

Bjørn, P. and N. Boulus (forthcoming) 'Dissenting in reflective conversations: critical components of doing action research', *Action Research Journal*.

Bjørn, P. and K. Rødje (2008) 'Triage drift: a workplace study in a pediatric emergency department', *Computer Supported Cooperative Work*, 17(4): 395–419.

Bjørn, P., S. Burgoyne, V. Crompton, T. MacDonald, B. Pickering and S. Munro (2009) 'Boundary factors and contextual contingencies: configuring electronic templates for health care professionals', *European Journal of Information Systems*, 18: 428–41.

Boulus, N. (2009) 'Socio-technical changes brought about by electronic medical records', in *Proceedings of the Fifteenth Americas Conference on Information Systems, San Francisco, August 2009*, Paper 781.

Boulus, N. (2010) 'A journey into the hidden lives of electronic medical records (EMRS): action research in the making', unpublished PhD thesis, Simon Fraser University.

Boulus, N. and B. Bjørn (2010) 'A cross-case analysis of technology-in-use practices: EPR-adaptation in Canada and Norway', *International Journal of Medical Informatics*, 79(6): 97–108.

Gärtner, J. and I. Wagner (1996) 'Mapping actors and agendas: political frameworks of systems design and participation', *Human–Computer Interaction*, 11: 187–214.

Green, E., F. Griffiths and A. Lindenmeyer (2009) 'It can see into your body: gender, ICTS and decision making about midlife women's health', in E. Balka, E. Green and F. Henwood (eds) *Gender, Health and Information Technology in Context*, Hampshire: Palgrave, 157–76.

Harris, R. (2009) 'Cyber-burdens: emerging imperatives in women's unpaid care work', in E. Balka, E. Green and F. Henwood (eds) *Gender, Health and Information Technology in Context*, Hampshire: Palgrave, 72–87.

Hart, F. and M. Bond (1995) *Action Research for Health and Social Care: A Guide to Practice*, Buckingham: Open University Press.

Henwood, F. and S. Wyatt (2009) 'All change? Gender, health and the internet', in E. Balka, E. Green and F. Henwood (eds) *Gender, Health and Information Technology in Context*, Hampshire: Palgrave, 17–33.

Henwood, F., R. Harris, S. Burdett and A. Marshall (2008) 'Health intermediaries? Positioning the public library in e-health discourse', in N. Wathen, S. Wyatt and R. Harris (eds) *Mediating Health Information: The Go-Betweens in a Changing Socio-Technical Landscape*, Hampshire: Palgrave, 38–55.

Holmes, B. (2005) 'Me on-line: narrative identities of people with arthritis', unpublished thesis, Simon Fraser University.

Holter, I. M. and D. Schwartz-Barcott (1993) 'Action research: What is it? How has it been used and how can it be used in nursing?', *Journal of Advanced Nursing*, 128: 298–304.

Jensen, C. B. (2007a) 'Sorting attachments: usefulness of STS in health care practice and policy', *Science as Culture*, 16(3): 237–53.

Jensen, C. B. (2007b) 'The wireless nursing call system: politics of discourse, technology and dependability in a pilot project', *Computer Supported Cooperative Work*, 15(5–6): 419–41.

Knorr-Cetina, K. and A. V. Cicourel (eds) (1981) *Advances in Social Theory and Methodology: Toward an Integration of Micro- and Macro-Sociologies*, Boston, MA: Routledge and Kegan Paul.

Korpela, M., A. Mursu, H. A. Soriyan and A. Eerola (2002) 'Information systems research and information systems practice in a network of activities', in Y. Dittrich, C. Floyd and R. Klischewski (eds) *Social Thinking – Software Practice*, Cambridge, MA: MIT Press, 287–308.

Kyng, M. (2010) 'Bridging the gap between politics and techniques: on the next practices of participatory design', *Scandinavian Journal of Information Systems*, 22(1): Article 5.

Le Jeune, G. (2009) 'Ungendering women's health: information systems and occupational health indicators', in E. Balka, E. Green and F. Henwood (eds) *Gender, Health and Information Technology in Context*, Hampshire: Palgrave.

McCulloch, A. (2007) 'Informed choice? English- and French-speakers' use of the Canadian health network', unpublished thesis (MA), Simon Fraser University.

Messing, K., A. Seifert, M. Vézina, E. Balka and C. Chatigny (2005) 'Qualitative research using numbers: analysis developed in France and used to transform work in North America', *New Solutions*, 15(3): 245–60.

Randall, D., J. Hughes and D. Shapiro (1991) 'Systems development – the fourth dimension perspectives on the social organization of work', paper presented at the SPRU CICT Conference at Sussex University.

Reidl, C. and M. Tolar (2007) 'Lost in implementation? Lessons learned from a complex IT implementation project', in CD-ROM Proceedings of Information Technology and Communications in Health (ITCH2007), Victoria, British Columbia February, 2007.

Reidl, C., M. Tolar and I. Wagner (2008) 'Impediments to change: the case of implementing an electronic patient record in three oncology clinics', in D. Hakken, J. Simonsen and T. Robertson (eds) Proceedings of PDC 2008, Bloomington, Indiana, October 2008, New York: ACM, 1–10.

Robertson, T. (1996) 'Participatory Design and participative practices in small companies', in J. Bloomberg, F. Kensing and E. Dykstra-Erickson (eds), PDC '96: Proceedings of the Participatory Design Conference, Cambridge, MA: Computer Professionals for Social Responsibility, New York: ACM, 35–43.

Sætnan, A. R., H. M. Lomell and S. Hammer (eds) (2010) By the Very Act of Counting: The Co-construction of Statistics and Society, New York: Routledge.

Schmidt, K., I. Wagner and M. Tolar (2007) 'Permutations of cooperative work practices: a study of two oncology clinics', in Proceedings of the 2007 International ACM Conference on Supporting Group Work, Sanibel Island, Florida, November 2007, New York: ACM, 1–10.

Schuurman, N. and E. Balka (2009) 'Ontological context for data use and integration', Journal of Computer Supported Cooperative Work, 18(1): 83–108.

Shapiro, D. (2005) 'Participatory Design: the will to succeed', in O. W. Bertelsen, N. O. Bouvin, P. G. Krogh and M. Kyng (eds) Proceedings of the Fourth Decennial Aarhus Conference of Critical Computing – Between Sense and Sensibility, New York: ACM, 1–10.

Sharman, Z. (2009) 'Nursing technologies? gender, care, and skill in the use of patient care information systems', in E. Balka, E. Green and F. Henwood (eds) Gender, Health and Information Technology in Context, Hampshire: Palgrave, 88–103.

Smith, K. L. (2006) 'A wired waiting room: interventions to enhance access to online health information', unpublished thesis (MA), Simon Fraser University.

Star, Susan Leigh (1991) 'Invisible work and silenced dialogues in representing knowledge', in I. V. Eriksson, B. A. Kitchenham and K. G. Tijdens (eds) Women, Work and Computerization: Understanding and Overcoming Bias in Work and Education, Amsterdam: North-Holland, 81–92.

Suchman, L. and B. Jordan (1988) 'Computerization and women's knowledge', in K. Tijdens, M. Jennings, I. Wagner and M. Weggelaar (eds) Women, Work and Computerization: Forming New Alliances, Amsterdam: North-Holland, 97–105.

Turner, J. H. (1991) The Structure of Sociological Theory, fifth edition, Belmont, CA: Wadsworth.

Wathen, N., R. Harris and S. Wyatt (2008) 'Reflections on the middle space', in N. Wathen, S. Wyatt and R. Harris (eds) Mediating Health Information: The Go-Betweens in a Changing Socio-Technical Landscape, Hampshire: Palgrave, 182–93.

Wathen, N., S. Wyatt and R. Harris (eds) (2008) Mediating Health Information: The Go-Betweens in a Changing Socio-Technical Landscape, Hampshire: Palgrave.

Wise, L. C., J. Bostrom, J. Crosier, S. White and R. Caldwell (1996) 'Cost benefit analysis of an automated medication system', Nursing Economics, 14(4): 224–38.

Wood-Harper, A. T., S. Corder, J. R. G. Wood and H. Watson (1996) 'How we profess: the ethical systems analyst', Communications of ACM, 39(3): 69–77.

Wyatt, S., R. Harris and N. Wathen (2008) 'The go-betweens: health, technology and info(r)mediation', in N. Wathen, S. Wyatt and R. Harris (eds) Mediating Health Information: The Go-Betweens in a Changing Socio-Technical Landscape, Hampshire: Palgrave, 1–17.

Index

Aarts, E. and Grotenhuis, F. 51
Abelson, R. and Friquegnon, M.-L. 68
absolutist ethical theories 68
accountability: ethics and 64; systems of 80
ACTION for Health 257–77; Assessment of
    Technology in Context Design (ATIC) work
    258; background to current approach 259–61;
    collaborative work 275; colleagues, need for
    271–72; communications to audiences,
    importance of tailoring 275; discussion 275–76;
    ethics 69; flexibility, importance of 275;
    frankness, difficulties in 271–72; influencing
    technology through participatory design 257–;
    integration into senior decision-making and
    policy environments 273–74; intellectual
    property and autonomy 274–75; limitations of
    participatory design practice 276; Mid-Main
    Clinic and the wireless call system, perils of
    staffing changes 269–71; partnerships,
    collaborative working with 275; partnerships,
    complexity in 275–76; partnerships, intellectual
    property and 274–75; project overview 258–59;
    reformist participatory design, reflection of
    challenges 275–76; researchable problems,
    finding in unexpected places 272–73;
    simplification of complexities, need for 271–72;
    summary and learning objectives 257; Tower
    Move project, supporting operational needs
    while collecting data 262–69; working with
    health sector management 261–62
action research 26; inspiration for interventions 44
activist and hobbyist communities 190–91
Agar, M. 87
Aging@Work project 161
agnostic democracy, concept of 200
aims of the book 1, 2–3
Akama, Y. and Ivanka, T. 185
Alexander, C. 45
Altman, I. 80
ambient intelligence (AmI) 51
Ambrosino, N. and Vianello, A. 81
analysis and design, intertwining of 134–35

Andersen, N.E. et al. 43, 46, 118, 119, 146
Andersen, T., Halse, J. and Moll, J. 102
Anderson, Benedict 92, 95, 96, 184
Anderson, R.J. 96
application areas 119; addressing new areas 135–36
appropriation 50–51
Archer, B. 45
architectures, participatory design in 251–52
Argyris, C. and Schön, D.A. 133
Aristotle 67
Armstrong, P. et al. 259
art, role in design process 47–49
Artful Integrators Award 203–4
Ås, B. 130
Asad, T. 107
Asplund, G. et al. 38
Assessment of Technology in Context Design
    (ATIC) work 258
Australia, Federal Chancellery of 81
Austrian Federal Chancellery 81
Avison, D.E. and Wood-Harper, A.T. 121

Bader, G. and Nyce, J.M. 96
Baek, J.-S. and Lee, K.-P. 156
Bakhtin, M.M. 68
Balka, E. 102, 104, 259, 260, 261, 262
Balka, E. and Butt, A. 258
Balka, E. and Freilich, J. 259
Balka, E. and Kahnamoui, F. 9
Balka, E. and Kahnamoui, N. 261, 262
Balka, E. and Wagner, I. 262
Balka, E. and Whitehouse, S. 259, 264, 271
Balka, E. et al. 69, 138, 258, 259, 262
Balka, E., Mason, S. and Elfring, N. 262
Balka, E., Wagner, I. and Jensen, C.B. 9, 259, 262
Balka, Ellen x, 257–77
Bannon, L. et al. 136
Bannon, Liam J. xiv, 37–58
Bannon, L.J. and Bødker, S. 47
Bansler, J. 120
Bansler, J. and Havn, E. 9
Baskerville, R.L. and Wood-Harper, A.T. 264, 275

281

Bauhaus 37, 38–39
Beck, E.E. 65, 78, 81, 89, 199, 233, 275, 276
Bella, L. 258
Bella, L. et al. 259
Benston, M. and Balka, E. 185
Bentley, R. et al. 94, 97
Benyon, D. et al. 156
Berg, M. 80
Berg, M. and Bowker, G. 76
Bergo, Olav Terje 24, 43
Berman, M. 38
Bertalanffy, Ludwig von 42
Beyer, H. and Holtzblatt, K. 27
Binder, T. 54, 58
Binder, T. et al. 39, 147, 148, 172
Binder, T., Gregory, J. and Wagner, I. 14n1
Binder, Thomas xvi, 145–77
Bjerknes, G. and Bratteteig, T. 6, 8, 29, 30, 43, 87, 126, 128, 131, 132
Bjerknes, G., Ehn, P. and Kyng, M. 2
Bjerknes, G. et al. 43, 237
Björgvinsson, E. et al. 53, 54, 58, 192, 193, 196, 200
Bjørn, P. and Balka, E. 259, 262, 270, 277n5
Bjørn, P. and Boulus, N. 262, 270, 277n5
Bjørn, P. and Rødje, K. 259, 264, 271
Bjørn, P. et al. 259, 271, 273
Blacksburg Electronic Village (BEV) 191, 197
Bleecker, J. 51
Blomberg, J. and Burrell, M. 93
Blomberg, J. and Henderson, H. 92, 99
Blomberg, J. and Trigg, R. 92, 99
Blomberg, J. et al. 30, 31, 78, 87, 88, 90, 92, 93, 99, 101, 151
Blomberg, J., Giacomi, J. et al. 8, 12
Blomberg, J., Kensing, F. and Dykstra-Erickson, E. 14n1
Blomberg, Jeanette xi–xii, 30, 58, 76, 86–109
Bloomington Participatory Design Conference (2008) xx, 48
Blythin, S. et al. 93
Boal, A. 164
Bødker, K. and Granlien, M.S. 137
Bødker, K. and Kensing, F. 87
Bødker, K. and Pedersen, J.S. 151
Bødker, K., Bratteteig, D. et al. 14n1
Bødker, K. et al. 123, 126, 130, 133, 135, 166
Bødker, K., Kensing, F. and Simonsen, J. 3, 5, 6, 9, 49
Bødker, Keld xiii–xiv, 49, 117–40
Bødker, S. 71, 75, 149
Bødker, S. and Buur, J. 168
Bødker, S. and Grønbaek, K. 155, 221
Bodker, S. and Iverson, O.S. 189
Bødker, S. et al. 28, 29, 39, 43, 90, 91, 93, 146, 155, 238
Boehner, K. et al. 158

Bogdan, C. and Bowers, J. 190
Boland, R.J. 121
Boland, R.J. and Collopy, F. 39
Borchorst, N.G. et al. 137
Borning, A. et al. 199
Borum, F. and Enderud, H. 130
Bossen, C. et al. 104, 105
Botero, A. and Saad-Sulone, J. 52
Boulus, N. 259, 269, 270
Boulus, N. and Bjørn, B. 259
boundaries: boundary objects 148–49; hierarchical boundaries 72; professional boundaries 72
Bowen, S.J. et al. 184
Bowers, J. et al. 95
Bowker, G. and Star, S.L. 76, 77
Braa, J. and Hedberg, C. 204, 237
Braa, J. et al. 104, 106, 204, 236, 243
Braa, Jørn xiii, 235–56
Brandt, E. 175, 195
Brandt, E. and Grunnet, C. 164, 165
Brandt, E. and Messeter, J. 174
Brandt, E. et al. 175
Brandt, Eva x, 145–77
Bråten, S. 129
Bratteteig, T. and Wagner, I. 136, 137
Bratteteig, T. et al. 73, 137
Bratteteig, Tone xvi–xvii, 78, 117–40
Braverman, H. 32
Brereton, M. and Buur, J. 78
Brereton, M. and Redhead, F. 163
Brereton, M. et al. 161
Brereton, M., Redhead, F. et al. 191
Brodersen, C. et al. 153
Brown, T. 55
Brun-Cottan, F. et al. 30, 95
Bucciarelli, L. 95
Buchenau, M. and Fulton Suri, J. 168
Burns, C. 165
Burns, C. et al. 165
Büscher, M., Eriksen, M.A. et al. 9
Büscher, M. et al. 72, 77, 99, 195
Button, G. 87, 97
Button, G. and Harper, R. 87, 96
Buur, J. and Bødker, S. 47, 102
Buur, J. and Larsen, H. 53
Buur, J. and Matthews, B. 53
Buur, J. and Mitchell, R. 160
Buur, J. et al. 102
Byrne, E. and Alexander, P.M. 71, 72
Byrne, E. and Sahay, S. 106

Card, S. et al. 47
Carroll, J. 165, 166
Carroll, J. and Rosson, M.B. 188, 191
Carroll, J.M. et al. 134, 183, 185, 202
Carstensen, P. Schmidt, K. and Wiil, U.K. 200
case-based prototypes 99

Castells, M. 252
CAVEAT (justice system reform organisation) 186
Cefkin, M. 104, 107
CESD (Cooperative Experimental System Development) 125–28; activities 126; concerns 126; cooperative techniques 125; design ideas, expandability of space for 127; experimental techniques 125; guidelines 128; methods 125–28; use-oriented design 126–28
Chambers, R. 253, 254
Chambers, T. 72
change: Mid-Main Clinic and the wireless call system, perils of staffing changes in 269–71; MUST method and coherent visions of 124; in participatory design contexts 137–38; perspectives on, casting new light through 152–53
Change Laboratory 105
Chaplin, Charlie 24
Characteristics of Infrastructure (Star, S.L. and Bowker, G.) 202
Chatfield, R.H., Kuhn, S. and Muller, M. 14n1
Checkland, P. 118
Checkland, P. et al. 43
Checkland, Peter 43
Cherkasky, T., Greenbaum, J. et al. 14n1
Chesbrough, H. 53
Chomsky, N. 159
Christensen, M. et al. 126
Churchman, C. West 43, 44
Ciborra, C. and Schneider, L. 28
Ciborra, Claudio 46
Ciolfi, L. and Bannon, L. 136
Civic Nexus 188–90, 199
civil society: ethics and 68; rising importance of 183
Clausen, H. 166
Clement, A. and van den Besselaar, P. 9, 23, 188
Clement, A., Cindio, F.D. et al. 14n1
Clement, A. et al. 52, 184
Clement, Andrew ix, 182–205, 233
Clifford, J. 74, 98
Clifford, J. and Marcus, G. 98
cloud, participatory design in 248–51
co-authorship 76–77
co-design: cooperative prototyping and 90; generative tools for 159–60; tools and techniques 148
co-realisation: ethnography 99–100; methods 133
Coleman, S. and van Hellermann, P. 105
collaborative *gesamtkunstwerk* 40–41
collaborative inquiry 171
collaborative work in ACTION for Health 275
collective designer, notion of 67–68
COMIT project 167, 174
commercial settings, opportunities for participatory design in 107–8

communications: to audiences, importance of tailoring 275; community communications, participatory design for 191–92; information and communications technologies 2, 6, 51, 261; invention communication strategy 267–69; with users 131–32
communities 182–205; activist and hobbyist communities, participatory design in 190–91; agnostic democracy, concept of 200; Artful Integrators Award 203–4; Blacksburg Electronic Village (BEV) 191, 197; CAVEAT (justice system reform organisation) 186; Civic Nexus 188–90, 199; civil society, rising importance of 183; community, concept of 183; community-based organisations, participatory design with and by 185–90; community based participatory design, emergence of 183; community-based participatory design, topics shaping the development of 199–204; community communications, participatory design for 191–92; Community-Driven Development (CDD) 198; community learning network (CLN) at St Christopher House 186–88, 203; community networking (CN) initiatives 185–86; content management system (CMS) 189; creativity and cultural production, participatory design for enabling and fostering 192–96; Democratising Technology (DemTech) 195–96, 200; designing with activists 191; District Health Information Software (DHIS) 204; free/open source software (FOSS) 187, 203, 204, 245, 255; Global Fund for Women (GFW) 203–4; globalisation 183; Health Information System Project (HISP) 204; IBIS method 198–99; identity, importance of 184; infrastructuring 201–4; Laboratory for Computer-Supported Collaboration and Learning (CSCL), Penn State University 188; learning in course of everyday activities 189–90; Malmö Living Labs 192–93; Media Centre Software 197–99; Moggill community partnership 191–92; Neighbourhood Networks 193–95, 200; neighbourhoods 184; open access approaches 204; plurality within, challenge of 184–85; political and commercial environments, participatory design for enhancing public deliberation in 196–99; politics, new forms of 199–200; publics, notion of 200–201, 203; Seattle Community Network (SCN) 191; shared interests, focus on 184; social services, rising importance of 183; Societyware 199; summary and learning objectives 182; topics shaping the development of community-based participatory design 199–204; User Parliament 198, 199; varieties of 184–85
'Community Help in Context' (Stevens, G. and Wiedenhöfer, T.) 199

computer-based systems 3–4
Computer Human Interaction (CHI) 23; *see also* Human-Computer Interaction (HCI)
Computer Professionals for Social Responsibility (CPSR) 23
computer science, systems analysis and 23
Computer-Supported Cooperative Work (CSCW): design process 41; ethnography 94, 95; heritage 23; participatory design 7–8
Computers and Democracy – A Scandinavian Challenge (Bjerknes, G. et al.) 237–38
concretising of ideas 131
configurability 9, 80, 138–39
Conklin, J. and Begemann, M.L. 198
content management system (CMS) 189
contexts: change in participatory design contexts 137–38; enacting scenarios in real-use contexts 168–69; participatory design in Global Fund for Women (GFW) 214–15, 215–16; political context in tradition of participatory design 23; tools and techniques, use of 146–47
Contextual Design and User Driven Innovation 27
cooperative design, Scandinavian tradition of 150
Costabile, M.F. et al. 50, 139
Crabtree, A. 95
Crabtree, A. et al. 95, 101
creativity: participatory design for enabling 192–96; in worker involvement 32
critical design studies, role of 47–49
critical reflection: ethical questions for 82; reflexivity in design and ethnography 102–4
Cross, N. 2, 45, 58n1, 147
Cross, N. and Müllert, N. 147
Cuba 241–42
cultural probes and animation of design space. 101

Danielsson, K. and Wiberg, C. 184
data processing 22
Davies, C.A. 103
Dearden, A. and Rizvi, H. 102
decision-making: Global Fund for Women (GFW) 224–25; having a say in 129, 130; integration into senior decision-making and policy environments 273–74; rights to, ethics and 65
decoding documents 76
DELTA language 43
Demarco, T. 23
democracy: democratic practices 33; voice and 31–33
Democratising Technology (DemTech) 195–96, 200
DEMOS project (Sweden) 25, 27, 29
Deshpande, P. 58
design: design-after-design 138–39; Design and Intervention projects 24, 28–30; design ethnography 100–102; ethnography as resource for 87; involvement of workers in 65; practices in, proliferating family of 146
Design Anthropological Innovation Model (DAIM): design process 47; ethnography 101, 102
Design at Work (Greenbaum, J. and Kyng, M., Eds.) xx, 4
Design Council 55
design games: as particular framing of design participation 171–73; tools and techniques 146, 171–75
Design Noir 158
The Design of Inquiring Systems (Churchman, C. W.) 43–44
design process 8–10, 37–58; action research, inspiration for interventions from 44; ambient intelligence (AmI) 51; appropriation 50–51; art, role of 47–49; Bauhaus 37, 38–39; challenges for participatory design 49–55; collaborative *gesamtkunstwerk* 40–41; Computer-Supported Cooperative Work (CSCW) 41; concept of design 40–41; core themes of design 41–49; critical design studies, role of 47–49; DELTA language 43; Design Anthropological Innovation Model (DAIM) 47; design anthropology, emergence of 47; Design History Society 56; design intelligence, notion of 45–46; Design Research movement 44–45; design science 45; design things and drawing things together 55–58; design thinking, centrality of 55–58; design thinking, fundamental to business strategies 40–41; design thinking, reflective practice and 58; drawing things together and opening up controversies 56–57; end-user participation 53–54; ethnography and design anthropology 47; Fabrication Laboratories (Fab Labs) 54–55; Global Village Set 55; Human-Computer Interaction (HCI) 39, 41, 48, 53; Human-Computer Interaction (HCI), user-centred design approaches to 47; IDEO Design 55–56; importance of design 40; infrastructural variations 51; innovation, open and user-driven 52–53; Internet of Things (IoT) 51; knowledge systems 43–44; Living Labs 53–54; MIT Media Lab 54; MUST method (Roskilde University) 49; Neighbourhood Networks Project 54; Norwegian Metal Workers project 39, 43; open innovation 52–53; open production, fabrication laboratories and 54–55; Open Source Ecology 55; open source software packages 50–51; organisational information systems 49–50; participatory production, forms of 52; problem-solving rationality *versus* reflective practice 46; public participation, social innovation and 55; reflection and iteration during 82; reflective design 48; reflective practice *versus* problem-solving rationality 46;

resign research and participatory design 44–45; Scandinavian approach to systems design 43; Scandinavian Participatory Design projects 44; Scandinavian systems development tradition 42; Situationist International movement 48; social innovation 55; social media 51–52; socio-technical systems 42; 'soft' systems 43–44; stakeholder engagement 57; summary and learning objectives 37; systems design, influences on 43–44; tailorability 50–51; Tavistock Institute 42, 44; technology substrates, systems and infrastructures 49; user-centred design approaches to human–computer interaction (HCI) 47; user-driven innovation 52–53; UTOPIA project 39; Young Foundation 55

design research, participatory design and 44–45

Design Research Society 2, 147

Design Things (Binder, T. et al.) 172

designing: with activists 191; design games and 173–75; roles of designers 2–3, 4

Designing with Video: Focusing the User-centered Design Process (Ylirisku, S. and Buur, J.) 167

developing countries: lessons from 252–56; 'networks of actions,' responding to challenges in 243–44; opportunities for participatory design in 106–7; *see also* Cuba; India; Mozambique; Sierra Leone; South Africa

Dewey, J. and Latour, B. 201

Dewey, John 32, 33, 46, 58, 69, 70, 189, 200, 201, 203

diagnostic narratives 151–52

Dindler, C. 153, 154, 155

Dindler, C., Brodersen, C. et al. 153

Dindler, C. et al. 136

DiSalvo, C. et al. 54, 58

DiSalvo, Carl ix, 182–205

distributed participatory design, proposal for 106

District Health Information Software (DHIS) 204; design and development 236–37

Dittrich, Y. and Lindeberg, O. 137

Dittrich, Y. et al. 104, 106

Dittrich, Yvonne xvii–xviii, 117–40

Dott Cornwall 55

double silencing 77

Dourish, P. 95, 161

drawing things together 56–57

Dreyfus, H. and Dreyfus, S. 32

Droste, M. 38

Druin, A. 156

Druin, A. and Fast, C. 136

DUE project (Denmark) 25, 28, 29

Dunne, A. 48, 158

Dunne, A. and Raby, F. 48, 158

early action projects 24

In the Name of Efficiency (Greenbaum, J.) 32

Eglash, R. et al. 51

Ehn, P. and Badham, R. 67

Ehn, P. and Kyng, M. 4, 25, 28, 43, 125, 164

Ehn, P. and Sandberg, A. 25, 27

Ehn, P. and Sjögren, D. 149, 151, 164, 171

Ehn, P. et al. 172, 173

Ehn, Pelle xiv–xv, 4, 6, 7, 8, 25, 28, 29, 31, 37–58, 78, 90, 97, 125, 128, 134, 146–48, 153, 155, 192, 196, 200, 201

Elovaara, P. et al. 107

Emery, F. and Thorsrud, E. 42

Emery, Fred 42

Emery, M. 130

Emilsson, A. 58

empirically-based experience 118

empowerment: Global Fund for Women (GFW) 214; Health Information Systems Programme (HISP) 252–53

Enacted Scenario Game 175

end-user participation 53–54

engagement with project participants 71–75

Engeström, Y. et al. 105

envisioning 131

Eriksson, J. and Dittrich, Y. 50, 139

ethics 3–5, 64–83; absolutist ethical theories 68; accountability 64; accountability systems 80; ACTION for Health 69; civil society and 68; co-authorship 76–77; collective designer, notion of 67–68; constitutive relations between ethics and participatory design 65–66; critical reflection, questions for 82; decision-making rights 65; decoding documents 76; design, involvement of workers in 65; design process, reflection and iteration during 82; double silencing 77; engagement with project participants 71–75; ethical case deliberation 69; ethical problems of technology use, contribution to participatory design 80–81; ethical theories 67–68; hierarchical boundaries 72; home care technologies 80–81; identity, development of 70; indigenous knowledge management system, development of 74; informed consent 73; litigation support 76; misrepresentation 76; mobile technologies 80; moral philosophy and subject matter of 66–71; moral sensitivity 68–69; narrative ethics 68–69; normative ethical theories 68; participatory design and 65–66; phronesis, virtue of 67–68; practical, situated ethics 68–69; professional boundaries 72; project participants, identification and engagement with 71–72; project participants, practice of engagement with 72–75; project participants, reflection on what can be offered to 77–78; relativist ethical theories 68; representation of participants and their work 75–77; responsibility and 64, 66, 67, 68, 69–70, 71, 72, 78, 81, 83; social

technologies 80; stakeholder engagement
73–75; summary and learning objectives 64;
technology, ethics and 69–71; technology
design, ethical issues of 78–81; tools and
processes, development of 65, 70; users,
ethical issues of working with 71–78; virtue
theory 67–68; working with users, ethical issues
of 71–78
ETHICS design tool 121
ethnography 8, 12, 22, 86–109; case-based
prototypes 99; Change Laboratory 105; co-
design and cooperative prototyping 90; co-
realisation 99–100; commercial settings,
opportunities for participatory design in 107–8;
commitments and guiding principles of
participatory design and 88–91; Computer
Supported Cooperative Design (CSCW) 94,
95; critical reflection – reflexivity in design and
ethnography 102–4; cultural probes and
animation of design space. 101; in design, turn
to 91–92; Design Anthropological Innovation
Model (DAIM) 101, 102; design anthropology
and 47; design ethnography 100–102;
developing countries, opportunities for
participatory design in 106–7; distributed
participatory design, proposal for 106;
ethnographer as mediator 97–98; ethnographic
work, guiding principles for 30–31;
ethnographic workplace studies unencumbered
by design 95; ethnographically informed design
as interdisciplinary research 95; ethnography
and focus on everyday settings 88–89;
ethnomethodology and 87–88; exploration of
ethnographic perspective in (participatory)
design 91–94; foregrounding user/practitioner
98; Human-Computer Interaction (HCI) 94,
95; informed design and 93–94, 95–96; as input
to design 95–96; institutional and disciplinary
affiliations 94; (inter)disciplinary difference,
reconciliation of 96–97; interdisciplinary
research, ethnographically informed design as
94–95; intervention in 87, 88, 90, 91, 93, 97,
101, 102, 103, 104, 105, 108; joining
ethnography and (participatory) design 94–98;
large-scale information systems 106; 'lay'
participants 97; methodological
interdisciplinarity 96; methodology of
participatory design and 93; multi-perspectival
collaboration with participatory design 97;
MUST method (Roskilde University) 93;
mutual learning 89, 91, 98; opportunities and
challenges 104–8; participatory design and
mutual learning 89–90; power and hierarchy,
notions of 107; principles of 88; principles of
participatory design 89; reflective practice,
notion of 102–3; reflexive relation,
ethnography and participatory design in 92;
(re)positioning ethnography within
participatory design 99–102, 108; resource for
design 87; spatial scaling 105–6; summary and
learning objectives 86; synergies between
participatory design and 90–91; temporal
scaling 104–5; Xerox PARC 92, 103
Ethnography and the Corporate Encounter (Cefkin,
M.) 107
exploration: of ethnographic perspective in
(participatory) design 91–94; experience, probes
for exploration of 158–59

Fabrication Laboratories (Fab Labs) 54–55
Falzon, M.-A. 105
Farooq, U. et al. 188, 189, 190
Farrington, C. and Pine, E. 191
feminism and participatory actions 32–33
fictional narratives 153–55
Finken, S. 102, 103
Fischer, G. 139
Fischer, G. and Scharff, E. 199
flexibility, importance of 43, 70–71, 79, 118, 139,
166, 187, 214–15, 221, 227–28, 243, 275
Florence project 28, 29–30, 131, 134
Floyd, C. et al. 189
Floyd, C., Reisin, F.-M. and Schmidt, G. 121,
122
Floyd, C.A. 121, 122, 149, 156
Focus Troupe approach 165
foregrounding user/practitioner 98
Forsythe, D.E. 97
Forum Theatre 164
Foucault, M. 70
Foverskov, M. and Binder, T. 156, 168
Frankena, W. 67
frankness, difficulties in 271–72
free/open source software (FOSS) 187, 203, 204,
245, 255
Frodeman, R. et al. 94
Fuller, Buckminster 45
further reading 15
future directions, opportunities and 175–77
future workshops 145–46, 152–53

Garabet, A. et al. 165
Gardiner, M. 68
Garfinkel, H. 100
Gärtner, J. and Wagner, I. 131, 232, 260, 261,
274
Gatens, M. 64
Gauntlett, D. 52
Gaver, B., Dunne, T. and Pacenti, E. 153
Gaver, B. et al. 78, 137, 155, 158
Gaver, W. 48
Gaver, W. et al. 101
generative tools for co-designing 159–60
Gershenfeld, N.A. 52, 54

Gerson, E.M. and Star, S.L. 95
Gibson-Graham, K.K. 75
Gilligan, C. 66, 67, 69
Global Fund for Women (GFW) 213–34;
    beginnings of 214; communities 203–4; context
    for participatory design 214–15, 215–16;
    decision-making 224–25; empowerment 214;
    grant classification 216–18; identification of
    appropriate liaisons 222–23; in-house
    participatory design, reflections on 218–19;
    information management (IM), example of
    216–18; participatory design process and
    product 219–22; process control 225; respect
    214–15; Salsa project, shared information space
    in 'cloud' 230–31; shared access 227–29; shared
    information 229–30, 230–31; shared
    information, stakeholder participation and 231;
    shared information space 226; shared ownership
    226–27; summary and learning objectives 213;
    trust 214–15; value of participation 223–24;
    work practice knowledge 225–26; working
    within, information management liaisons and
    222; workplace democracy 232–33
Global Village Set 55
globalisation 50, 140, 183
Gordon, T.F. and Karacapilidis, N. 198
grant classification 216–18
Green, E. et al. 259
Greenbaum, J. and Kyng, M. 4, 10, 46, 49, 90,
    147, 149, 186
Greenbaum, Joan xii–xiii, 4, 21–34, 65, 71, 276
Greenfield, A. 51
Greenwood, D. and Levin, M. 26
Gregory, S.A. 45
Grønbaek, K. 149
Grønbaek, K. and Morgensen, P.H. 126
Grønbaek, K. et al. 90, 99, 125
Grønbaek, K., Grudin, J. et al. 6
Gropius, W. 38
Grudin, J. 6, 119, 123, 127, 230
Grudin, J. and Grinter, R.E. 96
Gulliksen, J. et al. 47
Gurstein, M. 184

Habraken, H.J. and Gross, M.D. 171
Hagen, P. and Robertson, T. 52, 80
Hagen, P. et al. 137
Hall, K. 68
Hall, T. and Bannon, L. 136
Halloran, J. et al. 71
Halse, J. 47, 102
Halse, J. et al. 47, 53, 100, 101, 153, 169, 170,
    171
Halskov, K., Simonsen, J. and Bødker, K. 14n1
Hammersley, M. 87
Hannerz, U. 105
Hansen, T.R., Bardram, J.E. and Soegaard, M. 9

Haraway, D. 68
Harper, R. and Hughes, J.A. 93
Harper, R. et al. 95
Harris, R. 259
Hart, F. and Bond, M. 264, 265
Hartswood, M. et al. 98, 99, 100, 104
Harvey, L.J. and Mayers, M.D. 92
Health Information Systems Programme (HISP)
    204, 235–56; architectures, participatory
    design in 251–52; cloud, participatory design in
    248–51; community-level participatory design,
    rationale and experience 246–47; in Cuba
    241–42; current trends, looking forward and
    248–52; cyclic and evolutionary participatory
    design in 253–54; District Health Information
    Software (DHIS), design and development
    236–37; empowerment 252–53; in India
    242–43, 247–48; lessons from developing
    countries and 252–56; in Mozambique 243;
    'networks of actions,' participatory design in
    first wave extension (Phase 2) 240–44;
    'networks of actions,' responding to challenges
    in developing countries 243–44; open source,
    empowering the South through 255–56; open
    source web-based environments, participatory
    design in new technological paradigm (Phase 3)
    244–48; opportunities for participatory design
    in Africa 255; outsourcing software-based
    services from Africa, threat of 255; politics
    252–53; in Sierra Leone 245–46; in South
    Africa 238–40; summary and learning objectives
    235; traditional participatory design and (Phase
    1) 237–40; traditional participatory design and
    (Phase 1), learning from 240; users,
    identification of 252–53
Heath, C. and Luff, P. 95
Hegel, Georg W.F. 43
Held, V. 66
Henderson, A. and Kyng, M. 50, 100, 138
Henderson, K. 95
Henwood, F. and Wyatt, S. 258
Henwood, F. et al. 259
Herbsleb, J.D. et al. 138
heritage 21–34; action research 26; Computer
    Human Interaction (CHI) 23; Computer
    Professionals for Social Responsibility (CPSR)
    23; computer science, systems analysis and 23;
    Computer Supported Cooperative Work
    (CSCW) 23; Contextual Design and User
    Driven Innovation 27; data processing 22;
    democracy, voice and 31–33; democratic
    practices 33; DEMOS project (Sweden) 25, 27,
    29; Design and Intervention projects 24; design
    and intervention projects 28–30; DUE project
    (Denmark) 25, 28, 29; early action projects
    24; ethnographic work, guiding principles for
    30–31; feminism and participatory actions

32–33; Florence strategy 28, 29–30; influential thinkers, works of 31–33; Iron and Metal project 24, 25–27, 27–28, 29, 32; knowledge strategy projects 24–25; mutual learning 33; NJMF project (Norway) 25; Norwegian Computing Centre (Norsk Regnesentral) 24; participation, need for 22–23; participation, theoretical roots of 31–33; political context 23; power relations, equalization of 33; pragmatic philosophy and participatory actions 32; reflections on 33–34; roots 21–23; Scandinavia, exemplary cases in (1970s) 22, 24–25; Scientific Management 24; situation-based actions 33; summary and learning objectives 21; Tavistock Institute 25; technology, alternative visions about 34; tools and techniques 33; User Centred Design 27; UTOPIA project 28, 29; voicing participation 27–28; work and technology, ethnography of relations between 30–31; work-oriented design, early struggles 21–23; worker involvement, creativity in 32; working principles and practices, roots of 31–32; Xerox Palo Alto Research Center (PARC) 24, 30, 31
Hess, J. et al. 199
Hess, K. 54
Hevner, A.R. et al. 58n2
Heyer, C. and Brereton, M. 161, 163, 164
hierarchical boundaries 72
Hillgren, P.-A. et al. 53, 54, 55, 58
Hinds, P. and Mortensen, M. 137
Hine, C. 105
Hirsch, T. 190, 191, 199
Holmes, B. 258
Holquist, M., Liapunov, V. and Brostrom, K. 68
Holter, I.M. and Schwartz-Barcott, D. 264
home care technologies 80–81
Hornecker, E. and Stifter, M. 136
Hovorka, D. and Germonprez, M. 58n2
Howard, S. et al. 165
Hughes, J. et al. 87, 93, 94, 95, 96, 97, 98, 99
Human-Computer Interaction (HCI): design process 39, 41, 48, 53; ethnography 94, 95; tools and techniques 156; user-centred design approaches to 47
Human Relations 44
Hussain, S. and Sanders, E.B.-N. 157
Hutchins, E. 95

Iacucci, G. and Kuutti, K. 168, 169
Iacucci, G. et al. 195
IBIS method 198–99
identity: development of 70; importance in communities of 184
IDEO Design 55–56
The Imperative of Responsibility (Jonas, H.) 69–70

improvisational theatre techniques, inspiration from 164–65
in-house participatory design, reflections on 218–19
India 242–43, 247–48
indigenous knowledge management system, development of 74
influence levels 131–32
influential thinkers, works of 31–33
Info Block and Info Tree 156
information and communications technologies (ICT) 2, 6, 51, 261
information management (IM), example of 216–18
information systems: large-scale information systems 106; organisational information systems 49–50; *see also* Health Information Systems Programme (HISP)
information technology design 120
informed consent 73
informed design 93–94, 95–96
infrastructure: design process, infrastructional variations 51; development of 137; infrastructuring, communities and 201–4
innovation: open and user-driven 52–53; social innovation 55; in tools and techniques, discussion on and dissemination of 146; *see also* Design Anthropological Innovation Model (DAIM)
institutional and disciplinary affiliations 94
intellectual property and autonomy 274–75
Interactive Institute, Malmö 173
interdisciplinarity: (inter)disciplinary difference, reconciliation of 96–97; interdisciplinary research, ethnographically informed design as 94–95; methodological interdisciplinarity 96
Internet of Things (IoT) 51
intervention 87, 88, 90, 91, 93, 97, 101, 102, 103, 104, 105, 108
Iron and Metal project 24, 25–27, 27–28, 29, 32
Ishimaru, Karen xiii, 13, 213–34
Iversen, O.S. and Dindler, C. 153, 154

Jacucci, G. et al. 14n1
Jakobsen, H. et al. 25
Jansson, M. et al. 137
Jégou, F. and Manzini, E. 55
Jenkins, H. 52
Jensen, C.B. 259, 262, 269, 270, 277n5
Jeremijenko, Natalie 48
Johansson, M. 152
Johansson, M. and Linde, P. 78, 152
Johansson, M. et al. 153
Johnson, M. 68
joining ethnography and (participatory) design 94–98
Jonas, H. 69, 70, 80
Jones, J.C. 45, 149

Jordan, B. 97, 103
Jordan, B. and Henderson, A. 30
Joy, J. 276
Jungk, R. and Müllert, N. 23, 152

Kanstrup, A.M. and Christiansen, E. 137
Kanstrup, A.M. et al. 137
Kant, Immanuel 67, 68
Karasti, H. and Baker, K.S. 52, 57, 104
Karasti, H. and Syrjänen, A.-L. 104, 190, 202
Karasti, H. et al. 104
Karasti, Helena xi, 58, 86–109
Kattegat Marine Centre 153, 154, 155
Kavanaugh, A.L. et al. 195
Keller, E. 32
Kensing, F. and Blomberg, J. 6, 28, 65, 90, 151
Kensing, F. and Madsen, K.H. 152, 205n2
Kensing, F. and Munk-Madsen, A. 133, 150
Kensing, F. and Winograd, T. 93
Kensing, F. et al. 93, 101
Kensing, Finn x–xi, 9, 21–34, 90, 120, 121, 123,
    130, 149
Kindermann, A. 97
Klein, J.T. 95, 96
Knorr-Cetina, K. and Cicourel, A.V. 261
knowledge domains in design projects 133
knowledge strategy projects 24–25
knowledge systems 43–44
Koestler, A. 160
Kohlberg, L. 69
Korpela, M. et al. 104, 106, 264
Koskinen, I. et al. 159
Kraft, P. and Bansler, J.P. 131
Kunz, W. and Rittel, H.W.J. 198
Kyng, M. and Mathiassen, L. 25, 28
Kyng, Morten 3, 4, 90, 97, 103, 104, 106, 126,
    166, 252, 273, 274, 275

Labor and Monopoly Capital (Braverman, H.) 32
Laboratory for Computer-Supported
    Collaboration and Learning (CSCL), Penn State
    University 188
Lainer, R. and Wagner, I. 137
The Lancet 247
Landscape Game 174
language: methods 134; tools and techniques
    148
Lanzara, Giovanni Francesco 46
large-scale information systems 106
Latour, B. and Weibel, P. 57, 201
Latour, Bruno 39, 56, 57, 75, 201
Lave, J. and Wenger, E. 148, 184, 190
Lawson, B. 45
'lay' participants 97
Le Dantec, C.A. and Edwards, W.K. 200
Le Dantec, C.A. et al. 200
Le Jeune, G. 259

learning in course of everyday activities 189–90;
    see also mutual learning
Lee, Y. and Bichard, J.-A. 136
LEGO Serious Play 160
Levinas, E. 68
Lewin, Kurt 44
Lieberman, H. et al. 138
Light, A. et al. 184, 195, 196, 200
Lilienfeld, S.O. et al. 159
Linde, C. 152
Lindström, K. and Ståhl, Å. 52
litigation support 76
Living Labs 53–54
Loewy, E. 81
Loi, D. et al. 137
Löwgren, J. and Stolterman, E. 46, 146
Luff, P. et al. 95
Luke, R. et al. 186, 187
Lundsgaard, C. 156

McCulloch, A. 258
MacDonald, S. and Clement, A. 186
McGuigan, J. 84
McNaughton, D. 67
McPhail, B. et al. 185, 186, 221
'magic if' technique 165
making: telling and enacting, investigation of
    relationships between 176; of things as means of
    design participation 155–64
Making Use: Scenario-based Design of Human-
    Computer Interactions (Carroll, J.) 166
Malmö Living Labs 192–93
Mambrey, P. et al. 97
Maquil, V. et al. 136
Marcus, G.E. 105
Markussen, R. 103
Marres, N. 58
Mathiassen, L. and Nielsen, P.A. 104
Mathiassen, L. et al. 28, 129
Mattelmäki, T. 155, 159
Mattelmäki, T. et al. 161
Mazé, R. and Redström, J. 158, 159
Mazé, R. et al. 158
Mazzone E. et al. 184
Media Centre Software 197–99
Merkel, C.B. et al. 104, 106, 185, 188, 189
Messeter, J. et al. 167
Messing, K. 276
Messing, K. et al. 259, 260
meta-method 118–19
methods 117–40; accessing private spaces 137;
    addressing new application areas 135–36;
    analysis and design, intertwining of 134–35;
    application area 119; CESD (Cooperative
    Experimental System Development) 125–28;
    challenges to 135–39; changes in participatory
    design contexts 137–38; co-realisation 133;

communication with users 131–32; concept of method 118–19; concretising of ideas 131; decision-making and having a say 129, 130; design-after-design 138–39; empirically-based experience and 118; envisioning 131; ETHICS design tool 121; ethnography and participatory design 93; examples 120–28; expansion of participatory design perspective 138; Florence project 131, 134; guidelines 119; influence levels 131–32; information technology design 120; infrastructure development 137; knowledge domains in design projects 133; language 134; meta-method 118–19; mixed realities, migrating users and transitory commitments 136–37; model monopoly 130; models and concepts 119–20; MUST method (Roskilde University) 123–25; mutual learning 132; perspectives 119, 128–35; power, addressing and sharing 130–31, 139; problem-setting 130; prototypes, use of 135; STEPS (Software Technology for Evolutionary Participatory Systems Development) 121–23; summary and learning objectives 117; system development 118; techniques 119; tools 119; two-way learning 132–33; use-oriented design cycle 128; UTOPIA project 131, 134; voice and having a say 129–30; *see also* tools and techniques
Mid-Main Clinic and the wireless call system, perils of staffing changes 269–71
Mill, John Stuart 67
Millen, D.R. 96
Mind over Machine (Dreyfus, H. and Dreyfus, S.) 32
misrepresentation 76
MIT Media Lab 54
mixed realities, migrating users and transitory commitments 136–37
mobile technologies 80
models: CESD (Cooperative Experimental System Development), conceptual model 126, 127; concepts and 119–20; Design Anthropological Innovation Model (DAIM) 47, 101, 102; model monopoly 130; Velcro-modelling toolkit 161
Modern Times (Chaplin film) 24
Mogensen, P. 153
Mogensen, Preben Holst xv, 117–40
Moggill community partnership 191–92
Moholy-Nagy, L. and van der Rohe, L.M. 38
Monson Haefel, R. 228
mood boards 159
moral philosophy 66–71
moral sensitivity 68–69
Mørch, A.I. and Andersen, R. 139
Morgensen, P. and Robinson, M. 101
Morgensen, P. and Trigg, R. 101
Morgensen, P.H. 101, 102, 125

Mörtberg, C. et al. 102
Mörtberg, C.M. and Elovaara, P. 78, 128, 137
Mouffe, C. 200
Mozambique 243
Muller, M. 149, 151
Muller, M. and Druin, A. 148
Muller, M.J. et al. 14n1
multi-perspectival collaboration with participatory design 97
Mumford, E. 23, 25, 41, 121
Mumford, E. et al. 25
Murray, R. et al. 55
Mursu, A. et al. 104, 106
MUST method (Roskilde University) 123–25; anchoring visions 125; change, coherent visions of 124; conceptual framework 123; core idea of research 123; design process 49; ethnography 93; genuine user participation 124; methods 123–25; resources 124; tools and techniques 146; work practices, first-hand experiences with 124–25
mutual learning: ethnography 89, 91, 98; heritage 33; methods 132; participatory design and 6

Namioka, A. and Schuler, D. 14n1
Nardi, B.A. 50
narrative ethics 68–69
Naur, P. 122
Neighbourhood Networks 54, 193–95, 200
neighbourhoods, communities and 184
Nelson, H. and Stolterman, E. 44, 46
'networks of actions' 240–44; responding to challenges in developing countries 243–44
New York Times 79
Nielsen, J. 138
Nilsson, J. et al. 168
NJMF project (Norway) 25
Nnub project (digital community noticeboard) 161–64
Noble, B. 108
Nokia Design Manifesto 56
Norman, D.A. and Draper, S.W. 26, 47
normative ethical theories 68
Norwegian Computing Centre (Norsk Regnesentral) 24
Norwegian Metal Workers project 39, 43
The Not Quite Yet: On the Margins of Technology (Exhibition) 196
Nuojua, J. et al. 52
Nurminen, M.I. 121
Nyce, J.M. and Löwgren, J. 96
Nygaard, K. and Bergo, O.T. 2, 24, 25, 26, 27, 43, 44
Nygaard, Kirsten 24, 42, 43, 132, 134, 238

Obendorf, H. et al. 105
Öberg, K.D. et al. 138

Oostveen, A.-M. and van den Besselaar, P. 9, 104
open access approaches 204
open innovation 52–53
open production, fabrication laboratories and 54–55
Open Source Ecology 55
open source software: empowering the South through 255–56; open source web-based environments 244–48; packages of, design process and 50–51
oral narratives 152
organisational information systems 49–50
origins of: Global Fund for Women (GFW) 214; participatory design 1–2, 7, 9
Orlikowski, W. and Hofman, D. 8
Orr, J.E. 30, 92, 148, 151, 152
Oulasvirta, A. et al. 168
outsourcing software-based services from Africa 255

Palo Alto Participatory Design Conference (1994) 103–4
participation: as themselves; with themselves; for the task and the project 5; core of participatory design 5–7; need for, tradition of 22–23; reification and 148; theoretical roots of 31–33; through enacting possible futures 164–70
participatory design 109n1, 109n2, 109n3; applications see ACTION for Health; Global Fund for Women; Health Information Systems Programme; beginnings of 1–2, 7, 9; commitments and guiding principles of 88–91; communities 182–205; computer-based systems 3–4; Computer Supported Cooperative Work (CSCW) 7–8; conceptual inspiration for 4–5; configurability 9, 80, 138–39; core principles (and commitment to) 3, 4, 117–40; definition of 2–3; design process 8–10, 37–58; designers, roles of 2–3, 4; distributed participatory design, proposal for 106; ethical stand of 3–5, 64–83; ethnography and 8, 12, 22, 86–109; expansion of 9–10, 138; further reading 15; heritage 21–34; in-house participatory design, reflections on 218–19; information and communications technologies 2; introductory summary 1; methods of 117–40; mutual learning and 6, 89–90; opportunities in Africa for 255; participation at core of 5–7; political rationale for participation 6–7; practice, approach to 7–8; practice of participation 147–49; pragmatic rationale for participation 6; 'reflection in action' 8–9; socio-technical approach 7; tailorability 9; technology-enabled systems 2; theoretical inspiration for 4–5; tools and techniques for 145–77; tradition of 2, 21–34; users, roles of 2–3, 4; value of user participation 5–6; Xerox Palo Alto Research Center (PARC) 7–8

Participatory Design (Schuler, D. and Namioka, A., eds) xx
Participatory IT Design: Designing for Business and Workplace Realities (Bødker, S. et al.) 166
participatory production, forms of 52
participatory prototyping techniques 155–57
partnerships: collaborative working with 275; complexity in 275–76; intellectual property and 274–75
Patel, N. 138
Pederson, J. 72
performance staging 168
Peritz, L. 276
perspectives 119, 128–35
phronesis, virtue of 67–68
Piaget, J. and Inhelder, B. 189
Pink, S. 107
Pipek, V. and Syrjänen, A.-L. 190, 202
Pipek, V. and Wulf, V. 50, 57, 202
Pipek, Volkmar xvii, 83n1, 182–205
Plans and Situated Actions (Suchman, L.) 30, 31
Plato 67
Plowman, L. et al. 92, 95, 103
plurality within communities, challenge of 184–85
Polanyi, M. 134
politics: commercial and political environments, participatory design for enhancing public deliberation in 196–99; Health Information Systems Programme (HISP) 252–53; new forms of 199–200; participation, political rationale for 6–7; tradition and political context 23
Pollock, N. and Williams, R. 50, 104
Pors, J.K. et al. 92
power: addressing and sharing 130–31, 139; and hierarchy, notions of 107; power relations, equalization of 33
practice: approach to 7–8; concept of 147–48; situated and practical ethics 68–69; see also reflective practice
pragmatic philosophy: participatory actions and 32; rationale for participation 6
Pralahad, C.K. and Krishnan, M.S. 53
Principles of Biomedical Ethics (Beauchamp, T.L. and Childress, J.F.) 67
principles of ethnography 88
probes as a means of exploring experience 158–59
probing kits 158, 161
problem-setting 130
problem-solving rationality versus reflective practice 46
process control 225
professional boundaries 72
project participants: identification and engagement with 71–72; practice of engagement with 72–75; reflection on what can be offered to 77–78
prototypes: case-based prototypes 99; co-design, cooperative prototyping and 90; participatory

prototyping techniques 155–57; prototyping 145–46, 153; use of 135
The Public and Its Problems (Dewey, J.) 200
publics: notion of 200–201, 203; participation of, social innovation and 55
Puri, S.K. et al. 106, 107, 242

Raghvendra, R.C. and Sahay, S. 242
Randall, D. et al. 99, 265
Rauhala, M. 74
Read, J.C. et al. 184
Redhead, F. 163
Redhead, F. and Brereton, M. 161, 163, 191, 192
Redström, J. 57
'reflection in action' 8–9; *see also* reflective practice
Reflective Agile Iterative Design framework 162–63
reflective design 48
reflective practice: notion of 102–3; problem-solving rationality *versus* 46
The Reflective Practitioner (Schön, D.A.) 31, 46
reflexive relation, ethnography and participatory design in 92
reformist participatory design, reflection of challenges 275–76
rehearsal of new roles and relations 169–70
Reidl, C. and Tolar, M. 259
Reidl, C. et al. 72, 259
relativist ethical theories 68
representation of participants and their work 75–77
researchable problems, finding in unexpected places 272–73
respect 41, 67, 72–73, 81, 129, 204, 214–15, 225; mutual respect 89, 132, 136, 137
responsibility and ethics 64, 66, 67, 68, 69–70, 71, 72, 78, 81, 83
Rittel, H. and Webber, M. 45
Robertson, T. et al. 107
Robertson, Toni xvii, xix–xx, 1–15, 58, 64–83, 264
Rogers, Y. 103
Rogers, Y. and Bellotti, V. 92
Roskilde Participatory Design Conference (2012) xx
Rouncefield, M. et al. 93
Royce, W. 123

Sahay, Sundeep xv–xvi, 235–56
Salsa project, shared information space in 'cloud' 230–31
Salter, L. and Hearn, A. 96
Salvador, T. et al. 107
Samis, P.S. 136
Sandberg, Å. 2, 44, 90
Sandberg, Å. and Ehn, P. 149
Sandberg, Å and Greenbaum, J. 24
Sanders, E.B.-N. and Simons, G. 177

Sanders, E.B.-N. and Stappers, P.J. 146, 155
Sanders, E.B.-N. and William, C.T. 160
Sanders, E.B.-N. et al. 155
Sanders, Elizabeth B.-N. xiv, 145–77
Sandiford, P. et al. 238
Sanoff, H. 2, 156
Sato, S. and Salvador, T. 165
Scandinavia: approach to systems design in 43; exemplary cases in (1970s) 22, 24–25; Participatory Design projects 44; systems development tradition 42
scenarios: enacting scenarios in real-use contexts 168–69; scenario-based techniques 165–68, 168–69
Schmidt, K. 79, 92
Schmidt, K. et al. 7, 8, 259
Schön, D. and Wiggins, G. 134
Schön, Donald A. 2, 8, 31, 37, 46, 58, 102, 131
Schuhman, D. 44
Schuler, D. 184, 185, 191
Schuler, D. and Namioka, A. 10, 12, 49, 147
Schuurman, N. and Balka, E. 259
The Sciences of the Artificial (Simon, H.) 46
Scientific Management 24
Seattle Community Network (SCN) 191
Sefyrin, J. and Mörtberg, C.M. 137
Sengers, P. et al. 48
Seravalli, A. 54, 55, 58
Shaping Things (Sterling, B.) 51
Shapiro, D. 79, 81, 96, 97, 98, 106, 131, 276
Shapiro, D. et al. 93, 99
shared access 227–29
shared information 229–30, 230–31; shared information space 226; stakeholder participation and 231
shared interests, focus on 184
shared ownership 226–27
Sharman, Z. 259
Sharrock, W. and Anderson, B. 95
Shilton, K. et al. 184
Shneiderman, B. 138
Sidlar, C.L. and Rinner, C. 198
Sierra Leone 245–46
SILK 55
Silverstone, R. and Haddon, L. 138
Simon, Herbert 37, 45, 46
Simonsen, J. and Hertzum, M. 9, 50, 104, 139
Simonsen, J. and Kensing, F. 75, 93, 96, 97
Simonsen, J. et al. 14n1
Simonsen, Jesper xii, xix–xx, 1–15, 58, 104, 117–40
simplification of complexities, need for 271–72
Singer, P. 67
situation-based actions 33
Situationist International movement 48
Sleeswijk Visser, F. et al. 160, 177
Smith, K.L. 258

Snyder, C. 156
social innovation 55
social media 51–52
social services, rising importance of 183
social technologies 80
Societyware 199
socio-technical approach 7
socio-technical systems 42
'soft' systems 43–44
Sommerville, I. et al. 95
Sorting Things Out (Bowker, G. and Star, S.L.) 76
South Africa 238–40
spatial scaling 105–6
Spinuzzi, C. 50
stakeholder engagement: design process 57; ethics 73–75
Stålbröst, A. 53
Stanislavskij, K. 165
Star, S.L. 4, 148, 277n10
Star, S.L. and Bowker, G.C. 49, 77, 202
Star, S.L. and Greismer, J.R. 148, 149
Star, S.L. and Ruhleder, K. 95, 202, 230, 231
Star, S.L. and Strauss, A. 76, 130
Star, S.L. et al. 201
Statler, M. et al. 160
Steinkamp, N. and Gordijn, B. 69
STEPS (Software Technology for Evolutionary Participatory Systems Development) 121–23
Sterling, B. 51
Stevens, G. and Wiedenhöfer, T. 199
Stevens, G. et al. 51
Stolterman, E. 46
Storm Jensen, O. 5
Storni, C. 51, 58
structure of the book 11–14
Stuedahl, D. et al. 103
Suchman, L. and Jordan, B. 263, 265
Suchman, L. and Trigg, R. 7, 30, 92, 97
Suchman, L. and Wynn, E. 30, 92, 95
Suchman, L. et al. 87, 88, 92, 99, 103
Suchman, Lucy A. 4, 7–8, 25, 30, 57, 80, 95, 98, 103, 123, 203
summaries and learning objectives: ACTION for Health 257; communities 182; design process 37; ethics 64; ethnography 86; Global Fund for Women (GFW) 213; Health Information Systems Programme (HISP) 235; heritage 21; methods 117; tools and techniques 145
Surowiecki, J. 53
Sydney Participatory Design Conference (2010) xx
synergies between participatory design and ethnography 90–91
Syrjänen, A.-L. 97, 190
systems design: influences on 43–44; iterative process of rethinking on 149–50; system development methods 118; systems design tradition 146

tailorability: design process 50–51; participatory design 9
target audience 10–11
Tavistock Institute: design process 42, 44; heritage 25
Taxén, G. et al. 136
techniques 119; *see also* tools and techniques
technology: alternative visions about 34; design of, ethical issues in 78–81; ethics and 69–71; participatory design, influence on 257–77; substrates of, systems and infrastructures in 49; technology-enabled systems 2; Technology Game 174
Telier, A. 9–10, 51, 57, 139
telling activities: as drivers for participation 149–55; tell-make-enact framework 149, 150, 162–63, 168; 'tell-techniques' 163–64
temporal scaling 104–5
Thackara, John 55
third space, notion of 148
Thrift, N. 39
Titlestad, O.H. et al. 106, 138, 248
Tjørnehøj, H. 25
tools and techniques 119, 145–77; Aging@Work project 161; boundary objects 148–49; change perspectives casting new light on well known, introduction of 152–53; co-design 148; co-designing, generative tools for 159–60; collaborative inquiry 171; COMIT project 167, 174; conception of 146; contexts for use, focus on 146–47; cooperative design, Scandinavian tradition of 150; design game as particular framing of design participation 171–73; design games 146, 171–75; Design Noir 158; design practices, proliferating family of 146; designing (with) design games 173–75; diagnostic narratives 151–52; Enacted Scenario Game 175; enacting scenarios in real-use contexts 168–69; existing (work) practices, investigation of 151–52; experience, probes for exploration of 158–59; fictional narratives 153–55; Focus Troupe approach 165; Forum Theatre 164; future directions and opportunities 175–77; future workshops 145–46, 152–53; generative tools for co-designing 159–60; heritage 33; Human-Computer Interaction (HCI) 156; improvisational theatre techniques, inspiration from 164–65; Info Block and Info Tree 156; innovation in, discussion on and dissemination of 146; Interactive Institute, Malmö 173; Kattegat Marine Centre 153, 154, 155; Landscape Game 174; language 148; LEGO Serious Play 160; 'magic if' technique 165; making, telling and enacting, investigation of relationships between 176; making of things as means of design participation 155–64; mood boards 159; MUST method (Roskilde

University) 146; Nnub project 161–64; oral narratives 152; participation and reification 148; participation through enacting possible futures 164–70; participatory design is practice of participation 147–49; participatory prototyping techniques 155–57; performance staging 168; practice, concept of 147–48; probes as a means of exploring experience 158–59; probing kits 158, 161; processes and tools, ethics and development of 65, 70; prototyping 145–46, 153; refinement of design participation framework 176–77; Reflective Agile Iterative Design framework 162–63; rehearsal of new roles and relations 169–70; scenario-based techniques 165–68, 168–69; specific tools and techniques, continued exploration and application of 175–76; summary and learning objectives 145; systems design, iterative process of rethinking on 149–50; systems design, tradition in 146; Technology Game 174; tell-make-enact framework 149, 150, 162–63, 168; 'tell-techniques' 163–64; telling activities as drivers for participation 149–55; third space, notion of 148; tradition and transcendence, fictional narratives and challenge to 153–55; transformative generative grammar, theory of 159; User Game 174; UTOPIA project 151, 155–56; values strategically guiding participatory design 147; Velcro-modelling toolkit 161; wellbeing at work, improvement of 160–61; see also methods

Tower Move project, supporting operational needs while collecting data 262–69; ACTION for Health 262–69; background 263–64; data collection, novel approaches to 265–67; invention communication strategy 267–69; methodology 264–65; Technology Trouble 258, 259, 263–70

tradition: in participatory design 2, 21–34, 237–40; transcendence and, fictional narratives and challenge to 153–55

transformative generative grammar, theory of 159

Trigg, R. and Bødker, S. 9

Trigg, R. et al. 14n1, 90, 92, 99

Trigg, Randy xv, 13, 204, 213–34

Trist, E. 25

Trist, E. and Bamforth, K. 42

Trist, E. et al. 25

Trist, E.L. and Lewin, K. 44

Trist, E.L. et al. 42

Troxler, Peter 54

trust 66, 72–73, 74–75, 189–90, 214–15, 268; mutual trust 72, 132, 138

Turner, J.H. 261

Twidale, M. and Floyd, I. 57

Twidale, M. et al. 94

two-way learning 132–33

Understanding Computer and Cognition: A New Foundation for Design (Winograd, T. and Flores, F.) 31, 32

User Centred Design 27; approaches to Human-Computer Interaction (HCI) 47

User Game 174

User Parliament 198, 199

users: communication with 131–32; ethical issues of working with 71–78; foregrounding user/practitioner 98; identification in Health Information Systems Programme (HISP) of 252–53; roles in participatory design 2–3, 4; use-oriented design cycle 128; user-driven innovation 52–53

UTOPIA project 238, 256; design process 39; heritage 28, 29; methods 131, 134; tools and techniques 151, 155–56

Vaajakallio, K. and Mattelmäki, T. 161, 162

values: participation in Global Fund for Women (GFW) 223–24; strategically guiding participatory design 147; user participation in design 5–6

van Kranenburg, R. 51

Velcro-modelling toolkit 161

Verganti, R. 55

Verran, H. 104, 107

Vina, Sandra 52

virtue theory 67–68

voices: democracy, voice and 31–33; voice and having a say 129–30; voicing participation 27–28

von Hippel, E. 53

Voss, A. 99, 100, 103, 104

Vygotsky, L.S. 190

Wagner, I. 58, 276

Wagner, I. and Gärtner, J. 26

Wagner, I. and Jensen, C.B. 262

Wagner, I. et al. 71, 102, 136

Wagner, Ina xi, 64–83

Wathen, N., Harris, R. and Wyatt, S. 259

Webster, P.C. 247

Wenger, E. 147, 205n1

Westerlund, B. 159, 168

White, S. 23

Whitehouse, S. 276

Willems, D. 81

Willigen, J.V. 88

Winograd, T. 39

Winograd, T. and Flores, F. 4, 5, 31, 32, 150

Winschiers-Theophilus, H. et al. 74, 104, 107, 184

Wise, L.C. et al. 265

Wittgenstein, Ludwig 66, 171

Wolfe, T. 38

Wood-Harper, A.T. et al. 121, 264, 275

work and workplaces: creativity in worker involvement 32; ethical issues of working with users 71–78; existing (work) practices, investigation of 151–52; Global Fund for Women (GFW) work practice knowledge 225–26; health sector management, working with 261–62; information management liaisons in Global Fund for Women (GFW) 222; technology and work, ethnography of relations between 30–31; wellbeing at work, improvement of 160–61; work-oriented design, early struggles 21–23; working principles and practices, roots of 31–32; workplace democracy 232–33

Work-oriented Design of Computer Artifacts (Ehn, P.) 31
Wyatt, S. et al. 259
Wynn, E. 30
Wynn, E.H. 95

Xerox Palo Alto Research Center (PARC): ethnography and 92, 103; heritage and 24, 30, 31; participatory design and 7–8

Ylirisku, S. and Buur, J. 152, 167, 168
Young Foundation 55
Yourdon, E. 23

Printed in Great Britain
by Amazon